D1454289

PRINCELIE MAJES
THE COURT OF JAMES V OF SCOTLAND,

PRINCELIE MAJESTIE

The Court of James V of Scotland, 1528–1542

Andrea Thomas

JOHN DONALD

First published in Great Britain in 2005 by
John Donald, an imprint of Birlinn Ltd
West Newington House
10 Newington Road
Edinburgh EH9 1QS

www.birlinn.co.uk

ISBN 10: 0 85976 611 X
ISBN 13: 978 0 85976 611 1

British Library Cataloguing-in-Publication Data
A catalogue record for this book is available from the British Library

The publisher gratefully acknowledges subsidy from the
Dr Jamie Stuart Cameron Trust towards the production of this volume

Typeset by Hewer Text UK Ltd, Edinburgh
Printed and bound by Bell and Bain Ltd, Glasgow

Contents

List of Illustrations

Colour plates

1. James V by an unknown artist
2. Portraits of James V and Queen Madeleine from the *Seton Armorial*
3. Mary of Guise by Corneille de Lyon
4. Double portrait of James V and Mary of Guise
5. The four orders of chivalry on the Linlithgow Palace foregate
6. The arms of Queen Madeleine and Mary of Guise from Sir David Lindsay's Armorial (1542)
7. The royal arms of Scotland from Sir David Lindsay's *Armorial* (1542)
8. *O Bone Jesu* from the *Scone Antiphonary/Carver Choir Book*
9. The Honours of Scotland

Black and white plates

1. The royal arms and heraldic badges with James V's cipher, c.1540, on the main gateway at Holyrood
2. James V's tower and forework at Holyrood depicted by James Gordon of Rothiemay
3. The entrance tower built for James V at Falkland Palace
4. The fountain in the courtyard of Linlithgow Palace, c.1540
5. John Slezer's view of Linlithgow Palace from the west, from *Theatrum Scotiae* (1693)
6. Falkland Palace, the Renaissance east and south ranges
7. David Pollock's conjectural reconstruction of James IV's forework at Stirling Castle, c.1500-08
8. Facades of the James V palace block at Stirling Castle, 1538-42
9. James V's presence chamber, Stirling Castle, a conjectural restoration
10. Two of the Stirling Heads: Hercules and Jester

Acknowledgements

This book began in the mid-1990s as a doctoral thesis at the University of Edinburgh. I am very grateful for the work of my supervisors, Professors Michael Lynch and Anthony Goodman, and my examiners, Doctors Roger Mason and Andrew Brown. They were generous with their time, constructive with their comments and patient with my inadequacies. John Bannerman, Robert Morris, John Dunbar, Athol Murray, Rosalind Marshall, Alison Rosie, Aonghus Mackechnie, Pat Dennison, Theo van Heijnsbergen, Alasdair Macdonald, Amy Juhala, Robin MacPherson, Janet Foggie, Alan MacDonald, Ruth Grant, Sharon Adams, John Finlay and Mark Godfrey all provided invaluable assistance, advice and encouragement in areas where my research overlapped with their specialisms. The staff of the Scottish Record Office (now the National Archives of Scotland), the National Library of Scotland, Edinburgh University Library and the British Library, and Doris Williamson, formerly at the Scottish History Department of Edinburgh University, were unfailingly courteous and helpful in dealing with my enquiries. The University of Edinburgh Arts Faculty Research Fund, the Jeremiah Dalziel Prize Committee and the Scottish History Department Conference Fund provided some valuable financial assistance. I also benefited hugely from the camaraderie generated by my fellow members of the Scottish History Department's Postgraduate Seminar. Tim Hands and Ashley Null were kind enough to do some proof-reading for me, but the greatest burden in this task fell upon the shoulders of my husband, David, whose wizardry with recalcitrant computer software also smoothed my path. His support and encouragement have been tremendous, but naturally any lingering errors contained in the book are entirely my own.

The manuscript was prepared for press in 1999 but publication was then unfortunately delayed. I am thus enormously grateful to Hugh Andrew and Neville Moir of Birlinn/John Donald for rescuing it from limbo. Absolutely no blame attaches to them for the fact that the book contains no citations later than 1999/2000; I did not wish to delay matters further by attempting another revision of the text at this stage. It is a great relief to see *Princelie Majestie* finally get into print and I hope that the many friends and well-wishers who have enquired about its progress over the years will feel that it has been worth the wait.

Andrea Thomas
Reigate, March 2005

Abbreviations

Abbreviations have, where possible, followed the guidelines set by the 'List of Abbreviated Titles of the Printed Sources of Scottish History to 1560', *SHR*, xlii (1963), pp. vii–xxix.

Abdn. Counc.	*Extracts from the Council Register of the Burgh of Aberdeen* (Spalding Club, 1844–48)
ADCP	*Acts of the Lords of Council in Public Affairs 1501–1544: Selections from Acta Dominorum Concilii*, ed. R. K. Hannay (Edinburgh, 1932)
APS	*The Acts of the Parliaments of Scotland*, eds. T. Thomson and C. Innes (Edinburgh, 1814–75)
Balcarres Papers	*Foreign Correspondence with Marie de Lorraine Queen of Scotland, from the Originals in the Balcarres Papers* (SHS, 1923–25)
Bannatyne Misc.	*The Bannatyne Miscellany* (Bannatyne Club, 1827–55)
Bann. MS	*The Bannatyne Manuscript*, ed. W. Tod Ritchie (STS, 1923–25)
Chron. Perth.	*The Chronicle of Perth* (Maitland Club, 1831)
Cronique de Roy	*Cronique du Roy Françoys Premier de ce nom*, ed. Georges Guiffrey (Paris, 1860)
CSP Scot.	*Calendar of State Papers Relating to Scotland, 1509–1603*, ed. M. J. Thorpe (2 vols., London, 1858)
CSP Ven.	*Calendar of State Papers and Manuscripts relating to English affairs, existing in the Archives and Collections of Venice*, eds. T. Brown et al., (London, 1864–)
Diurnal of Occurrents	*A Diurnal of Remarkable Occurrents that have passed within the country of Scotland, since the death of King James the Fourth till the year 1575* (Bannatyne and Maitland Clubs, 1833)
DNB	*Dictionary of National Biography* (London and Oxford, 1885–1900)
DSCHT	N. M. de S. Cameron et al., *Dictionary of Scottish Church History and Theology* (Edinburgh, 1993)
Edin. Recs.	*Extracts from the Records of the Burgh of Edinburgh* (SBRS, 1869–92)
EETS	Early English Text Society
Excerpta e Libris	*Excerpta e Libris Domicilii Domini Jacobi Quinti Regis Scotorum* (Bannatyne Club, 1836)
ER	*The Exchequer Rolls of Scotland*, eds. J. Stuart et al. (Edinburgh, 1878–1908)
Hamilton Papers	*The Hamilton Papers*, ed. J. Bain (Edinburgh, 1890–92)
HMC	*Reports of the Royal Commission on Historical Manuscripts* (London, 1870–)
IR	*The Innes Review* (1950–)

James IV Letters	*The Letters of James the Fourth 1505–13*, eds. R. K. Hannay and R. L. Mackie (SHS, 1953)
James V Letters	*The Letters of James V*, eds. R. K. Hannay and D. Hay (Edinburgh, 1954)
JR	*Juridical Review* (1889–)
L&P Henry VIII	*Calendar of Letters and Papers, Foreign and Domestic, Henry VIII*, eds. J. S. Brewer et al. (London, 1864–1932)
MB	*Musica Britannica* (London, 1950–)
Maitland Misc.	*Miscellany of the Maitland Club* (Maitland Club, 1833–47)
MW	*Accounts of the Masters of Works*, eds. H. M. Paton et al. (Edinburgh, 1957–)
Nat. MSS. Scot.	*Facsimiles of the National Manuscripts of Scotland* (London, 1867–71)
NLS	National Library of Scotland
PSAS	*Proceedings of the Society of Antiquaries of Scotland* (1851–)
Prot. Bk. Johnsoun	*Protocol Books of Dominus Thomas Johnsoun 1528–78* (SRS, 1920)
RCAHMS	*Reports of the Royal Commission on the Ancient and Historical Monuments and Constructions of Scotland* (Edinburgh, 1909–)
RMS	*Registrum Magni Sigilii Regum Scotorum*, eds. J. M. Thomson et al. (Edinburgh, 1882–1914)
ROSC	*Review of Scottish Culture* (Edinburgh, 1985–)
RSCHS	*Records of the Scottish Church History Society* (1923–)
RSS	*Registrum Secreti Sigilli Regum Scotorum*, eds. M. Livingstone et al. (Edinburgh, 1908–)
Sadler's Papers	*State Papers and Letters of Sir Ralph Sadler*, ed. A. Clifford (Edinburgh, 1809)
SBRS	Scottish Burgh Record Society
SHR	*The Scottish Historical Review* (1903–28, 1947–)
SHS	Scottish History Society
SHS Misc.	*Miscellany of the Scottish History Society* (SHS, 1893–)
SP	*The Scots Peerage*, ed. Sir J. Balfour Paul (Edinburgh, 1904–14)
Spalding Misc.	*Miscellany of the Spalding Club* (Spalding Club, 1841–52)
SRO	Scottish Record Office [now the National Archives of Scotland]
SRS	Scottish Record Society
STS	Scottish Text Society
TA	*Accounts of the Lord High Treasurer of Scotland*, eds. T. Dickson and Sir J. Balfour Paul (Edinburgh, 1877–1916)
TDGAS	*Transactions of the Dumfries and Galloway Natural History and Antiquarian Society*
TRHS	*Transactions of the Royal Historical Society*
TSES	*Transactions of the Scottish Ecclesiological Society*
Wardrobe Inventories	*A Collection of Inventories and other Records of the Royal Wardrobe and Jewelhouse; and of the Artillery and Munitioun in some of the Royal Castles, 1488–1606*, ed. T. Thomson (Edinburgh, 1815)

Conventions and Conversions

All sums of money are in pounds Scots unless otherwise stated (a merk was two-thirds of a pound). The exchange rate during the 1530s was approximately three pounds Scots to one pound Sterling, and two and a quarter livres Tournois to one pound Scots. The French crown was current at roughly one pound Scots.

The Scottish ell was approximately thirty seven inches.

The year is deemed to have started on 1 January, although the Scottish records of the period begin a new year on 25 March and the French at Easter Sunday.

The spellings of names have generally been modernised as in G. F. Black, *The Surnames of Scotland: Their Origin, Meaning, and History* (Edinburgh, 1836).

The spellings of place-names have generally been modernised as in F. H. Groome, *Ordnance Gazetteer of Scotland* (Edinburgh, 1885–1901).

All references give the page/folio numbers except citations from *RMS*, *RSS* and *L&P Henry VIII*, which give the document numbers.

James V's second wife is referred to in all the contemporary documents as Mary of Lorraine, but to avoid confusion the convention of calling her Mary of Guise has been adopted.

Texts of the period are quoted in the original spelling except that *yogh* is rendered as 'y', *thorn* as 'th' and i/j and u/v/w are modernised for greater clarity. Contractions have been expanded and punctuation modernised.

The histories of Bishop John Leslie and Robert Lindsay of Pitscottie are both available in two different editions, deriving from different manuscript sources. Both versions of each text have been referred to at various points; they are differentiated thus:

John Lesley, *The History of Scotland* (Bannatyne Club, 1830) [Lesley, *History* (Bann. Club)]

Jhone Leslie, *The Historie of Scotland* trans. James Dalrymple, ed. E. G. Cody and W. Murison (2 vols., STS, 1888–95) [Leslie, *Historie* (STS)]

Robert Lindsay of Pitscottie, *The Chronicles of Scotland*, ed. John Graham Dalyell (2 vols., Edinburgh, 1814) [Pitscottie, *History*, ed. Dalyell]

Robert Lindsay of Pitscottie, *The Historie and Cronicles of Scotland*, ed. Æ. J. G. MacKay (3 vols., STS, 1899–1911) [Pitscottie, *Historie* (STS)]

All knights are styled 'Sir' (e.g. Sir James Hamilton of Finnart), whilst priests who have not obtained university degrees are styled 'sir' (e.g. sir George Clapperton).

Courts, Courtiers and Courtesy

One of the bestsellers of sixteenth-century Europe was a handbook of courtly deportment: Baldassare Castiglione's *Il Libro del Cortegiano* [*The Book of the Courtier*], which was first published in Venice in 1528 but subsequently ran to many editions and translations. The book provides advice on all aspects of a courtier's life gleaned from Castiglione's own experience of the courts of Italy and Spain in the first quarter of the century. His discussion ranges from the trivial to the profound, but above all he wished to demonstrate that there was a moral purpose behind the ephemeral existence of a court favourite:

> In my opinion, therefore, the end of the perfect courtier . . . is, by means of the accomplishments attributed to him . . . so to win for himself the mind and favour of the prince he serves that he can and always will tell him the truth about all he needs to know, without fear or risk of displeasing him. And, if he knows that his prince is of a mind to do something unworthy, he should be in a position to dare to oppose him, and make courteous use of the favour his good qualities have won to remove every evil intention and persuade him to return to the path of virtue. Thus if the courtier is endowed with the goodness . . . attributed to him, as well as being quick-witted and charming, prudent and scholarly and so forth, he will always have the skill to make his prince realise the honour and advantages that accrue to him and his family from justice, liberality, magnanimity, gentleness and all the other virtues befitting a ruler, and on the other hand, the infamy and loss that result from practising the vices opposed to these virtues. Therefore I consider that just as music, festivities, games and other agreeable accomplishments are, so to speak, the flower of courtiership, so its real fruit is to encourage and help his prince to be virtuous and to deter him from evil.[1]

In this passage Castiglione places his discussion of the nature and purpose of the Renaissance court firmly within the context of an 'advice

---

1 Baldassare Castiglione, *The Book of the Courtier*, trans. George Bull (Harmondsworth, 1983), 284–5.

to princes' tradition with a long pedigree in western European thought and in the book as a whole he is also able to demonstrate his humanist training. There are echoes of Aristotle's *Politics* in the discussion of the best and worst forms of government; Castiglione quotes freely from Plato's *Republic*, Cicero's *De Oratore* and other classical texts. He also draws upon biblical stories and the great writers of the Tuscan vernacular: Dante, Petrarch and Boccaccio.[2] His debt to the conventions of late-medieval discourse is also apparent in his awareness of the long-standing stereotypical images of the decadent and corrupting courtly environment, where the unseemly scramble for favour and preferment was said to encourage men to display all their base instincts. This may also be seen in his use of the moral framework of the search for good government delivered by the virtuous prince.[3] Furthermore, his discussion is enriched by an appreciation of the chivalric culture of the northern courts of France, the Netherlands and England and by the lingering appeal of a pan-European crusading movement against the Turk.[4] Thus he informs his readers that prowess at the martial sports of the lists and tiltyard is to be nurtured for the opportunities it provides to exhibit manly virtues and to impress potential patrons. Likewise, the chivalric orders of the Garter, St. Michael and the Golden Fleece are mentioned with approval, and Monsieur d'Angoulême, Prince Henry and Don Carlos (the future Francis I, Henry VIII and Charles V) are presented as the incipient heroes of a courtly revival.[5]

However, in pursuit of these exalted universalist ideals Castiglione is also fastidious in his attention to detail. He provides the budding courtier with a recipe for 'how to win friends and influence people' which advises him on such matters as his clothing (dignified and restrained for everyday wear, colourful and conspicuous for sports and festivals), his sense of humour (collect light and witty anecdotes for

2 Richard Firth Green, *Poets and Princepleasers: Literature and the English Court in the Late Middle Ages* (Toronto, 1980), 135–67; Peter Burke, *The Fortunes of the* Courtier: *The European Reception of Castiglione's* Cortegiano (Cambridge, 1995), 8–18.

3 Burke, *Fortunes of the* Courtier, 55, 106–15. Similar comments can be found in works by Peter of Blois, John of Salisbury, Walter Map, William of Malmesbury, Aeneas Sylvius Piccolomini and others: Sydney Anglo, 'The Courtier: The Renaissance and Changing Ideals', in A. G. Dickens (ed.), *The Courts of Europe, 1400–1800* (New York, 1984), 33–4; C. Stephen Jaeger, *The Origins of Courtliness: Civilizing Trends and the Formation of Courtly Ideals, 939–1210* (Philadelphia, 1985), 54–66.

4 See Cecil H. Clough, 'Francis I and the Courtiers of Castiglione's *Courtier*', in *European Studies Review*, xviii (1978), 23–50.

5 Castiglione, *Courtier*, 115–16, 208–09, 312–13.

suitable moments but avoid being coarse or blasphemous) and his approach to playing chess (aim for mediocrity, since mastery of the game requires such dedicated application that it suggests that playing the game has become an end in itself, whereas it should be simply an agreeable way of ingratiating oneself with persons of quality). Once the skills and accomplishments of the ideal courtier have been acquired they should, if possible, be deployed in the service of the ideal prince. The good lord not only exhibits the standard attributes of enforcing justice, securing victory in warfare, protecting true religion, rewarding good service according to merit, and accepting wise counsel but, for Castiglione, he should have other characteristics too. He should have an appreciation of art, music, literature, oratory and scholarship; he must appear to be a splendid and generous patron, who holds 'magnificent banquets, festivals, games and public shows', and who keeps 'a great many fine horses for use in peace or war, as well as falcons, hounds and all the other things that pertain to the pleasures of great lords and their subjects' and he should also 'erect great buildings, both to do him honour in his lifetime and to be memorials after his death'. Such are the marks of a truly great Renaissance prince.[6]

Castiglione had had personal experience of the courts of Urbino, Mantua, Milan, Rome and Spain and contacts with people from the courts of France, England and the Netherlands. Presentation copies of his book were sent to many of the great princes of the age and his text was thus widely disseminated even before translations were undertaken, such as that of Jacques Colin into French (c.1537) and that of Sir Thomas Hoby into English (1561).[7] Thus *The Courtier* may well have been known to some of the educated and globe-trotting members of the Scottish court of the period (later in the century it appeared in the library of James VI)[8] but, even if this were not the case, many of the ideals it expounds can be detected at work in the courtly culture of the reign of James V. This is hardly surprising since the popularity of Castiglione's work rested not upon its novelty or particularity but on its compendious and eloquent insight into many of the general concerns, ideals, and customs of the political élite of the age. Indeed, many of the authorities cited by Castiglione were known in Scotland, and so were other texts on similar themes of courtliness, good lordship and chivalric

---

6 Castiglione, *Courtier*, 134–6, 154–203, 140, 310.

7 Castiglione, *Courtier*, 9–19; Clough, 'Courtiers of Castiglione', 23–50; Burke, *Fortunes of the* Courtier, 55–80, 158–78.

8 George F. Warner, 'The Library of James VI, 1573–1583, from a Manuscript in the hand of Peter Young, his Tutor' in *Miscellany of the Scottish History Society* (SHS, 1893), vol. i, p. lii.

virtue. For instance, Dante and Boccaccio were known to Sir David Lindsay of the Mount, the foremost vernacular poet of James V's court, and other courtly texts appeared in Scottish versions in the manuscripts of Sir Gilbert Hay and John Asloan. [9]

The importance of Castiglione's work for the purposes of this study is twofold: firstly, in that his eclectic use of a wide range of sources and influences is reflected in the cultural developments of European courts of the period, a pattern to which the court of James V largely conforms; and secondly, because his emphasis on the impression created by such apparently trivial details, such as clothing, manners, conversation, etiquette, sports and games and so forth, indicates clearly just how important such things were for the Renaissance court, in which the lifestyle of the prince and his circle can possibly be seen as a work of art in itself (albeit one with high political and moral purposes).

The chapters that follow attempt to explain in some detail how many diverse cultural influences came to be inter-twined in the Scottish royal court of the period, and how the domestic routine provided by such elements as a hierarchical household, a regular itinerary, palatial surroundings and the staging of occasional public spectacles all combined to create a courtly culture which imitated in miniature those of France, England and the Netherlands, and which carried important political messages for consumption at home and abroad. Thus it is possible to detect the influence of humanist scholarship and its concern with the revival of antiquity in the classical decorative details applied to the courtyard façades of Falkland palace, or in the translation of Livy's *History of Rome*, commissioned by the king. The imperial theme, which became a mainstay of political iconography of the period, is reflected in the refashioning of the royal regalia and in the images struck on coins, whilst the national identity of the Scottish realm was stirred by the rhetoric of Hector Boece's *Scotorum Historia* (1527), also translated for the king.[10] Similarly, the cult of chivalry was fostered at the court,

---

9 Sir David Lindsay of the Mount, *The Works*, ed. Douglas Hamer (4 vols., STS, 1931–36) i, 3–38, 131, 265; Sir Gilbert Hay, *The Prose Manuscript*, ed. J. H. Stevenson (2 vols., STS, 1901–14); *The Asloan Manuscript*, ed. W. A. Craigie (2 vols., STS, 1923–25).

10 John MacQueen (ed.), *Humanism in Renaissance Scotland* (Edinburgh, 1990), 10–19, 32–5; Frances A Yates, *Astraea: The Imperial Theme in the Sixteenth Century* (London, 1985), 1–28; R. A. Mason, 'Scotching the Brut', in Mason (ed.), *Scotland and England, 1286–1815* (Edinburgh, 1987), 60–84; Mason, 'Chivalry and Citizenship: Aspects of National Identity in Renaissance Scotland', in R. A. Mason and N. Macdougall (eds.), *People and Power in Scotland: Essays in Honour of T. C. Smout* (Edinburgh, 1992), 50–73.

which mounted jousts and tournaments, gave prominence to the art of
heraldry and honoured the European orders of knighthood. Also the
medieval customs of the Scottish monarchy were maintained: the king
toured his realm relentlessly, showing himself to the people in regal
magnificence and dispensing justice in person; he both supported and
exploited the church simultaneously whilst presenting himself as the
ideal Christian knight, eager (in principle but not in practice) for
crusading duties; he led his feudal host on military campaigns in
which the crown supplied the latest artillery and naval technology;
and his genealogy as a descendant of an ancient line of kings was
stressed. Within this brimming melting-pot of the Scottish court, a rich
and heady brew was concocted in which fine art, architecture, scholarship, literature, music and piety jostled for attention alongside hunting,
hawking, dancing, feasting, fighting, flirting, archery, tennis, cards,
chess and the other routine activities of aristocratic life. Indeed, the
patronage of learning and the arts at court seems to have been aimed
essentially at providing the scenery, props and 'sound-bites' for the
theatrical confection of royal pageantry and spectacle. The men of
talent were probably regarded with little more reverence than other
servants of the king, their artistic creations valued only in so far as they
served to entertain people of rank, propagate the images of power, and
enhance the honour, dignity and fame of the court.[11] This book,
therefore, is a consideration of cultural activity in its widest possible
sense, which attempts to portray the totality of the courtly experience in
the Scotland of the adult James V.

The format adopted is thematic rather than chronological in order to
facilitate a detailed consideration of each of the main areas of cultural
activity of the period, but within each chapter attempts have been
made to indicate changes in the use and form of courtly patronage over
time and therefore, where appropriate, some explanation is offered of
the most significant events of the reign. Unlike the other Stewart
monarchs, James V still awaits a full scholarly biography to make
the story of his life and times widely known. The sixteenth-century
accounts of the reign are so frustratingly terse and selective, that they
are of very limited use to historians. The *Chronicle of Perth* and the
Chronicle of Aberdeen both have very narrow, parochial perspectives
and whilst the *Diurnal of Occurrents* is a little broader in its interests it
scarcely elaborates on the rather bald sequence of dates and events it

11 Sydney Anglo, 'Humanism and the Court Arts', in Anthony Goodman and
    Angus MacKay (eds.), *The Impact of Humanism on Western Europe* (London,
    1990), 66–98.

records.[12] Friar Adam Abell's *Roit and Quheill of Tyme* ranges in its scope from the Ottoman incursions into the Balkans and central Europe to the conversion of the pagans in Mexico and muses at length on the wickedness of the world, epitomised by the heretic king of England, but tells us very little about events in Scotland, and in any case it ventures no further in time than 1537.[13] The idiosyncrasies and 'hobby-horses' of the later sixteenth-century narratives by Knox, Leslie, Pitscottie and Buchanan are well known and colour vividly all subsequent accounts by commentators from the seventeenth to the twentieth centuries, including Caroline Bingham's popular biography of James V.[14] However, recent research has attempted to unravel the history from the mythology by close examination of the surviving record sources and two important theses now provide a narrative of the reign, which both extends and challenges the analyses of the most successful general histories of the period, those of Gordon Donaldson and Jenny Wormald.[15] The work of the late Jamie Cameron on the personal rule of James V has been published recently and makes a valuable contribution to the historical perspective, but unfortunately Kenneth Emond's account of the minority regimes remains unpublished.[16]

12 *The Chronicle of Perth* (Maitland Club, 1831); 'The Chronicle of Aberdeen', in *Miscellany of the Spalding Club*, ii (1841); *A Diurnal of Remarkable Occurrents that have passed within the country of Scotland since the death of king James the Fourth till the year MDLXXV* (Bannatyne Club, 1833).

13 NLS MS 1746; Alasdair M. Stewart, 'The Final Folios of Adam Abell's "Roit or Quheill of Tyme": An Observantine Friar's Reflections of the 1520s and '30s' in Janet Hadley Williams (ed.), *Stewart Style, 1513–1542: Essays on the Court of James V* (East Linton, 1996), 227–53.

14 John Knox, *The Works*, ed. David Laing (6 vols., Woodrow Society, 1846–64), i (*The History of the Reformation in Scotland*); Jhone Leslie, *The Historie of Scotland* trans. James Dalrymple, ed. E. G. Cody and W. Murison (2 vols., STS, 1888–95); John Lesley, *The History of Scotland* (Bannatyne Club, 1830); Robert Lindsay of Pitscottie, *The Historie and Cronicles of Scotland*, ed. Æ. J. G. MacKay (3 vols., STS, 1899–1911); Robert Lindsay of Pitscottie, *The Chronicles of Scotland*, ed. John Graham Dalyell (2 vols., Edinburgh, 1814); George Buchanan, *The History of Scotland*, trans. J. Aikman (4 vols., Glasgow, 1827–9); Caroline Bingham, *James V, King of Scots, 1512–1542* (London, 1971). See also *Extracta e variis cronicis Scocie*, ed. W. B. D. Turnbull (Abbotsford Club, 1842).

15 Gordon Donaldson, *Scotland: James V-James VII* (Edinburgh, 1990), 3–62; Jenny Wormald, *Court, Kirk and Community: Scotland, 1470–1625* (Edinburgh, 1992), 3–108.

16 James S. Cameron, 'Crown-Magnate Relations in the Personal Rule of James V, 1528–1542' (University of St. Andrews Ph.D., 1994) is now in print as Jamie Cameron, *James V: the Personal Rule, 1528–1542*, ed. Norman Macdougall (East Linton, 1998); W. K. Emond, 'The Minority of King James V, 1513–1528' (University of St. Andrews Ph.D., 1988).

The wide-ranging and incisive research of Carol Edington on Lindsay and the court has also made a significant addition to the published accounts of the period and the courtly theme is pursued in an important collection of essays edited by Janet Hadley Williams and entitled *Stewart Style*.[17]

The most important aspects of the sequence of events of the reign need to be borne in mind when considering the cultural analysis of the following chapters. James V was the only surviving child of King James IV and Queen Margaret Tudor, who was the eldest daughter of King Henry VII of England. He succeeded to the throne in September 1513, at the tender age of seventeen months, after the defeat and death of his father by the armies of the earl of Surrey at the battle of Flodden. He thus inherited a realm in which the political community was by and large (but not unanimously) instinctively hostile to the English crown, whilst himself having a prominent place in the line of succession to that same crown. He also inherited a long-standing alliance with the French kingdom which was widely considered to have served the interests of France more effectively than those of Scotland. The international standing of the Scottish realm was placed under further pressure in the early 1530s when the English king renounced his allegiance to the church of Rome but simultaneously entered a period of uncharacteristically warm relations with the king of France, which endured until the Most Christian King and the Holy Roman Emperor buried their differences in 1538. This *rapprochement* created a Habsburg-Valois alliance which for two years threatened to develop into a crusade against Henry VIII, but which had collapsed in acrimony by 1540–41. In the see-sawing international diplomacy of the period, the friendship of the Scottish realm was seldom prized for its own sake, but could be alternately cultivated or disregarded according to how useful it might have become to an opposing power.[18]

The shifting sands of international relations made the long minority of James V (1513–28) a particularly unstable period, since the official lord governor (because he was the closest adult male heir to the throne)

17 Carol Edington, *Court and Culture in Renaissance Scotland: Sir David Lindsay of the Mount* (East Linton, 1995); Hadley Williams (ed.), *Stewart Style*.

18 Emond, 'Minority'; R. G. Eaves, *Henry VIII's Scottish Diplomacy, 1513–1524: England's Relations with the Regency Government of James V* (New York, 1971); Eaves, *Henry VIII and James V's Regency, 1524–1528: A Study in Anglo-Scottish Diplomacy* (London, 1987); D. M. Head, 'Henry VIII's Scottish Policy: A Reassessment', *SHR*, lxi (1982), 1–24; C. Patrick Hotle, *Thorns and Thistles: Diplomacy between Henry VIII and James V, 1528–1542* (Lanham, 1996).

was a man who styled himself Jehan Stuart, duc d'Albanie. He was the son of James III's exiled brother, Alexander, by his French wife; he was married to a French heiress, Anne de la Tour d'Auvergne; he was a peer of the French realm; and until 1515 he had neither set foot in Scotland nor spoken a word of Scots.[19] He exercised his governorship in person only for brief periods from May 1515 to September 1517, from November 1521 to October 1522, and from September 1523 to May 1524 and this timetable was dictated largely by the needs of French foreign policy (in particular relations with England) rather than Scottish domestic needs. In Albany's absence, power was wielded by Queen Margaret, the earl of Arran and other lords with varying degrees of incompetence, until in 1525–26 Archibald Douglas, sixth earl of Angus, achieved hegemony by the simple expedient of acquiring and retaining custody of the king. Angus's regime was partial and heavy-handed but was sponsored by Henry VIII, who was keen to counteract the francophilia of the duke of Albany. It came to an end in the summer of 1528 when the sixteen-year-old James V slipped away from his Douglas captors and proclaimed his personal rule. He set up camp at Stirling Castle (one of his mother's dower houses, which she made over to him) and called to his side all those lords who had been alienated by the Angus regime. A parliament was swiftly convened in which the Douglases were forfeited for treason, and this was followed by an attempt to enforce the ruling through a siege of Tantallon Castle, which failed. In March 1529 a deal was done with Henry VIII which secured exile in England for Angus and possession of his properties for James V.[20]

In the early 1530s the king stamped his authority on his realm by launching raids on the Borders and the Highlands and by successfully defending Scotland from English incursions in 1532–33. A Frenchbrokered peace treaty followed in May 1534. James also obtained papal agreement to tax the church heavily, ostensibly to fund the college of justice (which was established in Edinburgh in 1532 as a body of professional judges to staff the court of session for regular terms), but in reality much of the money raised went into the royal palacebuilding programme.[21] Other concessions secured from the papacy included the extension of the period for which the crown could draw

19 Marie W. Stuart, *The Scot who was a Frenchman* (Edinburgh, 1940).
20 Emond, 'Minority'; Cameron, *James V*, 9–69.
21 See W. S. Reid, 'Clerical Taxation: the Scottish Alternative to the Dissolution of the Monasteries', *Catholic Historical Review*, xxxiv (1948), 129–53.

the revenues of vacant benefices from eight months to one year (granted in March 1535), permission for the king to bestow five of the major Scottish abbacies upon his illegitimate and underage sons (and therefore to have access to their revenues until the boys came of age), and the gift of the blessed cap and sword, presented to the king in February 1537.[22] After many years of involved negotiations with several foreign governments, James V's marriage was agreed in March 1536. He was betrothed to a lady of the French blood royal, Marie de Bourbon, daughter of the duke of Vendôme. However, she was very much the consolation prize, since according to the treaty of Rouen (1517, ratified 1522) James should have married a daughter of King Francis I. In September 1536 James sailed to France to claim his bride, and having inspected her at her father's residence at St. Quentin, he rejected the match and managed to secure the hand of the Princess Madeleine instead. They were married in Paris on 1 January 1537 amid lavish festivities and pageantry. Upon Queen Madeleine's early death in July 1537, a second French marriage was arranged with Marie de Lorraine (otherwise known as Mary of Guise), eldest daughter of Claude de Lorraine, duke of Guise. She arrived in Scotland in June 1538 and produced two princes of Scotland who died in April 1541, before she gave birth to the future Mary, queen of Scots, in December 1542, just a week before the death of the king.[23]

By then relations with England, which had been cordial from 1534 to 1536, and increasingly tense from the time of the first French marriage, had broken down completely. The excuses offered for Surrey's cross-border raids were that James V had refused repeated invitations to meet his uncle in a face-to-face encounter designed to settle the differences between them, and that the king of Scots had been harbouring English rebels. The real reason was that Francis I and Charles V were at war again and that Henry VIII was in the process of reviving his imperial alliance and his claims to the throne of France. He was therefore impatient to take his armies to the continent, where he was convinced that a glorious victory awaited them. However, the French marriages and the papal favour bestowed upon James V had convinced Henry that if England launched a cross-channel invasion of France the Scots would attack its northern border, as had happened in

22 *The Letters of James V*, ed. R. K. Hannay and D. Hay (SHS, 1954), 279, 285, 327–9, 342–3, 357, 399, 423–7.

23 Cameron, *James V*, 131–6, 263–5, 323–5; Edmond Bapst, *Les Mariages de Jaques V* (Paris, 1889); Rosalind Marshall, *Mary of Guise* (London, 1977), 40–107.

1513. To avoid this potentially dangerous situation the English king decided on a pre-emptive strike in the summer and autumn of 1542 (there was no risk that an invasion of Scotland would precipitate a French assault on the English south coast), which he hoped would inflict sufficient damage upon the Scots to ensure that they did not venture a military campaign on behalf of the French. In the event, the decisive blow against potential Scottish action was delivered not by the English victory at Solway Moss on 24 November (although this was undoubtedly a humiliation for the Scots) but by the untimely death of King James on 14 December, leaving as his heir a baby girl only six days old. From the English point of view, this was a remarkable stroke of luck, and one which delayed Henry's continental adventures for a further year, whilst he tried to exploit the situation. From the Scottish point of view it was a calamity, which brought an abrupt halt to a period of relatively stable and effective government and of remarkable cultural development, plunging the realm into yet another long and traumatic minority.[24]

Setting politics and diplomacy aside, the reign of the adult James V has long been seen as an important period of development for the legal and fiscal aspects of Scottish government.[25] This may be largely a result of the accidental survival of official records, which are substantially more complete for the sixteenth century than for any earlier period, but it is also clear that this interpretation has at least some basis in reality. The financial administration of the period has been effectively dissected in the works of Athol Murray and it is not necessary to rehearse his findings in detail.[26] However, it is clear that during the minority of James V the accounts of the comptroller and treasurer were often 'superexpended' (in deficit). This was largely

24 Cameron, *James V*, 70–97, 131–60, 286–327; Head, 'Scottish Policy', 13–21; Hotle, *Thorns and Thistles*, 141–91.

25 Donaldson, *James V – James VII*, 43–8, 53, 56–8; Wormald, *Court, Kirk and Community*, 12–13, 15–16, 20–26. See also Cameron, *James V*, 1–7, 255–62.

26 A. L. Murray, 'Exchequer and Crown Revenue of Scotland, 1437–1542' (University of Edinburgh Ph.D., 1961); Murray, 'Exchequer and Council in the reign of James V', *Juridical Review*, v (1960), 209–25; Murray, 'The Procedure of the Scottish Exchequer in the early Sixteenth Century', *SHR*, xl (1961), 89–117; Murray, 'Accounts of the King's Pursemaster, 1539–40', *SHS Misc.*, x (1965), 13–51; Murray, 'Financing the Royal Household: James V and his Comptrollers, 1513–43', in I. B. Cowan and D. Shaw, *The Renaissance and Reformation in Scotland: Essays in Honour of Gordon Donaldson* (Edinburgh, 1983), 41–59; Murray, 'Exchequer, Council and Session, 1513–1542', in Hadley Williams (ed.), *Stewart Style*, 96–117.

because of the difficulties of regularly extracting full payments for rents, customs and other dues during a period of political instability, a problem which was compounded by the heavy expenditure of the regimes of the duke of Albany, Queen Margaret and the earl of Angus, which had to be met in addition to the household expenses of the young king. The problems continued into the early years of the adult reign because, as we have seen, there was still some unrest as well as military campaigns in the Borders and Isles during the period 1528 to 1534 and, even though the expenditure on the royal household was brought under firmer control, the king embarked on a lavish building programme and replenished the royal arsenal at considerable expense.[27] However, by the end of the reign the crown finances had been put on a relatively sound footing by a combination of tighter general management and the use of several effective expedients: the raising of taxation (both clerical and lay) when opportunities presented themselves (as they did for the foundation of the college of justice in 1532, or for the expenses arising from the arrangements for the king's marriage in 1535–36), the annexation of the lands of forfeited lords (those of the earl of Angus, Lord Glamis, Sir James Colville of East Wemyss and Sir James Hamilton of Finnart) and the control of monastic revenues held *in commendam* by the king's under-age and illegitimate sons (those of the abbeys of Melrose, Kelso and Holyrood and the priories of St. Andrews and Coldingham). Crown revenues were also augmented by the large dowries brought by the two French queens (£100,000 with Queen Madeleine and 100,000 merks with Queen Mary), as a result of the king's traditional act of revocation upon reaching his 'perfect age' of twenty-five years (an act originally made in Rouen in April 1537 and confirmed by the parliament of 1540–41), and following the resumption of Queen Margaret's jointure lands after her death in October 1541.[28] Cameron's consideration of James V's financial circumstances concluded that the king managed the collection and expenditure of his revenue well and generally lived within his means, and it was certainly the case that he left a cash surplus of £26,000 or more within his treasure chests on his death.[29] This contrasts markedly with the enormous debts left by both Francis I and Henry VIII in 1547, which

---

27 See chapters 2 and 5.
28 Murray, 'James V and his Comptrollers', 49–59; Murray, 'Pursemaster's Accounts', 24–7.
29 Cameron, *James V*, 255–62; *RSS*, iii, 383; Murray, 'Pursemaster's Accounts', 27.

they had managed to accumulate despite having considerably larger incomes than the king of Scots.[30]

Consideration of legal developments during the reign of James V has, quite naturally, focused on the establishment of the college of justice in May 1532.[31] This was presented as a royal initiative and James attended the opening ceremony in person, although Chancellor Dunbar and Secretary Erskine are usually credited with devising the scheme.[32] It certainly suited the king's financial ambitions to support the plan since it provided him with an excuse to levy regular taxation on the Scottish church with papal permission. It may also have appealed to him in principle as a means of fulfilling his royal duty to provide justice by establishing a professional body of judges in civil causes (and a group of licensed advocates) sitting for regular terms.[33] A detailed legal history of this period has yet to be written but recent research at the University of Edinburgh should improve our understanding of the processes and personalities involved considerably: Mark Godfrey has just produced a thesis on the jurisdiction and operation of the court of session in the 1520s and 1530s and John Finlay's work is on the development of the legal profession in the same period.[34] It would be premature to venture much

30 R. J. Knecht, *Renaissance Warrior and Patron: The Reign of Francis I* (Cambridge, 1994), 505; J. J. Scarisbrick, *Henry VIII* (1990), 453–4, 456. The exact extent of James V's income at the end of his reign is impossible to calculate, since much of it bypassed the official accounts; it has been estimated at something approaching £100,000 Scots p.a. (Cameron, *James V*, 262) which would equate to about £33,000 Sterling or £225,000 livres Tournois. Henry VIII's ordinary income (i.e. excluding taxes) reached about £300,000 Sterling in the late 1530s (C. S. L. Davies, *Peace, Print and Protestantism, 1450–1558* [London, 1990], 195) and Francis I's total revenue (including taxes) at the beginning of his reign was roughly 4.9 million livres (Knecht, *Warrior and Patron*, 59). These figures are only very approximate but suggest that the Scottish king's financial resources were possibly only a tenth those of the English monarch and a twentieth those of the French king.

31 R. K. Hannay, *The College of Justice*, ed. Hector L. MacQueen (Stair Society, 1990), 27–78.

32 Ibid., 49–54; D. E. Easson, *Gavin Dunbar, Chancellor of Scotland and Archbishop of Glasgow* (Edinburgh and London, 1947), 41–53.

33 *APS*, ii, 335–6; Donaldson, *James V – James VII*, 46–8.

34 Andrew Mark Godfrey, 'The Lords of Council and Session and the Foundation of the College of Justice: A Study in Jurisdiction' (University of Edinburgh Ph.D. thesis, 1998); John Finlay, 'Professional Men of Law before the Lords of Council, c.1500 – c.1550' (University of Edinburgh, Ph.D. thesis, 1998). I am very grateful to both of them for discussing some of their findings with me.

further comment on the subject at this point, but an examination of the published accounts of the period seems to suggest some links between the legal developments of the 1530s and the royal court.

Of the men who served on the bench before 1542, many were very close servants of the king and familiar figures within the court and household, and in that the court of session seems to have evolved as a sub-committee of the royal council, to which body the council's judicial functions in civil cases had devolved, this should not be particularly surprising.[35] Yet the number of names which can be located both within the royal court or household and within the court of session may nevertheless raise a suspicion that the foundation of the college of justice may have been, at least in part, intended to extend the operation of the royal prerogative rather than solely to formalise the disinterested administration of impartial justice. This impression is reinforced by the power which the king exercised to appoint extraordinary lords to sit alongside the ordinary judges at the royal pleasure, and by the fact that the court of session had an exclusive competence in all cases involving the crown.[36] Senators of the college with dual roles included the first lord president, Alexander Mylne, abbot of Cambuskenneth, who acted as the administrator of the lands of two of the king's illegitimate sons from June 1540; Sir James Colville who was also the comptroller between 1530 and 1538; whilst John Dingwall, William Gibson, Sir John Campbell of Lundy and Nichol Crawford of Oxgangs had all acted as auditors of exchequer at some point.[37] Likewise the extraordinary lords of session included many royal familiars such as Lord Erskine, appointed in November 1532, who was the captain of Stirling Castle; two successive deans of the chapel royal were appointed in 1533 and 1541 (Henry Wemyss and Andrew Durie); the king's secretary, Sir Thomas Erskine of Brechin was appointed in 1533; and Sir James Hamilton of Finnart was the master of the king's stables when he was appointed in 1534.[38] Some of the advocates licensed to plead before

---

35 Hannay, *College of Justice*, 1–25; A. M. M. Duncan, 'The Central Courts before 1532', in G. C. H. Paton (ed.), *An Introduction to Scottish Legal History* (Stair Society, 1958), 330–39.

36 Hannay, *College of Justice*, 28, 128–30.

37 *James V Letters*, 399; ER, xv, 84, 357, 373, 550; xvi, 127, 402; xvii, 155; *TA*, v, 99, 111, 280, 454, 463.

38 ADCP, 389; G. Brunton and D. Haig, *An Historical Account of the Senators of the College of Justice* (Edinburgh, 1836), 41–2, 68–9, 43–4, 52–5. For their offices in the royal household see Andrea Thomas, 'Renaissance Culture at the Court of James V, 1528–1542' (University of Edinburgh Ph.D. thesis, 1997), Appendix A, pp. 299–375.

the court of session also moved in royal circles (and many were subsequently raised to the bench): Robert Galbraith had been treasurer of the chapel royal between 1528 and 1532; Henry Lauder became king's advocate in 1538; whilst Thomas Marjoribanks, Henry Balnaves and James Carmuir had all worked as royal clerks.[39] Thus, whilst it is certainly possible to interpret the establishment of the college of justice as a significant step along the road to the development of a centralised, bureaucratic and professional judicial system, it may also be viewed in a rather different light. The multiple activities and interests of the personnel of the court of session of the period might also suggest that this was something less than a professional body, an offshoot of the royal court and council which consisted of men experienced in legal matters, but who were not dedicated to a career in the law to the exclusion of all other possibilities. Adam Otterburn is perhaps a prime example of this: he was one of the original fifteen senators appointed in May 1532 (having already served as a lord of session for some years prior to that date), he was also the king's advocate (and *ex officio* of his council) between 1524 and 1538, he was frequently appointed to one or both of the parliamentary committees of the period (the lords of the articles and of causes), he served as a parliamentary commissioner (for instance as a searcher at the ports to prevent the export of specie in 1535), and was repeatedly sent to England on diplomatic missions as a royal envoy and expert negotiator. Furthermore, he was also a burgess of Edinburgh who engaged in a trade in cloth and iron and served seven terms as provost of the burgh.[40]

Alongside Otterburn's wide-ranging legal, commercial, diplomatic and public activities, there is also a suggestion that he had some literary talent: in June 1538 he was one of three men commissioned by the burgh of Edinburgh to compose a French oration, the text of which has not survived, to welcome Mary of Guise on the occasion of her royal entry to the town. The others were David Lindsay and James Foulis of Colinton and the speech was to be delivered by Henry Lauder. Otterburn has also been credited with composing some Latin hexam-

---

39 *RMS*, iii, 605; *RSS*, ii, 1104, 2714; *TA*, vi, 327–32; *RMS*, iii, 2116; *RSS*, i, 4090. For the advocates of the period see F. J. Grant (ed.), *The Faculty of Advocates in Scotland, 1532–1943* (SRS, 1944), 10, 13, 14, 26, 46, 78, 82, 110, 114, 117, 118, 121, 123, 128, 132, 144, 179, 197, 203, 218, 225–6; G. W. T. Omond, *The Lords Advocate of Scotland* (3 vols., Edinburgh, 1883), i, 9–24. See also Thomas, 'Renaissance Culture', Appendix A, pp. 299–375.

40 *ADCP*, 177; *RSS*, ii, 2714; *APS*, ii, 336, 285, 292, 304, 322, 333, 334, 341, 343; *ADCP*, 293, 405, 450–51; J. A. Inglis, *Sir Adam Otterburn of Redhall* (Glasgow, 1935), 1–3, 5–6, 15–16, 35–6, 41–3, 61–2, 66–7, 77, 82–9.

eters which were later used by George Buchanan as the basis of a poem.[41] It is easy to imagine that Castiglione would have approved of the administrative and artistic skills developed by Otterburn in his distinguished career, although the Italian would have found the trading activities inappropriate for a courtier and would have lamented the lapses in political judgement which led to dismissal from the post of king's advocate in 1538.[42] Nevertheless, it is clear that the concept of the *uomo universale* as propounded by Castiglione was not alien to the Scottish court of the period and, as the following chapters will attempt to demonstrate, James V recruited into his service many multi-talented 'Renaissance men' who contributed in various ways to a vibrant, assertive and cosmopolitan courtly culture.

41 *Extracts from the Records of the Burgh of Edinburgh, 1528–1557* (SBRS, 1871), ii, 89; Inglis, *Adam Otterburn*, 116–18.
42 See Inglis, *Adam Otterburn*, 67–70 and Cameron, *James V*, 256.

ONE

Magnificence and Domesticity: the Royal Household

The early-modern royal court was an important 'point of contact' for those people engaged in all aspects of political, diplomatic, religious, social and cultural activities, and the royal household, at the centre of the court, was therefore of considerable significance.[1] Recent household studies for France and England in the fifteenth and sixteenth centuries have greatly assisted a fuller appreciation of the physical and social environment in which the political and administrative developments of the period took place and traced the interaction of the mechanisms of domestic service with the wider world.[2] The study of the household of Scottish monarchs is still in its infancy, so this consideration of the household of James V is a preliminary sketch against which to set the cultural developments discussed in later chapters.[3] It is also an attempt to place the Scottish experience within the wider context of the northern European Renaissance court. In so doing, this chapter is primarily concerned with the personnel, organisation and routine of the domestic life of the Scottish court, but it also sheds some light on the networks of patronage and clientage which can be discerned dimly in the surviving records. Later chapters pursue the cultural themes in more detail and

1 G. R. Elton, 'Tudor Government: The Points of Contact, III: The Court', *TRHS*, xxvi (1976), 211–28.
2 A. R. Myers, *The Household of Edward IV: The Black Book and the Ordinance of 1478* (Manchester, 1959); D. R. Starkey, 'The Rise of the Privy Chamber, 1485–1547', in Starkey (ed.), *The English Court* (London, 1987), 71–117; Kate Mertes, *The English Noble Household, 1250–1600: Good Governance and Politic Rule* (Oxford, 1988); R. J. Knecht, 'The Court of Francis I', *European Studies Review*, viii (1978), 1–18 and Knecht, *Renaissance Warrior and Patron: the Reign of Francis I* (Cambridge, 1994), 117–33.
3 Published works which have touched on aspects of this field so far include: Murray, 'Financing the Royal Household', 41–59; Murray, 'Procedure of the Scottish Exchequer', 89–117; Murray, 'The Comptroller, 1425–1488', *SHR*, lii (1973), 1–29; Murray, 'Pursemaster's Accounts' 1539–40', 13–51; John Warrack, *Domestic Life in Scotland, 1488–1688* (Edinburgh, 1920); 'The Scottish King's Household', ed. M. Bateson, *SHS Misc.*, ii (1904), 3–43; the prefaces to the relevant volumes of *TA* and *ER*. Research into the royal household of James VI is being undertaken by Amy Juhala at the University of Edinburgh and I am grateful to her for discussing her preliminary findings with me.

further illuminate the operation of patronage within the royal household, in the wider court circle, and beyond into the local communities and international arena.

In an age of personal monarchy, the household of a sixteenth-century king fulfilled several overlapping functions and that of James V was no exception. It provided a permanent staff to perform services for the monarch and his entourage, ranging from the ceremonial to the menial. It provided opportunities for subjects to develop direct relationships with their sovereign, fostering ties of mutual trust, affection and loyalty, which could be utilised by both parties in pursuit of personal, dynastic and political goals. The household could also act as a cultural focus for the court, adding lustre and prestige to the monarch and the rituals of monarchy by accommodating favoured artists, writers, craftsmen and musicians in lucrative and influential posts. Finally, the household frequently provided sinecures for the clerks, lawyers, bureaucrats and other functionaries involved in the management of the crown lands and revenues and in the administration of the realm (two areas of responsibility which inevitably overlapped at this period).[4] In all these functions the royal household was a many-faceted support system designed to help the king reconcile the many contradictory demands and expectations placed upon a 'good lord': it was concerned with economy and liberality, with the humdrum and the majestic, with the private and the public, with security and accessibility. The *Liber Niger* of Edward IV of England (1471–72) expressed this duality of function in the way in which it described the two main divisions within the English royal household: the *domus providencie* and the *domus magnificencie*.[5] This arrangement was borrowed by the English king from the Burgundian tradition and such terms do not appear in the Scottish sources but the Scottish household was nevertheless a multi-purpose organisation in a similar mould.

The natural starting point for most household studies is the record of rules and regulations governing the organisation, such as the *Liber Niger* (which was a draft of proposed reforms) or the *Eltham Ordinances*

---

4 See David Starkey, 'The age of the household: politics, society and the arts c.1350–c.1550', in Stephen Medcalf (ed.), *The Context of English Literature: The Later Middle Ages* (London, 1981), 225–90; David Loades, *The Tudor Court* (Bangor, 1992), 1–84; Richard Firth Green, *Poets and Princepleasers: Literature and the English Court in the Late Middle Ages* (Toronto, 1980), 13–70; Chris Given Wilson, *The Royal Household and the King's Affinity: Service, Politics and Finance in England, 1360–1413* (New Haven and London, 1986), 258–62.

5 Myers, *Household of Edward IV*, 15.

of 1526.[6] Unfortunately, very few household ordinances survive in the
Scottish record, and what little information is available is not always as
full or as explicit as one might wish. However, analysis of the available
evidence is not a totally unrewarding task and does suggest areas in
which the Scottish practice conformed to, and differed from, the
conventions of other courts. The earliest Scottish document which
bears any resemblance to the English ordinances dates from January
1508 and may suggest that James IV was intending to impose greater
discipline on his household than had previously been the case. It opens:

> The haill place and residens of the kingis quharever it be to be
> clengit of all maner of rascall and boyis weill & onhonest personis
> quhatsumever ['quheddir tha be on the bill or nocht' struck out].
>
> Item ilk lord extra ordinar out of the bill of houshald to enter
> witht ii personis witht hym and to be nemmyt quaht he was at the
> nixt compt be name be the mercheall.
>
> Item ilk knycht i persoun sic lyk & ony honest gentilman of
> reputacioun providing alway tha be nemmyt.
>
> Item that na maner person haf ma entering na thar ordinar in
> the kingis bill of houshald & the extra ordinar be admittit as is
> befor said.
>
> Item that na officiar kep ma in his offis housis than is conteint &
> allowit in the bill of houshald.[7]

It then proceeds with the 'bill of houshald' which lists the members of
the household both 'ordinar' and 'extraordinar' (i.e. those receiving
fees, wages and/or livery clothes and those who served unpaid) and
catalogues the number of personal servants each would be allowed to
keep at court, with the implication that they would be fed and housed
at the king's expense, a privilege known as 'bouche of court'. The list
ranges from the hereditary master of the household, the earl of Argyll
(who was allowed eight servants), down to the pages, clerks of the
chapel royal, and other lesser figures (who do not seem to have been
permitted any). This document is important for several reasons: firstly,
it indicates a concern for maintaining the proper dignity of members of
the court, according to their rank, whilst at the same time limiting the
population in the interests of economy and discipline. It also suggests

---

6 For these and other examples see *Household Ordinances* (London, Society of
  Antiquaries, 1790).
7 SRO, Misc. Household Papers, E.34/1, fo. 1r. The full text is transcribed in
  Thomas, 'Renaissance Culture', App. B, pp. 376–83, by kind permission of
  the Keeper of the Records for Scotland.

that the king felt some responsibility for the moral welfare of his entourage. Both of these concerns can also be detected in the household ordinances of other courts of the period.[8] More significant is the indication it provides of the number and quality of the extraordinary members of the household. There is no surviving 'bill of household' for the reign of James V and because the extraordinary lords and knights did not receive fees or livery, they hardly feature in the accounts of the king's expenditure, except when they received an occasional payment by special precept. For example, at Yule 1538, the following received 'livery extraordinar': George Steel, John Hamilton of Colmskeith, William Durham (the heir of the laird of Grange in Angus), John Denniston (the parson of Dysart), sir Michael Dysart, sir William Drummond (both of the chapel royal) and a French apothecary. Thus, if the precedent set by James IV was followed by his son (and, as we shall see, James V did seek to emulate his father in many things), we should expect to add the nobles and prelates, who usually served on the king's council, as well as a body of knights and squires of attendance (numbering forty-eight men on the 1508 list) to the list of the recorded household members. Indeed, in August 1526 (admittedly before James V was ruling in his own right), the king's auditors of exchequer were instructed to 'caus our officiaris to have siclyk wagis and dewitis lyk as thai had in our said derrest fadiris tyme and eftir the tenour of his saidis bukis'.[9]

There are only two surviving examples of (partial) household ordinances from the reign of James V. The first is undated but signed by the king's own hand and is a set of instructions to his master of household concerning the smooth running of the organisation. The king insists that his master of household should ensure that no one enters or leaves the court without proper authority (especially 'laddis or vyle boyis'), that his servants are decently housed, fed and clothed and that any complaints about non-payment of wages or allowances are dealt with swiftly and fairly. The second document seems to have been drafted c.1582 by one of James V's former masters of household, Sir James Learmonth of Dairsie, as guidance for the reform of the household of

8 Mertes, *English Noble Household*, 57–8, 188; Myers, *Household of Edward IV*, 40–9; Firth Green, *Poets and Princepleasers*, 18–21; Starkey, 'Age of the Household', 255–7; Loades, *Tudor Court*, 85–95.

9 *TA*, vii, 127; *ADCP*, 251. Many of the councillors are identified and discussed in Emond, 'Minority' and Cameron, *James V*. See also *ADCP* and SRO, Transumpt of Council Sederunts, 1518–1553, RH.2/1/9. For the full list of James V's recorded household see Thomas, 'Renaissance Culture', App. A, pp. 299–375.

James VI.[10] However, it concerns only the duties and responsibilities of the king's steward or senior caterer, and presumably it was once accompanied by similar descriptions of other key offices. It indicates that the steward was responsible for supervising the provision and distribution of all food and drink within the household (particularly supplies which had to be purchased at market), for obtaining value for money, for keeping in good order household items such as pots and pans and for answering for all relevant expenditure at the daily accounts. Incidentally, this document also reveals that there was no established formal system of purveyance, such as was enforced in England, for the steward was advised to buy supplies with ready cash whenever possible and to be very cautious when obtaining supplies on credit; but certain crown revenues were still paid in kind rather than cash, since grain, herrings, beef-cattle and so forth were regularly received as the king's dues.[11] Other sources of information on the household of James V are primarily records of expenditure: the accounts of the king's pantry, buttery, kitchen, wine cellar, spice-house, and avery are still in manuscript form[12] but the *Treasurer's Accounts*,

---

10 SRO, Instructions for the Master of Household, E.34/6; The Office of Steward, E.34/7: also transcribed in Thomas, 'Renaissance Culture', App. B, pp. 383–5. The household records of the reign of James VI are much fuller than those of the earlier period, see 'The Estate of the King and Quenis Majesties Houshald Reformit', in *Papers Relative to the Marriage of King James the Sixth of Scotland with the Princess Anna of Denmark, 1589*, ed. J. T. Gibson Craig (Bannatyne Club, 1828), App. 3, pp. 23–38; A. Gibson and T. C. Smout, 'Food and Hierarchy in Scotland, 1550–1650', in Leah Lenman (ed.), *Perspectives in Scottish Social History: Essays in honour of Rosalind Mitchison* (Aberdeen, 1988), 33–52. See also Rosalind Marshall, 'The Queen's Table', in Hugh Cheape (ed.), *Tools and Traditions: Studies in European Ethnology Presented to Alexander Fenton* (Edinburgh, 1993), 138–43. The household of James VI will be considered by Amy Juhala in her forthcoming thesis and she kindly allowed me to preview some of her findings.

11 E.g. SRO, Liber Domicili, E. 31/3, fos. 36v.-66v.

12 SRO, Libri Domicilii, 1525–39, E.31/1–8; SRO, Libri Emptorum, 1531–42, E.32/2–8. See also SRO, Misc. household papers, 1508–82, E.34/1–7; SRO, Wardrobe Inventories, 1539–42, E.35/1; and the (fragmentary) household accounts of Mary of Guise: SRO, Despence de la Maison Royale, 1538–42, E.33/1–2; SRO, Misc. household papers, 1538–43, E.34/8; NLS, Balcarres Papers, Adv. MS. 29.2.5, fos. 104, 105, 107, 127. Short extracts from some of these manuscripts are printed in *Excerpta e Libris Domicilii Domini Jacobi Quinti Regis Scotorum* (Bannatyne Club, 1836); *Facsimiles of the National Manuscripts of Scotland*, (3 vols, London, 1867–71), iii, nos. xvii, xviii & xxiii; *A Collection of Inventories and other Records of the Royal Wardrobe and Jewelhouse: and of the Artillery and Munitioun in some of the Royal Castles, 1488–1606*, ed. T. Thomson (Edinburgh, 1815), 29–113. See also *cont'd over/*

Exchequer Rolls, Pursemaster's Accounts and *Masters of Works' Accounts* are in print.[13] The financial records can also be supplemented by information taken from the legal, administrative and narrative sources of the period (as subsequent references will demonstrate), but these usually provide only tantalising glimpses of a wider picture, which is now very difficult to reconstruct with great confidence.

Heavy reliance on financial accounts brings dangers for the historian: the terminology used by the clerks may have been developed more to suit their own convenience than to represent the realities of domestic arrangements and warnings have been sounded against accepting the evidence of such sources too literally.[14] However, even if the surviving records appear to suggest a more coherent departmental structure for the household than was actually the case, it is clear that such places as 'the stable' and 'the wardrobe' did have real physical locations and specialist members of staff serving in them. Thus, although listing recorded household members by their 'department' is a rather clumsy analytical method, yielding results which must be tentative and subject to further qualification and elaboration where possible, it is nevertheless a useful exercise in that it enables us to place the wider developments of the political, economic, religious, social and cultural spheres in a personal and domestic context. A study of the royal household therefore sheds considerable light upon the daily routine and environment of the men of power and influence within the Scottish realm.

The royal household provided the close personal body servants, such as the king's barber, or the attendants who would sleep on pallet beds in the king's bedchamber (Henry VIII even had a lavatorial attendant, the groom of the stool)[15] as well as the more distant menials, who served the king and his court (the stable-lads, kitchen-boys, footmen and the like). It also provided, in its more ceremonial and honorific positions, opportunities for men of influence in the localities to be drawn into the orbit of the court, opening channels of communication and patronage useful to both parties. In this respect James V may not have used his household as successfully as his father had done, at times relying too heavily on a narrow group of favoured lairds rather than encouraging personal service from a wide range of influential fa-

Note in right margin: method & limitations

cont'd   Henry Ellis, 'Observations upon a Household Book of King James the Fifth of Scotland', *Archaeologia*, xxii (1829), 1–12, and Murray, 'The Comptroller', 16–19.

13 *TA*, v-viii; *ER*, xiv-xvii; Murray, 'Pursemaster's Accounts'; *MW*, i.

14 Mertes, *English Noble Household*, 17–8, 37–8.

15 Starkey, 'Age of the Household', 250–1.

milies.[16] However, this impression may have been created by the patchy survival of relevant sources and it has been argued recently that the king's relations with his magnates were far from being as antagonistic as they have been represented traditionally.[17] If the surviving household records understate the noble presence at court (as the 1508 bill of household, considered above, would appear to suggest), it may have been the case that James V was more successful in implementing the established conventions of household politics than he is generally given credit for. One suggestive reference is in Sir Ralph Sadler's description of his reception at the court of James V in February 1540, when he was sent there on a rather delicate embassy by Henry VIII. He was entrusted to the care of Sir David Lindsay of the Mount, Robert Hart, Sir Walter Ogilvy and Sir John Borthwick: only the first two of whom, as heralds, feature in the household accounts of the period. Furthermore, when Sadler dined at court he was entertained by Cardinal Beaton, the archbishop of Glasgow, the bishop of Aberdeen, Lord Erskine, the earls of Huntly, Errol, Cassilis, Atholl and other lords and gentlemen. The three prelates, the earl of Errol and Lord Erskine all held household posts but none of the others had an official role, except as great magnates of the realm. Without Sadler's testimony we would be unable to detect their presence at court at this time and this may well apply to the periods for which we lack an ambassador's report too.[18]

Foreign parallels include the fifteenth-century dukes of Burgundy (who were kings in all but name), who regarded this aspect of their household management as so important that key posts were held by provincial magnates for three or six months of the year in rotation, and when they returned home they were expected to promote the 'party-line' in their localities.[19] Likewise, in Tudor England, the possession of a household office conferred such status and influence on a country gentleman that he would be eager to advertise his court connections by

16 Michael Lynch, *Scotland: A New History* (London, 1992), 165–6.
17 Cameron, *James V*, especially pp. 328–35.
18 *The State Papers and Letters of Sir Ralph Sadler*, ed. A. Clifford (3 vols, Edinburgh, 1809), i, 17–45. See also A. S. Slavin, *Politics and Profit: A Study of Sir Ralph Sadler, 1507–1587* (Cambridge, 1966), 68–93 and Humphrey Drummond, *Our Man in Scotland: Sir Ralph Sadleir* [sic], *1507–1587* (London, 1969), 23–60. Saddler actually names one of his contacts as captain Borthwick, but since he died before 1532 (*RSS*, ii, 1213) this is probably a reference to Sir John Borthwick.
19 C. A. J. Armstrong, 'The Golden Age of Burgundy', in A. G. Dickens (ed.), *The Courts of Europe* (New York, 1984), 63; R. Vaughan, *Valois Burgundy* (London, 1975), 97.

embellishing his house with the Tudor arms, heraldic badges and livery colours (green and white), as did Sir Richard Clement at Ightham Mote and Sir William Compton at Compton Wynyates, both in the 1520s.[20] Similar conditions probably existed in Scotland as well, where the *Register of the Privy Seal* stands as prime testimony to the rewards garnered by faithful royal servants. Grants of lands, titles, offices and exemptions (benefices for clerics) conferred financial and social privileges on many members of James V's household, the most outstanding example of which was Sir James Hamilton of Finnart (an illegitimate son of the first earl of Arran), who accumulated the posts of master sewer (from 1526 to 1539), master of the stables (from 1527 to 1536), principal master of works (from 1539 to his death), captain and keeper of the palace of Linlithgow (from 1526 until his death), and captain of Dumbarton Castle (from 1527 to 1531) before his forfeiture and execution on trumped-up charges in August 1540.[21] His fate, like those of Wolsey and Cromwell in England or Semblançay in France, also illustrates graphically how the continuing rewards of service were dependant on maintaining the favour of the king (and not provoking his covetousness), again underlining the very personal nature of the monarchy of the period.

Among the chamber servants of James V's household were the men who came as close as was possible to being the king's friends. These were the high-spirited gallants, who would join him in riding, hunting, playing tennis and other amusements: men such as Oliver Sinclair of Pitcairn (who was the king's cupbearer and reputedly housed one of the king's mistresses for him), or John Tennent of Listonshiels (the king's pursemaster and yeoman of the wardrobe, who is supposed to have swapped roles with the king when James wanted to visit incognito his affianced bride, Marie de Vendôme, in 1536).[22] There are hints in the *Treasurer's Accounts* that the courtiers' amusements were sometimes rather boisterous. In 1533 James paid compensation to Elizabeth Macall, the wife of the keeper of the park of Stirling, whose cow he killed with a culverin, presumably accidentally. Similarly, compensation was paid in April 1540 to the owner of two lambs slain

20 Starkey, 'Age of the Household', 272–3; Starkey, 'Ightham Mote', *History Today*, xxx (Jan. 1980), 58–60.
21 *TA*, v, 307; vii, 302; *RMS*, iii, 2021, 2194; *ER*, xv, 380; xvi, 480E; *RSS*, i, 3523, 3778, 3779; ii, 890, 3144; Charles McKean, 'Hamilton of Finnart', *History Today*, xliii (Jan. 1993), 42–7. A sewer was a table servant. For more on James V's distribution of patronage to magnates and household men see Cameron, *James V*, 266–74.
22 *Hamilton Papers*, i, 329; Bapst, *Mariages*, 289.

by John Tennent.[23] There are also references to egg-throwing, which are reminiscent of the accounts of Francis I and his gentlemen careering through the streets of Paris hurling insults, stones and eggs at the common people for a lark.[24] Entertainment was also provided by dwarves, fools and a juggler and the king owned a splendid chess set, the board made of silver and gold and the pieces of jasper and rock crystal.[25] There is a scarcity of narrative sources illustrating the day to day pastimes of the court of James V but it is likely that wagers were laid on games of cards, dice and tennis as well as on archery contests and jousting matches, which featured in the life of other courts of the period.[26] According to Pitscottie, such a match was arranged at St. Andrews by Queen Margaret in February 1536, when the gentlemen accompanying the English embassy of Lord William Howard and William Barlow, bishop elect of St. Asaph, were challenged to an archery contest against a team of Scottish lairds and yeomen. The prize, supplied by the queen, was a purse of one hundred crowns and a tun of wine – the Scots won.[27] One indication of some of the favourite pastimes of James V is given by David Lindsay in *The Testament of the Papyngo*:

> Quharefor, sen thou hes sic capacitie
> To lerne to playe [music] so plesandlie, and syng,
> Ryde hors, ryn speris with gret audacitie,
> Schute with hand bow, crosbow, and culveryng,
> Amang the rest, schir, lerne to be ane kyng.[28]

In addition to providing personal service and companionship for the king, the household could be used as a method of bestowing patronage on favoured artists, writers, craftsmen and musicians. The cultural patronage of the court will be considered in more detail in subsequent chapters but at this stage it is probably useful to indicate that such matters seem to have had a considerable impact on the Scottish royal household. Many contemporary kings were far better placed to use

---

23 *TA*, vi, 96; Murray, 'Pursemaster's Accounts', 44.

24 *TA*, v, 257, 275; Knecht, 'Court of Francis I', 15–16; E. Hall, *The Union of the Two Noble and Illustre Famelies of Lancastre and York*, (London, 1809, originally 1519), 597.

25 SRO, Wardrobe Inventories, E.35/1, fo. 21v.

26 Loades, *Tudor Court*, 96–113.

27 Pitscottie, *History* (STS), i, 340–41; SRO, Liber Emptorum, E.32/5, unnumbered folio between fos. 64v. and 65r.

28 Lindsay, *Works*, i, 64.

their households in this field than James V: Francis I had both Leonardo da Vinci and Benvenuto Cellini on his payroll for brief periods and many other artists, architects and humanists, Italians, French and Flemish were employed in his *châteaux*, libraries and lectureships. Likewise, Henry VIII employed Hans Holbein, Nicolaus Kratzer, Thomas Tallis and others in household posts.[29] In comparison, James V's artistic patronage was rather low-key, but lacking as he did the superior financial resources of the Valois and Tudor monarchs, he nevertheless made a creditable effort in some areas. As will be seen, Scottish architecture, music, poetry, humanism and the sciences of ballistics, navigation and fortification all benefited from the interest of the king; and masons, sculptors, minstrels, writers, scholars, gunners and shipwrights all appear in the household records in considerable numbers. If the names of these men are not all amongst the foremost of the period, their achievements are nevertheless worthy of note and some, such as the herald-poet Sir David Lindsay, or the humanist-historian Hector Boece, were figures of international standing.

There is another very important aspect to the functions of the royal household in this period. Many of the chaplains, lawyers, clerks and scribes that served the king were also servants of the crown in its administrative, judicial and financial activities, manning as they did the exchequer, the chancery, the treasury and other offices. There was considerable movement of personnel between the two areas and experience and expertise developed in one field was clearly regarded as valuable in the other. The boundary between service to the monarch in person and service to the crown in matters of government was very indistinct in the sixteenth century; indeed every subject of the king was also, in a sense, his servant. Just as the sheriffs and justices were charged with enforcing the king's laws, and the various treaties or conflicts of the reign were considered to be the king's causes, so too the officers of state were understood to be his men. In England, privy councillors (whether holding official posts or the magnatial status which entitled them to offer counsel to the king as of right) were considered to be 'ordinary of the chamber' with 'bouche of court' and, as we have seen, the 1508 bill of household suggests that the councillors of the Scottish king may well have had similar privileges.[30] Certainly, it is sometimes very difficult to

29 D Seward, *Prince of the Renaissance: The Life of Francis I* (London, 1973), 88, 215; Knecht, *Warrior and Patron*, 425–77; D. Starkey (ed.), *Henry VIII: A European Court in England* (London, 1991), 58–63, 70–73, 104–6.

30 D. Hoak, 'The King's Privy Chamber, 1547–53' in D. J. Guth & J. W. McKenna (eds.), *Tudor Rule & Revolution* (Cambridge, 1982), 91.

discern from the contemporary records exactly who was a member of the government, or of the household, or both. Many of the clerics recommended for ecclesiastical preferment to the pope and the cardinal protector at Rome by the king were described as his 'familiar' or 'well-loved servitour' or something similar, even if their names never appear in the surviving household accounts.[31] Moreover, it would be wrong to imagine that only those people whose names do appear in the household accounts can be categorised as household members. Some posts were clearly unpaid (such as John Tennent's post as yeoman of the crossbow), whilst grants of fees or pensions to clergymen entering the king's service were often made as an interim measure until they obtained benefices worth a specified minimum sum, after which time they might cease to appear in the records, even though they would continue to carry out their duties (such an arrangement was made for sir James Nicholson, chaplain, as master of works in Stirling Castle).[32]

In England, the nominal distinction between the personal and the governmental servants of the crown is somewhat easier to define since, by the late-fifteenth century, several offices had 'gone out of court' (such as the chancery, the exchequer, the judicial benches and even the great wardrobe) and become permanently established in regular premises at Westminster or nearby.[33] Yet this does not seem to have been the case in Scotland; indeed, far from being a permanent office or court, the Scottish exchequer, for example, was convened anew each summer, with lords of exchequer appointed only for the duration of a specific audit.[34] Offices such as the exchequer and the treasury thus straddled the (modern) boundary between personal and governmental service and so did their staff. The comptroller collected the rents and dues from the royal lands and paid the main expenses of the king's household but also handled customs revenues and the expenses of some officials. The treasurer received the payments due to the king as a feudal lord and paid out for the royal alms, liveries, palaces and stables, but he also collected the profits of justice and of the mint and paid for messengers, munitions and ships. The roles of the lords of council were also very wide-ranging, with the same officers deliberating on matters of policy, finance, justice and the king's personal affairs, apparently indiscriminately.[35] The only separation and specialisation of power in the period

31 For instance, *James V Letters*, 195, 225, 251, 260, 270.
32 *ER*, xv, 548; *RSS*, ii, 487.
33 Loades, *Tudor Court*, 38.
34 Murray, 'Exchequer and Council', 209–25.
35 J. M. Thomson, *The Public Records of Scotland* (Glasgow, 1922), 82–3; *ADCP*, pp. xxxiii & xliv.

came when the college of justice was established in 1532 to take responsibility for civil cases; and even then many of the early senators were also royal familiars, as we have seen.[36] The boundaries between church and state were also hopelessly blurred in a manner typical of the age, with many of the senior Scottish prelates achieving their exalted positions largely as a result of their services to the king in both public and private matters. Indeed, by bestowing five of the major abbeys or priories on his under-age, illegitimate sons, James ensured that the Scottish church became 'not so much a department of state as a sub-department of the royal household.'[37]

Some of the officers wearing several different 'hats' included Sir James Kirkcaldy of Grange, who received livery from 1534 to 1542, was described as 'servitor regis' in October 1537, 'steward' (dapifer) of the king in 1538 and 1540, 'sewer' in 1542 and was treasurer from 24 March 1538 until August 1543, in which capacity he was also an auditor of exchequer.[38] Likewise, David Wood of Craig was the king's master lardner from 1528 until 1537, his carver from 1538 until 1542, and comptroller from 14 September 1538 until 17 March 1543, and therefore also an auditor of exchequer.[39] Of the clergy, David Beaton was perhaps the most active: he was abbot of Arbroath from June 1524, bishop of Mirepoix from July/August 1538, a cardinal from December 1538 and archbishop of St Andrews from February 1539, as well as being keeper of the privy seal from January 1529, an ambassador to France on several occasions from 1524 onwards, receiver of the dowries of Madeleine de Valois and Mary of Guise and, shortly after James V's death, chancellor.[40] There are also many other examples of men of all ranks holding offices within the church, government and household of the king, using their service at court to further their career in other fields and *vice versa*.

Because of the multiplicity of roles undertaken by some individual officers and the indistinct nature of the boundaries of those offices, it is also rather difficult to be precise about the size, structure and organisation of the royal household in this period. A manuscript belonging to Corpus Christi College, Cambridge, gives some indication of how the

---

36 Brunton and Haig, *Senators of the College of Justice*, 1–72.

37 Lynch, *Scotland*, 155.

38 *TA*, vi, 202; viii, 150; *RMS*, iii, 1718; *ER*, xvii, 164, 279; *TA*, viii, 100, 150; vi, 380; *ER*, xvii, 155, 269.

39 *ER*, xv, 460; *TA*, vi, 464; vii, 125; *ER*, xvii, 164; *TA*, viii, 100; vii, 65, 313; SRO, Liber Domicili, E.31/8, fo. 4r.; Liber Emptorum, E.32/8, fos. 71v., 72r.

40 M. H. B. Sanderson, *Cardinal of Scotland: David Beaton, c.1494–1546* (Edinburgh, 1986), 16, 17, 39, 68, 72; *RSS*, ii, 4019; iii, 21.

households of the Scottish kings were ordered in the early fourteenth century, and may have been prepared as a summary for Edward I of England in 1305.[41] The document lists the chief officers of the king, both 'denzeins' and 'foreins' (i.e. those receiving 'bouche of court' and those paid with other allowances), with each office described briefly. Although the manuscript is short, it is quite revealing. The chancellor heads the list as 'head of the king's council', to be assisted in his legal duties by the keeper of the privy seal and some clerks. Then follows the chamberlain, who was to deal with all revenue and expenditure, the auditors of exchequer, who would join the chancellor and chamberlain to check the accounts once a year, and the clerk of the rolls, who would keep the records of the chancery and exchequer. There follow notes on the steward, who was to order the household and be answerable to the chamberlain; the constable, who was in charge of the king's bodyguard of twenty-four sergeants or doorwards, presided at the court of the verge (which had jurisdiction for twelve leagues around the royal court) and was jointly responsible with the marshal for the ordering of trials by battle at the lists; and the marshal, with two valet-marshals, who was to be responsible for ordering the service of meals in the king's hall and, in wartime, presided over a court 'under the banner'. Also listed are an almoner (with one clerk), clerks of the liverance, provender, wardrobe and kitchen, a pantler, butler, larderer, baker, naperer, chandler, waterer and their respective ushers. Those not receiving 'bouche of court' ('foreins' rather than 'denzeins') are listed as three justices (in addition to the hereditary justices) with their coroners, who were to hold twice yearly ayres, and the sheriffs with their sergeants, making a total of about eighty officers. Many of these posts continued into the fifteenth and sixteenth centuries, although James I abolished the offices of the clerks of the liverance, provender, wardrobe and kitchen and sidelined the chamberlain, vesting his authority to collect and expend revenues in the new posts of comptroller and treasurer. He also replaced the lord steward with the master of the household (a change of title rather than substance), a post that would became hereditary with the earls of Argyll from the 1460s. The responsibilities of the clerks of the wardrobe and kitchen, as detailed in the Corpus Christi manuscript, seem to have been exercised by the master of the wardrobe and the master cook by the late-fifteenth century.[42]

In his preface to the first volume of the *Treasurer's Accounts*, Thomas Dickson listed about 160 officers of the household of James IV and

41 Bateson (ed.), 'Scottish King's Household', 3–43.
42 Thomson, *Public Records*, 82 & 84; *TA*, i, pp. cci & clxxxix.

grouped them by 'departments'.[43] The establishment he envisaged appears to be very similar in structure to the household of his son, but is rather smaller. During the 1530s, James V's household accounts generally record between 300 and 350 named officers in any one year, although there were many more people listed as receiving payments for unspecified duties or services.[44] In comparison, the households of Henry VIII and Francis I are estimated to have contained approximately 500 and 600 persons respectively.[45] Even the rough totals for the households of James IV and James V are likely to be understatements. Occasionally payments made to household officers were recorded as being for the named servant and his assistants or junior officers or 'childer', who were seldom listed separately.[46] Such entries were rare but since the sums paid out on such occasions were no larger than the usual payments, it is likely that the accounting conventions of the time required the senior household officers to take sole responsibility for paying the fees, allowances and rations of their subordinates, without specifically stating this in the record, thus distorting the numbers of servants listed. Furthermore, some of the letters of appointment for household officers specify the numbers of servants and horses they can keep at the king's expense, and these servants rarely appear in the accounts either.[47] In February 1540 some sort of reform of the arrangements for supporting the servants of servants within the royal household seems to have been attempted, when the treasurer and comptroller, each of whom had previously been allowed to keep six servants at the king's expense, were henceforth to be paid an additional cash allowance of £333 6s 8d (500 merks) a year to make their own arrangements.[48] There is no reference to similar changes being made to the allowances for other household officers at this time but it is unlikely that the treasurer and comptroller would have been singled out for special treatment, and a wider reform was probably intended.

43 *TA*, i, pp. clxxxviii – cxcii.
44 See Appendix A. Included in this average figure are those people listed in the chamber, musical posts, stable, wardrobe, hall, kitchens, provisioning departments, chapel royal and miscellaneous servants. Not included are the clerks and writers of the exchequer and casualty, the keepers, masons et al. working in the different residences, the office of arms (heralds, pursuivants et al.), gunners, armourers and shipwrights, who also appear in the accounts.
45 N. Williams, *Henry VIII and his Court* (London, 1971), 33–4; Knecht, 'Court of Francis I', 4.
46 For instance, *ER*, xv, 538, 549, 550.
47 For instance, *RSS*, ii, 4073. See also SRO, Liber Domicili, E.31/5, fo. 96v.
48 *TA*, vii, 362–3.

It is also very noticeable that virtually all (about ninety per cent) of the household officers listed in the accounts were men. Many of them had wives and children and there are occasional glimpses of these family members assisting a man in his duties, which would certainly have swelled the numbers of people present within the establishment, if not those actually receiving fees and allowances. Wives sometimes received expenses or payments, perhaps on behalf of their husbands: for instance, James Akinhead's wife did so in 1529 (he was master of the avery and cuphouse at the time) and so did David Bonar's wife in 1540 (whilst he was a groom in the wardrobe).[49] Sons often succeeded their fathers in their household posts, apparently without any previous experience, so it is perhaps not unreasonable to infer that they had earlier served as unpaid (and therefore unrecorded) assistants to their fathers. For example, Thomas Duddingston of Kilduncan was master of the silver vessels between January 1531 and August 1540, when he was appointed master of the household to the baby Prince James. His son, Stephen, took over his former post and received livery as master of the silver vessels in August 1541 and July 1542 but in December 1542 it was the father alone who received this livery (both had been recipients in July), having returned to the king's household after the death of the prince, and the son disappeared from the record again.[50] Thus the likelihood of the numbers of people within the household being swelled by the families of servants and the servants of servants is high, and several dynasties seem to have established themselves in some departments: amongst the king's trumpeters were seven different men, all with the surname Drummond; there were three Purveses in the stable, and three Cunninghams on the staff of Stirling Castle. Nepotism and opportunism were certainly problems at the English court, where a succession of ministers from Wolsey to Burleigh consistently battled to reduce the number of unofficial hangers-on in the interests of economy. Likewise, in France it was generally admitted that anyone who dressed respectably and claimed acquaintance with a member of the court could gain ready access, and efforts were made to correct this.[51]

However, if the number of people in the household can be calculated only very roughly, it is perhaps possible to obtain a clearer picture of the structure and organisation of the establishment. Four of the most senior posts (which dated back at least to the fourteenth-century manuscript discussed above, and almost certainly earlier) were held heritably by

---

49 *TA*, v, 383, 378, 372; Murray, 'Pursemaster's Accounts', 46.
50 *RMS*, iii, 986; *TA*, vii, 332, 475; viii, 100.
51 Loades, *Tudor Court*, 86–7; Knecht, 'Court of Francis I', 13.

members of the nobility, who would probably not have performed their duties in person, except on ceremonial occasions. These were the master of the household (formerly the steward), who was the earl of Argyll; the constable, who was the earl of Errol; the chamberlain, who was Lord Fleming; and the marshal, who (as his title suggests) was William Keith, the Earl Marischal. The chancellor was usually a senior prelate and throughout James V's adult reign it was his former tutor, Gavin Dunbar, archbishop of Glasgow. The comptroller and treasurer could be clergy-men or secular officers and usually served for between one and eight years at a time. James V had four treasurers and three comptrollers during his adult reign, with Robert Cairncross, abbot of Holyrood, as treasurer, and James Colville of Ochiltree (later of East Wemyss) as comptroller, each serving two separate terms of office and Robert Barton of Overbarnton filling both jobs simultaneously in 1529 and 1530. James V's secretary was Thomas Erskine of Haltoun and Brechin; his clerk register was Gavin Dunbar, bishop of Aberdeen (and uncle of his namesake the archbishop of Glasgow), until his death in March 1532 and thereafter Sir James Foulis of Colinton; the king's advocate was Sir Adam Otterburn of Oldham and Redhall until September 1538 and thereafter Henry Lauder of St Germains. These men also served the king as lords of council and auditors of exchequer as well as fulfilling the specific duties of their official posts.

During his minority James V's household was, of necessity, rather small, although the duke of Albany's household expenses put the exchequer and treasury into deficit whenever he was in Scotland. As a small child, the king was in the care of a nurse (first Christian Wille and then Elizabeth or Marion Douglas), his usher or master of the household (Sir David Lindsay of the Mount) and his tutor or preceptor (Gavin Dunbar).[52] Among his other servants, some are specifically listed as serving him from the very beginning of the reign: such as sir James Haswell, who was appointed by James IV to be his son's personal chaplain from birth; Andrew Edgar, the master tailor, served the king from the time of Flodden and so did the furrier, James Winchester, whilst the cordiner (shoemaker), John Davidson, was said to have served the king for four years by July 1517 and the coalman, Duncan Dawson, had served James III, James IV and James V in the same post. The king's laundress, Mavis Acheson, appears in the record from 1517.[53] There are no surviving treasurer's accounts for 1513 to

52 Murray, 'James V and his Comptrollers', 42–4; *ER*, xiv, 250, 350; *TA*, v, 146, 111–12.

53 *James V Letters*, 155; *TA*, v, 147, 131, 112; *ADCP*, 419, 470; *ER*, xiv, 287–8.

1515 so many other names may be missing from this list, but it is clear that there are no grounds for accusing Albany of neglect. The young king was well dressed, provided with a mule to ride and even had his own minstrel, James Graham, a taborer. He was housed at the castles of Edinburgh, Stirling and Craigmillar, where minor repairs were carried out and precautions taken for his security. The instructions issued to Lord Erskine concerning his responsibilities for keeping the king at Stirling in 1522 included inspecting the credentials of all visitors, supervising a guard of twenty footmen with a captain and a lieutenant on a round-the-clock watch and ensuring that when James went riding in the park he was accompanied by between twelve and twenty of the best men, with outriders checking that the way ahead was safe. By then the king's household had expanded to include a carver, cupbearer, cook, pantryman, clerk of expenses, stableman, grooms, chamber servants, a seamstress and a barber.[54] In April 1524 Albany returned to France for good and in August Queen Margaret 'erected' her son as king in his own right. Unfortunately, there are no surviving treasurer's accounts for this period, so the full impact of these changes on the king's household is rather unclear. However, James V's change of status did mean that all offices lapsed and had to be regranted by the new regime, in which Margaret was keen to reward her own supporters, and also that an 'adult' king required an appropriate household establishment.[55] One of the casualties was Sir David Lindsay, who was replaced as master usher by Andrew, Lord Avandale, the brother of Margaret's third husband, Henry Stewart, later to be Lord Methven.[56] In the absence of the full *Treasurer's Accounts*, the *Exchequer Rolls* and the *Libri Domicilii* show a large expansion of the household between 1524 and 1526. The chamber took on a more ceremonial aspect with an expanded staff of sewers, carvers, cupbearers, ushers, yeomen and grooms. The stable became a sizeable department as well, with an esquire, a stirrupman, between three and six yeomen, five or six henchmen, between three and five grooms, a master and yeoman of the avery, a sumpterman (in charge of the pack-horses), a saddler, a farrier and two falconers. The expansion of the wardrobe was more modest at this stage, rising from a staff of eight people in 1524 to eleven in 1526. Meanwhile the kitchens and hall were set up as fully-functioning departments for the first time, their staffs growing from four men

---

54 *TA*, v, 82, 117, 196–7; *HMC Mar and Kellie*, xlviii (1904), 11.
55 Emond, 'Minority', 406–23.
56 *RSS*, i, 3267; Edington, *Court and Culture*, 37–8; Emond, 'Minority', 534, 553, 554.

each in 1524 to eighteen and twenty men respectively by 1526. This expansion is confirmed by Athol Murray's summaries of the comptroller's expenditure on the royal household, which rose from £6,810 in 1524–25 to £8,829 in 1525–26.[57] Such an expansion was only to have been expected at this stage in the life of a royal prince, even if he had not been a reigning monarch, since the achievement of one's fourteenth year was seen as a significant milestone at this period: it marked the completion of the second 'age' of man and the entry into the third age, that of young adulthood. It was at this point that James was 'erected' as king (ostensibly in his own right) for second time, and by then the power behind the throne was no longer his mother but his stepfather, the earl of Angus.[58]

Angus had ousted Queen Margaret from power and had the king in his keeping, legally from July 1525 and illegally from November of that year until his rule was confirmed by parliament in June 1526. As a result, several of the most influential and lucrative offices in the household and state were held by the Douglases and their adherents until the king broke away from their control and asserted his authority between May and July 1528. James V's hatred for the Douglases was implacable and many offices were therefore re-assigned between the summers of 1528 and 1529. In particular, Gavin Dunbar, archbishop of Glasgow, replaced Angus as chancellor, Robert Cairncross replaced Archibald Douglas of Kilspindie as treasurer, Lord Maxwell replaced George Douglas of Pittendreich as master carver, Sir John Stirling of Keir took over from James Douglas of Drumlanrig as master of the wine cellar and David Wood of Craig replaced James Douglas of Parkhead as master lardner.[59] However, it is clear from the records that the majority of those officers serving the king under Angus's regime were not tainted with his treason, for of the people listed as serving in 1527 about two-thirds continued to serve into 1529 and beyond, with only a quarter losing their posts in 1528–29. Nevertheless, many of the displacements were in key posts and because the household of 1529 was larger than that of 1527 by about one-third, the proportion of 'new' men in 1529 was quite significant, at about thirty per cent.[60]

In many respects the household of the mature James V was very

---

57 Thomas, 'Renaissance Culture,' Appendix A, pp.299–375; Murray, 'James V and his Comptrollers', 45, 47.

58 M. Dove, *The Perfect Age of Man's Life* (Cambridge, 1986), 20; Emond, 'Minority', 499–500.

59 Emond, 'Minority', 472–555; Cameron, *James V*, 9–69; *RMS*, iii, 601; *ADCP*, 281; *ER*, xv, 459, 463, 460.

60 Thomas, 'Renaissance Culture,' Appendix A, pp. 299–375.

similar to those of his contemporaries, Francis I and Henry VIII, although there were important differences too, not least those of scale, mentioned above. James V had very close personal links with the court of Francis I through the duke of Albany, his two queens and his own visit in 1536–37, as well as the usual complement of ambassadors and envoys. The _maison du roy_ had had a long evolution, with a distinction between service to the king's person (_bouche_) and to his entourage (_commun_) apparent as early as the thirteenth century and with household officers organised into a hierarchical structure of departments and paid wages and/or allowances of food, fodder and fuel. By the time of Francis I, the entire establishment was subject to the authority of the _grand maître_, who was also one of the senior ministers of the crown. Between 1525 and 1541 this post was held by Anne de Montmorency, constable of France, but the routine duties were actually delegated to a staff of _maîtres de l'hôtel_. Other senior household officers, responsible for their own departments were the _grand chambellan_ in charge of the bedchamber, the _grand écuyer_ in charge of the stables and messengers, the _grand véneur_ in charge of the royal hunt, the _grand fauconnier_ in charge of the royal mews, the _premier médecin_ responsible for medical care, the _grand aumônier_ responsible for the king's chaplains and charity and the _prevôt de l'hôtel_, who was expected to maintain order at court with his company of archers. Other departments included several troops of guards such as the _garde Ecossaise_, the _cent Suisses_, the _archers de la garde_ and the _gentilhommes de l'hôtel_ and a purchasing office, the _argenterie_. Early in the reign Francis introduced the office of _gentilhomme de la chambre_ for his closest noble companions, leaving the older title of _valet de chambre_ for commoners undertaking more menial duties. The numbers of _gentilhommes_ expanded rapidly and they were often sent abroad as the personal envoys of the king, sometimes accompanying more traditional ambassadors, usually gaining entry into the chamber of the foreign prince as favoured guests. Under Jean de la Barre the influential post of _premier gentilhomme de la chambre_ was combined with that of _maître de la garderobe_, ensuring that he had charge of the king's clothes, jewels, purse and contracts for work on royal _châteaux_ as well as an intimate proximity to the monarch.[61]

There are many parallels between this system and that operated by

---

61 Knecht, 'Court of Francis I', 2–4, 7; Seward, _Prince of the Renaissance_, 99–100, 103; Knecht, _Warrior and Patron_, 109–28. See also David Starkey, 'Representation Through Intimacy: A Study in the Symbolism of Monarchy and Court Office in Early Modern England', in Ioan Lewis (ed.), _Symbols and Sentiments: Cross-Cultural Studies in Symbolism_ (London, 1977), 187–224.

James V between 1528 and his death. Like Francis, James rewarded his servants with a combination of wages and payments in kind; fodder being particularly valuable for such a peripatetic court. Also the descriptions of some household members in the *Treasurer's Accounts* and *Exchequer Rolls* imply that, as in France, there was some distinction made between those who served the king and those who served his entourage (variously referred to as the court, the household or the hall) but the references are sometimes sporadic or inconsistent.[62] There seem to have been separate kitchens and pantries for the king and his court/ hall/household as well as separate groups of cupbearers and sewers. It is also possible that this division accounts for the distinct offices of the silver vessels and the pewter or tin vessels and the great and petty larders, perhaps even the wine cellar and the ale cellar, but the sources are not precise enough to confirm this.[63] Other parallels with the French household are in the titles accorded to some of the senior officers, although it is not clear to what extent a similarity of terminology reflected a similarity in function. James V's chief officer was the earl of Argyll as hereditary master of the household, whose position seems to have been analogous to that of Anne de Montmorency. Like the Frenchman, Argyll also held offices of state, not constable but justice general and lieutenant in the west (the latter only until 1531). He also delegated his household duties to deputies: William Hamilton of Sanquhar and Maknairston was named as such between 1526 and 1529, whilst Patrick Wemyss of Pittencrieff and James Learmonth of Dairsie were described as masters of the household (presumably 'depute' being understood) between 1537 and 1542.[64] The Scottish royal stable was nominally headed by Sir James Hamilton of Finnart as master of the stable between 1527 and 1536 but the real work was done by the esquire (the linguistic equivalent of *écuyer*). From 1525 this was James Erskine and from 1538 Robert Gib, who had worked his way up through the jobs of stirrupman (from 1524) and principal yeoman (from 1531).[65] Although he hunted frequently and enthusiastically (see below) James V did not have a senior officer designated as master huntsman and his master falconers were of a much lower social rank

---

62 E.g. *ER*, xvi, 480G, 480H.
63 See Appendix A.
64 *RMS* iii, 972, 2343; *TA*, v, 308, 382; vi, 354; viii, 100; *RMS*, iii, 1733; *TA*, viii, 150.
65 *ER*, xv, 95, 206, 380; xvi, 480E; *TA*, vi, 18; vii, 9. See also Sir George Duncan Gibb, *The Life and Times of Robert Gib, Lord of Carriber, Familiar Servitor and Master of the Stables to King James V of Scotland* (2 vols, London, 1874).

than the nobles employed by Francis I; nor did he have a principal doctor (although sir Duncan Omay was described as his principal surgeon) but the master almoner was an influential and favoured clergyman in the French manner.[66]

Much of the daily routine service of both kings was carried out by the staff of their chambers. Both Francis and James regarded the office of great chamberlain as an honorific post to be held by a favoured noble; in France, Louis de la Tremouille and in Scotland, Malcolm, third Lord Fleming.[67] The two chambers seem to have had similar structures although the terminology is not identical. James V's equivalents of Francis's *gentilhommes de la chambre* were probably his yeomen of the chamber, many of whom (such as John Leslie of Cleish) were certainly of sufficient social standing to be considered gentlemen; and the *valets de chambre* were mirrored in the Scots grooms of the chamber, who were also referred to as 'varlets'. However, James's yeomen were not used as envoys to foreign courts since they were considerably less aristocratic than Francis's *gentilhommes*; indeed, there were very few nobles holding official posts within the Scottish chamber. In addition to Lord Fleming, Robert, Lord Maxwell was principal carver and in the *Register of the Great Seal* was once described as the first gentleman of the inner chamber (*primus regis thalami generosus*), whilst Norman Leslie, the master of Rothes, was a yeoman from 1538.[68] The rest of the chamber staff were favoured knights or lairds and rather humble menials. However, there was a parallel with the career of Jean de la Barre in John Tennent of Listonshiels, who combined the office of king's pursemaster (and was therefore *ex officio* a senior officer of the chamber) with that of yeoman of the wardrobe. He was once described as 'keeper of the king's wardrobe' and he might well have headed that department in fact since no-one else was listed as master of the wardrobe after 1536.[69]

Perhaps surprisingly, there was no equivalent in Scotland of Francis's many bands of bodyguards. During the minority, the king had been protected at Stirling Castle by a guard of twenty footmen paid for by the duke of Albany and appointed by him and Lord Erskine. These men were replaced by a larger bodyguard paid for by Henry VIII and appointed by Queen Margaret in 1524–25, and during the hegemony of

---

66 See Thomas 'Renaissance Culture', Appendix A, pp. 299–375; *RSS*, ii, 3416.
67 Seward, *Prince of the Renaissance*, 103
68 *RMS*, iii, 2164; *TA*, vii, 125; *ER*, xvii, 415.
69 *ER*, xvii, 280; Murray, 'Pursemaster's Accounts'; *TA*, v, 145, 192. See also Thomas, 'Renaissance Culture', App. A.

the earl of Angus the king was attended by such a heavily armed retinue that it was able to withstand two attempts to liberate the king by force in the summer of 1526.[70] However, from the moment that James began to rule in his own right he seems to have had only a crossbowman in the chamber with the status of yeoman or groom and a team of ushers and porters numbering up to eight or nine men in any given year and apparently no other regular protection. It is possible that the servants described as 'footmen' were also guards of some sort, but there are very few of them actually recorded in the accounts either (only two or three at any one time).[71] The lack of a designated body-guard has also been noted as a feature of English noble households of the period but the English royal establishment included the yeomen of the guard (founded by Henry VII) and the gentlemen pensioners (founded by Thomas Cromwell), who could be supplemented by extraordinary levies in times of crisis.[72] Maybe the king of Scots expected all of his able-bodied servants to act as an *ad hoc* bodyguard when necessary.

The similarities between the Scottish and English households are perhaps less striking than those between the establishments of Scotland and France but all three organisations shared a common purpose, ethos and origin. In England, as in Scotland and France, there were separate kitchens and table servants for the king and his entourage but the clearest distinction within the household was not between *bouche* and *commun* but between the *domus regie magnificencie* and the *domus providencie* (the 'above-stairs' and 'below-stairs' households), the former headed by the lord chamberlain with the assistance of the vice-chamberlain and treasurer; the latter under the lord steward assisted by the treasurer, the comptroller, the cofferer and the counting house, which was known as the board of the green cloth for much of the Tudor period. Early in the reign of Henry VII the chamber (which was actually a suite of apartments rather than just one room) was the core of the *domus magnificencie* and was staffed by knights and esquires of the body, who were the closest personal servants, sewers, carvers and cupbearers, who attended the king at meals, and the gentlemen and yeomen ushers, grooms and pages, who 'kept' the doors. Also within,

---

70 *HMC Mar and Kellie*, 11; *RSS*, i, 3283; Wood, *Letters*, i, 341–5; Strickland, *Lives*, i, 196–8; *L&P Henry VIII*, iv, I, 600, 637, 656, 657, 658, 674, 767, 797, 803, 805, 806, 809, 811, 813, 817, 823, 835, 889, 1026; Emond, 'Minority', 507–13.

71 *RSS*, ii, 324; *ER*, xv, 548; *RMS*, iii, 1008; Thomas, 'Renaissance Culture,' Appendix A.

72 Loades, *Tudor Court*, 91–3; Mertes, *English Noble Household*, 48–9.

or closely associated with, the _domus magnificencie_ were the yeomen of the guard, the office of arms (i.e. heralds, pursuivants and the like), the privy wardrobes (of the robes and of the beds), the physicians, chaplains, chapel royal, minstrels, jewel house and the king's purse. The _domus providencie_ consisted of the provisioning departments (the kitchens, bakehouse, pantry, cellars, chaundry, confectionary, larder, acatry, poultry, pastry and purveyors), the ancillary departments (the ewery, laundry, almonry, scullery, woodyard, porters and cart-takers) and the staff of the great hall (the knight marshal, provost marshal, harbingers, sewers, cupbearers and surveyors of the dresser). Other departments financed directly by the exchequer and therefore outside the structure of _domus magnificencie_ and _domus providencie_ were the stables, kennels, toyles (mews), great wardrobe, tents and revels, royal barge, keepers of the palaces and their staffs, works and ordnance.[73]

The English royal household was full of vested interests protecting their ancient perks and perquisites and therefore highly resistant to reform and rationalisation. Nevertheless, some changes did occur during the period, the most significant of which concerned the chamber and have been expounded by David Starkey. In 1495 Henry VII's most trusted household officers, the lord chamberlain and lord steward (Sir William Stanley and John Radcliffe, Lord Fitzwalter) were shown to have had treacherous communications with the pretender, Perkin Warbeck. Starkey postulates that the resulting shock and suspicion aroused in the king prompted him to establish informally a privy chamber staff of relatively lowly grooms and pages separate from the more public and political atmosphere of the lord chamberlain's domain. Henry VIII brought well-born young men into his privy chamber as his 'minions' and, following a visit by some of Francis I's *gentilhommes de la chambre* in 1518 (as part of a larger embassy), they were accorded the corresponding title of gentlemen of the privy chamber. By the time of Wolsey's *Eltham Ordinances* of 1526 the gentlemen, grooms and pages of the privy chamber were established as a department of the household independent of the lord chamberlain and had been put into wages.[74] The head of the privy chamber was the groom of the stool, who was also chief gentleman, keeper of the privy purse and sometimes in charge of the privy coffers (the private hoards of cash and plate kept in chests at Whitehall). Towards the end of Henry's reign and into

---

73 Williams, *Henry VIII and his Court*, 33; D. A. L. Morgan, 'The Late Plantagenet Household, 1422–1485', in Starkey (ed.), *English Court*, 31–33; Loades, *Tudor Court*, 38–72, 210–11, 62–5.
74 Starkey, 'Privy Chamber', 71–117; Loades, *Tudor Court*, 48–9.

the minority of Edward VI, the groom of the stool and his staff became the powerbrokers of the realm as they controlled access to the king and the application of the royal sign manual or dry stamp (a facsimile of the sign manual) to documents and could therefore heavily influence the opinions and actions of the monarch. The other major development in the household of Henry VIII was the programme of reforms introduced by Thomas Cromwell in 1539–40. He abolished the post of lord steward, eroded the authority of the lord chamberlain and introduced the office of lord great master with four masters of the household in an attempt to re-model the household along French lines. The plans were only partially implemented, and Mary abolished the great mastership and the other masters and reinstated the lord steward in 1553. More durable was Cromwell's creation of the gentlemen pensioners as an additional royal guard, again on the French model.[75]

Although many of the departments within the English royal household were also found in Scotland, the terms *domus regie magnificencie*, *domus providencie* and privy chamber do not occur in the Scottish records. Nor was there a cofferer nor a board of the green cloth, and the Scottish treasurer and comptroller had much higher status and authority than their English counterparts, as they were officers of state as well as of the household. Furthermore, the English lord chamberlain and lord steward had real responsibilities within the household, whereas the Scottish chamberlain and master of the household had become honorific titles. The Scottish chamber did not have a separate privy chamber offshoot but the accounts do contain references to an inner and outer chamber, which may imply a similar pattern. Certainly, in staffing the chamber with lairds and gentlemen rather than with nobles, James was adhering more closely to the example of the English privy chamber than to the French equivalent. Another parallel with English practice was the use of privy coffers for hoarding ready cash for the king's use. There was a Scottish precedent in that James III had assiduously gathered coin and plate in private chests for many years but James V had so many extraordinary sources of revenue that by-passed the treasurer and comptroller that his 'poise' (treasure) was of unprecedented proportions. Indeed he was able to provide £19,000 from his 'boxes' to pay the expenses of his visit to France in 1536–37, and in August 1543 £26,000 of his hoard was still remaining. Yet even these sums pale into insignificance beside Henry VIII's coffers,

---

75 Starkey, 'Privy Chamber', 93–100, 116–17; D. Hoak, 'The Secret History of the Tudor Court: The King's Coffers and the King's Purse, 1542–1553', in *Journal of British Studies*, xxvi (1987), 208–31; Loades, *Tudor Court*, 51–2.

which handled £246,405 (Sterling) between 1542 and 1548.[76] There is no evidence that James V had an equivalent of the groom of the stool nor a dry stamp and the key political manoeuvres at the end of his reign and the beginning of Mary's minority were carried out by the traditional nobles and prelates (in particular, the earl of Arran and Cardinal Beaton) rather than the servants of the chamber. However, there is a Scottish parallel for the clandestine political manipulation of Henry VIII's will at his deathbed in Beaton's failed attempt to exclude Arran from the regency council, which relied on a notarial instrument which purported to be the king's will and was witnessed by the dying king's familiars gathered in his inner chamber at Falkland Palace: James Learmonth of Dairsie (the master household depute), Henry Kemp of Thomaston (cupbearer), Michael Durham (the king's doctor), John Tennent (the pursemaster), William Kirkcaldy (a son of the king's sewer), sir Michael Dysart (a canon of the chapel royal), John Jordan (the almoner's chaplain), Francis Aikman (the king's apothecary), John Sinclair and George Bard (who were probably grooms of the chamber) and sir David Christison (the steward of the household).[77]

Some of the most difficult figures to detect in the surviving household records are the king's many mistresses. Their presence, at least somewhere within the orbit of the court, usually has to be deduced from the recorded provision made for their children. It is speculation to suggest that these would have been housed with their mothers, at least when they were very young, yet Maurice Lee and Peter Anderson agree that both James and Robert Stewart (afterwards earls of Moray and Orkney respectively) retained strong links with their mothers and maternal kin throughout their lives, so perhaps this is not too unrealistic a suggestion.[78] However, it was also a common practice of the period to send royal and noble children to board at the households of great magnates or prelates where they would be educated and trained in the etiquette appropriate to their station in life.[79] Since James V intended his sons to rule the church (or at least the most important church lands), one might expect to find them being brought up in

---

76 N. Macdougall, *James III: a Political Study* (Edinburgh, 1982), 254–5; *RSS*, iii, 383; Murray, 'Pursemaster's Accounts', 27; Hoak, 'Secret History', 212–13.

77 *HMC 11th Report & Hamilton MSS*, vi, 219–20; Andrew Lang, 'The Cardinal and the King's Will', *SHR*, iii (1906), 410–22.

78 M. Lee, *James Stewart, Earl of Moray* (New York, 1953), 18; P. D. Anderson, *Robert Stewart, Earl of Orkney, Lord of Shetland, 1533–93* (Edinburgh, 1982), 1–2.

79 Nicholas Orme, *From Childhood to Chivalry: The Education of the English Kings and Aristocracy, 1066–1530* (London, 1984), 44–80.

clerical households but this is quite difficult to establish with any certainty. The lands and revenues of the prior of St. Andrews (the second Lord James) were administered by sir James Kincraigie, provost of the collegiate church of St. Mary of the Rock, until his death in 1539–40, when he was replaced in this task by Alexander Mylne, abbot of Cambuskenneth, and at the same time Mylne was also appointed to act for Lord Robert Stewart, commendator of the abbey of Holyrood. It is possible that these clerics may have acted as guardians or foster fathers to the boys as well but we have no firm evidence of this. Indeed, the curators of the eldest Lord James, commendator of Kelso and Melrose, were secular men of the court: Sir Thomas Scot of Pitgormo (the justice clerk) and Sir James Hamilton of Finnart (the king's master sewer).[80]

James V's amorous career really was quite spectacular. Lindsay and Buchanan both imply that as a fourteen or fifteen year old he was deliberately encouraged into promiscuity by the Angus regime in order to distract him from wanting to exercise political power.[81] His subsequent behaviour suggests that he thought he could do both. James's list of conquests included Elizabeth Shaw, the daughter of Alexander Shaw of Sauchie, master of the king's wine cellar. She bore him a son, Lord James Stewart, in 1529 when the king himself was only seventeen. We know nothing more of her except that she received a payment of £20 and the nurse's fee in 1532, and seems to have died sometime before 31 August 1536.[82] However, one account suggests that the Elizabeth Shaw who produced the king's first child was the sister (rather than the daughter) of Alexander, laird of Sauchie, the wife of Robert Gib of Carribber (esquire of the stable to James V), the mother of a large family by her husband; and that she did not die until 1559. It is typical of the scarcity and ambiguity of the sources concerned with women at this period that it is impossible to distinguish which of the two Elizabeth Shaws, who died more than twenty years apart, was the mistress of the king, and indeed one reference even confuses her name and calls her Marion Shaw.[83] Her son was probably the Lord James who spent his infancy at Cupar, Fife, and his childhood primarily at Stirling Castle where, in December 1536, in the absence of his father in France, he held court at the Christmas feast with the rump of the royal entourage. In November 1538 he moved to St. Andrews and by 1542 he was in

80 *ADCP*, 492; *RMS*, iii, 2611; *James V Letters*, 399; Cameron, *James V*, 205n., citing SRO, ADCS, vii, fo.108.

81 Lindsay, *Works*, i, 46; Buchanan, *History*, ii, 324.

82 *RSS*, ii, 336; *HMC 6th. Report, Moray Muniments*, App. p. 670; *TA*, vi, 40; *RMS*, iii, 1620.

83 Gibb, *Robert Gib*, i, 233; *TA*, vi, 180.

residence at Holyrood. The boy was made commendator of the abbeys of Kelso and Melrose and granted some of the forfeited Douglas lands.[84] Another mistress was Lady Margaret Erskine, the daughter of John, fourth Lord Erskine, captain of Stirling Castle. She was already married to Sir Robert Douglas of Lochleven before James became interested in her. She bore the king a son, another James, in 1531 and seems to have been his favourite mistress. In 1536, whilst he was in theory engaged to Marie de Bourbon, daughter of the duke of Vendôme, James made an attempt to divorce Margaret Erskine from her husband so that he could marry her but the petition was refused. She was then granted a gift of 500 merks a year from the Edinburgh customs, perhaps as some sort of compensation. Their son was granted the lands of Tantallon and made commendator of the priory of St. Andrews. He seems to have spent his infancy at Alloa (a property belonging to his maternal grandfather) and was also lodged in St. Andrews from 1538, probably in the priory lodging, which had become his property.[85] These sons were clearly accorded some dignity and status, given lands, preferment and a good education (George Buchanan was tutor to the elder Lord James for three years) and one might speculate that perhaps their mothers would have shared some of the glory.[86]

Other mistresses included Christina Barclay, perhaps from the family of the captains of Falkland. She produced a son, probably in 1532, the third James, who seems to have died young. There was also Euphemia Elphinstone, daughter of the first Lord Elphinstone, who produced a son, Robert, in 1533 who was appointed commendator of the abbey of Holyrood. Elizabeth Carmichael, daughter of Sir John Carmichael, the captain of Crawford, and later the wife of Sir John Somerville, gave birth to a son, John, in 1531 who became commendator of the priory of Coldingham. Eleanor Stewart (or Helen or Elizabeth: the sources are inconsistent), daughter of John, third earl of Lennox, produced yet another son, Adam, who was given a pension from the charterhouse of

84 *TA*, vi, 190, 205, 390; vii, 102–3, 312–3; SRO, Libri Domicilii, E.31/5, fos.
    17r., 29r., 37r., 50r., 70r., 81v., 99r.-102v.; E.31/6, fos. 105r.-110v. and
    elsewhere; SRO, Liber Emptorum, E.32/6, fo. 28r.; *James V Letters*, 279, 287,
    425; *RMS*, iii, 1425. See also Thomas, 'Renaissance Culture', 72 nn.42 & 43.
85 *SP*, vi, 369; Lee, *James Stewart*, 17; HMC, *Moray*, App. p.670; *James V Letters*,
    320, 343; *RSS*, ii, 2138; *RMS*, iii, 1620; *TA*, vi, 255, 282, 297, 384, 437; vii,
    89–90. See also Thomas 'Renaissance Culture', 73 n.50. For the priory
    lodging see David Hay Fleming, *The Reformation in Scotland; Causes,
    Characteristics, Consequences* (London, 1910), 608–12.
86 *TA*, vi, 289, 353, 430; I. D. McFarlane, *Buchanan* (London, 1981), 48–9.

Perth.[87] Finally, there was Elizabeth Beaton, the daughter of Sir John Beaton of Creich and a cousin of Cardinal David Beaton, James's keeper of the privy seal and one of his ambassadors to France. She produced the king's only illegitimate daughter, Lady Jane Stewart, who as a child was placed in the household of Mary of Guise and then in that of her legitimate half-brother, the short-lived Prince James. As an adult she married the fifth earl of Argyll, a match that was possibly arranged within her father's lifetime.[88] There may have been a second Robert, who became commendator of Whithorn Priory in 1568, but his mother is not recorded.[89]

Other than this catalogue of names, kinship connections and births virtually nothing is known about James V's mistresses. They were almost all the daughters of nobles or lairds in the king's service and so, presumably, were present at least on the periphery of the court even before they became the mothers of royal bastards. It is perhaps not unreasonable to suspect that these mistresses are only known to us precisely because of their social status, and that the king may have sired offspring by humbler women about which we know nothing at all. Indeed, Lindsay's *Answer to the Kingis Flyting* describes the king's encounter with a kitchen wench in an account which barely stops short of accusing him of rape, and suggests that such episodes were regular occurrences.[90] The acknowledged children were suitably pro-vided for (as we have seen), although their appointment to the com-mendatorships of wealthy abbeys was also to the king's personal advantage since he retained their revenues whilst they were underage. Certainly, James does not seem to have contemplated the expense of setting up any of them in a great secular lordship as was done for Anthony, the 'great bastard' of Burgundy, in the fifteenth century, or for Henry Fitzroy, duke of Richmond, in the 1520s.[91] Very little is recorded about the king's arrangements for the financial support of

---

87 *RMS*, iii, 558; *ER*, xvi, 470; *TA*, vi, 180; Anderson, *Robert Stewart*, 1–6, 154, 156–8; *James V Letters*, 357, 426–7; *ADCP*, 502; *RSS*, ii, 3127; v, 915.

88 *SP*, i, 25, 342; iv, 155; ix, 21; *TA*, vi, 205; vii, 94, 101, 410, 433–4, 463, 477–8. See also Thomas, 'Renaissance Culture', 74 n.57.

89 *SP*, i, 25; G. Donaldson, 'The Bishops and Priors of Whithorn', *TDGAS*, 3rd Series, xxvii (1950), 147.

90 *Works*, i, 102–04. Lindsay had no sympathy for the victim; she is called a 'ladron', a 'caribald' and a 'duddroun' (slut, oik, slattern) and his concern is entirely for the king: 'On your behalf I thank God tymes ten score,/ That you preservit from gut & frome grandgore.'

91 *Biographie Nationale de Belgique* (28 vols., Brussels, 1866–1944), i, 838–42; Scarisbrick, *Henry VIII*, 147, 151, 350–51, 425n., 508.

their mothers either. Some of the mistresses subsequently made respectable marriages, and Elizabeth Beaton and Eleanor Stewart appear to have entered the service of Mary of Guise, but if they had any significant role within the court circle the sources do not mention it.[92] A possible exception might be Lady Margaret Erskine, who perhaps masterminded the downfall of George Buchanan in 1539. However, there is certainly no suggestion that James ever imitated the French practice of having an official mistress with luxurious apartments in the royal palaces, a rich endowment of lands and titles and considerable influence in politics and diplomacy.[93]

In one respect James V's household for much of his reign lacked facets that were very familiar to both Henry VIII and Francis I, that is, the provision of household establishments for a queen consort and an heir apparent.[94] There was no queen consort in Scotland between 1513 and 1537 and no heir apparent that survived for longer than a few months between 1488 and 1594. James's mother, Margaret Tudor, was expected to live off her jointure lands after the death of James IV and although she frequently had difficulties in collecting her revenues (as we will see), neither the treasurer nor the comptroller were ever authorised to pay her household expenses, even during the brief periods when she was regent. A few of her servants received occasional rewards from the king and James sometimes made cash gifts to the

---

92 Euphemia Elphinstone married John Bruce of Cultmalindie, Elizabeth Beaton married Lord Innermeith, and Eleanor Stewart married the sixth earl of Errol: Fraser, *Elphinstone*, i, 83; *RSS*, ii, 2206, 4016, 4525. See also *TA*, vii, 131, 136–9, 149, 166, 328, 438; viii, 63–4, 93 and Thomas 'Renaissance Culture', 75 nn.63 & 64.

93 McFarlane, *Buchanan*, 67; Buchanan, *History*, i, 4–8; Knecht, 'Court of Francis I', 9–10; Knecht, *Warrior and Patron*, 117, 290, 396, 407, 421, 498, 551, 558.

94 For the Scottish queens of the period see Patricia H. Buchanan, *Margaret Tudor, Queen of Scots* (London and Edinburgh, 1985); M. A. E. Green, *Lives of the Princesses of England from the Norman Conquest* (6 vols., London, 1849–55), iv, 475–505; Hester W. Chapman, *The Sisters of Henry VIII* (Bath, 1974), 1–156; Louise O. Fradenburg, 'Troubled Times: Margaret Tudor and the Historians' in Sally Mapstone and Juliette Wood (eds.), *The Rose and the Thistle: Essays on the Culture of Late Medieval and Renaissance Scotland* (East Linton, 1998), 38–58; Rosalind K. Marshall, *Mary of Guise* (London, 1977); E. M. H. McKerlie, *Mary of Guise-Lorraine, Queen of Scotland* (London, 1931); Agnes Strickland, *Lives of the Queens of Scotland and English Princesses* (8 vols, Edinburgh and London, 1850–59), i & ii; Andrea Thomas, '"Dragonis baith and dowis ay in double forme": Women at the Court of James V, 1513–1542' in Elizabeth Ewan and Maureen M. Meikle (eds.), *Women in Scotland c.1100–c.1750* (East Linton, 1999), 83–94.

queen dowager but the royal accounts do not contain enough information to establish the pattern of her household at this period.[95] There is also very little surviving information on the household of James's first queen, Madeleine de Valois. The couple were married in Paris on 1 January 1537 but did not arrive in Scotland until 19 May, following which Madeleine survived only a few weeks until her death on 7 July. After such a brief period of residence, references to her servants in the accounts are understandably few, with only eleven names recorded: her former governess and chief lady (Anne de Boissy, Madame de Montreuil), another lady (Madame de Bren), her secretary (Jean de Langeac, bishop of Limoges), her *maître de l'hôtel* (Jean de St. Aubin), her *écuyer d'écurie* (Charles de Marconnay), her doctor (Maître Patrix), two pages (John Crammy and Pierre de Ronsard), the furrier (Gillan), the butcher (John Kenneth) and the barber (Anthony).[96] The latter may seem a curious servant for a queen but in all probability he was a barber-surgeon and therefore served her medically. After Madeleine's death Pierre de Ronsard, who in later life became a celebrated poet, stayed on in Scotland with Mme. de Montreuil, to welcome Mary of Guise. Mme. de Montreuil and her entourage then departed for France overland, through England, in August 1538, although an undated letter to Mary of Guise (1538 x 1542) suggests that Ronsard remained in Scotland after this date and was taken into the service of James V. He later wrote a glowing account of the king of Scots as a vigorous, gracious and regal monarch.[97]

It was only after the arrival of James's second French wife, Mary of Guise, in June 1538 that the records of the queen's household appeared in any detail. Her establishment probably mirrored the king's in structure but seems to have been on a smaller scale and naturally her closest personal servants would have been female. She arrived with a retinue of French attendants, some of whom remained with her in Scotland and appeared in the accounts receiving items of clothing and trifling expenses but not wages or fees.[98] These were paid from the revenues of her French lands as dowager duchess of Longueville, which were supplemented by an annuity from Francis I. The records

95 Emond, 'Minority', 113, 163, 214–26; *ADCP*, 133, 148; *TA*, v, 434; *ER*, xvii, 597–9, 712–13.

96 *TA*, vii, 21, 61; *Balcarres Papers*, vol. i, p. xix; Teulet, *Inventaire*, 80, 85; *TA*, vi, 343; *Balcarres Papers*, i, 231; *TA*, vii, 61; vi, 334; *RSS*, ii, 2260; *TA*, vi, 354. See also *L&P Henry VIII*, xiii, II, pp. 69–70, 90.

97 *Balcarres Papers*, i, 231; *TA*, vii, 61; Michel Simonin, *Pierre de Ronsard* (Mesnil-sur-l'Estrée, 1990), 52–77.

98 E.g. *TA*, vii, 114–16, 420.

of her household from the period 1538–42, when she was consort, are fragmentary but they reveal the names of some of her French servants and indicate the existence of a French departmental structure of *bouche* and *maison* under the control of the *maître d'hôtel* (Charles de la Haye, sieur de Curel) and the *contrerolleur des finances* (François du Fon). Her only servants to receive funding from the exchequer and casualty were the native Scotsmen of her chamber, stable, avery, kitchen, pantry and spice-house.[99] Mary of Guise took her household responsibilities very seriously. Many of her accounts are checked and signed with her own hand and she has the reputation of taking a keen interest in the marriages of her ladies, such as Marie Pierris, who married George, fourth Lord Seton, and Jehanne Gresmor, who married Robert Beaton of Creich.[100] She is also credited with treating her husband's illegitimate offspring with some consideration and even affection.[101] If this were so, it underlines the fact that however robust, capable and overwhelmingly masculine these children may have been, they were no threat to the rights of her own children by James V.

On 22 May 1540 Mary gave birth to a short-lived prince of Scotland, christened James, who died in April 1541 within a few days of the death of his even more fragile newly-born brother, Robert, duke of Albany.[102] Prince James's household was established soon after his birth, with his earliest recorded servant, Margaret Maccombie, his laundress, appearing in the record in June 1540. She was joined by a team of other women attendants, presumably nurses, a master of the household (Thomas Duddingston), a master almoner (sir William Laing), a master usher (the 'auld laird'), a steward (Master Alan Lamont), a keeper of the silver vessels and collier (William Methven), a master cook (John Mount), a patissier (Patrick Marshall) and five other servants. Also attached to the prince's household, presumably in

---

99 SRO, Despence de la Maison Royale, E.33/1–E.33/2 & E.34/8/1; NLS, Balcarres Papers, Adv. 29.2.5, fos. 104r., 105r., 107r., 127r.; *Balcarres Papers*, i, 1–87, 228–31, 245. See Rosalind Marshall, 'Hir Rob Ryall', *Costume*, xii (1978), 1–12 and Marshall, 'Queen's Table'. *TA*, xi, 24–7 lists payments to 104 members of her household at her death in June 1560. See also Appendix A.

100 *Balcarres Papers*, i, 245; *TA*, vii, 166, 328. Her French household of 1539 is listed in SRO, Despence de la Maison Royale, E.33/1, fos. 8r.-15v. References to her Scottish servants are scattered through *TA*, vii & viii and *ER*, xvii. See Appendix A.

101 SRO, Despence de la Maison Royale, E.33/1, fos. 3v.-8r.; E.34/8/1; E.34/8/3; Marshall, *Mary of Guise*, 73; Anderson, *Robert Stewart*, 8.

102 *Diurnal of Occurrents*, 23; SRO, 'Despence de la Maison Royale', E.33/1, vii, fo. 11v. For the christening and funeral of the prince see chapter 6.

a ceremonial capacity, was his illegitimate half-sister, Lady Jane Stewart, and two of her attendants.[103] James V clearly intended his heir to enjoy every advantage of his rank but the plans were thwarted by mortality and James had no opportunity to repeat the exercise for his third (legitimate) child, who became queen of Scots in December 1542, when she was only a week old.

In addition to their maternal and household responsibilities, queens were also great territorial magnates with all the attendant rights, privileges and duties. As life-expectancy was so unpredictable in the sixteenth century, a queen's jointure lands might have to support her through many years of widowhood, and so the details of the estates to be settled upon her, and of the dowry she would bring with her, were often the most controversial aspects of the negotiations surrounding a marriage contract, particularly since both items were seen as status symbols as well as objects of greed for the parties concerned. In Scotland, where the crown patrimony was in any case smaller and less productive than that of the kings of England and France, making appropriate provision for a daughter of these wealthier realms could cause problems, especially when the queens of two generations over-lapped, as was the case between 1537 and 1541. Indeed, James II's struggle to meet the terms of Mary of Guelders' jointure settlement in 1449–50 contributed to the fall of the Livingstons and of the Black Douglases and the confiscation of their lands[104]

When Margaret Tudor married James IV in 1503, her jointure consisted of the earldom of March, the lordship of Dunbar (excluding Dunbar Castle), the lordship of Cockburnspath, the lordship of Ettrick Forest with the tower of Newark, the lordship of Methven with the castle of Methven, the earldom of Menteith, the lordship and castle of Doune, the castle of Stirling and lordship of the shire, and the palace of Linlithgow and lordship of the shire; all of which were supposed to raise for her total revenues of £6,000 a year (£2,000 Sterling). In addition, she received the lordship and castle of Kilmarnock as a 'morrowing gift' the day after the wedding. She brought with her a dowry of £30,000 (£10,000 Sterling) which was paid in three annual instalments between 1503 and 1505. Whilst her husband was alive he administered these lands on her behalf and paid her household ex-

103 *RSS*, ii, 3557; *TA*, vii, 477–78. See Appendix A.
104 Rosalind K. Marshall, *Virgins and Viragoes: a History of Women in Scotland from 1080 to 1980* (London, 1983), 29–36; Christine McGladdery, *James II* (Edinburgh, 1990), 49–55; Michael Brown, *The Black Douglases: War and Lordship in Late Medieval Scotland, 1300–1455* (East Linton, 1998), 286.

penses from the revenues, giving her £1,000 a year 'pocket money' to spend as she pleased.[105] However, as soon as he died she had to fend for herself, and was almost immediately in difficulties. In the aftermath of Flodden, raising revenues from Ettrick, East Lothian and the Merse, would have been extremely difficult even for a confident, efficient and forceful male, but for an inexperienced and rather pampered foreign princess with nursing infants and an ambitious, volatile new husband, engaged in a power struggle for the regency of Scotland, it was virtually impossible.[106] Throughout the turbulent minority of her son she repeatedly tried and failed to obtain access to her assigned income. Her exile in England between September 1515 and June 1517 allowed Angus to appropriate many of her revenues for himself and appeals for justice to Arran and Albany did not result in any lasting settlement.[107] During Angus's own hegemony between 1525 and 1528 her position was even more difficult, since she was seeking to divorce him, and the Douglas-dominated council tended to uphold his rights over her lands rather than hers. During this period he seems to have secured possession of Stirling, Doune, Linlithgow, Methven, Newark and Cockburnspath.[108]

When James V asserted his personal rule in 1528 he did so by establishing his power-base at Stirling Castle, which his mother re-signed into his hands, and although he subsequently recovered all the properties formerly held by Angus and his adherents, they were not invariably returned to Margaret's personal use. During the 1530s the king seems to have treated the palace and lordship of Linlithgow as his own property, even though we have no record of a formal resignation by Margaret, and in 1537 she assigned him her revenues from the lordship of Dunbar as a bribe to try to persuade him to agree to her divorce from her third husband, Lord Methven. The king accepted the revenues but blocked the divorce.[109] The lordship of Kilmarnock was

---

105 *APS*, ii, 271–73; Norman Macdougall, *James IV* (Edinburgh, 1988), 155; *TA*, ii, 243; iii, 37 and elsewhere.

106 James V was seventeen months old in Sept. 1513; his brother, Alexander, duke of Ross, was born in Apr. 1514 and died in Dec. 1515; his half-sister, Lady Margaret Douglas, was born in Oct. 1515. Margaret married Archibald Douglas, earl of Angus, in Aug. 1514.

107 Emond, 'Minority', 113, 163, 200, 214–18, 224, 232, 289, 334, 390, 466, 533, 535; *ADCP*, 133, 136–8, 148.

108 Emond, 'Minority', 466, 533, 535, 554; *ADCP*, 224–5, 241, 257–8.

109 Emond, 'Minority', 554; M. A. E. Wood, *Letters of the Royal and Illustrious Ladies of Great Britain* (3 vols, London, 1846), ii, 333–5, 336–8, 338–41; *Hamilton Papers*, i, 65; Strickland, *Lives*, i, 259–60, 261.

also returned to the crown, by arrangement with Methven, who seems to have assigned Doune to his landless brother, James Stewart. The only property to which Margaret appears to have had relatively easy access was Methven Castle (which was her main residence between 1528 and her death), and even this was closed to her during her divorce campaign of 1537, when she set up home in a town house in Dundee.[110] This being the case, it is hardly surprising that she continued to be financially embarrassed for almost all of the period 1513–41.

Since some of Margaret's jointure lands had already reverted to her son before 1537, James had more freedom of manoeuvre in providing for a potential bride than might have been the case if his mother had been more effective at protecting her own interests. Nevertheless, his first attempt at a marriage contract did not touch any of the lands formerly held by the dowager queen, relying instead on crown properties in some of the furthest reaches of the realm. In March 1536 he agreed to a marriage with Marie de Bourbon, daughter of the duke of Vendôme, a match that was sponsored by Francis I. She was to bring to Scotland a dowry of 200,000 livres Tournois (nearly £90,000 Scots) and was to be assigned lands worth 15,000 livres Tournois a year (£6,666 or 10,000 merks Scots) for her jointure. In other words, although she would bring a dowry worth three times that of Margaret Tudor, her income would be only slightly larger. The lands named in the contract were Falkland Palace and its contents, the lordships of Ross, Ardmannach, Orkney (including Kirkwall), Strathearn, and Galloway, with the castle of Threave. In addition, the duke of Albany was to return Dunbar Castle to the Scottish crown.[111] This marriage never took place and instead the king married Madeleine de Valois in January 1537. The contract for this marriage was agreed at Blois on 26 November 1536. As the eldest surviving daughter of the king of France, Madeleine's dowry was a little larger than Marie's: 225,000 livres (£100,000 Scots), and her jointure was to be double the value of the previous offer: 30,000 livres a year (£13,333 or 20,000 merks Scots). However, the lands assigned for this purpose were almost the same as those offered to the jilted Marie de Bourbon: the earldom of Fife and castle of Falkland with its moveables, the earldom of Strathearn with the castle of Stirling, the earldom of Ross with the castle of Dingwall, the earldom of Orkney, the lordship of Galloway with the castle of Threave, the lordship of Ardmannach

110 Cameron, *James V*, 176, 198; Strickland, *Lives*, i, 237–8, 261; *APS*, ii, 361; Sir William Fraser, *The Red Book of Menteith* (2 vols, Edinburgh, 1880), ii, 369–400; Wood, *Letters*, ii, 338–41.
111 Teulet, *Papiers*, 109–21.

and the lordship of the Isles, plus any other lands necessary to reach the required total income. In assigning Stirling Castle to his new wife, the king was making use of property recovered from his mother's jointure and one suspects that he would have had to surrender more in order to reach the requisite sum. In this context, Madeleine's early death was something of a mercy for the crown finances, but had she lived, she would have enjoyed an opulent lifestyle unprecedented for a queen of Scots with an income four-times that allocated to her predecessor, since Francis I had also agreed to pay her an annual pension of a further 30,000 livres.[112] In the event, the contract which really mattered was that made with Mary of Guise in 1538. Her dowry was only 150,000 livres (100,000 merks Scots) but coming as it did only a year after Madeleine's it was nevertheless a windfall for James V. The property assigned to her for her jointure was exactly the same as that destined for Madeleine, but the target income was set at the more realistic level offered to Marie de Vendôme: 15,000 livres or 10,000 merks a year. Even so the promised revenues had to be raised and financial necessity may have been a contributory factor in prompting the king's voyage to the Northern and Western Isles of June 1540 and the formal annexation of these lands in December of the same year.[113]

The king, his family, his household and court led a peripatetic existence, constantly on the move from one castle or palace to another, often staying no more than three or four days and seldom more than three or four weeks in one place. The usual itinerary circulated between Edinburgh, Linlithgow, Stirling, Perth, Falkland and St. Andrews, but there were also regular forays into the Borders, Argyll and Angus and occasional visits to the north east. James was also an enthusiastic sailor and he made two voyages to the outer extremities of his realm, taking in Orkney and the Hebrides, and (as we have seen) one trip to France. The details of his daily movements during a sample year of his adult reign (1538), have been outlined in Appendix B. Whilst on his travels, he sometimes lodged as the guest of abbots, bishops, earls and other men of standing, but more frequently he would make use of one of his own residences. There were royal castles scattered at intervals across the length and breadth of the kingdom: from Dingwall to Threave, from Rothesay to Dunbar, and many points in between. In addition the king maintained minor residences in key burghs such as Montrose and Haddington: these are described as 'lodgings' in the accounts, and so

---

112 *L&P Henry VIII*, xi, 1183; *James V Letters*, 325–6; Teulet, *Inventaire*, 84–5.
113 Teulet, *Relations*, 115–18; Teulet, *Papiers*, 131–4; *APS*, ii, 361. For the voyage see chapter 5.

were presumably fairly modest.[114] The royal household and its para-
phernalia often spent days on horseback and James was fond of
abandoning the main entourage in a major residence and striking
out with a much smaller retinue for more remote destinations, often
in pursuit of game. These excursions are clearly detectable in the
accounts of the pantry, cellar and kitchen, where *Rege Absenti* is marked
in the margin and a consolidated account of the king's total living
expenses whilst away usually appears in the ledger a few folios later.[115]
Such constant perambulations would have brought the king and court
into regular contact with a wide range of humble people. As we have
seen, the king's steward or caterer offered valuable business to burgesses and other traders, and private individuals feature in the accounts (often unnamed) receiving payments for goods and services or
rewards for gifts.[116] The penchant for travelling without the full household also lends some credence to James's popular reputation as 'the
poor man's king': the monarch who wandered incognito to learn about
the lives of his subjects.[117]

A study of the royal itinerary reveals that the pattern of use of the
royal residences changed over time.[118] Holyrood, as the palace in the
capital, was overwhelmingly associated with events of political importance. It was where James based himself when there was a session of
parliament to attend, or an important embassy to receive, or a show
trial of heretics to observe. As a result, it features strongly on his
itinerary of 1528–29, when he was struggling to establish his independence of the Douglases, and it was still quite important in 1530–33,
when he was stamping his authority on the Borders and negotiating a
major peace treaty with England. From 1534 to 1539, when his power
was more firmly established and his confidence high, Holyrood was
not used so frequently, but from 1540 to 1542 it featured more regularly
again, as the tensions heightened and warfare resumed against England. Stirling seems to have been the king's preferred residence in the
years 1529 to 1533. The emphasis then shifted in 1534 to Fife, when
James spent long periods in the burgh of Cupar, away from the main
household establishment. The exact reason why the king spent so much
time in Cupar at this period is rather mysterious but it is possible that a

114 *RSS*, ii, 519, 947.

115 Buchanan, *History*, ii, 309; E.g. SRO, Liber Domicili, E.31/5, fos. 73r.-79v.

116 E.g. *TA*, v, 373, 379.

117 Bingham, *James V*, 95; J. Paterson, *James the Fifth: or the "Gudeman of
Ballangeich:" his Poetry and Adventures* (Edinburgh, 1861), 155–61.

118 See Thomas, 'Renaissance Culture', Appendix C, pp. 386–423 for the full
itinerary.

hint may be found in the stable and avery accounts, where it is revealed that his young son, Lord James Stewart, had two horses kept at Cupar. The king seems therefore to have been visiting his son, and possibly the boy's mother too, at this time.[119] In 1535 the emphasis returned to Stirling, and the son seems to have moved to the castle. Whilst the king was in France, the Christmas feast of 1536 was kept at Stirling by this son, who continued to reside primarily at Stirling even after his father married.[120] However, the palaces of Linlithgow and Falkland seem to have attracted more attention in the years after 1538 than they did before James's second marriage. In the early years of the adult reign, Linlithgow tended to be used primarily to break the journey between Edinburgh and Stirling, rather than for long periods of residence. Technically, Linlithgow was the property of Queen Margaret until her death in October 1541, but his building activities seem to indicate that James treated it as one of his own possessions and it also seems to have become a favoured residence of Mary of Guise, even though it was not a part of her jointure.[121] Falkland was a part of her jointure and its profile on the itinerary of 1538 to 1542 seems to have been raised as a result. Indeed, almost the whole of the summers of 1539 and 1540 were spent in Fife, with the time divided between Falkland, St. Andrews[122] and a residence at Pitlethie, near Leuchars.[123] In fact, the long-awaited heir was born and baptised at St. Andrews in May 1540, just before James set sail for the Northern and Western Isles.

As well as indicating how the movements of the Scottish household and court changed over time, the royal itinerary also suggests a regular pattern of seasonal perambulations. The observance of religious feasts and fasts will be considered in detail in chapter three, but at this point it may be useful to observe that the celebration of the great festivals seems to have followed a regular pattern: Christmas and Epiphany (Yule and Uphaliday) were usually kept at Holyrood, although in 1539–40, the festive season was spent at Linlithgow; much of Lent and Easter itself were usually spent at Stirling; and Stirling was also the most likely location for the Whitsun feast in the earlier years of the reign, but after the arrival of Mary of Guise, it was celebrated at St. Andrews. Hunting

---

119 SRO, Libri Domicilii, E.31/5, fos. 99r.-102r.; E.31/6, fos. 105r.-110v.

120 SRO, Liber Emptorum, E.32/6, fo. 28r.

121 See chapter 2.

122 The second Lord James was appointed commendator of the priory of St. Andrews in 1538 and the king seems to have treated his son's property as his own: *RMS*, iii, 1620; *James V Letters*, 343.

123 My thanks are owed to Athol Murray, who located Pitlethie for me. It lies to the north-east of Leuchars village NO 459220 on the 1:25124 OS map.

expeditions were also a regular feature on the itinerary: these could be arranged at any point during the summer and early autumn but September seems to have been the favoured time for the lengthier hunting parties.[124] James V, like his father, maintained a large staff of falconers and dog-handlers as well as an extensive stable, which included horses bred for specialist functions. His falconers were sent regularly into the Highlands and Isles to capture birds of prey and these men were so close to the king that by the late 1530s they were receiving many of their fees and expenses directly from the king's purse rather than from the treasurer.[125] Hawking was a sport which could be pursued for most of the year and which was easily arranged within the royal parks of Holyrood, Linlithgow, Stirling or Falkland. The summer hunting parties which took the king into Meggetland, Menteith, Strathearn and Argyll with tents (pavilions), bows and spears were likely to have been major drives targeting larger game such as deer and boar, since the chase (stalking, coursing and hunting *par force*) was not as popular in Scotland as in England and France.[126] The only narrative account we have of James V's hunting parties is in one of Pitscottie's somewhat far-fetched stories. He states that the king took 12,000 men with him to the Borders in 1529 (the 'raid' actually took place in 1530 and almost certainly involved a much smaller and more mobile entourage), when he slew eighteen-score (360) of harts and hanged Johnnie Armstrong of Gilnockie and other outlaws. Pitscottie also describes a three-day excursion into Atholl in September 1532 (although he dates it to 1528) at which the earl of Atholl is said to have spent £1,000 a day entertaining the king, his mother and the papal envoy, Sylvester Darius. They were apparently lodged in an almost fairy-tale palace built from green timber in the middle of a remote meadow, furnished with tapestries and plate and supplied with luxurious delicacies. The hunting seems to have been a great success, for the party killed 'xxx scoir of heartis and hyndis witht wther small beistis as re and rebuke, wolf and fox, and wyldcattis.' Once the party was over, the highland servants of the earl of Atholl, in an extravagant show of conspicuous consumption, set the palace ablaze, to the astonishment of

---

124 See Appendix B.
125 See Appendix A and Murray, 'Pursemaster's Accounts', 29–51.
126 John M. Gilbert, *Hunting and Hunting Reserves in Medieval Scotland* (Edinburgh, 1979); R. S. Fittis, *Sports and Pastimes of Scotland Historically Illustrated* (Wakefield, 1975), 1–105. See also Nicholas Orme, 'Medieval Hunting: Fact and Fancy', in Barbara A. Hanawalt (ed.), *Chaucer's England: Literature in Historical Context* (Minneapolis, 1992), 133–53 and Simon Thurley, 'The Sport of Kings', in Starkey (ed.), *A European Court*, 163–6.

the departing legate.[127] Thus ended a most remarkable Scottish version of a *fête champêtre*, the significance of which will become clearer when it is set alongside the other cultural and ceremonial activities of the court to be considered in the following chapters.

127 Pitscottie, *History* (STS), i, 335–8; *TA*, vi, 103, 105; SRO, Liber Emptorum, E.32/2, fo. 149v. For Darius see *James V Letters*, 206, 211, 223–4, 229, 237–8.

TWO

Regal Display: The Visual Arts

In western Europe as a whole the 1530s was a decade of lavish expenditure on royal patronage of the visual arts. In England Henry VIII was building at Hampton Court, Whitehall and elsewhere, employing Hans Holbein to produce portraits and decorative schemes for his palaces and pageants and the king also imported some of the finest tapestries and *objets d'art* from the continent. In France the palaces of Chambord, Fontainebleau and Madrid were being constructed and embellished for Francis I and stocked with masterpieces by Rosso, Primaticcio, Cellini, the Clouets and Corneille de Lyon, among others.[1] In both cases there was a dual source of inspiration; architects, artists and craftsmen could draw upon the flamboyant and dazzling late-Gothic style of the Burgundian tradition with its emphasis on magnificence, finesse and chivalric courtesy but they were also influenced by the more restrained classicism of Renaissance Lombardy and Tuscany which stressed the virtues of proportion, harmony and imitation of the antique.[2] As the French kings had been active in Italian politics since 1494 and Francis I particularly coveted the duchy of Milan, the Italian influence was felt heavily in France where, for instance, the essential form of the château of Chambord was based on the villa of Poggio a Caiano, built for Lorenzo de Medici a generation earlier. In England on the other hand, the long-standing links with the ports of the Netherlands established by the medieval woollen-cloth trade, and reinforced by Edward IV's alliance and exile, made the Burgundian fashions irresistible, even to Henry VII, who had spent his period of exile at the courts of Brittany and France, at a time when they were also heavily influenced by Burgundian tastes. The Burgundian influence was reinforced by Henry VIII's marriage to Katherine of Aragon, which effectively locked England into the Habsburg orbit while it lasted, but the advent of Anne Boleyn not only transformed the religious and diplomatic position of the English realm but also created a new mood in the

1 Starkey, *A European Court*; Seward, *Prince of the Renaissance*, 87–167.
2 Peter and Linda Murray, *The Art of the Renaissance* (London, 1986), 89–180, 227–45.

culture of the English court, which quickly adopted French and Italian fashions.[3]

(The Scottish court was somewhat constrained by geographical and economic factors in the extent to which it could participate in such developments but just as the Stewart kings of the fifteenth century had signalled their intention to cut a dash on the international stage by their prestigious marriages, so James V seems to have made a concerted effort to 'keep up with the Joneses' as far as he was able, and his first marriage was the most prestigious and lucrative of all.)As we have seen, James V had a French regent, two French queens, and had visited France in person in 1536–37. The 'auld alliance' was therefore considerably reinforced during his reign and French artistic influences were strong. Nevertheless, Scotland also had its own links with the Burgundian Netherlands: James II's queen had been Mary of Guelders (a niece of Duke Philip the Good), and trading links were well established with the Scottish staple located at Veere in Zeeland from 1477.[4] The Burgundian influence was also felt through the relations with England which, though strained, were relatively peaceful for most of James V's adult reign. James's English mother, Margaret Tudor, may well have had some impact on the taste of the Scottish court and, although her only personal experience of the English court since her marriage was her sojourn there in 1516–17, she was in frequent correspondence with her brother, as indeed was James himself, for ambassadors and envoys shuttled constantly between the two monarchs.

Thus it would seem to be fair to consider the artistic achievements of the court of James V within a European context,)for the king's own actions, as we shall see, suggest that he relished such comparisons. Certainly, the evidence for his enthusiasm for building schemes is manifest and his architectural programme is considered to be 'unparalleled either in interest or intensity by that of any other Scottish

---

3 R. J. Knecht, 'Francis I: Prince and Patron of the Northern Renaissance' in Dickens (ed.), _Courts of Europe_, 109; Knecht, _Warrior and Patron_, 398–461; Simon Thurley, _The Royal Palaces of Tudor England: Architecture and Court Life, 1460–1547_ (New Haven, 1993), 11–37; Eric Ives, _Anne Boleyn_ (London, 1988), 22–46, 273–301; Maria Dowling, 'Anne Boleyn as Patron' in Starkey (ed.) _A European Court_ , 107–11.

4 Lynch, _Scotland: A New History_, 147–8, 155–6; John Davidson and Alexander Gray, _The Scottish Staple at Veere: A Study in the Economic History of Scotland_ (London, 1909), 144–63.

monarch'.[5] He was also an avid collector of tapestries, plate and jewels and there is some evidence to suggest an interest in paintings and illuminated manuscripts too, although this is more difficult to establish from the surviving sources. Undoubtedly the artistic patronage of the court of James V was at its most active and innovative in architectural endeavours. All the major royal residences and several minor ones underwent extensive redevelopment during his adult reign, with the most significant work focused on Falkland and Stirling where the palace blocks represent the earliest examples of the Renaissance style in Britain.[6]

Holyrood was the most important location for the court when it was present within the capital since Edinburgh Castle was used chiefly as an arsenal by the adult James V, who was presumably unimpressed by its potential when, as a child, he had been lodged securely within the fortress. The Augustinian abbey of Holyrood was a royal foundation (by David I in 1128), had regularly lodged fifteenth-century kings, and James II had built some lodgings there before the first palace was constructed for James IV from 1501. The motive seems to have been to create a suitably regal location for the reception of his bride, Margaret Tudor, whom he married in the abbey kirk on 8 August 1503. Their betrothal had been celebrated in January 1502 at another new palace, Henry VII's showpiece residence at Richmond, Surrey, the main phase of which was complete by 1501.[7] The new palace of Holyrood presumably compared relatively favourably to Richmond, for the account of the marriage festivities produced for the Tudor court by John Young, Somerset herald, is glowing in its appreciation of the splendours of the halls and chambers and their rich furnishings.[8] The actual structures of James IV's palace have long since vanished beneath the building works of later generations and no contemporary drawings of the place have survived, but some tantalising glimpses of the architectural scheme are

5 John G. Dunbar, *The Historic Architecture of Scotland* (London, 1966), 17. At the time of writing, John Dunbar is putting the final touches to a major new work arising from his Rhind lectures of 1998: *Scottish Royal Palaces: The Architecture of the Royal Residences during the Late Medieval and Early Renaissance Periods* (East Linton, 1999), and I am extremely grateful to him for allowing me to view some of his drafts prior to publication.

6 Richard Fawcett, *Scottish Architecture from the Accession of the Stewarts to the Reformation, 1371–1560* (Edinburgh, 1994), 323; George Hay, 'Scottish Renaissance Architecture' in D. J. Breeze (ed.), *Studies in Scottish Antiquity presented to Stewart Cruden* (Edinburgh, 1984), 205.

7 *TA*, v, 122, 129; *ER*, v, 26, 346–7; *TA*, ii, 87f.; Thurley, *Tudor Palaces*, 28.

8 John Leland, *De Rebus Britannicis Collectanea* (6 vols, London, 1770), iv, 258–300.

provided by the financial records. The first phase included a foregate, a forework, a chapel, a gallery and royal apartments costing at least £2,500 and constructed by Leonard Logy, overseer, Walter Merliene, master mason, and Walter Turnbull, mason.[9] The palace occupied the site to the west of the monastic cloister on which the current palace now stands and is likely to have been arranged on the quadrangular plan that still persists. Young, who accompanied Margaret Tudor on her progress northwards and was therefore an eye-witness, described the king and queen occupying matching apartments consisting of a hall, great chamber and inner chamber and other rooms included oratories for the king and queen, a king's closet and a queen's gallery. In 1505 a tower was added to the complex and later the gardens received attention: a lion house was built which housed a pair of bears as well as a lion and 'the loch beside the abbay' was drained.[10] There is no contemporary evidence of the precise arrangement of all these elements but the accounts of James V's rebuilding work imply that the chapel was in the north range running westwards from the west front of the abbey kirk and that the queen's chambers were in the south range on the opposite side of the close.[11] The great hall had a door which led from the abbey cloister, had a south-facing roof line and seems to have stood immediately to the east of the chapel so was perhaps the former monastic refectory appropriated for the king's use.[12] The site of the tower of 1505 is unknown but the later accounts refer to a south tower, the governor's tower (which is listed in a roofing account for buildings on the east side of the palace) and the old tower. These may be references to separate structures or perhaps represent different names for the same building. John Dunbar has speculated that James IV's tower may have been at the southern end of the west front on the site of the tower built for Charles II in the 1670s.[13]

From the death of James IV at Flodden in 1513 to the assumption of power by James V in 1528 little seems to have been done at

 9 *RCAHMS (Edinburgh)*, 146; John Sinclair, 'Notes on the Holyrood "Foir-yet" of James IV', *PSAS*, xxxiv (1904–5), 352–62; *TA*, ii, 269f., 273f., 280, 344, 383, 419; J. G. Dunbar, 'The Palace of Holyrood during the first half of the sixteenth century', *Architectural Journal cxx* (1963), 242–54.

10 Leland, *Collectanea*, iv, 295–6; *TA*, ii, 269, 299, 417, 419; iii, 86, 191, 200; iv, 276, 529.

11 *MW*, i, 42, 43, 188, 191.

12 *MW*, i, 72, 103, 193; John G. Dunbar, 'Some Aspects of the Planning of Scottish Royal Palaces in the sixteenth century', *Architectural History*, xxvii (1984), 16–17.

13 *MW*, i, 10f., 188, 225, 242, 290; Dunbar, 'Palace of Holyrood', 244.

Holyrood other than repairs and maintenance. When writing in 1591 about the events of 1514, George Marjoribanks made a passing reference to 'the auld touer of Holyrudhouss, wich wes foundit by the said ducke [of Albany]' but there is no reference to it in the surviving accounts, which appear to be quite full for 1515 to 1517.[14] However, the accounts covering the period of Albany's second and third visits to Scotland in 1521–2 and 1523–4 are incomplete, so it is just possible that some building work was done then but this is unlikely because his visits were brief and directed primarily towards military action.[15] It is just conceivable that Albany built a tower at Holyrood which he financed from his own revenues, as he was a very wealthy man in his own right and certainly commissioned building work at his own castle of Dunbar, but this is also unlikely since he seems to have utilised the crown revenues to finance his office as governor of the king. It seems more likely that Marjoribanks was aware that there was a structure at Holyrood called the governor's tower and concluded that Albany had built it, without considering the possibility that this was an older building where he had merely lodged.[16]

In any event, the adult James V clearly regarded the facilities provided at Holyrood as deficient, for building work seems to have started there almost as soon as he began to rule in his own right in the summer of 1528. The first surviving account book of his master of works, John Scrymgeour, covers the period from 21 August 1529 to 28 August 1530 but is headed *Secundus Liber* and makes reference to an earlier account. Presumably the missing *Primus Liber* ran from August 1528; that is within weeks of James asserting his personal rule and before he had secured the forfeiture and banishment of the Douglases, a process that was of fundamental importance for the reign as a whole. The fact that the king embarked on a building programme so early, during a period of political and financial crisis, says much about how

14 G. Marjoribanks, *Annals of Scotland from the yeir 1514 to the yeir 1591* (Edinburgh, 1814), 1–2. In fact Albany did not arrive in Scotland until May 1515. *TA*, v, 1–131. Repairs were made to a tower at Holyrood in 1516: *ER*, xiv, 162.

15 Emond, 'Minority', 288–394. Minor repairs to the palace during Albany's regency are noted in *TA*, v, 10–16, 41, 78–9, 95, 113–16, 118, 120, 219–20.

16 Murray, 'Financing the Royal Household', 41–59; *MW*, i, 290. There is a reference to Albany paying out of his own coffers for the guard which was established to protect the king in 1522. It is not clear whether this refers to money that he had brought from France, or to his revenues from Dunbar: *HMC Mar and Kellie*, 11. For the Dunbar works see chap. 5.

important he thought it was to express his new power and dignity in stone.[17]

The *Secundus Liber* reveals that a new tower was being built at Holyrood and had already progressed beyond the vaulted ceilings of the ground floor rooms, which were probably intended as storage cellars, and onto the first floor chamber windows and doors. It used to be thought that this tower, which still survives at the north-west corner of the current building, was started by James IV or Albany and only completed by James V but the original accounts clearly attribute its construction to the period 1528–32.[18] It is also specifically stated that whilst it was being built, James V was residing in the south tower, which was obviously an earlier structure.[19] The new tower (or 'new werk') was probably designed by John Ayton, the king's master mason, working under Scrymgeour's supervision, and follows a simple rectangular plan (68' x 35') with circular turrets in each corner.[20] The south-east turret no longer survives and had already disappeared by the time of the earliest surviving plan of the palace which was made in 1663, but it may have been removed as early as 1535–6 when work was underway on the adjoining west range.[21] The tower seems to have been a free-standing structure at first (part of James IV's chapel was demolished to make room for it and had to be shored up) and may even have been moated. It certainly had a drawbridge leading to the main entrance on the first floor where there was both a wooden door and an iron gate.[22] These features, combined with gun loops and crenellations, suggest that James V was intending his new residence to be a well-fortified, defensible structure (which is understandable considering the turbulent events of his minority and his campaign against the Douglases, which was then at its height) but there is an alternative view. Crenellations and gun-loops were fashionable accessories often used for decorative impact at this period and a monarch's retreat into a tower residence separated from the public rooms of a palace by a moat and drawbridge may simply indicate a desire for greater privacy, as seems to have been the case for Henry V and Henry VII of England at

17 *MW*, i, 1; Cameron, *James V*, 31–69.
18 *MW*, i, 3–4; *RCAHMS* (*Edinburgh*), 144; John Sinclair, 'Notes on James V's Towers, Holyrood Palace', *PSAS*, xxxiv (1899–1900), 227.
19 *MW*, i, 27.
20 Ibid., i, 1f., 22, 55; *RCAHMS* (*Edinburgh*), 146.
21 Bodleian Library, Gough Maps, 39, fo. Iv. reproduced in Dunbar, 'Holyrood Palace', plate vi & p. 248; *MW*, i, 132f.
22 *MW*, i, 18, 33, 40, 42, 43; John Harrison, *The History of the Monastery of the Holy-Rood and of the Palace of Holyrood House* (Edinburgh, 1919), 58.

Sheen/Richmond.[23] It is also worth noting that at exactly the same time as James V was building his Holyrood tower, Henry VIII of England was moving into a 'stacked lodging' at Hampton Court Palace where the queen's apartments were above the king's, as at Holyrood. However, after 1533 Henry abandoned this arrangement and reverted to matching apartments on the same level, which was the pattern favoured in Scotland by James IV and by James V in his later work at Stirling. A similar development can also be detected in France where 'stacked lodgings' were in use until about 1530 (e.g. at Blois and Chambord) but thereafter royal apartments were arranged on one level (e.g. at Fontainebleau).[24]

Scrymgeour's account book for 1529–30 shows the work progressing rapidly.[25] The first floor contained two main rooms: the drawbridge led directly into 'the uter chalmer nixt the woltis' (also known as 'the gret chalmer of the tour') on the east side of the tower and to the west there was 'the inner chalmer nixt the woltis' with closets in the turret space (the 'roundis'). There was a turnpike stair ('turngreis') in the north-east turret and a straight stair with an iron gate in the north wall from the inner chamber to the next floor ('the passage betwix the laicht and height chalmeris'). By the summer of 1530 the work had moved on to the second floor where a matching pair of rooms was built: 'the uter myd chalmer' and 'the inner myd chalmer' with a stair to the third floor, 'the trans betuex the myd inner chalmeris and the wardrop' (the third floor still housed the wardrobe in 1611).[26] Scrymgeour's third book for August 1530 to September 1531 is lost and by the start of the fourth book the tower was being roofed. The corner turrets were built one storey higher than the battlements and capped with conical lead roofs and a platform roof (also of lead) provided a wall-walk in a circuit between the turrets ('allering').[27] Attention then turned to the fittings and decorations. Wooden floors, ceilings and wall panels were in-

23 Emond, 'Minority', 486–560; Cameron, *James V*, 31–69; Fawcett, *Scottish Architecture*, 322; Thurley, *Tudor Palaces*, 10, 36. Nevertheless it is also worth bearing in mind that munitions of some sort were kept at Holyrood during this period (it is not clear whether the accounts refer to small arms or larger weapons): *TA*, vi, 438; vii, 350. I am grateful to John Dunbar for alerting me to the significance of these references.

24 Thurley, *Tudor Palaces*, 52–3; Jean-Pierre Babelon, *Châteaux de France au siècle de la Renaissance* (Paris, 1989), 110–17, 159–67, 198–206.

25 It has been examined in detail by Dunbar, 'Palace of Holyrood', 242–54, and this account largely follows his article.

26 *MW*, i, 3, 10, 25, 29, 33, 93, 94, 331.

27 Ibid, i, 64–67, 71, 74.

stalled, all the iron work of the gates, doors and window frames was painted red, the two west turrets were topped with heraldic badges (lions and towers) that were gilded and painted and the windows of the main chambers were fitted with painted or stained glass showing the royal arms within chaplets, a description which is very reminiscent of the pieces of heraldic glass surviving from English royal works and of the glass roundels in the Magdalen Chapel, Edinburgh, c.1542. Finally, in 1536, the two 'gret howsings' on the west turrets, which today hold stone armorial panels, were fitted with lead panels, one bearing the king's arms and the other an image of St. Andrew with arms. These would probably have been painted, although payment for this work does not appear in the surviving records.[28]

The new tower clearly had a practical function as a princely lodging, but it seems to have been designed almost as a piece of theatre or an item of propaganda: it was built to impress. The solid, imposing mass rose through its three floors in a form very reminiscent of the forework built at Stirling Castle by the new king's father and the resemblance may well have been quite deliberate.[29] James V and his masons were employing all the colourful, exuberant, heraldic elements of late-Gothic regal display as a statement of intent. In constructing this new tower in a style worthy of James IV, as an extension to a palace created by James IV, James V seems to have been making a clear political point, announcing his determination to be as effective a king as his father had been and predicting a glorious future for himself. However, we should be wary of overplaying the significance of this point; it has been suggested that James IV's Stirling forework constituted a Renaissance triumphal arch, but this interpretation is not wholly convincing. It would appear to be based upon the proportions of the gateway as it stands today, rather than as it was initially built (the towers were originally much higher). Also there seems to be no evidence to suggest that the Stirling gateway ever possessed the classical pilasters and other decorative features visible on the Italian

28 *MW*, i, 69, 76, 79, 86, 94, 194; Hilary Wayment, 'Stained Glass in Henry
    VIII's Palaces' in Starkey (ed.), *A European Court*, 28–32; G. Seton, 'Notice
    of Four Stained Glass Shields of Arms and a Monumental Slab in St.
    Magdalene's Chapel, Cowgate', *PSAS*, xxi (1886–87), 266–74; Hay, 'Scottish
    Renaissance Architecture', 206. See also C. P. Graves, 'Medieval Stained
    and Painted Window Glass in the Diocese of St. Andrews', in John Higgit
    (ed.), *Medieval Art and Architecture in the Diocese of St. Andrews* (London,
    1994), 125–36.

29 Richard Fawcett, *Stirling Castle* (London, 1995), 48–51; Fawcett, *Scottish
    Architecture*, 321.

gateway cited as a parallel example.[30] James IV's forework was essentially a late-medieval fortification, redolent with <u>chivalric but not classical</u> imagery. Nevertheless, at Holyrood in the first months and years of the adult rule of James V, his new tower simultaneously signalled a new departure and harked back to a chivalric golden age in the not so distant past.

James V's next phase of building at Holyrood seems to have been inspired by the imminent prospect of marriage (which is another parallel with the works of James IV). As we have seen, throughout the early 1530s negotiations were conducted for the hand of a French princess (amongst others) and James eventually married Madeleine in Paris on 1 January 1537. She resided briefly at Holyrood until her death there on 7 July and she was buried in the abbey kirk, but in 1538 the palace was made ready for the reception of her successor, Mary of Guise. Most of the new work was undertaken between June 1535 and December 1536 for which period quite detailed accounts survive; thereafter we have only a few pages recording small scale repairs and maintenance.[31] These works were in the hands of John Brownhill, the king's master mason in succession to John Ayton, who was dead by January 1532[32]. They involved converting the old queen's chambers in the south range into a new chapel, making the old chapel in the north range presentable as a chamber or chambers, and constructing a new west range known as the fore-entry or fore-work. James IV's work on this site seems to have been demolished; there were payments to workmen for 'brekand down auld wallis, berand stanis and makand red, serwand the masonis and kastand the ground [digging the foundations?] of the fore entray' and purchases of 'auld schip tymmer for certane spilis and brandry to the ground of the fore entre'.[33] The building that was erected on the site was demolished in turn when Charles II's palace was built in the 1670s but its west front is depicted on an engraving by Gordon of Rothiemay c.1649 and its first floor plan is shown in John Mylne's survey of 1663. This indicates that a south-west tower was planned by James V to balance the north-west one but

30 Aonghus MacKechnie, 'Stirling's Triumphal Arch', *Welcome: News for Friends of Historic Scotland* (Sept. 1991), unpaginated. See also Miles Glendinning, Ranald MacInnes and Aonghus MacKechnie, *A History of Scottish Architecture from the Renaissance to the Present Day* (Edinburgh, 1996), 14, where the curious term 'neo-chivalric' is used to describe James IV's architectural style.

31 *MW*, i, 132–95, 222–27, 242, 288–90.

32 *RSS*, i, 1119; *MW*, i, 153–65.

33 *MW*, i, 167, 179, 186–91.

not built until the 1670s.[34] The range extended southwards from the
tower of 1528–32 on two storeys surmounted by crenellations and a
pitched roof. There was an arched entry in the centre under a stone
armorial panel flanked by a pair of semi-circular turrets and a rectilinear turret at each end.[35] The ground floor contained 'laich chalmers'
and the 'gret yet' leading into the central courtyard or close. The first
floor suite was reached from a great stair in the south-west corner of the
close, which also gave access to the chapel, and consisted of an outer,
mid and inner chamber (also identified, perhaps inaccurately, as the
wardrobe).[36] These apartments were more spacious than those in the
north-west tower and were probably used for formal, public occasions.
Certainly Sir Ralph Sadler, the English ambassador, was received by
James at Holyrood in 1540 in a suite of rooms near the chapel, at least
one of which overlooked the inner courtyard, where Henry VIII's gift of
six geldings was paraded before the king.[37] This description strongly
suggests the forework chambers, perhaps in conjunction with the north
chamber(s) and this would have allowed James to use the tower rooms
as a private retreat, which was a practice adopted by Henry VIII on a
much larger scale in the late 1530s.[38] It is perhaps worth noting that the
forework as depicted by Gordon bears some resemblance to views of
the queen's gallery at Hampton Court Palace, built in 1537, so that
James may have been adopting English fashions in architectural design
as well as function at this point.[39]

The new apartments were certainly embellished in a grand style. The
great arms above the main entrance were cut from a single block of
stone by masons working day and night to a design by sir John Kilgour

34 Reproduced in Dunbar, 'Palace of Holyrood', facing pp. 232 & 242.
35 A rectilinear turret feature with full-height windows closely resembling
    those on the Rothiemay engraving was later built on the chapel façade of
    Heriot's Hospital, Edinburgh (1628–93), and was perhaps inspired by the
    Holyrood design. Indeed the entire scheme at Heriot's seems to owe much
    to James V's Holyrood.
36 *MW*, i, 185–6, 187, 190–1.
37 *Sadler's Papers*, i, 40–1. In 1579 the same courtyard was possibly used for
    'running at the ring' by James VI and his companions: see Chambers,
    Domestic Annals of Scotland (Edinburgh, 1858–61), i, 142. I am grateful to
    Professor Lynch for this point.
38 By 1579 the north range probably housed 'the auld hall' (*MW*, i, 305)
    which was perhaps used as a council chamber: Harrison, *History of
    Holyrood*, 61; *MW*, i, 306; Thurley, *Tudor Palaces*, 52–3.
39 See Thurley, *Tudor Palaces*, plate 172, p. 134; Hugh Murray Baillie,
    'Etiquette and the Planning of the State Apartments in Baroque Palaces',
    Archaeologia, ci (1967), 169–99.

and gilded and painted. The king's arms also appeared in stone on the east quarter of the palace and in timber within the chapel and the queen's arms were cast in lead; all were painted and gilded. Some of the glass from James IV's forework was salvaged and reset in the hall and chapel, whilst the new glass included stained or painted panels: 'Flanderis roundis and squair antik peces' and 'bordouris and antik faces'. The term 'antique' appeared frequently in the English accounts of the 1530s too and referred to decorations in the grotesque style which had originated in Italy in the 1490s. The ceilings of the fore-entry chambers and chapel were decorated with about two hundred pendant bosses ('gret hingand knoppis') that were gilded and coloured and the mouldings ('millouris') were painted azure. All the iron work of window frames and fittings was also painted, the roof line was set with six copper gilt weather vanes ('thanis') and the 'roundis' were adorned with twenty-two gilded and coloured 'manikynnis' with twenty-two more 'thanis'. The chapel interior was fitted with oak stalls ('deskis'), turned wooden decoration above the high altar (gilded and coloured), azure mouldings and hangings of Milan fustian. Tapestries and hangings were presumably used elsewhere too, although there are no specifics in the accounts apart from occasional references to the hooks from which they were hung. The altar may also have had a painted timber retable, as such an item ('a chabyll') was removed from the chapel in May 1559.[40]

The records also mention work on the old oratory and the queen's oratory, the great hall, several galleries, the gatehouse and the gardens, the precise locations of which are unclear.[41] Renovations were also undertaken on most of the office houses which were probably sited to the south of the palace block. Reference is made to the wardrobes, stables, avery, forge, armoury, coining house, tapisier's house, kitchens, bakehouse, dressory, vesselhouse, brewhouse, napery house, larders, spicehouse, Thomas Peebles' house (he was the king's glazier) and chambers for Dr. Arbuthnot (the king's mediciner), the sangsters (i.e. choristers of the chapel) and Lady Drummond.[42] This list corresponds very closely to the records of household personnel discussed in chapter one, indicating that the full household establishment could probably operate here.

Taking the two main phases of the Holyrood works together, James

---

40 *MW*, i, 99, 138, 162, 170, 184, 189–91, 224, 298; *TA*, vi, 352; Thurley, *Tudor Palaces*, 86–7.

41 *MW*, i, 226, 227, 191, 166f., 132, 191–2.

42 Ibid., i, 27, 103, 242, 96–7, 290, 226, 222, 103, 189, 225.

V seems to have spent about £12,000 on this palace.[43] The expenses seem to have been directed at a largely traditional structure: the only suggestions of innovation come in the references to 'antik' decoration on glass (see above), a design for 'ane dowbill turngrece', which calls to mind Francis I's double-spiral stair at Chambord but is not recorded as ever having been built at Holyrood, and the repeated use of large bay windows running virtually the full height of the west façade, which is a final flourish of late-Gothic design rather than a foretaste of Renaissance style.[44] However, this does not mean that the Holyrood works were somehow inferior to the later experiments at Falkland and Stirling, for the palace as it was created for James V seems to have successfully reproduced the flamboyant grace of the best of English and Flemish court architecture of the period.

The next royal palace to receive attention was Linlithgow but the accounts are less extensive for this project than for Holyrood. The work was in the hands of Sir James Hamilton of Finnart, captain and keeper of the palace and park, and sir Thomas Johnson, chaplain and overseer of the work, but only one of their account books survives, recording £1973 11s 3d of expenses for 1 February 1535 to 31 January 1536.[45] However, reference is made to superexpenses (i.e. deficit) of £1198 4s 2d from the previous account, which presumably ran from February 1534. There were also accounts for February to August 1536 and for 1537 (£133 6s 8d) which have been lost, the latter including expenditure on Blackness Castle, which was also under Finnart's control because Blackness was the port for the burgh. In May 1538 Finnart was also given four hundred French crowns of the sun from Mary of Guise's dowry for the repairs at Linlithgow.[46] Thus the total expenditure on Linlithgow and Blackness in the mid-1530s may have reached more than £5000. The master mason at Linlithgow was Thomas French (or Franche), whose surname obviously suggests that he was of French extraction. He may well have been a second-generation Scot for his father, John French, was apparently buried in St. Michael's Kirk in 1489. Thomas seems to have worked for Bishop Gavin Dunbar of Aberdeen on the brig of Dee and the cathedral where his son, also called Thomas,

---

43 Ibid., i, 55, 114, 195 plus an estimate for the missing books. See Dunbar, 'Palace of Holyrood', 247.

44 *MW*, i, 191. See Gordon of Rothiemay's engraving, reproduced in Dunbar, 'Palace of Holyrood', facing p. 232.

45 *RSS*, i, 3523; *MW*, i, 115–31. Johnson was from a Linlithgow burgess family, acted as a public notary and held several chaplaincies, see *Prot. Bk. Johnsoun*, pp iii–v.

46 *MW*, i, 130; *RSS*, ii, 2147; *TA*, vi, 304; vii, 60.

was buried in 1530. By 1531–32 he was back in Linlithgow working on St. Michael's Kirk, by 1534 he was working at the palace and in April 1535 he was appointed master mason to the king for life, this appointment running concurrently with that of John Brownhill, who continued to receive his fee for the same post.[47]

(Unlike the works at Holyrood, James appears to have adapted and developed existing structures rather than building from scratch.) Like Holyrood, Linlithgow was arranged on a quadrangular plan, with defensive features that were probably more decorative than functional. The east quarter dates almost entirely from the reign of James I and contained in its basement cellars, kitchens, larders and a brewhouse, and on the ground floor, more cellars and the main entrance across a drawbridge from James IV's 'bulwerk'.[48] Above this was the great hall (or lion chamber) built by James I and remodelled by James IV; the imposing, carved triple-fireplace dates from his reign. James IV was also probably responsible for most of the work on the other three ranges although some parts of the south and west quarters may be older.[49] The south range (like all the others) had cellars at ground level, with the chapel on the first floor and chambers at either end, the purpose of which is uncertain, although the eastern rooms presumably served as withdrawing rooms from the great hall and the western ones were perhaps ante-chambers to the chapel or royal lodgings. There was also a three-storey gallery running along the courtyard front of this range, its design exhibiting a strong English influence.[50] The first floor of the west range seems to have held the king's apartments (the two western rooms of the south range may

47 R. S. Mylne, *The Master Masons of the Crown of Scotland* (Edinburgh, 1893), 36–9; *ER*, xvi, 234; J. S. Richardson, *The Medieval Stone Carver in Scotland* (Edinburgh, 1964), 57; John Ferguson, *Ecclesia Antiqua or the History of an Ancient Church (St. Michael's, Linlithgow) with an account of its chapels, chantries and endowments* (Edinburgh, 1905), 33; *MW*, i, 122; *RSS*, ii, 1643, 1119; *TA*, vi, 315. See also Thomas, 'Renaissance Culture', 104 n.98.

48 *RCAHMS (Mid and West Lothian)*, 219–31.

49 Fawcett, *Scottish Architecture*, 305–9. Ian Campbell, 'Linlithgow's "Princely Palace" and its Influence in Europe', *Architectural Heritage*, v (1995), 1–20, argues that the quadrangular plan of the palace was devised for James III on Italian models by Anselm Adornes, a merchant and traveller from Bruges of Genoese extraction, who was keeper of the palace between 1477 and 1483. Campbell also believes that the palace exerted considerable influence on other buildings in Europe.

50 C. Wilson, 'Linlithgow Palace' in C. McWilliam (ed.), *The Buildings of Scotland: Lothian except Edinburgh* (London, 1978), 297–8; D. McGibbon and T. Ross, *The Castellated and Domestic Architecture of Scotland* (5 vols, Edinburgh, 1887), i, 497.

also have been part of this arrangement). The names of these chambers are known only from a seventeenth-century source. They ran *en suite* from the south-west tower as the king's hall, presence chamber and bed chamber and from this latter room there was access to a strong-room below and a closet and oratory on the same level in the north wall of the north-west tower.[51] The second floor contained a matching set of *en suite* apartments which may have served the queen but these chambers are not as well-lit as the first floor rooms (they lack windows to the west) and may have served a different function.[52] The other possible location for the queen's apartment is the first floor of the north quarter, but this building collapsed in 1607 and was rebuilt to a new design in 1618–20, so the fabric of this part of the sixteenth-century palace has been lost. However, a clue survives in the fragmentary remains of an oriel window adjoining the king's oratory in the north-west tower which may have been the queen's oratory, in which case the queen's chambers would have run at right angles to the king's as was the case in the palace block at Stirling.[53] James V may have done some work on the now-vanished north quarter as there is a record of a purchase of timber for 'proping' it in 1541: this perhaps implies that the structure was already becoming unstable, although an account of May 1583 suggests that it was the west quarter that was at risk of collapse but this may be an error for the north quarter.[54]

Because so many accounts are missing it is difficult to be precise about the extent of the work undertaken at Linlithgow by James V. He was certainly responsible for abandoning the east entrance and creating a new approach to the palace from the south. This involved cutting an arched 'pend' through James IV's transe and cellars (one of which was converted into a guard-room) and building an outer gate beside the west end of St. Michael's Kirk, with a cobbled 'causeway' running between the outer and inner gates and around the courtyard. This 'causeway' was laid between April and July 1535, when the two new gates were already standing, so they had presumably been built sometime during 1534.[55] The outer gate consists of two octagonal

51 Wilson, 'Linlithgow Palace', 300; *MW*, ii, 126, 262–9, 273; *RCAHMS* (*Mid and West Lothian*), 229.

52 In the Rhind lectures for 1998 John Dunbar stated that he now believes this to have been the location of the queen's apartments, although he had previously argued to the contrary: Dunbar, 'Aspects of Planning', 21. See Dunbar, *Scottish Royal Palaces*, 138–40.

53 *RCAHMS* (*Mid and West Lothian*), 223; *TA*, iv, 524; Dunbar, 'Aspects of Planning', 21, but cf. above.

54 *TA*, vii, 444; *MW*, i, 311.

55 *RCAHMS* (*Mid and West Lothian*), 220–26; *MW*, i, 123.

towers with an archway between and originally had a drawbridge over a ditch. The crenellated parapet that can be seen there today is a nineteenth-century reconstruction of the earlier work and is adorned with the insignia of the four chivalric orders to which James belonged: those of the Garter, the Thistle, the Golden Fleece and St. Michael. John Slezer's view of the palace (c.1678) also shows a pitched roof above the parapet but this has since vanished.[56] John Leslie noted the adornment of the Linlithgow gate with the orders of chivalry thus:

> . . . for an evident sygne and takne to al posteritie the kingis armes upon the port of the palice of Lithquowe, with the rest of the armes fra quhome he receivet thame, with the ornamentis of S. Andro quilkes ar the proper armes of our natioune, our king selfe causet thair til affix verie artificiouslie with cunning craft of gret commend.[57]

The inner gate was flanked by circular turrets provided with gunloops and crenellations and was also decorated with carved badges and figures that were painted and gilded. These are detailed in a painter's account of 1535 as a lion and two unicorns on the outer face (presumably the royal arms with supporters) and an annunciation scene ('the salutation of our lade with the wle [sic] pege' i.e. the 'lile pege' or pot of lilies) on the inner face. The same painter, John Ross, was also paid for colouring the statuary on the inner face of the old east entrance, which was probably a representation of the three estates: the church ('the pape'), the nobility ('the knycht') and the burghs ('the laborius man'), and perhaps a reference to James I's interest in developing the Scottish parliament.[58] Finally, Ross painted the iron window frames with red lead and vermilion (as at Holyrood), gilded the weather vanes which were in the shape of 'crossis and ballis' and painted the chapel ceiling azure and the twelve 'ballis' under the chapel loft. The new paint in the chapel was part of a redecoration programme that involved either replacing or renovating the ceiling above the altar and reglazing the five windows with painted or stained glass depicting 'ymagis'. The great hall was also redecorated, receiving new painted glass into its western windows and new benches and tables ('formes and burd'). Other work was carried out on the ceiling of the king's kitchen in 1535 and in 1539 a new chimney piece and oven were installed and a silver vessel house, coalhouse and 'grete librall' (library?) were built.[59] These

---

56 Keith Cavers, *A Vision of Scotland: The Nation Observed by John Slezer, 1671 to 1717* (Edinburgh, 1993), 27.

57 Leslie, *Historie* (STS), ii, 230.

58 *MW*, i, 128; Michael Brown, *James I* (Edinburgh, 1994), 122.

59 *MW*, i, 124, 127, 128; *TA*, vii, 195.

were perhaps in the now vanished north quarter and if this is a reference to a library, it is the only mention of such a facility in all the works accounts of this period.[60]

The only other Linlithgow structure that is usually attributed to James V is the fountain in the centre of the courtyard. It is generally ascribed to the late 1530s for stylistic reasons because some of the statuary resembles the decoration on the palace block at Stirling (c.1540) although the three-tiered octagonal design and architectural framework are of a somewhat different character to the Stirling scheme and rather reminiscent of the ornate, tiered, late-Gothic font covers which can still be seen in many English churches. In 1894 the lead pipe serving the fountain was dug up in the Kirkgait and the date 1538 was found marked upon it and in the *Treasurer's Accounts* of April 1542 one payment relating to it is recorded so the stylistic analysis would appear to be roughly correct. Courtyard fountains were fashionable features abroad at this time too. Henry VIII had them at Greenwich and Hampton Court, although made of wood rather than stone.[61] It was perhaps intended as the finishing touch to a palace fit for a new queen, for Linlithgow was a favoured residence of Mary of Guise even though it was not a part of her jointure. She apparently declared herself delighted with the palace, comparing it favourably (and, one suspects, tactfully) with those of France.[62] However, Linlithgow Palace (as we have seen) was heavily influenced by the architecture of Tudor England and the Habsburg Netherlands, which is hardly surprising since it was a dower house of Queen Margaret Tudor and had previously been in the care of Anselm Adornes of Bruges. It is still visibly distinct from the contemporary *châteaux* of the Loire and Ile de France, although an attempt has recently been made to establish Italian influences on the design.[63] It was only at Falkland and Stirling (both of

60 John Dunbar has suggested in a private communication that this might actually be a reference to a great balance or scales rather than a library.
61 Wilson, 'Linlithgow Palace', 297; *TA*, viii, 72; Thurley, *Tudor Palaces*, 167; Thurley, 'Henry VIII and the Building of Hampton Court Palace: A Reconstruction of a Tudor Palace', *Architectural History*, xxxi (1988), 24.
62 Pitscottie, *History*, ed. Dalyell, 378.
63 Campbell, 'Linlithgow's "Princely Palace"', 3–7; Campbell, 'A Romanesque Revival and the Early Renaissance in Scotland, c. 1380–1513', *Journal of the Society of Architectural Historians*, liv (1995), 314–18; Miles Glendinning, Ranald MacInnes and Aonghus MacKechnie, *A History of Scottish Architecture from the Renaissance to the Present Day* (Edinburgh, 1996), 9–11. See also Alan Macquarrie, 'Anselm Adornes of Bruges: Traveller in the East and Friend of James III', *IR*, xxxiii (1982), 15–22. Adornes was keeper of Linlithgow between 1477 and 1483 but the only record of building work by him there relates to the construction of a mill: *ER*, ix, 400, 466; *RSS*, i, 417.

which were included in Mary's jointure) that James V began to develop a
new Renaissance style for the Scottish court.

[The oldest structure at Falkland was the thirteenth- and fourteenth-
century castle, where the duke of Rothesay was imprisoned and
starved to death in 1402] and which has long since vanished.[64] At
least part of this structure was still standing in 1532 and it might have
contained the old chapel which appears in the records between 1532
and 1538 and which seems to have been demolished by 1540–41.[65] To
the south of this castle a quadrangular royal palace evolved after 1437,
the castle having become crown property on the forfeiture of Murdac,
duke of Albany, in 1425.[66] The north range, which has also disappeared, was probably started by James II, worked on by James IV and
contained the great hall. In 1538 it probably housed 'the inner lying
chalmer on the cloce syd of the nether north luging quhare the kingis
grace lyis' and 'the north galry and kingis grace closat' for which new
window frames were provided. There is also reference to a 'north
wardrup' in 1540–41. The west range no longer survives either but in
1539 it contained office houses.[67] The unfinished appearance of the
masonry on the north wall of the south-west tower perhaps implies that
James V intended to build a new west wing adjoining the tower but that
death intervened. In 1532 workmen were engaged on 'thekin poynting
and beting of the new galryis and corssis', which is perhaps a reference
to the gallery and cross-house of the east range, as well as building a
new stable and avery block (the old one was demolished) to the north-
east of the palace. From December 1538 a tennis court ('caichpule') was
also built in this area.[68]

However, the most intensive and innovative work was undertaken
on the south and east ranges between 1537 and 1541, when nearly
£13,000 was spent on improvements and extensions to buildings begun
by James IV at the beginning of the century.[69] A new entrance tower
was built containing a pair of chambers on each of its three floors, with
turrets, crenellations and gunloops in a design very similar to the
Holyrood tower of 1528–32, and was constructed by the master mason

64 *RCAHMS* (*Fife, Kinross and Clackmannan*), 135; Brown, *James I*, 12.
65 *MW*, i, 111–217, 280. However, *ER*, xiv, 175 suggests that the old chapel
   was in the east quarter, but it is difficult to see how the correct orientation
   could have been achieved within the width of a range which runs north-
   south. The chapels of all the royal palaces face east.
66 Brown, *James I*, 73, 113.
67 *ER*, v, 338, 347; *TA*, ii, 87–9; *MW*, i, 217–18, 260, 285.
68 Dunbar, 'Aspects of Planning', 22; *MW*, i, 112–14, 244f., 288.
69 *MW*, i, 207, 213, 221, 263, 292; *TA*, ii, 87–9 and elsewhere.

who had previously worked at Holyrood, John Brownhill. The adjoining south front of the palace was embellished with crenellations extending across the roof line from the tower and a foreign sculptor, Peter Fleming, produced five statues to adorn the buttress niches. The interior of the chapel on the second floor of the south range acquired new wooden fittings made by Richard Stewart, a wright sent from Edinburgh Castle, which included floor boards, wall panels, a panelled ceiling, loft, stalls, altarpiece and screen. Much of this woodwork survives, although heavily restored, and the ceiling was painted in 1633 to celebrate the Scottish coronation of Charles I. A mason from Holyrood, John Merliene, 'reformed' seven chambers and various office houses in the east range and two master masons, James Black from Holyrood and Thomas French from Linlithgow were paid for building the gallery extension to the south range. There is also a reference to a fountain in the courtyard, perhaps similar to the one at Linlithgow, and to a clock bought from Alexander Lindsay of Kinghorn.[70]

All of the work to this point seems to have been in the traditional late-Gothic style that was also used at Holyrood and Linlithgow and it included the usual painted iron work, weather vanes and even gargoyles,[71] but a dramatic new departure came with the employment of two French master masons to decorate the courtyard façades of the east and south ranges. James V was not the first to employ foreign masons; an Italian had worked for James IV in 1511–12 and the duke of Albany had used a Frenchman at Dunbar Castle.[72] Yet the courtyard façades at Falkland provide 'a display of early-Renaissance architecture without parallel in the British Isles.'[73] The east façade is inscribed with the date 1537 and was probably designed and executed by Mogin or Moses Martin, the French mason who had worked for Albany at Dunbar and accompanied James V on his visit to France in 1536–37. It was at Orléans on 1 December 1536 that he was appointed the king's master mason, a third appointee to this post alongside John Brownhill and Thomas French. It is perhaps significant that he acquired this office only five days after the marriage contract of James and Madeleine had been signed at Blois; certainly several French *châteaux* that were on the court

70 *MW*, i, 218f., 256–7, 261, 275, 279; *TA*, vii, 219–20; Gifford, *Buildings of Fife*, 214; *RCAHMS (Fife)*,138.
71 *MW*, i, 215, 246, 272 ('gargonis').
72 *TA*, iv, 271, 439; I. MacIvor, 'Artillery and Major Places of Strength in the Lothians and the East Border, 1513–1542' in D. H. Caldwell (ed.), *Scottish Weapons and Fortifications, 1100–1800* (Edinburgh, 1981), 115; *RSS*, ii, 2199.
73 M. Girouard, 'Falkland Palace, Fife I', *Country Life*, vol. cxxvi, no 3260 (27 Aug. 1959), 121.

itinerary of 1536–37 have been cited as sources for the Falkland design, for example, Bury (begun 1511) and Villers-Cotterêts (begun 1533).[74] Martin is first recorded in the Falkland accounts in December 1537 but the records of 1536 are missing and he may have started work earlier. The south façade is inscribed with the date 1539 and follows essentially the same design as the east façade but is more mature and accomplished in execution. Martin died in March 1538 and another Frenchman, Nicholas Roy, was appointed master mason to the king in his place on 22 April 1539, having been engaged for her son-in-law by the duchess of Guise. He features in the Falkland accounts from July 1539 to July 1541.[75]

The design divides the building vertically into five equal bays separated by shallow pilaster-buttresses supporting engaged Corinthian columns. The buttresses of the east range were topped by canopied niches containing statues and those of the south range by inverted consoles supporting carved heraldic beasts.[76] The vertical lines were also enhanced by projecting chimney stacks and by windows capped by semi-circular pediments and more statuary. Meanwhile the horizontal emphasis was delivered by evenly spaced window lintels and transoms and by a row of carved heads within roundels, arranged in ten pairs, flanking the windows at first floor level/Many of these are heavily weathered but the surviving examples indicate a desire to imitate the new Renaissance style. The overall effect is one of balanced elegance and near symmetry. Renaissance fashions were beginning to have an impact in England at this period too (for example in the terracotta roundels of 1521 at Hampton Court made by Giovanni da Maiano) but there, Italianate decorative details were applied to buildings that were still essentially Gothic, whereas the Falkland courtyard is the first British example of the wholesale utilisation of a Renaissance architectural scheme.[77] All the features at Falkland noted above are characteristic of the French Renaissance style developed for Francis I at

74 *RSS*, ii, 2199; *James V Letters*, 325–6; Cameron, *James V*, 133; D. Bentley-Cranch, 'An early Sixteenth-century French Architectural source for the Palace of Falkland', *ROSC*, ii (1986), 85–95; J. G. Dunbar, 'Some Sixteenth-century French Parallels for the Palace of Falkland', *ROSC*, vii (1991), 3–8.

75 *MW*, i, 208, 254–78. Martin had a son of the same name who worked at Holyrood and Falkland: ibid, i, 242, 254–5, 277–8. *RSS*, ii, 3002; *Balcarres Papers*, i, 20, 33.

76 These are visible in John Slezer's view of the courtyard: Cavers, *Vision of Scotland*, 29.

77 Thurley, *Tudor Palaces*, 106; Nicola Coldstream, 'Art and Architecture in the Late Middle Ages', in Medcalf (ed.), *Later Middle Ages*, 216–20.

Blois (begun 1515), Chambord (begun 1519), Madrid and Fontaine-bleau (both begun 1528) and elsewhere. It is even possible to detect parallels between the layout of the rooms in the Francis I wing at Blois and in the east range at Falkland, although uncertainties about the precise arrangement at both sites make this exercise very speculative.[78] Had James V lived beyond 1542 it is quite likely that the Falkland initiative would have been developed much further but in the event this was a false dawn. It is not possible to demonstrate the influence of the Falkland façades upon any other buildings in the British Isles and Renaissance classicism made a fresh start in the next century under the influence of Palladio transmitted through Inigo Jones.[79]

If the Falkland courtyard represents James V's imitation of the architectural style developed for Francis I, then the exterior walls of the palace block at Stirling Castle seem to owe more to the style of Louis XII of a generation earlier, even though Stirling was probably built slightly later than Falkland. Iain McIvor has speculated that the apparent anachronism of design at Stirling may have been because the palace block was planned and started for the duke of Albany c.1515 and simply completed by Finnart a quarter of a century later.[80] How-ever, no other commentator has adopted this line and evidence that Albany undertook any major construction work (other than the block-house at Dunbar Castle, which was his private property) has yet to be unearthed. Sufficient explanation of this anomaly probably lies in the influence of Hamilton of Finnart who had visited France in 1517, before most of Francis I's projects commenced. There is no evidence that he ever returned to France at a later period so he could not have seen the *François premier* style for himself.[81] He was appointed principal master of works to the king on 9 September 1539. Although this title gave him universal jurisdiction over the royal works, he appears in the records

---

78 A. Blunt, *Art and Architecture in France, 1500–1700*, (London, 1980), 26–34, 50–58; Dunbar, 'French Parallels', 6–7; Dunbar, 'Aspects of Planning', 22–3.

79 James Lees-Milne, *The Age of Inigo Jones* (London, 1953), 61–2.

80 C. McKean, 'Finnart's Platt' in *Scottish Architects Abroad: Architectural Heritage II: The Journal of the Architectural Heritage Society of Scotland* (1991), 16, referring to unpublished work by McIvor.

81 *TA*, v, 158; It is sometimes stated that Finnart travelled to France with James V in 1536–37 (e.g. C. McKean, 'Hamilton of Finnart', *History Today*, xliii [Jan. 1993], 44) but this is an error. A Sir James Hamilton certainly appeared in the king's French accounts of that period (*TA*, vii, 20) but this was Sir James Hamilton of Kincavil, the former sheriff of Linlithgow, who had gone into exile following an accusation of heresy. An English report on the king's movements in France is quite explicit about Hamilton of Finnart's absence: *L&P Henry VIII*, xi, 916.

only for Linlithgow and Stirling, where he was active from mid-1538.[82] Even if Finnart exerted a decisive influence on the decorative form of Stirling Palace, as Charles McKean believes, most of the day-to-day supervision would have been in the hands of sir James Nicholson who was vicar of the church in Stirling Castle from 19 May 1539 and master of works within the castle from 3 January 1530 until at least August 1541.[83] The only accounts of his to survive are for 23 September 1531 to 6 July 1532 and for January to May 1538 and the latter is John Scrymgeour's summary rather than the full account.[84] Neither account suggests any major work was being undertaken at that time, for the two together record expenditure of less than £300, with the emphasis on repairing the roofs and windows and making minor alterations. A new stable block was probably built in 1530–31, as this was roofed and fitted with stalls in 1531–32, but this was below the castle walls rather than within the fortress. The palace block must therefore have been built after May 1538 and is usually dated to c.1540. A possible reason for the lack of accounts for the palace works is that Hamilton of Finnart seems to have agreed to fund much of the project himself in return for his new barony of Avandale.[85]

The new palace block was constructed on the south side of the upper square within the castle. The other three sides of the square were formed by the free-standing great hall to the east (built by James IV), the chapel royal to the north (which was on a slightly different alignment to the existing chapel, built for Prince Henry's baptism in 1594) and a range of buildings to the west, some elements of which may survive within the existing structure, known today as the King's Old Building. This range probably contained the royal lodging built for James IV in the 1490s, which appears in the accounts of 1531–32 as consisting of a great chamber, outer chamber and wardrobe. To the south of the new palace block was the lower square with a well, a kitchen range (possibly built in 1542) and the main entrance to the castle through James IV's heavily fortified and imposing forework.[86] James V's palace formed yet another quadrangle around a small inner courtyard, traditionally known as the lion's den, and stood on a vaulted undercroft which accommodated the different levels of the sloping site.

82 *RSS*, ii, 3144; *MW*, i, 227–8.
83 C. McKean, 'Hamilton of Finnart', 42–7; *RSS*, ii, 3028; *TA*, vii, 479.
84 *MW*, i, 103–11, 227–8.
85 *RSS*, ii, 3199. See also Thomas, 'Renaissance Culture', 116 n.185.
86 Dunbar, 'Aspects of Planning', 19; Fawcett, *Stirling Castle*, 35–9; *MW*, i, 104–7; *TA*, vii, 72, 84; *RCAHMS (Stirlingshire)*, i, 183–219; Fawcett, *Scottish Architecture*, 314–17. See also Thomas, 'Renaissance Culture', 117 n.189.

We have no record of which master mason or masons designed and worked on the palace under Finnart's supervision but two likely candidates might be Thomas French and James Black, both of whom disappeared from the Falkland accounts after December 1539, when they each received a bounty payment, even though John Brownhill and Nicholas Roy continued working there until at least 1541. However, French masons may also have been involved, for the final whereabouts of the six who arrived in Scotland in July 1539 is unknown.[87]

Most of the west range of the new palace block was lost in the seventeenth century but the surviving building contains the principal royal apartments on the first floor. In the north quarter stands the king's outer hall and presence chamber *en suite* with the bed chamber and cabinet in the east quarter. The south quarter houses the queen's outer hall and inner hall, with her bed chamber and cabinet adjoining the king's in the east quarter. All of these chambers are spacious and well-lit, containing fireplaces with richly carved capitals, but the most impressive feature of the block is clearly the decorative scheme of the outer walls.[88] More flamboyant and whimsical than the comparatively restrained classicism of Falkland, it still exhibits French and also German influences and perhaps represents something of a hybrid work where continental designs were adapted to Scottish tastes and circumstances. Some of the sculptures are derived from a series of engravings of planetary deities by Hans Burgkmair but the architectural design of carved string-courses, moulded and cusped arches, twisted columns and sculpted gargoyles is very reminiscent of the buildings of Louis XII, such as his wing at the château of Blois.[89] Meanwhile the crenellated parapet and crow-stepped gables have impeccable Scottish credentials, perhaps with Burgundian overtones. An attempt has recently been made to construe the symbolism and iconography of the sculptural decoration in astrological and mystical terms but the surviving carvings are so weathered and mutilated that this must remain a tentative and speculative interpretation.[90]

It is tempting to think that some of the statues were intended to

87 *MW*, i, 256, 278–9; *TA*, vii, 184.

88 Dunbar, 'Aspects of Planning', 16, 20. The lintels may also have been intended to carry counter-sunk carvings which were never completed: McKean, 'Finnart's Platt', 10.

89 F. W. H. Hollstein, *German Engravings, Etchings and Woodcuts, c.1400–1700* (Amsterdam, 1954–), v, 94–5; Babelon, *Châteaux de France*, 41–7; McKean, 'Finnart's Platt', 11–12. See Thomas, 'Renaissance Culture', 118 n.196.

90 H. M. Shire, 'The King's House at Stirling: Its Carvings in Stone', in Hadley Williams (ed.), *Stewart Style*, 72–84.

portray real people active in the court and household, although in the absence of any documentary sources this must also remain speculation. However, the male statue at the east end of the north façade is traditionally identified as King James himself and other figures include a crossbowman, a cupholder, a pursebearer, a cook and a gunman, all of whom can be found in the records of the royal household.[91] Similar speculative identifications have also been attempted for the figures carved on the oak roundels known as the Stirling heads, which were at one time thought to represent the kings and queens of Scotland.[92] Thirty-eight of these survive along with drawings of two others out of an original set thought to have numbered fifty-six. They were set in the compartmented ceiling of the king's presence chamber, c.1542, until they were taken down in 1777. Many of the figures are shown in contemporary dress and may have been intended as portraits but others seem to be dressed in antique or fanciful costume and may represent mythological or historical characters. Alternatively, they might depict the members of the court dressed in their costumes for a pageant or entertainment, or in imaginary personas; indeed, such a fashion was certainly current at the French court of the period.[93] The style is robust and even grotesque, tending towards caricature, and they may have been brightly painted originally, like most of the sculpture and decoration in James V's palaces. As with the architecture, foreign sources for this design have been suggested such as the ceiling of the great watching chamber at Hampton Court (c.1535) or that of a staircase at Azay-le-Rideau (c.1518–28) but the closest parallel is with a ceiling built for Sigismund I in a hall at Wavel Castle, Cracow (c.1531–35). Since it is very difficult to establish that there was any intimate contact between the Scottish and Polish courts of the period, this coincidence serves to highlight the wide diffusion of ideas and designs inspired by Italian Renaissance developments by the 1530s and 1540s. Indeed, just as the Falkland and Stirling innovations seem to have been inspired by the advent of a foreign queen and undertaken by imported masons, the Wavel refurbishment has been linked to King Sigismund's marriage to Bona Sforza and was undertaken by an Italian architect.[94]

91 *RCAHMS (Stirlingshire)*, i, 220–23.
92 John Loveday of Caversham, *Diary of a Tour in 1732* (Roxburghe Club, 1890), 124.
93 J. G. Dunbar, *The Stirling Heads* (HMSO, 1975), 3–22; Bentley-Cranch, 'Architectural Source', 92–3.
94 Dunbar, *Stirling Heads*, 26; Dunbar, 'Carved Heads to Adorn a Ceiling', *Country Life* vol. cxxxii, no. 3418 (Sep. 1962), 528–9; Shire, 'King's House', 83.

It is thought that two or more craftsmen were responsible for the Stirling heads, one of whom may have been Robert Robertson who was appointed carver and principal overseer of his craft within Stirling Castle on 31 August 1541 and was still receiving payments for his work there in June 1542. He had previously worked at both Holyrood and Falkland, where he was described simply as a wright, and had worked on the panelling of the queen's inner chamber.[95] Another candidate is John Drummond of Mylnab, the king's principal carpenter, who was sent to France in 1538 as a member of Mary of Guise's escort-party for her 'homecoming' and had previously worked at Holyrood and Falkland. His main interest seems to have been artillery and there is no contemporary record specifically linking him to Stirling, but a seventeenth-century source asserts that he produced fine timber work there.[96] A French wright and carver, Andrew Manson, is also 'associated' with the Stirling works but does not appear in the relevant accounts either.[97] Other fragments of carved woodwork said to be from Stirling Palace contain twenty medallion panels similar to the Stirling heads which may have been set in the wainscoting and on aumbry doors, suggesting an extensive scheme of co-ordinating interior decoration.[98] The use of carved wooden panels for interior decoration may have been common in the residences of Scottish nobles of the period, for the Stirling heads and fragments are not the only examples to survive. Several oak panels using similar designs of medallion heads and inter-twined foliage in the *François premier* style have survived from Mary of Guise's houses on Castle Hill, Edinburgh and Quality Wynd, Leith but other contemporary fragments were still being produced in a medieval, Gothic style, such as those made for David Beaton, abbot of Arbroath, co-adjutor of St. Andrews and keeper of the privy seal, at Arbroath Abbey c.1530. He had clear opportunities to consider the latest French fashions for he served repeatedly as an ambassador to the French court and was

---

95 *RSS*, ii, 4191; *TA*, viii, 84; *MW*, i, 59, 214.

96 *MW*, i, 1f.-175, 213–4; *RSS*, ii, 1304; *TA*, viii, 133; W. Drummond, *The Genealogy of the Most Noble and Ancient House of Drummond* (Edinburgh, 1831, originally 1681), 62. See also Chapter 5.

97 Hay, 'Scottish Renaissance Architecture', 205, 207. Manson did carve the cradle for Prince James in 1540, the royal chambers on board a ship in 1539, and the inscription for James V's tomb (*TA*, vii, 307, 189; viii, 143).

98 J. S. Richardson, 'Unrecorded Scottish Wood Carvings', *PSAS*, lx (1925–6), 384–408.

later to become bishop of Mirepoix, yet he chose a traditional style for this commission.[99]

Another important aspect of the interior decoration of Stirling and all the other royal residences was the use of tapestries and hangings.[100] The great centres of tapestry production in the fifteenth and sixteenth centuries were the manufacturing towns of northern France and Flanders and the majority of the tapestries in the Scottish royal collection were probably imported from this area: James IV bought in bulk from Flanders for his wedding and James V made several similar purchases.[101] Among the office houses at Holyrood was the tapisier's house and James V employed two French tapisiers: Jacques Habet who is recorded from August 1539 to July 1542 and Guillaume who appears in the accounts from June 1538 to March 1540, as well as a Scottish tapestry maker, William Edbe or Hebbe (perhaps Hebden?) who is listed from 1536 to 1540.[102] There was also a 'broudstar' (embroiderer) who may have worked at least some of the time on hangings. His name was John Young; he appears in the accounts from June 1535 to March 1543 and he was specifically instructed to engage a French boy to assist him. This was perhaps the 'broudstar' called Robinet who was listed only once in December 1536.[103] With such staff it is possible that some simple tapestries or hangings were made at the court, although it is likely that these men were mainly employed in repairing and maintaining the imported cloths as well as supervising their carriage and installation as the court moved from one residence to another.

The architectural details at Falkland and Stirling demonstrate the king's taste for French Renaissance design and this is probably reinforced by the stories and themes depicted on his tapestries. James V's tapestries were listed on two inventories of 25 March 1539 and 3 March 1543.[104] The two lists are not identical and the second appears to be a selection from the full stock which had been in the keeping of George

99 *Renaissance Decorative Arts in Scotland, 1480–1650*, NMAS and SNPG exhibition catalogue (Edinburgh, 1959), p.18 no.39, p.22 no.50a, p.26 no.68, p.30 no.78, p.31 no.82; *Angels, Nobles and Unicorns: Art and Patronage in Medieval Scotland*, NMS exhibition handbook (Edinburgh,1982), p.108 no.F10; D. H. Caldwell, 'The Beaton Panels – Scottish Carvings of the 1520s and 1530s', in Higgit (ed.), *Diocese of St. Andrews*, 182.
100 They were suspended from walls by little metal hooks ('clekis'): *MW*, i, 99.
101 *TA*, ii, 214; vii, 17, 28, 257, 471.
102 *MW*, i, 222, 226, 290; *TA*, vi, 458; vii, 44, 193; viii, 90; Murray, 'Pursemaster's Accounts', 40; *ER*, xvii, 282.
103 *RSS*, ii, 1705; *TA*, vi, 457; viii, 173.
104 *Wardrobe Inventories*, 49–51 and 103–4 and SRO, Wardrobe Inventories, E.31/1, fos. 23r.-24v. and 54v.-55v.

Steel, 'a special favourite in the court and household' until his death sometime before 20 March 1542.[105] The lists include tapestries depicting the classical myths and legends: the stories of Aeneas, Perseus, the Trojan wars, Jason and the golden fleece, Hercules, Romulus and seven pieces of 'antik werk' brought home (presumably from the continent) by William Shaw, showing Venus, Pallas, Hercules, Mars, Bacchus and 'the moder of the erd'. Some of these images, such as the golden fleece or Hercules, also had chivalric overtones. There were also stories from the Bible: those of Solomon, Rehoboam and Tobit and themes which seem to be taken from medieval romance: 'the Citie of Dammys',[106] two sets of the story of the unicorn, the story of the apes and other beasts and 'verdouris' (floral and foliate patterns).[107] This list suggests that the styles probably ranged from the late-Gothic *mille-fleurs* tradition to the more fashionable antique designs of the 1530s as was also the case in Henry VIII's collection – but whereas the Tudor owned nearly 2000 pieces, James V's inventories list fewer than 200.[108] In addition to the narrative scenes, the inventories also list hangings made of cloth of gold, velvet and damask, including cloths of estate and altar cloths, 'ane miekle taip of turque' (a great Turkey carpet), canopies, curtains and covers for four great beds and several smaller beds, together with cushions, rugs and chair covers, all richly worked in bright colours. The household books also record purchases of 'dornik' (i.e. linen from Tournai, called Dornewyk in Dutch) and Holland cloth for use as household linens, napery etc.[109] Such a list inevitably gives the impression that the interiors of the Stewart palaces were sumptuously furnished but this image is slightly tarnished by an entry in one account which states that the floors of the chambers in Holyrood were strewn with bent (a coarse grass). However, this reference is perhaps to chambers other than the royal apartments, for the floors of the principal rooms at Linlithgow were certainly tiled.[110]

105 *James V Letters*, 166; *RSS*, ii, 4548.

106 This was perhaps the set of tapestries of the 'Triumphant Dames' bought in Paris in 1538: *TA*, vii, 28, 43–4.

107 Pieces from the stories of Aeneas, Troy, Rehoboam, Tobit and the unicorn were still listed on an inventory of 1578 but others had obviously been lost by then: *Wardrobe Inventories*, 211–12.

108 Thurley, *Tudor Palaces*, 222–4.

109 SRO, Wardrobe Inventories, E.35/1, fos. 17r.-19r.; SRO, Liber Domicili, E.31/3, fo. 106r. and elsewhere.

110 *MW*, i, 225; *RCAHMS (Mid and West Lothian)*, 229; Andrew Kerr, 'Notes of Ancient tile paving in Linlithgow Palace', *PSAS*, xv (1880–81), 194–8. See also C. Norton, 'Medieval Floor Tiles in Scotland', in Higgit (ed.), *Diocese of St. Andrews*, 150–63.

The impression of luxurious display persists in the scattered references to the gardens attached to all the palaces. Most entries in the accounts are for building and maintaining the garden 'dykes' (walls) and gates but the gardens at Falkland, Holyrood and Stirling also contained archery butts, lists were erected when required for jousting matches at Stirling and Holyrood, and there were tennis courts (catchpele) at all the palaces.[111] The gardens were also provided with turf banks, stone benches, flower beds (knots) and pools (stanks) and stocked with wildlife: partridges were kept at Holyrood, swans and cranes on the lake in Stirling Park, two bears and three wolves in Stirling Castle, a fox and some French wild boar at Falkland. In addition, the pools would probably have contained fish for the table.[112] There is very little evidence for the plants that were cultivated at this time but there are several references to orchards, which seem to have grown pears and plums as well as apples, and in 1532 the Stirling gardeners were supplied with lettuce and thyme seeds as well as a 'schoid schule' (probably a wooden shovel or spade, shod with a metal edge).[113] It is quite likely that onions, leeks, kale, peas, berries, thorns, willows, pansies, marigolds, wallflowers, peonies, poppies, violets and the like were grown in beds marked out in symmetrical patterns within walled or fenced enclosures, as was the practice of the period. Such a scheme is certainly visible on Gordon of Rothiemay's view of Holyrood of c.1647, which also shows formal beds within the former abbey cloister, perhaps the 'litill garding within the place' of 1538.[114] James V certainly had a large staff of gardeners; at Stirling the park was kept by members of the Cunningham family and there were at least two gardeners; at Falkland the Fernie family kept the park and the Strachans were the gardeners; at Linlithgow Loudons kept the park with at least one gardener; and at Holyrood a Glaswegian, John Auchter, was employed in succession to Bertrand Gallotre, a Frenchman who worked as the king's principal gardener in 1536–37 with three assistants.[115]

111 *MW*, i, 132, 191, 105, 112, 192, 222, 36, 227–8, 288–9; *RSS*, ii, 3394.

112 *MW*, i, 109–10, 191, 98; SRO, Libri Emptorum, E.32/3 fos. 120r., 134r.; E.32/5 fo. 138r.; E.32/4 fos. 153v., 137r.; *TA*, vii, 159, 472.

113 *RSS*, ii, 4929; *TA*, ii, 83, 358; *MW*, i, 110. Thanks to Dr. Alan MacDonald for helping to explain this term.

114 E. H. M. Cox, *A History of Gardening in Scotland* (London, 1935), 21–3; Peter Verney, *The Gardens of Scotland* (London, no date), 21. See also Kenneth Wood-bridge, *Princely Gardens: The Origins and Development of the French Formal Style* (London, 1986), 39–59; Deborah Howard (ed.), *The Architecture of the Scottish Renaissance*, RIAS exhibition handbook (Edinburgh, 1990), 11; *MW*, i, 225.

115 See Thomas, 'Renaissance Culture', Appendix A, pp.361–63.

In considering the architecture, interior decor and gardens of the major royal palaces an image is formed of the physical environment which James V and his court inhabited. The regular circuit of the court rotated between the four major residences discussed above[116] but the king also maintained minor residences and lodgings in other places and many of these received attention during the period. For instance, a new portal was made for the king's lodging at Perth in 1532 and there is a reference to 'the new werk of Letht' in 1541.[117] Minor work was also done at Cramalt Tower, a hunting lodge near Peebles, the priory of St. Andrews (held *in commendam* by the king's illegitimate son, Lord James Stewart, and used extensively by the court) and at the castles of Craignethan, Crawfordjohn and Glamis, which came into the king's possession between 1537 and 1540 by the forfeiture of their lords.[118] Work was also carried out on the fortifications of the castles of Edinburgh, Tantallon, Blackness, Dunbar, Rothesay, Dunaverty, Inchgarvy and Kinghorn and to the harbour at Burntisland. These developments are considered in chapter five, which deals with military technology. James V's contributions to the chapel royal at Stirling are discussed in chapter three, which considers religious observance at the court.

When one turns to consider the court patronage of fine arts such as portraiture and manuscript illumination, the evidence for the period is much less extensive than it is for the royal palaces, but it is unlikely that a king so active in one area would ignore the other completely. Many works of art from James V's collection were undoubtedly lost during the upheavals of his daughter's and grandson's minorities and other pieces went south after 1603 to be lost or dispersed during the civil war or other crises.[119] Nevertheless, there are scattered documentary references which provide a glimpse of what has been lost. There was certainly a collection of portraits at the court of James IV, for in September 1502 a painter called Mynours arrived from England with gifts of portraits of Henry VII, Elizabeth of York, Prince Henry (the

116 See Thomas 'Renaissance Culture', Appendix C, pp.386–423.
117 *MW*, i, 111, 290.
118 *TA*, vi, 210, 409; Fleming, *Reformation in Scotland*, 608–12; *ER*, xvii, 126f., 213f., 375f., 560, 570, 582–3; MW, i, 192, 198, 228; *TA*, vi, 334, 364; vii, 495–7; Cameron, *James V*, 169–81, 209–18. See also Thomas, 'Renaissance Culture', 125–6 nn.248, 249 & 251.
119 David McRoberts, 'Material Destruction caused by the Scottish Reformation', *IR*, x (1959), 126–72. The earl of Arran as governor for the infant queen Mary is recorded as having disposed of all of James V's treasure and valuables in the defence of the realm: *APS*, ii, 603 (1554).

1. The royal arms and heraldic badges with James V's cipher, c.1540, on the main gateway at Holyrood. (Courtesy of Historic Scotland)

THE ROYAL PALACE OF HOLY ROOD HOVSE.

2. James V's tower and forework at Holyrood depicted by James Gordon of Rothiemay, c.1649, before the redevelopment of the 1670s.

3. The entrance tower built for James V at Falkland Palace. (Courtesy of the National Trust for Scotland)

4. The fountain in the courtyard of Linlithgow Palace, c.1540. (Courtesy of
Historic Scotland)

Prospectus Regis Palatis LIMNUCHENSIS.
This plate is Most humbly Inscribd to the H...

5. John Slezer's view of Linlithgow Palace from the west, from *Theatrum Scotiae* (1693)

Profpect of Their Maj.ties Palace of LINLITHGOW.

D.r James Cunynghame of Milncraig Bar.tt -

10.

6. Falkland Palace, the Renaissance east and south ranges, completed in 1514 by James V. The design imitates the style of the court of Francis I and was created by French masons. (Courtesy of the National Trust of Scotland)

7. David Pollock's conjectural reconstruction of James IV's forework at Stirling Castle, c.1500-08. (Courtesy of the National Trust for Scotland)

8. Facades of the James V palace block at Stirling Castle, 1538-42. The Prince's Tower of c.1500-08 is on the left. (Courtesy of Historic Scotland)

future Henry VIII) and 'oure quene' (the Princess Margaret Tudor). He stayed until November 1503.[120] Protocol would have dictated that Henry Tudor should receive a portrait of his new son-in-law in return and it is possible that this was painted by Mynours before he left Scotland and was later copied by Daniel Mytens for Charles I (the copy survives today in a private collection but the original has been lost).[121] It is also possible that some of the drawings in a Flemish portrait album compiled in the fifteenth and sixteenth centuries, the *Receuil d'Arras*, were made from life or copied from portraits of people at the court of James IV. The subjects include James IV, Margaret Tudor, Elizabeth of York, Henry VII, Alexander Stewart (archbishop of St. Andrews), Perkin Warbeck, four Franco-Flemish knights who visited Scotland for the tournaments of 1507–8 and an 'Egyptian' woman (the term usually denoted a gypsy at this period) who was perhaps the mysterious 'black lady' of the tournaments.[122] The drawings were possibly made by Piers, a painter sent to Scotland by Andrew Haliburton (d. 1514), conservator of the privileges of the Scottish nation in the Netherlands. Piers worked at the Scottish court between 1505 and 1508.[123] Haliburton also had contacts with the Bening family of artists and may therefore have been instrumental in commissioning the *Book of Hours of James IV and Margaret Tudor*, a rare surviving masterpiece of the period, which contains portraits of James and Margaret at prayer very reminiscent of the portrayals of James III and Margaret of Denmark by Hugo van der Goes on the Trinity College altarpiece of c.1475–76.[124]

With two generations of fruitful artistic contacts between the

120 *TA*, ii, 341, 405; M. R. Apted and S. Hannabus, *Painters in Scotland, 1301–1700: A Biographical Dictionary* (SRS, 1978), 68–9; L. Campbell, *The Early Flemish Pictures in the Collection of Her Majesty the Queen* (Cambridge, 1985), p. xxxi.

121 Charles R. Beard, 'Early Stewart Portraits: A Discovery', *The Connoisseur*, lxxi (Jan.-Apr. 1925), 5–9. My thanks go to Professor Michael Lynch for alerting me to this article.

122 Ibid., 9–15. The *Receuil d'Arras* also contains a portrait identified as James I of Scotland. If genuine, this would be the earliest true portrait of a Scottish monarch. It is reproduced in Campbell, *Early Flemish Pictures*, p. xxxi, fig. 12.

123 Apted and Hannabus, *Painters in Scotland*, 70–2.

124 *Das Gebetbuch Jakobs IV von Schottland und seiner Gemahlin Margaret Tudor*, ed. Franz Unterkircher (Graz, 1987); L. MacFarlane, 'The Book of Hours of James IV and Margaret Tudor', *IR*, xi (1960), 3–21; David McRoberts, 'Notes on Scoto-Flemish Artistic Contacts', *IR*, x (1959), 91–6; C. Thompson and L. Campbell, *Hugo van der Goes and the Trinity Panels in Edinburgh* (NGS, 1974).

Scottish court and the Flemish *ateliers* already established, it would have been strange if James V had not acquired some pieces similar to those associated with his predecessors. According to Pitscottie, portraits of Dorothea and Christina of Denmark were commissioned from a painter living near Brussels and sent back to Scotland in the early 1530s when both ladies were being considered as potential brides for James V, and in 1535 the king bought five Flemish paintings from John Brown of Leith, but the artists and subjects of these pictures are unfortunately not recorded.[125] Only five apparently contemporary portraits of James V survive. Four are of unknown provenance, dated c.1538–40 and of poor quality; the figures are very stiff and apparently painted to a formula (what Dana Bentley-Cranch calls 'effigy-portraits'). They are to be found in the Scottish National Portrait Gallery, the royal collection at Windsor Castle (these two are solo portraits), the National Trust, Hardwick Hall, Derbyshire, and the duke of Atholl's collection at Blair Castle (these two are double portraits with Mary of Guise).[126] In addition there are numerous portraits which are derivative of these four prime images and of unknown date and provenance but probably of the later sixteenth or early seventeenth centuries.[127] None of these pictures reaches the standard set by the Trinity altarpiece, nor by Holbein at the English court, nor by Jean and François Clouet at the French court. However, the fifth picture is much more accomplished and worthy of a king with Renaissance ambitions. It survives in three versions: one is at the Weiss Gallery, London, a second was auctioned in Paris in 1921 and its current location is unknown, and the third is owned by the National Trust at Polesden Lacy, Surrey.[128] This image is attributed to Corneille de Lyon, c.1536–37, and was presumably painted when James was in France for his first marriage. It may well have been intended as a companion to the portrait of Madeleine de Valois

125 Pitscottie, *Historie* (STS), i, 354; *TA*, vi, 250.
126 Dana Bentley-Cranch, 'Effigy and Portrait in Sixteenth Century Scotland', *ROSC*, iv (1988), 9–19; Duncan MacMillan, *Scottish Art, 1460–1990* (Edinburgh, 1990), 32.
127 I am very grateful to Rosalind Marshall for compiling a dossier of these portraits for me.
128 Again, Rosalind Marshall kindly supplied me with this information. The Polesden Lacy portrait is reproduced in Dana Bentley-Cranch and Rosalind K. Marshall, 'Iconography and Literature in the Service of Diplomacy: The Franco-Scottish Alliance, James V and Scotland's two French Queens, Madeleine of France and Mary of Guise', in Hadley Williams (ed.), *Stewart Style*, fig. 2, between pp. 288 and 289.

(Château of Blois and Palace of Versailles) by the same artist. Corneille de Lyon also painted James's second queen, Mary of Guise (Scottish National Portrait Gallery, Palace of Versailles and the Clowes Fund, Indianapolis), and these three portraits again highlight the importance of French influences.[129] Indeed, Renaissance portraiture seems to have been a cultural weak-spot for the Scottish court. Not only is the sole effective portrait of James V a wholly French production but also it is a 'revealing fact' that his daughter, Mary, had herself painted when she was in both France and England but not when she was in Scotland.[130] James VI's court painters, Arnold Bronckhorst and Adrian Vanson, were both from the Netherlands, and Scotland did not produce an accomplished portraitist until George Jameson in the seventeenth century.[131] None of the painters listed by Apted and Hannabus for the reign of James V (twenty-one named and three anonymous entries) are recorded undertaking anything other than decorative tasks, with the sole exception of Andrew Bairhum, who painted murals at Kinloss for abbot Robert Reid c.1538–41 rather than at the royal court.[132] It is also possible that Pierre Quesnel, a painter in the service of Mary of Guise (who was also an usher of her chamber), may have been something more than just a decorator but this is unlikely. There is no record of any of his works but he spent £11 on paints for Falkland in February 1542, and his fee for the year 1539 as 'huissier de chambre' was only eighty livres tournois (twenty livres less than the queen's tailor and seventy livres less than her embroiderer), which seems to imply that he was a craftsman rather than a fine artist.[133] Nevertheless, James V's portrait on his gold 'bonnet-pieces' (ducats) of 1539–42 are of high quality and in the Renaissance tradition established by James III's silver groats.[134]

129 Bentley-Cranch, 'Effigy and Portrait', 16–17; Bentley-Cranch and Marshall, 'Iconography and Literature', 276–7, 287–8, figs. 3 & 7.

130 Jenny Wormald, *Mary Queen of Scots: a Study in Failure* (London, 1991), 195; Helen Smailes and Duncan Thomson, *The Queen's Image* (Edinburgh, 1987), 15.

131 Duncan MacMillan, 'Scottish Art' in Paul H. Scott (ed.) *Scotland: A Concise Cultural History* (Edinburgh, 1993), 210–11.

132 Apted and Hannabus, *Painters in Scotland*, 120–21, 25. For Reid see John Durkan, 'Giovanni Ferrerio, Humanist: His Influence in sixteenth-century Scotland', in *Religion and Humanism, Studies in Church History*, 17, ed. K. Robbins (Oxford, 1981), 181–94 and chapter 4. See also Thomas, 'Renaissance Culture', 130 nn. 270 & 271.

133 *TA*, viii, 59, 77, 84, 92; SRO, Despence de la Maison Royale, E.33/1, fo. 11v.

134 I. H. Stewart, *The Scottish Coinage* (London, 1955), 78 and see chapter five.

The references to illuminated manuscripts at the court of James V are also very scarce and may indicate only a fraction of what actually existed. The finest surviving examples of manuscript illuminations of Scottish provenance date from the reigns of James III and James IV but James V did commission John Bellenden's translation of Hector Boece's *Scotorum Historia* and the manuscript of 1531, which was written and decorated by David Douglas, is now in the Pierpont Morgan Library. MacMillan considers its decoration to be a lively and witty example of Scottish illumination.[135] When Bellenden's Boece was later printed by Thomas Davidson, it included a woodcut depiction of the arms of Scotland which is thought to have been designed by Sir David Lindsay of the Mount, Snowdon herald from c.1530 and Lyon king of arms from 1542. Lindsay was certainly responsible for the earliest known armorial register in Scotland, 1542 (National Library of Scotland), which is probably the finest illuminated manuscript from the royal court of this period. Also surviving is a mutilated copy of a French book of hours of c.1500 which once belonged to Mary of Guise (Fort Augustus Abbey) and a Flemish book of hours which perhaps belonged to Margaret Tudor (Bibliothèque Nationale, Paris).[136] Fourteen books from Holyrood were apparently looted in 1544 by an English soldier, Sir William Norris (along with some wooden panelling) but whether these were from the abbey or the palace is not clear. Perhaps one of them was the missal purchased for the chapel at Holyrood in 1541.[137] There is no record of the contents of the 'librall' (if indeed this was a library) built at Linlithgow Palace in 1539 by Finnart and no books or paintings are listed in the inventories of 1539 and 1542–43, even though the lists include 'chapel graith', but there are scattered references to books in the *Treasurer's Accounts*, mainly dealing with their covers of velvet and clasps of gold and silver. No mention is made of illuminations.[138]

135 MacMillan, *Scottish Art*, 27–9, 34–5.

136 NLS, Adv. MS, 31.4.3 and *Facsimile of an Ancient Heraldic Manuscript Emblazoned by Sir David Lyndsay* [sic] *of the Mount, Lyon King of Arms, 1542*, ed. W. D. Laing (Edinburgh, 1822); Edington, *Court and Culture*, 37–9; Mark Dilworth, 'Book of Hours of Mary of Guise', *IR*, xix (1968), 77–80; David McRoberts, *Catalogue of Scottish Medieval Books and Fragments* (Glasgow, 1953), p.19 no.117.

137 Harrison, *History of Holyrood*, 80; Robert Donaldson, 'The Cambuskenneth Books: The Norris of Speke Collection,' *Bibliothek*, xv (1988), 3–7; Priscilla Bawcutt, 'Crossing the Border: Scottish Poetry and English Readers in the Sixteenth Century,' in Mapstone and Wood (eds.), *The Rose and the Thistle*, 63; *TA*, vii, 459.

138 *TA*, vii, 195 (and see above n.59); *Wardrobe Inventories*, 29–113; e.g. *TA*, vii, 17, 19, 113, 132, 135, 197 etc.

However, the inventories do contain information about the plate
and jewels in the royal collection and many of these items were clearly
of the finest workmanship. The symbolic importance of the royal
regalia and the insignia of the chivalric orders is discussed in chapter
six, which deals with court ceremonial and pageantry, and the tapestries and furnishings have already been considered above. Other
treasures listed included a silver-gilt chessboard with chessmen of
jasper and 'cristallyne' (rock-crystal), a steel mirror with a silver frame
and a grey velvet case, a case of gold tooth-picks, a little gold box with
a relic of the holy cross sent by the duke of Albany, Robert Bruce's cup,
a 'quhinzear' (whinger or short sword) given to James by Francis I set
with a great sapphire, thirty-six rubies, six emeralds, nine diamonds,
pearls, gold and silver and the two little cups of gold, the basin of
agate, 'laver' (ewer) of jasper and flagon of rock-crystal made for
Queen Madeleine when she was a child. Also listed are eighteen pieces
of chapel plate such as bells, chalices and pattens of silver or silver-gilt,
over 400 pieces of silver/silver-gilt table ware, over 270 items of
jewellery including rings, chains and cap-badges ('tergattis') of gold
enamelled and set with precious stones, nearly 300 garments, mainly
of velvet, satin and taffeta, a chest containing nearly 190 ells of unmade
fabric brought to Scotland by Madeleine, and sixty items of horse gear
such as saddles, harnesses, caparisons and feather head-dresses.[139]
Many of these priceless objects disappeared from the records after the
king's death; indeed the collection of silver plate was already reduced
to a quarter of its former size by November 1543 when another
inventory was taken.[140] Apart from indicating the wealth of the king,
these inventories also suggest that James V was keeping up with
French fashions. As we have seen, many of his possessions were of
French origin and he favoured jewellery settings using prestigious
motifs such as unicorns, lions, thistles and so forth or mythological or
allegorical figures such as mermaids, just as Francis I favoured the
salamander (his personal badge) and *fleurs de lys*. On the other hand,
Henry VIII was fond of cameos, intaglios and ciphers. Two jewels of
the 1560s, the Aberdeen jewel and the Lennox jewel, perhaps give an
impression of how James V's pieces may have looked with their

139 SRO, Wardrobe Inventories, E.35/1 fos. 21v., 35r., 34v., 36r., 39r., 38r., 34v.;
     Rosalind K. Marshall, 'The Jewellery of James V, King of Scots', *Jewellery
     Studies*, vii (1996), 79–86; Marshall, '"To be the Kingis Grace ane Dowblett":
     The Costume of James V, King of Scots', *Costume: The Journal of the Costume
     Society*, xxviii (1994), 14–21; Marshall, '"Hir Rob Ryall": the Costume of
     Mary of Guise', *Costume*, xii (1978), 1–12.
140 *Wardrobe Inventories*, 107–13.

elaborate iconography and vivid use of enamels and precious stones.[141]

Explaining the consequences of James V's marriage to Madeleine, Bishop John Leslie wrote in 1570,

> Here is to be remembred, that thair wes mony new ingynis and devysis, alsweill of bigging of paleicis, abilyementis, as of banquating and of menis behaviour, first begun and used in Scotland at this tyme, eftir the fassione quhilk thay had sene in France. Albeit it semit to be varray comlie and beautifull, yit it wes moir superfluows and volupteous nor [than] the substaunce of the realme of Scotland mycht beir furth or susteine.[142]

As we have seen, there were French influences and French craftsmen at work in the Scottish court before 1537 yet the essence of Leslie's analysis rings true. The most innovative and modish manifestations of James V's patronage of the visual arts all date from after his visit to the French court, particularly the courtyard façades at Falkland and the exterior decoration of the Stirling palace block, and (along with his marriages) seem to indicate his desire to be taken seriously as a Renaissance prince on the European stage; whereas his earlier works seem to indicate his desire to be taken seriously as a true king of Scots within his own realm. In the early years of the adult reign, James was largely a patron of arts in the traditional, late-medieval, high-Gothic style, which would have recalled the glories of his father's court. After 1537 his patronage was infused with the Renaissance spirit and was on a much grander scale than Scotland had ever witnessed before. To re-apply a phrase associated with one of James's ancestors, he had become 'a king unleashed'.[143] Leslie was very pessimistic about the practicalities of such a policy in the long-term but whilst he was alive James made the most of the financial resources available to him, particularly the French dowries and the wealth of the Scottish church and, unlike Francis I and Henry VIII, he died unencumbered by colossal debts.[144]

---

141 *TA*, vi, 414; Anne-Marie Lecoq, *François Ier imaginaire: symbolique et politique à l'aube de la Renaissance Française* (Paris, 1987), 35–52, 342–50, 396–409; Hugh Tait, 'Goldsmiths and their work at the Court of Henry VIII' in Starkey (ed.) *A European Court*, 115–17; R. K. Marshall and G. R. Dalgleish (eds.), *The Art of Jewellery in Scotland* (Edinburgh, 1991), 12–17.

142 John Lesley, *The History of Scotland* (Bannatyne Club, 1830), 154. The STS edition of Leslie does not include this comment.

143 R. G. Nicholson, *Scotland, The Later Middle Ages* (Edinburgh, 1974), 317, referring to James I.

144 Cameron, *James V*, 255–74; Murray, 'Pursemaster's Accounts', 27.

No doubt from the perspective of the 1570s the exuberance of James V's court looked vainglorious and futile but if he had had an adult reign of twenty-five years (as his father had done) or forty years (as his grandson was to achieve) rather than fourteen, the verdict might not have been so severe. However, in the event it was certainly the case that 'native architecture as a whole remained unaffected by the achievements of the court school, and all creative enterprise ceased in the royal works after the king's death.'[145] The brief flowering of the visual arts at the court of James V was, within the Scottish context, spectacular and original but all the images and motifs were directed towards the glorification of a strong, adult, male ruler and until the realm was graced with such a monarch again the initiatives of James V lacked the focus and the security for further development.

145 Dunbar, *Historic Architecture*, 17.

THREE

'Plesand Armony':
Music and Religious Observance

Music played an important part in the courtly culture of late-medieval and early-modern Europe. Kings and princes would expect their presence to be signalled by fanfares, which would also be heard at military manoeuvres, tournaments and official proclamations. Meals, chapel services and dances would require musical accompaniments and so would state ceremonies such as royal entries or coronations. The pageants and entertainments staged to celebrate weddings, treaties and other festivals also utilised the musical talent of the court, and people from all walks of life would relax in private to the sound of the lute, harp, fiddle or voice.[1] Such customs demanded that a princely court should contain a staff of professional musicians capable of composing for, performing on, and providing tuition in a wide range of instruments, as well as a group of courtly amateurs capable of impromptu performances in which they would either play solo or accompany their own singing on the lute or clavichord. It was customary in fifteenth- and sixteenth-century European courts to categorise the instrumental staff according to whether they played instruments considered to be *haut* (loud) or *bas* (soft) and this demarcation indicated the social status of the players within the hierarchy of the household. The players of loud instruments such as trumpets and shawms, who usually performed as a band in the open air or large halls at public events, were considered inferior to the players of soft instruments such as recorders, clavichords, lutes and viols, who would play alone or as part of a small ensemble within the apartments and chambers of the royal palaces.[2] Indeed, the players of loud instruments at the court of Francis I were attached to the royal stable (*écurie*) and ranked as grooms, whilst the players of soft instruments were attached to the chamber and ranked as *valets*. At the Tudor court the distinction was between those musicians with access to the privy chamber and those without such

---

1 For a full discussion see John Stevens, *Music and Poetry in the Early Tudor Court* (London, 1961), 235–55.

2 Peter Holman, 'Music at the Court of Henry VIII', in Starkey (ed.), *European Court*, 106; Stevens, *Early Tudor Court*, 303–21; D. James Ross, *Musick Fyne: Robert Carver and the Art of Music in Sixteenth Century Scotland* (Edinburgh, 1993), 116–7. The shawm (or *hautbois* in French) was a double-reed instrument related to the modern oboe.

privileges.[3] The staff of princely chapels held the highest status of any professional musicians within the household since they were classed as clergymen (although very few entered the priesthood) and therefore were considered to be gentlemen, albeit rather lowly ones. The possession of a household post as a singer in the chapel or minstrel of the chamber did not necessarily involve constant attendance at court and musicians occasionally travelled a circuit of noble households and urban or ecclesiastical corporations, and sometimes visited foreign courts to obtain greater experience and training or to accompany diplomatic missions. Likewise, princes would often employ wandering minstrels and local musicians on a casual basis whilst traversing their lands and could also make use of the players attached to the households of nobles, prelates and other dignitaries who visited their courts. Thus the possible permutations of personnel for musical performances at court were diverse, particularly on special occasions when the regular staff could be augmented from other sources. For example, in Paris at new year 1537, many distinguished guests were at the court of Francis I for the marriage of his daughter, Madeleine, to James V and James made gifts of money to the minstrels attached to their households: payments were made to Francis I's trumpeters, *hautbois*, 'sisters' and cornets; to the queen of Navarre's *hautbois*; to the duke of Guise's two minstrels; to the queen of France's two minstrels and to Madeleine's taborer.[4]

Castiglione considered the ability to sing or to play soft instruments to be a social skill essential to a successful career as a courtier. Performances should not be given in public, he believed, but in the more private apartments of a prince, in select company, to give pleasure to persons of quality and to obtain their approval and favour. The courtly musician should be sufficiently adept to play or sing suitable tunes by ear but would not necessarily be expected to read or write music nor to perform in a virtuosic manner, since such skills might indicate a professional outlook.[5] Castiglione derived his principles from the practice at the Italian courts of Urbino and Mantua but a similar approach to music-making by the nobility can also be detected at the courts of Francis I, Charles V and Margaret of Austria.[6] However,

3 Knecht, *Warrior and Patron*, 459; Holman, 'Music at the Court of Henry VIII', 105.
4 *TA*, vii, 15–16.
5 Castiglione, *Courtier*, 95–6.
6 Richard Freedman, 'Paris and the French Court under François I', and Martin Picker, 'The Habsburg Courts in the Netherlands and Austria, 1477–1530', both in Iain Fenlon (ed.), *The Renaissance* (London, 1989), 174–96, 216–42.

Henry VIII displayed such an enthusiasm for music that he became a skilled practitioner on a number of instruments and also undertook some composition, although his achievements in this field have been exaggerated. At his death his musical staff (excluding the chapel royal) consisted of some fifty-eight persons, including many foreign 'stars' and whole consorts of violars and other instrumentalists. His inventories indicate that he owned numerous boxes of recorders, flutes, lutes, virginals, organs, viols and shawms for use by his staff, courtiers, family and himself.[7] Similarly, Francis I had a band of twelve trumpets, a band of eight shawms (*hautbois*), an organist, a lutenist, four singers, four violars and a chapel of thirty-six singers.[8] The Stewart kings of Scotland appear to have adopted the same approach to music at their courts as other European monarchs. James I has the reputation of having fostered up-to-date organ music and James IV could certainly play the lute and the clavichord and employed a large musical staff.[9] Considering his Tudor and Stewart ancestry, it would have been surprising if James V had not been a musical monarch. Musicians receiving livery and fees were prominent within his household and he could play the lute, sight-read vocal parts and seems to have been a discerning listener: c.1562 Thomas Wood of St. Andrews stated that 'the king had ane singular guid eir and culd sing that he had never seine before, bot his voyce wes rawky and harske.'[10] James appears to have transmitted his interest to at least some of his children as well: Mary, queen of Scots, was a noted music-lover and Lord James Stewart, prior of St. Andrews, was a patron of David Peebles after the Reformation.[11]

There are no surviving inventories listing the instruments possessed by James V but he is known to have purchased lutes and organs.[12] The lists of musicians within the household accounts suggest that there was a distinction between players of loud and soft instruments at his court too, since the latter seem to be attached to the chamber, whilst the

7 David Wulstan, *Tudor Music* (London, 1985), 70–71, 79, 80; Holman, 'Music at the Court of Henry VIII', 104.

8 Freedman, 'Paris and the French Court', 178–9.

9 David Calderwood, *History of the Kirk of Scotland*, ed. T. Thomson and D. Laing (8 vols., Wodrow Society, 1842–49), i, 48; Leland, *Collectanea*, iv, 284; *TA*, iii, 360.

10 John Purser, *Scotland's Music* (Edinburgh, 1992), 98; David Laing, 'An Account of the Scottish Psalter of A.D. 1566', *PSAS*, vii (1866–7), 445–58.

11 Ross, *Musick Fyne*, 128–32; Kenneth Elliot and Frederick Rimmer, *A History of Scottish Music* (London, 1973), 26.

12 *TA*, v, 276; vi, 18, 86–7, 89, 179–81, 185–6, 258, 281, 353; viii, 55; *MW*, i, 227–8. For details of these purchases see Thomas, 'Renaissance Culture', 138 n.18.

former are sometimes listed alongside armourers and messengers-at-arms. The most numerous minstrels in the records are the trumpeters, many of whom were foreigners. A band of Italian musicians, designated as minstrels, trumpeters (*tubicines*), players (*histriones*) and, occasionally, shawmers seem to have served as a coherent, family group at the Scottish court from the latter years of the reign of James IV into the minority of Mary.[13] They took the surname Drummond and are consistently described as Italians, even though the second generation would have had no first-hand experience of Italian courts. Such musical dynasties were not unusual in the courts of the period: the Bassano family (Venetian Jews fleeing the Inquisition) provided musicians at the English court from 1540 until the civil war and the English Hudsons served both Henry, Lord Darnley, and his son, James VI.[14] The Drummonds were possibly the four unnamed Italian musicians recorded in 1503 but names are listed in 1505, 1509, and 1515.[15] In 1524 the late Julian Richard/Drummond was replaced by a Scot, Henry Rudman, who was replaced in turn by Ninian Brown in 1529–30. In 1533 Michael Drummond took the place of Vincent Pace/Drummond, who had presumably died, and the individual members are last named in 1535 as George Forest, Ninian Brown and Julian, Sebastian and Michael Drummond.[16] Thereafter, there were regular livery payments to a group of five unnamed Italian minstrels (presumably the same ones) which were brought up to date at Christmas 1542, a few days after James V's death.[17] Payments to unnamed Italian and Scots trumpeters continued from the exchequer until 1561.[18] In addition, from June 1537 payments were made to a separate group of four trumpeters of war, who also received regular livery until 1546. Their

---

13 For two detailed accounts of this band, which nevertheless differ in emphasis see Anna Jean Mill, *Medieval Plays in Scotland* (Edinburgh and London, 1927), 42–3 and Helena Mennie Shire, 'Music for "Goddis Glore and the Kingis"', in Hadley Williams (ed.), *Stewart Style*, 120–22. Neither account traces the history of the Italian band beyond 1529.

14 Holman, 'Music at the Court of Henry VIII', 106; Ross, *Musick Fyne*, 133.

15 *TA*, ii, 395; *RSS*, i, 1185, 1189 (Julian Drummond, Julian Richard, Vincent Pais and Benedict Delmes); *RSS*, i, 1808 (Sebastian Drummond joined); *TA*, v, 53–4 (Vincent, old Julian, young Julian, Anthony and Sebastian Drummond, and George Forest, Scotsman). For more details see Thomas, 'Renaissance Culture', 139 nn. 24 & 26.

16 *RSS*, i, 3282; *ER*, xv, 220; xvi, 5, 240, 443; *TA*, v, 432. Brown may have been another Italian the records are ambiguous.

17 *TA*, vi, 301; vii, 199, 334–5, 478–9; viii, 103, 149–50.

18 *ER*, xvi, 474; xvii, 82–3, 374, 526; xviii, 98–9, 133–4, 316, 349; xix, 20, 49–50, 97, 102, 158–9.

names can be found in the *Register of the Privy Seal* for 2 July 1538, and two of the four were also called Drummond (John and James) and, although they are not specifically described as Italians, Julian certainly had two sons with these names.[19] James V also had the services of a band of three French trumpeters in 1532–33: Claude de la Vale, Guillaume Soudane and Vincent Violet were engaged for a year's service but decided to leave early.[20] No explanation is given for their departure but it is possible that they considered themselves to be too much in the shadow of the more established Italian band.

The trumpeters of the court are often recorded in conjunction with taborers, and the trumpeters of war are regularly listed alongside Swiss taborers. The tabor was a side-drum, usually played with the right hand whilst playing a pipe or fife with the left. Fife and tabor traditionally provided dance music, whilst the Swiss tabor was a variant used for military purposes.[21] The most prominent tabor player at the court was Anthony, a Frenchman, who took the occupational surname, Taburner or Taverner. From December 1541 he was named master of the king's minstrels but he may have held this post as early as December 1538 when he refused to wear the red and yellow livery provided for the other musicians and was given money to buy more suitable clothes instead. He seems to have had a French assistant, Jakis (probably Jacques), and two 'childer' or 'boys', John and William Thomson, who were 'quhisilarris' (whistlers, i.e. they played the pipe or fife).[22] The Swiss tabor was played by 'Tod' and 'auld Tod', presumably a father and son team, who were first recorded in May 1538 and served as a pair until 1542 with one Tod serving alone until 1544.[23] There are no clear references to the use of bagpipes at the court of James V; the 'pipers' listed in the accounts are almost certainly players of recorders, fifes or shawms; the term 'drone' (which would indicate bagpipes) is not mentioned.[24]

The trumpeters, shawmers, whistlers and taborers formed the 'loud' music of the court and the sources give a few hints of their

19 *TA*, vi, 327, 339–400; vii, 118–9, 199, 271–2, 334–5, 478–9; viii, 103, 149–50, 224, 462; *RSS*, ii, 2607, 2608, 2609, 2610; iii, 2496. James Drummond, trumpeter, son of Julian was engaged in December 1526 (ibid., i, 3382).

20 *RSS*, ii, 1552; *TA*, vi, 102.

21 M. G. A. Vale, *War and Chivalry* (London, 1981), 152–4.

22 *TA*, v, 256, 260; vi, 36, 92, 204; vii, 119, 290; viii, 150, 158; *RSS*, ii, 2621, 2622; *ER*, xvi, 375; xvii, 49, 61, 185, 305, 394, 464; xviii, 50, 90.

23 *TA*, vi, 399–400; viii, 149, 158, 248, 291.

24 Henry George Farmer, *A History of Music in Scotland* (London, 1947), 94. Drones are mentioned in the time of James IV: *TA*, ii, 131, 367; iii, 190.

activities. The minstrels were often provided with outfits of clothes, usually in the red and yellow livery colours of the Stewarts. These clothes were of fine materials such as satins, indicating that the exceptions made for minstrels in the fifteenth-century sumptuary laws were regularly exploited.[25] During the minority, the Italian trumpeters were in the service of both the young king and his governor; in September 1522 they were in attendance on Albany at the siege of Carlisle, and Julian was taken on 'raidis' (justice ayres) with the king and his lords in 1527. They seem to have been engaged on military duties again in January 1533, during the hostilities with England, when they were stationed at the castle of Dunbar.[26] Dunbar was one of the key coastal fortresses and at that time still in the ownership of the duke of Albany, who had been in France since 1524 and never again returned to Scotland. In the Autumn of 1536, on James V's departure for France, the Italians were given suits of clothing, which may suggest that they travelled with him and were being dressed to impress the French. However, other names on the same list clearly did not travel to France at this time, so perhaps the gifts were intended as compensation for a lack of work whilst the king was absent.[27] In June 1537, four unnamed trumpeters (perhaps the trumpeters of war) were clearly intended to take part in the royal entry that was planned for Queen Madeleine since banners were bought for their instruments. It is likely that her entry, had it taken place, would have been accompanied by minstrels employed by the burgh too, but no details are recorded. Her successor, Mary of Guise, was provided with a larger ceremonial band consisting of four trumpeters (probably the same ones), four taborers and three whistlers, who were sent by ship to France in May 1538 to collect her, along with a large escort.[28] It is reasonable to imagine that their services would also have been required at the many tournaments, ceremonies and military campaigns, such as those discussed in chapter six, but no specific details appear in the household sources. However, Pitscottie described the musical reception awaiting James V at the home of the duke of Vendôme (whose daughter he was engaged to marry) in 1536 thus,

25 TA, vi, 399–400, 404–5; APS, ii, 49. Heralds were similarly exempt.
26 TA, v, 87, 96, 203, 318; vi, 95.
27 TA, vi, 301, 303.
28 TA, vi, 327, 399–400; viii, 158; Farmer, Music in Scotland, 84. Town bands were common in other countries too; in Italy they were known as pifare, in England as 'waits': Gustave Reese, Music in the Renaissance (London, 1954), 545, 772; Stevens, Early Tudor Court, 299.

Then thair was nothing bot mirrienes, bancatting and great cheir
and lustie commoning betuix the kingis grace and ladyis witht
great musick and playing on instrumentis, that is to say trumpatis,
schalmes, luttis and violes, virginallis or pinattis [spinets] and all
uther kynd of instrumentis playand melodiouslie witht gallyart
[galliard] dancing in messerie [maskery] and prattie frassis
[farces] and playis.

His account of the wedding celebrations at St. Andrews in June 1538
includes references to 'schallmes, draught trumpattis and weir trumpatis
witht playing and phrassis' providing entertainment for the guests
between one feast and the next, and Leslie's description of James V's
funeral also mentions 'lamentable trumpetis' and 'qwisselis of dule'.[29]

The lutes, viols, virginals and spinets cited by Pitscottie were not part
of the 'loud' musical establishment of a Renaissance court, but formed
the 'soft' music of the chamber and James V was also exposed to this
type of music from an early age. Amongst the earliest surviving
household accounts of the reign are payments to James Graham, the
king's minstrel, Bontemps, a French minstrel, and John Crook (or
Craig), minstrel.[30] A popular chamber instrument of the fifteenth
century was the harp but James V did not have a harpist on his regular
staff; only three payments are recorded: to 'ane harpar' in 1520, to a
westland harper in 1529 and to an Irish (presumably Highland)
'clairsochtar' in February 1534.[31] The place of the harp was taken by
the lute, which became ever more popular as the sixteenth century
progressed.[32] As we have seen, James probably played the lute himself,
and he certainly employed several lutenists (or 'lutars' in Scots) in his
chamber. The peculiar name of 'Urre Schennek, lutair' appears in the
records for Christmas 1526 and this may have been the same person as
'Franche Orry, menstrale' who was listed at Easter of the same year.
The Scottish scribes always struggled to render foreign names coher-
ently and Helena Shire speculated that his real name might have been
Henri Jeannequin or Harry Senneck and that he may have been French,
Flemish or English. A payment to 'Hare, lutar' in the *Pursemaster's*

29 Pitscottie, *Historie* (STS), i, 359, 379. A draught trumpet (or slide trumpet)
    was a form of sackbut, related to the modern trombone: Farmer, *Music in
    Scotland*, 95; Leslie, *Historie* (STS), ii, 260.

30 *TA*, v, 44, 53, 82–3, 113, 114, 117, 128, 156, 373, 435; vi, 207. See also Shire,
    'Music for Goddis Glore', 125 and Thomas, 'Renaissance Culture', 143 n.53.

31 *TA*, v, 256, 373; vi, 207. The clarsach is the Gaelic harp: Farmer, *Music in
    Scotland*, 88.

32 Farmer, *Music in Scotland*, 91; Ross, *Musick Fyne*, 119; Stevens, *Early Tudor
    Court*, 278.

Accounts of March 1540 could conceivably have been to the same man as well and, if so, it would suggest that the loss of the records of the expenditure from the king's purse for all but a few months in 1539 and 1540 is a serious obstacle to the study of the musicians in the chamber, since Urre/Orry/Hare appears in neither the *Treasurer's Accounts* nor the *Exchequer Rolls* after 1526.[33] William Galbraith, a yeoman of the inner chamber and a singer, was probably a lutar as well, since he was responsible for buying lutes and strings for the king.[34] At the end of the reign, James had a lutar called Cunningham, who was also paid from the king's purse, but who received some clothing from the treasurer.[35] The king was also served by a fiddle player, John Cabroch, who was listed between 1530 and 1540 and who was another musician sent to France in May 1538 to escort Mary of Guise to Scotland.[36]

The most fashionable bowed instrument of the 1530s in the Italian and French courts was the viol, which was often played in a consort of four or six instruments of different sizes, and this trend can be detected at the Scottish court too.[37] In November 1535 an Englishman, Richard Hume, was employed to make viols for the king and from 1 August 1538 a consort of four viols, led by Jacques Columbell, a Frenchman, was employed in the household.[38] The fact that Columbell's appointment coincided with the arrival of Mary of Guise may be significant, for her family were notable patrons of musicians.[39] The French consort of viols

33 *TA*, v, 312, 256; Shire, 'Music for Goddis Glore', 127–8; Murray, 'Pursemaster's Accounts', 33.

34 *TA*, v, 276; vi, 18, 86–7. He was listed as a chamber servant between 1526 and 1533, when Henry Drummond was appointed in his place: *ER*, xv, 292, 387, 463; xvi, 136, 176, 296; *TA*, v, 260–1, 310, 324, 382, 375, 434. It is possible that he was still in the king's service at the end of the reign as William Galbraith, keeper/usher of the kitchen door, July 1542: *TA*, viii, 101.

35 Murray, 'Pursemaster's Accounts', 50; *TA*, vii, 288, 414; viii, 46.

36 *TA*, v, 431, 435; vi, 37, 91, 204, 399–400; vii, 152, 414. The 'fiddle' he played may have been a croud or rebec: both were late-medieval bowed instruments with between two and four strings: Farmer, *Music in Scotland*, 92.

37 The viol is not to be confused with the violin, since the two instruments were quite distinct. The viol had a fretted finger-board, six strings, a less resonant sound than the violin and was placed in the lap rather than on the arm: Thurston Dart, 'The Viols' in Anthony Baines (ed.), *Musical Instruments Through the Ages* (London, 1973), 184–90.

38 *TA*, vi, 261–2; *RSS*, ii, 2620; *TA*, vii, 118–9, 199, 271, 328, 334–5, 413, 478–9, 482; viii, 46, 55, 93, 103, 149–50.

39 Members of the family were among Janequin's patrons: Reese, *Music in the Renaissance*, 296.

remained in service until the end of the reign and unnamed violars were still receiving payments until 1550.[40] In 1542 there was also a payment to a Scottish musician, sir John Fethy, whose 'childer' played the viols. In later years Fethy was a famous organist and composer, who became master of the sang schools at Aberdeen and Edinburgh, but he had earlier spent some years studying abroad and was possibly in royal service from 1529–30 when a man of that name received livery.[41]

Thomas Wood believed that James V did not have a very good singing voice, as we have seen, but the fact that he could sight-read suggests that he may have enjoyed singing part-songs, presumably in private, and he clearly employed singing men or boys (sangsters), who may have been attached to the staff of his chamber or to the chapel royal or both. William Galbraith, mentioned above, was certainly a singer in the king's chamber between 1525 and 1528 and there was also a singing boy/henchman called George Coutts who was listed between 1531 and 1534, a sangster called John Turnet listed in 1536 and one by the name of Archibald Borthwick in 1541.[42] The most frequently noted singer was Richard Carmichael, who appears in the sources from 1534 to the end of the reign and features in Knox's *History* as a chorister of the chapel royal suspected of anti-clericalism and compelled to 'burn his bill'. He certainly suffered an escheat of his goods sometime before 25 March 1539, when his property was remitted to him. Carmichael was also one of the king's entourage for the visit to France in 1536.[43] Whilst on this trip, the king seems to have acquired the services of an unnamed, presumably French, organist. This was possibly the same man as the organist provided with mourning clothes ('dule') for Queen Madeleine's funeral in July 1537, but the only named organist in the king's service, William Calderwood, was probably a Scotsman.[44] Furthermore, sir John Fethy, who was also within the court orbit, introduced a new style of organ-fingering to Scotland.[45] There were

40 *TA*, viii, 149–50, 240; ix, 127, 461.
41 *TA*, viii, 54; John MacQueen (ed.), *Ballattis of Luve* (Edinburgh, 1970), xxx–xxxiii; H M Shire, *Song, Dance and Poetry of the Court of Scotland Under James VI* (Cambridge, 1969), 54 & 260; *TA*, v, 383.
42 *ER*, xv, 208–463; *TA*, v, 432; vi, 92–205, 289; *RSS*, ii, 4151.
43 *TA*, vi, 205–429, 454; vii, 22–477; viii, 100–105; *ER*, xvi, 167–282; Knox, *Works*, i, 44–5; *RSS*, ii, 2976.
44 *TA*, vi, 350, 353; vii, 20, 22, 25; viii, 55. Possibly the Frenchman was 'Sebastiano Capellano et organiste gallicis' who was given £30 in Nov. 1537 on his return to France: SRO, Liber Domicili, E.31/7, fo. 17r.
45 *TA*, v, 383; viii, 54; Ross, *Musick Fyne*, 100; Jim Inglis, *The Organ in Scotland before 1700* (Schagen, 1991), 60.

organs in the chapels at Stirling, Linlithgow, Falkland and Holyrood, and possibly in other royal residences too. The instrument bought for the king's chapel in 1537, and the one bought for Holyrood chapel in 1539 are both described as 'pairs' of organs in the accounts, which suggests that they included both flutes and reeds and would thus have had two manuals (as was common with the Dutch organs of the period), but there is no mention of pedals. The instruments in Holyrood, Stirling and Falkland were housed in organ lofts, which may have been located on the rood screen of the chapels. James, like his father, may also have owned portative organs for use in chamber music as well as the chapel.[46] Other than the paid professional musicians, mentioned above, music would also have been played in the king's chambers by the amateurs of the court. It is impossible to be sure which of the many well-connected visitors and attendants would have had any musical skills but it might be fair to guess that those men who are known to have written poetry may also have had some musical talent since the two arts were often combined. Some candidates might be George Steel (one of the king's favourites, who kept some of the royal tapestries) or sir George Clapperton (the king's master almoner and sub-dean of the chapel royal).[47] Sir David Lindsay of the Mount, who had been the king's usher in the minority, certainly claimed to have played the lute to the king when James was a child.[48]

It is very difficult to detect any indication of the repertoire performed by the large staff of chamber musicians, other than Pitscottie's references to dances and plays noted above. Pitscottie particularly mentions the galliard and this dance was popular in the courts of Italy, France, Flanders and England, especially in combination with the pavane.[49] Basse-danses and rounds were certainly performed at the court of James IV and may well have continued to be danced in Scotland at a

46 Inglis, *The Organ in Scotland*, 19, 20, 24–5, 29, 62–6; *TA*, vi, 353; viii, 55; Peter Williams, *A New History of the Organ from the Greeks to the Present Day* (London, 1980), 68. It is by no means certain that these royal chapels had rood screens as there is no specific mention of such structures in the works accounts.

47 MacQueen, *Ballatis of Luve*, xxxiii-xxxv, 68–72. Two songs with words by Steel have survived: *Absent I am* and *Support your Servand*: see *Musica Scotica: Editions of Early Scottish Music* (2 vols., Glasgow, 1996), ii, 1–4; *MB*, xv, 158–9. Steel's servant was twice engaged to provide clothes for choristers of the chapel royal: *TA*, vii, 151, 464.

48 Lindsay, *Works*, i, 42 (*The Complaynt*). Apparently the king's favourite tune was *Ginkerton*.

49 Reese, *Music in the Renaissance*, 523, 553, 564, 868.

later date.[50] This is implied in *The Complaynt of Scotland* (c.1550) where the shepherds in the story are said to have danced 'base dansis, pauvans, galyardis turdions, branlis, and branglis, buffons witht mony uthir lycht dancis.'[51] Although the sources are very reticent about dances at the court, it is likely that the repertoire included the branle and allemande as well as the pavane, galliard, basse-danse and round. Both the basse-danse and the pavane were stately, processional dances, which might be used as preludes to the allemande or the galliard, which were lighter, more sprightly dances. The branle and the round were both danced in circles with linked hands and had many variations.[52] It is also possible that the traditional Scottish epic song, *Greysteil*, was performed at court, since James V probably gave this nickname to one of his childhood servants[53] and *The Complaynt of Scotland* also includes a list of well-known songs, some of which may have been heard at court too.[54]

There seems to have been a Franco-Italian influence early in the adult reign, exerted by the visit to the Scottish court of Thomas de Averencia of Brescia, a servant of Maximilian Sforza, titular duke of Milan, between November 1529 and March 1530. Averencia became a favourite of the Scottish king because of his interest in music, and James sought to delay his departure, to encourage his early return and to reward him for his attentions by making him a feed member of the household (*famulus et stipendiarius*). Although obviously a native of Italy, Averencia may have been introducing James to the musical developments of the French court since his master had been deposed as duke of Milan by Francis I in the autumn of 1515, spent the rest of his life in France as a client of the French king and died in

---

50 Leland, *Collectanea*, iv, 283. Two pavanes and a galliard of the early- to mid-sixteenth century are printed in *MB*, xv, 190–4 and three songs with dance rhythms have also survived: *Musica Scotica*, ii, 17–19, 32–5, 75–9.

51 Robert Wedderburn, *The Complaynt of Scotland*, ed. A. M. Stewart (STS, 1979), 51–2.

52 George S. Emmerson, *A Social History of Scottish Dance: Ane Celestial Recreatioun* (Montreal and London, 1972), 33–45; Mabel Dolmetsch, *Dances of England and France from 1450 to 1600* (London, 1949), 1–49, 55–128, 144–58. See also Dolmetsch, *Dances of Spain and Italy from 1400 to 1600* (London, 1954).

53 John Purser, 'Greysteil', in Hadley Williams (ed.), *Stewart Style*, 145, 150–1. *Greysteil* was certainly sung to James IV: *TA*, i, 330; iv, 96.

54 Wedderburn, *The Complaynt*, 51. The list begins with Henry VIII's *Pastime with Good Company* and continues with over thirty other songs including two which have survived, *Alas that Same Sueit Face* and *O Lusty May*: printed in *Musica Scotica*, ii, 11–13, 75–9.

Paris in 1530.[55] Averencia seems to have arrived in Scotland in the company of William Stewart, 'Captain of Milan' (who was also in French service), and the archdeacon of St. Andrews and all three were probably on a mission from the duke of Albany, who had a personal interest in the state of the Scottish realm under its newly liberated king. It is possible that the visits of other foreign envoys (such as Raphael Cassanzeis, a Spanish gentleman, who received a pension from James in 1542) also exerted a musical influence on the Scottish court but no specific details are available.[56] It is therefore likely that the greatest impulse for musical developments (as in so many other cultural activities) came from the king's own visit to France in 1536–37 and from the foreigners he employed in his household.

It is certainly possible to detect French influence in some of the surviving Scottish part-songs of the 1530s and 1540s, some of which may have been performed at court. The French songs of the period were either *chansons rustiques*, adaptations of traditional, vernacular verses and tunes which were sometimes woven into medleys (*fricassées*), or settings of more courtly verses by Clément Marot, Pierre de Ronsard and even Francis I himself, set to music by composers such as Pierre Certon, Claude de Sermisy (known as Claudin) or Clément Janequin. Typically, they were written for three or four parts, with the tune in the tenor, in a simple, chordal style and with a dance-like rhythm. They are almost all strophic in form, with repeated refrains, and owe something to the inspiration of the Italian *frottole* of the late-fifteenth century. In turn, the French *chansons* exerted some influence upon the embryonic madrigal form, which was pioneered in Italy by composers of French or Flemish origin, such as Philippe Verdelot and Adrian Willaert.[57] Surviving Scottish songs display very similar features: *The Pleugh Sang* (anon. c.1500), *Trip and Goe, Hey* (anon. c.1530) and *All Sons of Adam* (anon. c.1540) are medleys of popular, and sometimes bawdy, verses in the manner of *fricassées* and perhaps bear some resemblance to the 'three-men's songs' and carols sung at the

55 *James V Letters*, 163, 169, 170; Shire, 'Music for Goddis Glore', 131–3; Knecht, *Warrior and Patron*, 77.

56 For Cassanzeis: *TA*, viii, 54, 106, 148.

57 Freedman, 'Paris and the French Court', 191–2; Helena M. Shire and Kenneth Elliot, 'La Fricassée en Ecosse et ses rapports avec les Fêtes de la Renaissance', in Jean Jacquot (ed.), *Les Fêtes de la Renaissance* (3 vols., Paris 1956, 1960, 1965), i, 335–45; Knecht, *Warrior and Patron*, 460–61; Reese, *Music in the Renaissance*, 288–323.

English court.[58] The first is associated with a significant date in the agricultural year, 'Plough Monday', the second would be suitable for performance at a Maying and the third is a Christmas song. May Day and Christmas were certainly celebrated at the Scottish court and it is possible that *The Pleugh Sang* was used in a theatrical parody of rural life presented there.[59] According to Kenneth Elliot, John Fethy's *O God Abufe* displays the influence of Josquin, perhaps acquired when on his travels in the early decades of the sixteenth century, and there is a scholarly consensus that songs such as *Richt Soir Opprest* (anon.), *O Lusty May* (anon.) and *Deperte, Deperte* (words, and possibly music also, by Alexander Scott, c.1547) were inspired by the style of Claudin; indeed *Support your Servand* is a Scottish version of Marot's *Sécourez moy ma dame*, a poem which was set to music by Claudin.[60] Similarly, the process of assimilating the Franco-Italian fashion for lute songs, consorts of viols and dances such as the pavane and galliard can also be traced at the English court of the same period.[61]

It is easy to see how the French influence could have been exerted on Scottish music, for there were many diplomatic and trading links between the two countries. After 1528 French music could travel as easily and cheaply as any other printed text, since a Parisian printer, Pierre Attaignant, developed a technique for printing musical notation in one impression rather than in multiple impressions (which had been the earlier, more expensive, approach). As a result, Attaignant built up a flourishing music-publishing business and in 1529 was granted a Parisian monopoly by Francis I, who appointed him his official printer

58 Purser, *Scotland's Music*, 67–70; Ross, *Musick Fyne*, 119–26; Elliot and Rimmer, *A History of Scottish Music*, 15, 21; *MB*, xv, 141–7, 152–4; Kenneth Elliot, 'Trip and Goe, Hey: "A Truly Scottish Song"', in Hadley Williams (ed.), *Stewart Style*, 153–78; Wulstan, *Tudor Music*, 73.

59 Ross, *Musick Fyne*, 119–20.

60 Kenneth Elliot, 'sir John Fethy', in Stanley Sadie (ed.), *The New Grove Dictionary of Music and Musicians* (20 vols., London, 1980), vi, 511; Elliot, 'Trip and Goe, Hey', 153; Elliot and Rimmer, *A History of Scottish Music*, 21–3; Ross, *Musick Fyne*, 123–7; *MB*, xv, 158–9. Alexander Scott was a member of the chapel royal in 1539 and was later connected with the priory of Inchmahome and the abbey of Inchaffray: *Musica Scotica*, ii, 86–90, 75–9, 17–19; John MacQueen, 'Biography of Alexander Scott', in D. J. McClure (ed.), *Scotland and the Lowland Tongue* (Aberdeen, 1983), 52–3.

61 Stevens, *Early Tudor Court*, 108. See also Paul Kast, 'Remarques sur la musique et les musiciens de la chapelle de François Ier au camp du drap d'or' and Hugh Baillie, 'Les musiciens de la chapelle royale d'Henri VIII au camp du drap d'or', both in Jacquot (ed.), *Fêtes de la Renaissance*, ii, 135–46, 147–59; Wulstan, *Tudor Music*, 109–10.

in 1537. Attaignant published the works of Claudin, Certon and Janequin, as well as the French metrical psalms of Marot, and his books were in demand all over Europe.[62] Some of them may have arrived in Scotland in the baggage of Thomas de Averencia, Queens Madeleine and Mary, Jacques Columbell or James V himself, who indulged in a spending spree whilst in Paris for his first wedding and may even have visited the Attaignant workshop in the Rue de la Harpe. It is known that James purchased books whilst in France but there is no indication of their titles.[63] It is quite likely that James met Certon or Claudin for they both held posts in Francis I's chapel royal and in the Sainte-chapelle (the chapel of the Palais de justice on the Ile de la Cité, in the great hall of which palace the wedding supper was held) and they (along with Attaignant) had close connections to Jean, cardinal of Lorraine, in whose Parisian residence, the Hôtel de Cluny, James was lodged for a while.[64] He certainly came into contact with their collaborator, Marot, who wrote a *Chant nuptial du Roy d'Ecosse et de Madame Magdelene Première Fille de France* to celebrate the wedding. He also met the young Ronsard, who went to Scotland as a page with Queen Madeleine, as we saw in chapter one. James had earlier visited Lyons, which was also a cultural centre of major importance, with a flourishing printing trade, thriving musical life and very strong Italian influences. He seems to have had his portrait painted whilst in this city, and may have bought some music here too.[65] Given all these intimate contacts with the poets and musicians of the French court it seems highly likely that the influential French *chanson*-style entered Scotland through the court of James V at this time.

If France was the model for developments in secular (and particu-

62 Fenlon, 'Music and Society', and Freedman, 'Paris and the French Court' both in Fenlon (ed.), *The Renaissance*, 47–8, 181, 184–7; Knecht, *Warrior and Patron*, 460; Reese, *Music in the Renaissance*, 557–8, 563–4.

63 *L&P Henry VIII*, xi, 916; *TA*, vii, 17, 19.

64 Freedman, 'Paris and the French Court', 180–1; *Cronique du Roy Françoys Premier de ce nom publiée par la première fois d'après un manuscrit de la Bibliothèque Impériale*, ed. Georges Guiffrey (Paris, 1860), 202–4; Teulet, *Relations*, 107–8. The cardinal was also one of the witnesses to the marriage contract: Bentley-Cranch and Marshall, 'The Auld Alliance in Iconography and Literature', 277, citing BL Harley MS 1244, fos. 159r.-163v. & Add. MS 30666, fos. 204r.-207v.

65 Bentley-Cranch and Marshall, 'The Auld Alliance in Iconography and Literature', 276–7, 279–80; Frank Dobbins, 'Lyons: Commercial and Cultural Metropolis' in Fenlon (ed.), *The Renaissance*, 197–215. Music was published in Lyons between 1532 and 1547 by Jacques Moderne, who was originally from Istria: ibid., 207.

larly chamber) music of the period, Flanders and England took the lead
in sacred music and strongly influenced the liturgical music of the
Scottish court. Flemish influence was exerted on the Scottish church by
Mary of Guelders, queen of James II, and through the many diplomatic
and trading links to the Netherlands. Mary introduced the Observant
Franciscans to the realm and they became established as an order
particularly associated with royal patrons. She also founded Trinity
College, Edinburgh, a religious house that still had very strong links to
the royal court at the time of James V.[66] The English influence also
operated through diplomatic exchange; however, it was exerted most
strongly through the person of Queen Margaret Tudor, who retained at
least one English musician in her service after her marriage to James
IV.[67] The Flemish school of Pierre de la Rue and Nicolas Gombert
specialised in writing dense and complex polyphony, which utilised
intricate melodies with long phrases presented in a uniform texture and
continuous flow of music. This contrasted with the French preference
for clearly defined sections and the use of repetition. Marian works
were particularly popular and there was also a tradition at the Burgundian court of the Valois dukes and their Habsburg successors of
composing masses based on the popular melody, *L'homme armé*. This
theme was closely associated with the Order of the Golden Fleece and
the crusading ideal. At the English court, the sacred works of William
Cornish, Robert Fairfax and John Taverner also involved complex and
extended polyphony, and English choirs specialised in very high,
virtuosic treble lines. There it was common to take a section from
an antiphon (particularly a Marian antiphon) to form the motif for a
mass, although one secular melody, *The Western Wind*, was also used as
the basis for masses by Taverner, Tye and Sheppard.[68]

Unfortunately, very little Scottish sacred music survived the Refor-

---

66 Farmer, *Music in Scotland*, 69; Michael Lynch, 'Scottish Culture in its
Historical Perspective', in Paul H. Scott (ed.), *Scotland: A Concise Cultural
History* (Edinburgh, 1993), 30; David McRoberts, 'Notes on Scoto-Flemish
Artistic Contacts', *IR*, x (1959), 91–6; Theo van Heijnsbergen, 'The Scottish
Chapel Royal as Cultural Intermediary between Town and Court', in Jan
Willem Drijvers and A. A. MacDonald (eds.), *Centres of Learning: Learning
and Location in Pre-Modern Europe and the Near East* (Leiden, 1995), 302, 304,
306.

67 *TA*, ii, 412, 428, 460, 472.

68 Reese, *Music in the Renaissance*, 343–8, 778–9; Picker, 'Habsburg Courts',
223, 229; Barbara Haggh, 'Music and Liturgy' in Christiane Van den
Bergen-Pantens (ed.), *L'ordre de la Toison d'or, de Philippe le Bon à Philippe le
Beau (1430–1505): idéal ou reflet d'une société?* (Brussels, 1996), 186; Wulstan,
Tudor Music, 233–9, 251–8.

mation and so it is possible that the extant fragments do not present a fair picture of the early sixteenth-century repertoire. However, the available sources are quite suggestive. The most extensive oeuvre is that of Robert Carver, alias Arnot (c.1484/5–c.1568), whose known works are contained in the *Scone Antiphonary*, also known as the *Carver Choirbook*.[69] It is possible that Robert Carver was the son of David Carver who was working on the gallery, loft and ceiling of the Stirling chapel royal between 1497 and 1504. If these men were related, it would be reasonable to explain the use of the alias by supposing that the family was from the kindred of Arnot and that Carver was applied as an occupational surname. Another possibility is that Robert was an illegitimate son of David Arnot, bishop of Galloway and dean of the chapel royal between 1508 and 1526, and was adopted or fostered by David Carver of Stirling.[70] Robert Carver may have engaged in the family business for a while, since a Robert Arnot, burgess of Stirling, held a series of local offices including master of works at the parish church of the Holy Rude between 1519 and 1529 and his name appears in the Stirling records between 1516 and 1551.[71] Carver had possibly entered the university of Louvain in 1504 (this would help explain the Flemish influence in his work); he was a canon of Scone from around 1511–13 and a canon of the chapel royal from 1543; his name appears in Scone documents until 1568.[72] In addition to five masses and two motets by him, the *Carver Choirbook* contains a copy of Dufay's mass, *L'homme armé*, and works by Cornish, Fairfax and other English composers. The Flemish and English influence on Carver is thus made explicit in this manuscript, which includes his own *L'homme armé* mass and settings of *Gaude Flore Virginali* and *O Bone Jesu*, which texts had been used by Fairfax as motifs for two of his masses.[73] Carver's works are difficult to date accurately but three of the masses and the two motets were probably written between c.1506 and 1513, and the

---

69 NLS Adv. MS 5.1.15. Carver's known output is published in *Musica Scotica*, i.

70 *TA*, i, 357, 364; ii, 318, 429. The James Carver who helped to construct the organ for the chapel of Linlithgow palace in 1512 may have been related too: *TA*, iv, 275; Purser, *Scotland's Music*, 85.

71 Isobel Woods, 'Towards a Biography of Robert Carvor [sic]', *The Music Review*, xxxxix, II (May 1989), 90–96. Kenneth Elliot doubts whether this can be the same man because he imagines that a cleric attached to the chapel royal would be of too high a status to engage in such activities (*Musica Scotica*, vol. i, p.v), however it is known that at least two others (Master John Scrymgeour and sir James Nicholson) also acted as masters of works: see chapter 2.

72 Woods, 'Towards a Biography', 86–96; *Musica Scotica*, i, xi.

73 Wulstan, *Tudor Music*, 258.

remaining two masses probably date from the mid-1540s although one of these, *Fera Pessima*, may be from the 1520s.[74] The gap in output probably indicates that a portion of the manuscript has been lost, rather than the existence of a thirty-year crisis in Scottish music.[75] It has been argued that the musical life of the chapel royal was at a low ebb in the 1520s and the political upheavals of the minority would make this a likely proposition, but this could hardly have been the case during the 1530s when the cultural life of the Scottish court, including its secular music, was so vibrant.[76] The choirbook may have been copied for the chapel royal or for Scone, but it seems more likely that the chapel royal would have been able to muster the forces necessary to perform the mass *Dum Sacrum Mysterium*, which is scored for ten parts, or the motet *O Bone Jesu*, which is scored for nineteen, including eleven tenors.[77] Tentative suggestions have been put forward for royal occasions for which some of the pieces may have been written (none of them from the adult reign of James V) but they remain entirely speculative.[78]

It is possible that Carver also wrote some of the unattributed pieces and fragments in the choirbook but no firm conclusions may be drawn from these.[79] It has been suggested that he was responsible for the anonymous mass, *Cantate Domino*, which appears in the *Dunkeld Antiphonary*, also known as the *Dowglas/Fischar part book*, alongside copies of works by Josquin and Willaert. If this was the case, it is an example of a mature and accomplished work.[80] The *Dowglas/Fischar* manuscript also contains another anonymous Scottish mass, *Felix Namque*, which seems to be from the pen of a composer working in a rather different idiom from Carver, that is, one strongly influenced by Josquin. It is likely that this piece was by David Peebles (fl.1530–76), a canon of St. Andrews Priory. He is the only composer of his generation

---

74 Purser, *Scotland's Music*, 90. However, Elliot suggests a different chronology in *Musica Scotica*, vol. i, p. vii-ix.

75 The fact that the mass, *Pater Creator Omnium*, is lacking its first page makes this explanation likely: Ross, *Musick Fyne*, 43; Elliot and Rimmer, *A History of Scottish Music*, 20.

76 Woods, 'Towards a Biography', 97–101. For further discussion see Thomas, 'Renaissance Culture', 156 n.131.

77 Ross, *Musick Fyne*, 14–5, 29–33, 35–9, 60. Woods, 'Towards a Biography', 88, 97; Kenneth Elliot, 'Robert Carver' in Sadie (ed.), *The New Grove Dictionary*, iii, 842.

78 Ross, *Musick Fyne*, 20–24, 27–8, 30–1, 34–9, 45–50; Purser, *Scotland's Music*, 87–90; Elliot, 'Robert Carver', 842–3; Woods, 'Towards a Biography', 85, 94–5. See also Thomas, 'Renaissance Culture', 156 n.134.

79 Ross, *Musick Fyne*, 51–2.

80 Ross, *Musick Fyne*, 51–54; *Musica Scotica*, vol. i, p. ix-x.

who can be linked to the court of James V with any certainty, for his beautiful motet, *Si quis diligit me*, was presented to the king in c.1530, according to Thomas Wood, who copied it into his part books after the Reformation. Wood preserved it as an example of the work of one of the foremost Scottish composers, despite the fact that it was written for the Catholic church.[81] The motet, *Descendi in hortum meum* (c.1520), which is also influenced by Josquin, was possibly by Peebles too, but another candidate might be Robert Johnson of Duns (c.1500–c.1560), a Scottish musician who fled to England when he came under suspicion of heresy, sometime in the late 1520s or early 1530s. All of Johnson's known works appear in English sources and he may have had an impact on the works of Sheppard and other English composers, but it is unclear to what extent his works were familiar to Scots before the Reformation.[82]

The composers and performers of sacred music were particularly vulnerable to the pressures arising from the Reformation. In England both John Taverner and John Merbecke came under suspicion of heresy for a time and Thomas Tallis found his abbey at Waltham dissolved around him in 1540.[83] There were similar problems in Scotland too: the first Scottish martyr, Patrick Hamilton, may have been a composer and, as we have seen, Robert Johnson went into exile for religious reasons.[84] If Thomas Wood's comments can be relied upon, David Peebles was dismayed at the rejection of the works he had written for Catholic worship and also found the restrictions imposed upon those composing for the reformed church to be burdensome.[85] Even Robert Carver, a master of florid polyphony, seems to have made some attempt to alter his style in response to the winds of religious change, since his mass, *Pater Creator Omnium* (1546), is a much simpler, more chordal and syllabic setting than any of his other works.[86] This may have been

81 *MB*, xv, 111–14; Ross, *Musick Fyne*, 65–71, 75–80; Elliot, 'David Peebles', in Sadie (ed.) *The New Grove Dictionary*, xiv, 333; Elliot and Rimmer, *History of Scottish Music*, 19–20.

82 *MB*, xv, 103–5; Elliot and Rimmer, *History of Scottish Music*, 19; Purser, *Scotland's Music*, 95–7; Farmer, *Music in Scotland*, 112–13; Wulstan, *Tudor Music*, 298; Elliot, 'Robert Johnson', in *The New Grove Dictionary*, ix, 680.

83 Wulstan, *Tudor Music*, 268–9.

84 Hamilton was precentor at St. Andrews, before his execution in 1528, and seems to have written a nine-part mass, *Benedicant Dominum omnes angeli eius*, which no longer survives: Peter Lorimer, *Patrick Hamilton* (Edinburgh, 1857), 238. See also John Durkan, 'Scottish Reformers: the Less than Golden Legend', *IR*, xlv (1994), 10–18.

85 Ross, *Musick Fyne*, 87–8.

86 *Musica Scotica*, i, 46–62; Ross, *Musick Fyne*, 40–44; Purser, *Scotland's Music*, 97; Woods, 'Towards a Biography', 94.

because he was writing for the limited choral forces of Stirling's parish church of the Holy Rude or possibly because he was responding to views such as those expressed by Robert Richardson, a canon of Cambuskenneth, in his *Exegesis in canonem divi Augustini* (Paris, 1530). In this tract Richardson, who later became a Protestant, decries the use of elaborate polyphony in acts of worship because it obscures the words of the liturgy and may serve the glory of composers and performers rather than of God. He recommends the use of simple musical settings where the words may be clearly distinguished and the music serves to enhance the worship rather than the other way around.[87] This is quite an early example of a view which influenced the development, or restriction, of sacred music in Germany from the 1520s, in England during the reign of Edward VI, and in Scotland after 1560, as well as the musical pronouncements of the Council of Trent in 1562.[88] However, by far the most damaging effect of religious fervour on the musical life of Scotland came from the destruction of Catholic liturgical books and manuscripts at the Reformation, in which the greater part of the nation's musical heritage was lost.

The chapel royal at Stirling was clearly one of the centres of Scottish musical life before the Reformation. There had been a chapel in Stirling Castle from at least the twelfth century but James III was the first king to plan the establishment of a collegiate chapel royal there. The model for his foundation was the English chapel royal of Edward IV and the plans were developed with the help of an English musician and court favourite, William Rogers. However, political difficulties prevented the implementation of the scheme and the foundation eventually went ahead under James IV in 1501, as he was approaching marriage with an English princess. The building in which the chapel royal was housed within Stirling Castle no longer survives but the foundations of a chapel probably begun by James III and embellished by James IV have been detected beneath the existing structure which was constructed in 1594 for the baptism of Prince Henry.[89] Although James V

87 Robertus Richardinus, *Commentary on the Rule of St. Augustine*, ed. G. G. Couton (SHS, 1935), 80–81; Elliot and Rimmer, *History of Scottish Music*, 19–20; Farmer, *Music in Scotland*, 100; Purser, *Scotland's Music*, 97.

88 David Baldwin, *The Chapel Royal, Ancient and Modern* (London, 1990), 150–51; Ross, *Musick Fyne*, 84–7; Reese, *Music in the Renaissance*, 448–50, 673–88, 781, 795–8.

89 Fawcett, *Stirling Castle*, 17, 28–32, 45–7; Norman Macdougall, 'Crown vs Nobility: the Struggle for the Priory of Coldingham, 1472–1488', in K. J. Stringer (ed.), *Essays on the Nobility of Medieval Scotland* (Edinburgh, 1985), 254–69.

undertook a major building project within Stirling Castle (the construction of the palace block), the chapel royal received no more attention to its fabric than repairs to doors and stalls, according to the surviving records.[90] The endowments and staffing underwent some adjustment in the early years but by the end of the reign the college consisted of a dean (*ex officio* the bishop of Galloway), sub-dean, sacrist, chanter or precentor, chancellor, treasurer, sub-chanter or master of the bairns, and archdeacon, with a further eleven prebendaries and nine lesser canons, who were provided with incomes from the appropriated lands of several churches including Ayr, Crieff, Balmaclellan, Glenholm, Kells, Strathbran and Castellaw. There were also six boy choristers. This establishment was thus very similar in size to the Danish chapel royal, which consisted of eighteen singers in 1519.[91] The jurisdiction of the dean-bishop extended over the king, his household, all the royal residences throughout the kingdom and all the appropriated parishes.[92]

Unfortunately, no list of the personnel of the chapel royal survives for the reign of James V, although some members can be identified from scattered references in sources such as the *Register of the Privy Seal*.[93] At the end of this reign the senior officers included Andrew Durie, bishop of Galloway and dean, sir George Clapperton, sub-dean, and Master John Scrymgeour of Myres, precentor, whilst among the prebendaries were Alexander Scott and Master Alexander Kyd. All of these, except Scrymgeour, have been identified as poets and probably their posts would have demanded some skill in music too, particularly singing, since the papal letter giving permission for the foundation in 1501 insisted that the prebendaries should be skilled in song.[94] Scrymgeour was the king's master of works and therefore concentrated on architectural interests but as precentor he should have had some musical talent, although this role may have been undertaken by a

90 *MW*, i, 106, 110, 228. See chapter 2 for the work on the palace block.

91 Reese, *Music in the Renaissance*, 712–3.

92 I. B. Cowan and D. E. Easson, *Medieval Religious Houses: Scotland* (London, 1976), 226–7; C. Rogers, *History of the Chapel Royal of Scotland* (Grampian Club, 1882), xii-xliv; van Heijnsbergen, 'The Scottish Chapel Royal', 299–301.

93 A list of James IV's canons in January 1508 is in SRO MS E.34/1, fo. 6, transcribed in Thomas, 'Renaissance Culture', App. B, pp. 378–79.

94 van Heijnsbergen, 'The Scottish Chapel Royal', 303–4; Rogers, *History of the Chapel Royal*, xxxii. At Dunkeld the prebendaries provided vicars to sing the services: *Rentale Dunkeldense being Accounts of the Bishopric (A.D. 1505–1517) with Myln's 'Lives of the Bishops' (A.D. 1483–1517)*, ed. and trans. R. K. Hannay (SHS, 1915), 320–31.

deputy.[95] Shortly after James V's death sir John Fethy, the organist, and Robert Carver, the composer, joined the college.[96] We have very little information about the choirboys employed at Stirling, other than that they were usually six in number. Any of the sangsters of the chamber mentioned above may have been choristers of the chapel royal, indeed Knox described Richard Carmichael as such, and the sons of Jacques Columbell, the violar, who were at school in Stirling at the king's expense may also have been members of the establishment but there are no specific details in the sources. If the English pattern was closely followed, one would expect the choristers to have been recruited (sometimes forcibly) from a wide geographical area on merit alone, to have been taught Latin, liturgy and music, and to have been sent to university when their voices broke until some further preferment could be found for them.[97] At Wolsey's Cardinal College in the 1520s the boys were also given a courtly training similar to that provided for pages, which included waiting at table during formal meals, and some of James V's singing boys appear to have had similar duties.[98]

What is not at all clear from the Scottish sources is the extent to which the staff of the chapel royal accompanied the king around the kingdom, or stayed at Stirling. Charles the Bold of Burgundy had permanent chapels at Dijon and Lille as well as the travelling ducal chapel, whilst Philip the Fair instituted a *petite chapelle* in 1501, which was intended to minister to his private devotions and was expected to perform only low mass. Francis I also had two chapels: the *chapelle de musique*, which was capable of performing polyphonic settings of the mass and other services, and the chapel of plainchant, which conducted smaller,

---

95 In most Scottish cathedrals and collegiate churches the precentor or chanter was in charge of the choir, responsible for choosing the music, keeping discipline and appointing the master of the sang school: Arthur Oldham, 'Scottish Polyphonic Music', *IR*, xiii (1962), 54; Farmer, *Music in Scotland*, 96. Alexander Paterson seems to have been in charge of the music at the chapel royal in 1530, so perhaps he was Scrymgeour's deputy: Richardinus, *Commentary on the Rule of St. Augustine*, 80–1.

96 Carver was prebendary of Ayr *sexto* from 13 July 1543; Fethy was precentor from at least 1545: *RSS*, iii, 359, 1026.

97 Wulstan, *Tudor Music*, 233–9; Knecht, *Warrior and Patron*, 458; Baldwin, *The Chapel Royal*, 46, 319–25; Stevens, *Early Tudor Court*, 303–04. In March 1539, two boys from Aberdeen entered the chapel royal and their clothes were provided by a servant of George Steel: *TA*, vii, 151

98 Wulstan, *Tudor Music*, 262; George Coutts, 'the boy that sings', was also a henchboy and Richard Carmichael had a place in the pantry: *TA*, vi, 92–205; viii, 100, 150.

simpler services. Similarly, cardinal Wolsey's chapels made a distinction between chanters and polyphonists. However, the main division in the chapel royal of Henry VIII, following the *Eltham Ordinances* of 1526, was between the chapel that travelled with him continually and the one that stayed in London.[99] There is a suggestion in Pitscottie that the Scottish chapel royal also had 'home' and 'away' teams but there is no indication in the surviving sources of how this might have been organised.[100]

James maintained chapels in all of his main residences and some of the minor ones, so a travelling chapel staff would have had access to appropriate facilities for most of the year. The chapel of Holyrood Palace was rebuilt in 1535–6; the chapel of Linlithgow Palace had been built by James IV but underwent some refurbishment in 1535; the chapel of Falkland Palace also dates from the reign of James IV and was extensively renovated between 1537 and 1541. At Edinburgh Castle, James maintained St. Margaret's chapel and the chapel of the Barres (under the south wall) but converted the church of St. Mary into a munitions house. At Stirling the old church of St. Mary continued in use even after the construction of the chapel royal and there was also a chapel of St. Michael in Rothesay Castle.[101] Each of these lesser chapels was provided with a permanent chaplain, who usually acted as keeper of the residence, but it is not clear if these men were considered to be members of the chapel royal proper. Sir John Sharp, who was listed as chaplain and keeper of Holyrood Palace between 1515 and 1538, was recorded as a prebendary of the chapel royal in 1508 but the lack of a staff list for the chapel royal of the 1530s prevents the investigation of any similar coincidences.[102] The 1508 bill of household lists twenty-four canons (with six unnamed choristers) of James IV's chapel royal and gives a separate list of nine chaplains of the closet, but no such lists exist for the reign of James V. However, the records of 1528 to 1542 do contain scattered references to household chaplains, chaplains of the closet and king's orators, who perhaps

99 Haggh, 'Music and Liturgy', 184–5; Picker, 'The Habsburg Courts', 221; Knecht, *Warrior and Patron*, 458; Freedman, 'Paris and the French Court', 179; Wulstan, *Tudor Music*, 261; Baldwin, *The Chapel Royal*, 46–7, 323–5.
100 Pitscottie, *Historie* (STS), i, 200.
101 Iain MacIvor, *Edinburgh Castle* (London, 1993), 28–30, 54; Fawcett, *Stirling Castle*, 45; *ER*, xvi, 53; xvii, 472. See chapter 2. James also maintained chaplains at Restalrig, Cambuskenneth and Tain and took an interest in preferments at Trinity College and St. Giles, Edinburgh.
102 *TA*, v, 13 – vi, 403; SRO, Bill of household, E.34/1, fo. 6; Thomas, 'Renaissance Culture', 378–9.

formed the staff of the travelling chapel and assisted the king's private devotions (conducted within the small rooms leading off from the inner chambers of most of the royal residences, which were variously described as closets, oratories and studies).[103] These clerics seem to have been subject to the authority of the king's master almoner, and from 1535 this appointment was held by sir George Clapperton, who was also the sub-dean of the chapel royal. Such snippets of information as can be gleaned from the sources thus suggest some duplication of roles amongst the clergy within the orbit of the court and the tentacles of the chapel royal may therefore have extended much wider than is immediately apparent.

Whatever the day-to-day arrangements may have been for religious observance at court, it is clear that for the major feasts of Christmas and Easter and for state occasions the full chapel royal establishment was expected to be in attendance. Easter was usually celebrated at Stirling, so the court came to the chapel royal for this festival, but Christmas was usually kept at Holyrood and payments were recorded to the sacristan of the chapel for transporting the relics, vestments and ornaments from Stirling for Yule and Uphaliday (Epiphany), and back again; the most precious items travelled in the 'black kist'. The chapel graith was also sent to Edinburgh for the opening of parliament in 1532, the reception of ambassadors at the ratification of the 1534 peace treaty with England, the planned entry of Queen Madeleine in 1537 and the coronation of Mary of Guise in 1540.[104] Both the chapel royal and the other religious foundations with royal connections seem to have been quite well provided with vestments and ornaments. The chapel royal inventory of 1505 lists several sets of richly embroidered vestments, altar cloths and hangings, silver plate, reliquaries and liturgical books, both printed and manuscript, which between them indicate that despite papal pressure to introduce the Roman rite into the new college, it was the Scottish variant of the Sarum use that was observed here. The inventory also includes three organs, one with wooden pipework and two of pewter or lead. By January 1562 the chapel of Mary, queen of Scots, was left with only handful of old vestment and altar-cloths, one parchment mass-book, one parchment antiphonal and a coffer. Unfortunately no equivalent record survives for the 1530s; the items of chapel graith listed in the wardrobe inventories of 1539 and 1542–43 being sufficient only for the private altars of the king's and queen's

103 See chapter 2 for the arrangement of the rooms.
104 *TA*, vi, 49, 50, 103, 214, 215, 279, 305, 442; vii, 131, 280, 297; viii, 46, 53.

oratories.[105] However, the king did purchase new items from time to time and present them to his clergy. Such purchases included a complete set of ornaments and vestments for the chapel of the Barres in February 1533 and four sets of vestments for the chapel royal at Easter of the same year, three sets of vestments for the chapel of Loretto in August 1534, a silver chalice and new vestments for the master almoner in 1535–36 and a complete set of plate and vestments for the chapel of the baby prince in October 1540.[106] Shortly before James V's death there was an unseemly dispute between the dean and sacrist of the chapel royal over possession of the mitre and staff, presumably because these items were so valuable.[107]

The liturgy observed by the chapel royal and other ecclesiastical foundations in pre-Reformation Scotland was a variant of the Sarum rite of medieval England, which had been adapted to suit national needs. The Roman rite was also known in Scotland but does not seem to have been widely practised.[108] To the Sarum framework was added the veneration of local saints and shrines and the absorption of some aspects of religious observance from the Low Countries where, in the fifteenth century, the brand of popular piety known as the *devotio moderna* had developed. Such borrowings included the use of sacrament houses to store the reserved host (rather than the pyx suspended over the high altar, which was the English practice), the adoption of the cult of the holy blood of Bruges, the introduction of the Observant Franciscans, and the use

105 F. C. Eeles, 'The Inventory of the Chapel Royal at Stirling, 1505', *TSES*, iii (1909–10), 310–25; Robertson, *Inventaires*, pp. cxli-cxlii & p. 59; *Miscellaneous Papers Principally Illustrative of Events in the Reigns of Queen Mary and King James VI*, ed. Andrew MacGeorge (Maitland Club, 1834), 9–12; *Wardrobe Inventories*, 51, 58, 112; *TA*, vi, 467; vii, 36–7. See also Thomas, 'Renaissance Culture', 164–5, nn. 178 & 180.

106 *TA*, vi, 93, 82, 200–201, 248, 278; vii, 396–7. The prince's chapel graith was provided from the plate acquired by the king on the forfeiture of Sir James Hamilton of Finnart, with the addition of some newly embroidered hangings. These would have been in the care of the prince's master almoner, sir William Laing.

107 *ADCP*, 521–2.

108 David McRoberts, 'The Medieval Scottish Liturgy Illustrated by Surviving Documents', *TSES*, xv, I (1957), 24–40; James Galbraith, 'The Middle Ages', in Duncan B. Forrester and Douglas M. Murray (eds.), *Studies in the History of Worship in Scotland* (Edinburgh, 1984), 17–22; Rogers, *History of the Chapel Royal*, p. xxxii & p. 3; Eeles, 'The Inventory of the Chapel Royal', 40.

of the rosary to assist private devotions.[109] In the reign of James IV, Bishop Elphinstone of Aberdeen had attempted to rationalise and standardise 'the use of Scotland' but his efforts had been frustrated by the ease with which cheap liturgical books could be imported from abroad to undercut the official service-books produced by the fledgling Scottish printing trade. This influx was disrupted only by the upheavals within the English church following Henry VIII's assertion of the Royal Supremacy in 1534, after which event French presses stopped producing books for the Sarum rite and English publications could be classed as heretical books banned by the Scottish parliament. However, instead of reverting to Elphinstone's grand plan, the Scottish church in the late 1530s and 1540s seems to have turned to the revised Roman rite developed by Cardinal Quignonez, since several examples of his work with Scottish provenance have survived from this period.[110]

Scottish shrines which received particular attention from the royal court in the time of James V included St. Ninian's at Whithorn, St. Duthac's at Tain, St. Adrian's on the Isle of May and that of the Virgin of Loretto near Musselburgh. The king made regular pilgrimages and offerings to each of these sites throughout his adult reign. He visited Whithorn in November 1529, July 1532, June 1533 and August 1536.[111] He went to Tain in March and April 1534, November and December 1535 and September 1537 and kept a relic of St. Duthac set in silver.[112] He sailed to the Isle of May in May 1538 and August 1539 (on the latter occasion accompanied by Mary of

109 David McRoberts, 'Scottish Sacrament Houses', *TSES*, xv (1965), 33–56; McRoberts, 'The Medieval Scottish Liturgy', 35; Galbraith, 'The Middle Ages', 20–1; J. Cameron Lees, *St. Giles, Edinburgh: Church, College and Cathedral from the Earliest Times to the Present Day* (Edinburgh and London, 1889), 90; McRoberts, 'The Fetternear Banner', 69–86; *Edin. Recs.*, ii, 392; John Durkan, 'The Observant Franciscan Province in Scotland', *IR*, xxxv (1984), 51–7; David McRoberts, 'The Rosary in Scotland', *IR*, xxiii (1972), 81–6.

110 McRoberts, 'The Medieval Scottish Liturgy', 31–37, 37–9; Galbraith, 'The Middle Ages', 23–9; *APS*, ii, 295, 341–2; McRoberts, 'Some Sixteenth-Century Scottish Breviaries and their place in the History of the Scottish Liturgy', *IR*, iii (1952), 43–6; McRoberts, 'Catalogue of Scottish Medieval Liturgical Books and Fragments', ibid., iii, 59–60.

111 SRO, Libri Domicilii et Emptorum, E.31/3, fo. 25v.; E.32/2, fo. 119v.; E.31/4, fo. 87r.; E.32/5, fo. 118v.

112 *TA*, vi, 211, 248; SRO, Libri Domicilii et Emptorum, E.31/5, fos. 45v. & 99v.; E.32/5, fos. 26v.-36r.; E.32/6, fo. 121r.; E.31/7, fo. 108r. Two or three of the Tain prebends were royal presentations: John Durkan, 'The Sanctuary and College of Tain', *IR*, xiii (1962), 147–56.

1. James V by an unknown, probably contemporary, artist. (Courtesy of the Scottish National Portrait Gallery)

James the fyft
began his raign
1514 He maryed first
Magdelena dochter
of francis ye first
& of france

2. Portraits of James V and Queen Madeleine from the late-sixteenth-century
Seton Armorial. James wears a chivalric collar and Madeleine's petticoat
depicts the royal arms of France. (Courtesy of Sir Francis Ogilvy Bart., and the
trustees of the National Library of Scotland)

3. Mary of Guise by Corneille de Lyon. The same artist also painted portraits of James V and Madeleine of France. (Courtesy of the Scottish National Portrait Gallery)

4. A double portrait of James V and Mary of Guise by an unknown, possibly contemporary, artist. The shield depicts the royal arms of Scotland impaled with the arms of Guise and is surmounted by an imperial crown. (Courtesy of the Scottish National Portrait Gallery)

5. The four orders of chivalry on the Linlithgow Palace foregate, c.1536, restored in the nineteenth century. From left to right: the Garter, the Thistle, the Golden Fleece and St Michael. Note that the Garter escutcheon does not acknowledge the English king's claim to the throne of France. (Courtesy of Historic Scotland)

The arms of ye twa queynis sporusit to king Iomes ye first
ye first was magdalene de france; ye seind marie de lozane.

Magstalene qbeynē.

Marie: queynē,

6. The arms of Queen Madeleine and Mary of Guise from Sir David Lindsay's Armorial (1542). (Courtesy of the trustees of the National Library of Scotland)

7. The royal arms of Scotland from Sir David Lindsay's Armorial (1542). (Courtesy of the trustees of the National Library of Scotland)

8. The opening of the motet, *O Bone Jesu*, from the *Scone Antiphonary/Carver Choir Book*. (Courtesy of the trustees of the National Library of Scotland)

9. The Honours of Scotland. The sword and sceptre were papal gifts to James IV. The sceptre and crown were remodelled for James V. (Courtesy of Historic Scotland)

Guise) and owned a relic of St. Adrian set in silver gilt.[113] James walked to Loretto in August 1536 shortly before setting out on his voyage to France and he made offerings to the Virgin of Loretto in April and May 1537 when on his return journey.[114] Mary of Guise also walked to Loretto in August 1542 and made provision to have offerings given to the shrines of St. Trygian (Ninian) and St. Adrian in the event of her death in childbirth.[115] James's and Mary's devotion to Scottish shrines continued a custom established by James's father, who was also a regular pilgrim at Whithorn, Tain and May.[116] However, the shrine at Loretto was a new one, established in about 1533 by Thomas Doughtie, a hermit who brought to Scotland relics from the shrine of Loretto in Italy, whither the house of the Virgin Mary was said to have been transported from the holy land by angels. The royal patronage accorded to this new venture was therefore instrumental in establishing the credibility and popularity of this cult, which was particularly resented by the reformers. Knox regarded Doughtie as a charlatan and the shrine as an abomination, which meant that he therefore considered James V and Mary of Guise to have been either dupes or willing collaborators in wickedness.[117] The other newly established cult of the reign of James V was that of the True Cross at Peebles, which was ratified by Archbishop Gavin Dunbar in 1530. This site also received some royal patronage, since James regularly hunted in the area from his lodge at Cramalt Tower, and this was another shrine which would have received an offering of wax in the event of Mary's death.[118]

Another indication of the piety fostered within the court was the king's patronage of certain religious orders and foundations. Like his great-grandmother and father, James V was a notable supporter of the Observant Franciscans, but he also took an interest in the development of Trinity College, Edinburgh, the collegiate church at Restalrig, the convent of Sciennes and the abbey of Cambuskenneth. The Observant Franciscans entered Scotland in the mid-fifteenth century and expanded

113 SRO, Libri Domicilii, E.31/7, fo. 60r.; E.31/8, fos. 99v.-100r.; *TA*, vii, 395–6. A relic of St. Mahago was also set in gilt at the same time.

114 SRO, Liber Domicili, E.32/5, fo. 120v.; *TA*, vi, 299; vii, 24.

115 Leslie, *Historie* (STS), ii, 253; SRO, Liber Emptorum, E.32/8, fo. 125r.; *Balcarres Papers*, i, 78–9.

116 Macdougall, *James IV*, 196–9; Denis McKay, 'The four heid pilgrimages of Scotland', *IR*, xix (1968), 76–7.

117 *Diurnal of Occurrents*, 17; Knox, *History*, i, 75.

118 Robert Renwick, *A Peebles Aisle and Monastery* (Edinburgh, 1893), 82–3; *Balcarres Papers*, i, 78–9.

with the support of Mary of Guelders.[119] In 1494 James IV founded the
house at Stirling, which he maintained with gifts of cash and provisions
and to which he would retreat at Easter for a period of spiritual renew-
al.[120] This foundation has English parallels in the foundation of a house of
Observant Franciscans at Greenwich by Edward IV in 1478 and there was
also a friary at Richmond Palace.[121] James V continued to make regular
gifts to the Stirling Greyfriars[122] and at one point took his confessor from
amongst them but, although he usually spent Easter at Stirling, there is no
evidence that he continued the custom of regular retreats.[123] There were
probably close contacts between the Stirling friary and the chapel royal
too, but only one definite link can be established: Alexander Paterson,
who was sacristan of the chapel royal in the 1530s, became warden of the
Stirling Observants in 1544.[124] Trinity College, Edinburgh, was still being
built in the 1530s, with royal approval, and a cleric prominent at the court,
sir George Clapperton was appointed provost in 1540.[125] The collegiate
church at Restalrig was a foundation of James III but James V still
maintained at least two of the prebends there, the chaplain of St.
Triduana and the chaplain of the King's Wark at Leith, who were to
pray for the souls of James III and James IV.[126] They were both supported

119 W. Moir Bryce, *The Scottish Greyfriars* (2 vols., Edinburgh and London,
    1909), vol. i, p. vii; Durkan, 'The Observant Franciscan Province', 51–7.
120 See A. A. MacDonald, 'Catholic Devotion into Protestant Lyric: The Case of
    The Contemplacioun of Synnaris', *IR*, xxxv (1984), 58–83; Bryce, *Scottish
    Greyfriars*, i, 62–66, 369.
121 Starkey, 'The Friar's Church: Christening and Marriage', in Starkey (ed.), *A
    European Court*, 26.
122 Bryce, *Scottish Greyfriars*, i, 76–80, 93–4, 370, 372, 374; *TA*, v, 430; vi, 32; *ER*,
    xiv, 39, 40, 41; xv, 465; xvii, 597, 598, 599. Many other friaries also received
    occasional donations.
123 *TA*, vi, 32. See also Thomas, 'Renaissance Culture', 169 n.216.
124 *TA*, vi, 214; viii, 46; Bryce, *Scottish Greyfriars*, i, 452.
125 *Charters and Other Documents Relating to the City of Edinburgh, 1143–1540*,
    ed. J. D. Marwick (SBRS, 1871), 209–10; Marwick, *The History of the
    Collegiate Church and Hospital of the Holy Trinity and the Trinity Hospital,
    Edinburgh, 1460–1661* (SBRS, 1911), 26–9; *RSS*, ii, 3146. See also George
    Hay, 'The Architecture of Scottish Collegiate Churches', in G. W. S. Barrow
    (ed.), *The Scottish Tradition: Essays in Honour of Ronald Gordon Cant*
    (Edinburgh, 1974), 63.
126 *TA*, vi, 33; *ER*, xv, 93, 200, 286, 379, 459, 532, 544; xvi, 133, 173, 293, 480K;
    xvii, 170; xvii, 283; *RSS*, ii, 1143; *MW*, i, 290. See also Iain MacIvor, 'The
    King's Chapel at Restalrig and St. Triduana's Aisle: A Hexagonal two-
    storied Chapel of the Fifteenth Century', *PSAS*, xcvi (1962–3), 247–62; Hay,
    'Architecture of Scottish Collegiate Churches', 63; Campbell, 'A
    Romanesque Revival', 310; Thomas, 'Renaissance Culture', 170 n.219.

with an income generated by the King's Wark, which was a property built by James I, part of which seems to have been used as a warehouse for storing supplies for the royal household which landed at Leith, and part of which was probably rented out.[127] The nuns of Sciennes received a pension from the king throughout the adult reign but it is not entirely clear why they should have been singled out for such special favour, although the house was endowed with lands during the king's minority with the support of the duke of Albany.[128] Cambuskenneth was the burial place of James III and Margaret of Denmark, and James V continued his father's practice of maintaining a chaplain (sir James Inglis) there to pray for the souls of his departed ancestors.[129] Abbot Alexander Mylne was also prominent at court, serving as an auditor of exchequer and casualty, administrator of the lands of the prior of St. Andrews and the abbot of Holyrood (two of the king's illegitimate sons) and first president of the college of justice on its foundation in 1532.[130] Cambuskenneth and other Augustinian houses also maintained links with the chapel royal.[131] Other religious houses with close royal connections included those held by the king's illegitimate sons (the priories of St. Andrews and Coldingham, and the abbeys of Holyrood, Melrose and Kelso) and the charterhouse of Perth, which had been founded by James I, became the burial place of Queen

127 *ER*, xvii, 170, 283, 741n.; *RCAHMS, Edinburgh*, 266; Sue Mowat, *The Port of Leith, its History and its People* (Edinburgh, no date), 32–3.

128 *TA*, v, 429, 430; vi, 32, 200; vii, 198, 473; viii, 99. See also *James V Letters*, 232–3 and *Liber Conventus S. Katherine Senensis Prope Edinburgum*, ed. James Maidment (Abbotsford Club, 1841), 36–41.

129 Inglis is recorded at Cambuskenneth from c.1522 to 1542: *TA*, v, 199, 438; vi, 48, 447; vii, 200, 479; viii, 107. He is not to be confused with James Inglis, commendator of Culross, who was also at court and was murdered in 1531: *James V Letters*, 164, 190.

130 *TA*, vi, 1–468 etc.; *ER*, xvi, 127, 165, 225, 286, 302, 356, 402, 447 etc.; *MW*, i, 55–234; *RMS*, iii, 2611; *James V Letters*, 399. For Mylne see also John MacQueen, 'Alexander Myln, Bishop George Brown, and the Chapter of Dunkeld', in J. Kirk (ed.), *Humanism and Reform: The Church in Europe, England and Scotland, 1400–1643. Essays in Honour of James K. Cameron* (Oxford, 1991), 349–60.

131 The Augustinian priories of Restenneth and Inchmahome were intended to be annexed to the chapel royal by James IV (Cowan and Easson, *Religious Houses*, 226–7) and, as we have seen, Robert Carver was both a canon of Scone and a prebendary of the chapel royal and Alexander Scott was attached to Inchmahome, Inchaffray and the chapel royal. The association of the Scottish Augustinian houses with musical developments was noticed by Mark Dilworth, 'Canons Regular and the Reformation', in MacDonald, Cowan and Lynch (eds.), *Renaissance in Scotland*, 170–71.

Margaret Tudor in 1541 and numbered another royal bastard amongst its dependents.[132]

In all of these examples of royal patronage of religious foundations, James V seems to have been acting out of conventional rather than convictional piety and indeed much of his patronage served personal and political purposes rather than spiritual ones. Similar motives may also have influenced his response to the spread of Lutheranism, which was rather an ambiguous one. James seems to have favoured a group of men within his household who would later become known as reformers and to have encouraged some criticism of ecclesiastical corruption and 'sleaze'.[133] At the same time he also patronised those of the opposite persuasion, exacerbated some abuses by his blatant misuse of his powers of nomination to benefices, and allowed heresy prosecutions to go ahead, sometimes attending in person. The king was present to observe a heresy trial at the abbey of Holyrood in August 1534 which resulted in the execution of two men (David Straiton and Master Norman Gourlay) and the abjuration or exile of several others. His interest on this occasion was probably aroused by the fact that one of the accused was of the royal blood, and an officer of the king: Sir James Hamilton of Kincavil, sheriff of Linlithgow, who was allowed to go into exile in France.[134] The king was present at another Holyrood heresy trial in February-March 1539 when six men were burned on the Castle Hill (three friars named Lyn, Beveridge and Keillor; sir Duncan Simson, Thomas Forret and Robert Forrester). However, the king's concern was probably for Richard Carmichael (a chorister of the chapel royal) and George Buchanan (the tutor of one of his sons): Carmichael recanted and Buchanan fled. The stories of the martyrs of James V's reign are well known from Knox's account and do not need repeating here but the king's strategy seems to have been essentially a pragmatic one. This involved maintaining a

---

132 See chapter 1 and Mary Black Verschuur, 'The Perth Charterhouse in the Sixteenth Century', *IR*, xxxix (1988), 1–11. Adam Stewart was not the prior of Perth but took a pension from the monastery.

133 The 'proto-Protestants' included Sir James Kirkcaldy of Grange (treasurer and sewer), John Macall (or MacKaw, the poultry-man) and Sir John Melville of Raith (captain of Dunbar Castle). See Sanderson, *Cardinal of Scotland*, 277–9. See also the discussion of Sir David Lindsay of the Mount and George Buchanan in chapter 4.

134 J. H. Burns, 'The Political Background to the Scottish Reformation, 1513–1625', in D. McRoberts (ed.), *Essays on the Scottish Reformation* (Glasgow, 1962), 6–9; Sanderson, *Cardinal of Scotland*, 47–51, 86–93; SRO, Liber Domicili, E.31/5, fo. 78v.; J. R. N. MacPhail, 'Hamilton of Kincavil and the General Assembly of 1563', *SHR*, x (1913), 156–61.

stance as a loyal but embattled son of the church, in opposition to his heretic uncle of England, in order to exploit the wealth and power of the Scottish church for his own ends. His successful extortion of concessions from the papacy extended to heavy taxation of the Scottish church (ostensibly for the foundation of the college of justice in 1532, but largely for the benefit of the royal coffers), the extension of the period during which the crown could benefit from the temporalities of vacant benefices from eight months to a year in 1535, and the presentation of the blessed cap and sword in 1537.[135] The Scottish king seems to have been content to maintain the customs and rituals of Catholic worship at his court and to allow a certain amount of religious persecution within his realm, but was apparently reluctant to endanger the lives of men whose service he valued (such as Kirkcaldy of Grange and Lindsay of the Mount) for theological reasons. As long as the papacy and the Scottish church continued to support his dignity and power, James would be faithful to Rome; but the threats he reportedly uttered at the performance of Lindsay's Linlithgow *Interlude* of 1540 were ominous. On this occasion James V is said to have approved of the criticisms levelled at the church and to have threatened to send recalcitrant clergy to England for a lesson in reform from Henry VIII.[136] One suspects that if the church had ever attempted to thwart James's ambitions, Henry would have welcomed him into the reformed fold with open arms and considerable relief, but the prelates of the period managed to ensure that James was never put to the test.

The ritual year of the Catholic church largely shaped the itinerary and customs of the royal court and the cycle of feasts and fasts observed in the household of James V was very similar to that followed by other courts and communities of the period. The ritual year began in Advent, a penitential season which nevertheless included some jollity in the celebrations surrounding the feast of St Nicholas, 6 December. In Aberdeen, where the parish church was dedicated to that saint, the boy bishop ruled over the celebrations from St. Nicholas's day until the feast of the Holy Innocents (28 December), but there is no clear indication that the court marked December 6 in any way during the

135 SRO, Liber Domicili, E.31/8, fos. 51r. & v.; Knox, *Works*, i, 44–90; Sanderson, *Cardinal of Scotland*, 72–93, 270–84; Lynch, *Scotland: A New History*, 154–5; Wormald, *Court, Kirk and Community*, 163–4; 84–6, 90–1, 98–9; Donaldson, *James V to James VII*, 54–8. See also chapter 6 for the blessed cap and sword.

136 Lindsay, *Works*, ii, 2–6; Edington, *Court and Culture*, 49–50, 92–3; *L&P HVIII*, xv, 114. See also chapter 4.

reign of James V, even though his father had celebrated it.[137] However, Christmas itself (Yule) was a major court festival which involved a large increase in the provisions supplied by the kitchen, pantry and similar departments and the payment of liveries to the household. The kitchen accounts also reveal that gifts of game were often sent to the king at Christmas by courtiers and clerics. For example, at Christmas 1532 the abbot of Lindores gave a swan, two geese, three partridges, six woodcocks, a grouse and a corncrake (*conturnix*); the bishop of Moray gave a swan and two geese; the laird of Burleigh gave a swan and George Ormiston gave a swan and a grouse. This may suggest that these men were present at court as guests of the king.[138] The Christmas court was usually held at Holyrood, which was the royal palace most capable of coping with a large gathering, although Christmas 1539 was held at Linlithgow. The Christmas season included the feast of the Holy Innocents, or Childermas, 28 December, which one would expect to be marked by the election of a boy bishop from amongst the choristers of the chapel royal but no specific details survive for the period. In English cathedrals and churches the boy bishop would have worn miniature vestments and officiated at all religious services except the mass; he might even preach a mock sermon and undertake mock visitations.[139] Although the calendar year began on 25 March (the feast of the Annunciation), the Roman custom of celebrating new year on 1 January (the feast of the Circumcision) persisted. The accounts contain records of new year gifts purchased by the king and queen to present to the senior courtiers and they were usually items of gold, silver or jewels: for example James spent £400 19s on gold and silver items, intended to be new year gifts, supplied by Thomas Rhind, John Kyle and John Mossman, goldsmiths, in December 1538 and January 1539.[140] In January 1537, when the king was in Paris, he gave costly new year gifts to the French royal family and some of the senior household-officers and minstrels. Gold and jewelled daggers (whingers) were given to the dauphin, the duke of Orléans and the king of Navarre; a pair of gold and ruby bracelets to the dauphine; an

137 See Ronald Hutton, *The Rise and Fall of Merry England: The Ritual Year, 1400–1700* (Oxford, 1994); *Extracts from the Council Register of the Burgh of Aberdeen, 1398–1570*, ed. John Stewart (Spalding Club, 1844–48), vol. i, p.xxv; David McRoberts, 'The Boy Bishop in Scotland', *IR*, xix (1968), 80–82; *TA*, ii, 128, 349, 409, 410; iii, 175, 176, 356.

138 SRO, Liber Domicili, E.31/4, fos. 35r.-37v.; *TA*, vi, 35–7, 91–3, 203–5 etc.

139 St. Innocent's bishop features in the reign of James IV: *TA*, iii, 285; Hutton, *Merry England*, 10–11.

140 *TA*, vii, 123.

expensive coffer to the queen of Navarre; and cash to the servants and minstrels.[141] The season of Christmas ended with Twelfth Night, Epiphany eve, also known as Uphaliday, which is the date on which the king or queen of the bean might make an appearance at court. This was a person selected to preside over the festivities because they happened to receive a piece of cake in which a bean had been concealed.[142] This was also the occasion for which Sir David Lindsay of the Mount produced his entertainment in 1540, which seems to have been a fore-runner of *Ane Satyre of the Thrie Estatis*.[143] In addition to the boy bishop and the queen of the bean, the season of Yule might also see the appearance of such characters as the abbot of bonaccord or of unreason and Robin Hood and Little John, who might preside over other festivals as well.[144] General merry-making at this time is indicated by references to mumming after supper on new year's night 1526, the purchase of play-coats for Yule 1526, a red and yellow play-coat provided for the king's son in January 1534, black and white cloth for 'certane play gounis to the kingis grace to pas in maskrie' in December 1535 and red and yellow play-coats made for Uphaliday 1540.[145] Such activities may well have involved the men and boys of the chapel royal, since their English counterparts were central to the festivities at the court of Henry VIII.[146]

The feast of the Purification of the Virgin Mary, otherwise known as Candlemas, 2 February, was the next one to be marked at court, with candles purchased especially for the day.[147] Candlemas was another feast which was marked by religious processions involving the guilds of many Scottish burghs, and something similar may have happened at the chapel royal.[148] This was swiftly followed by Shrove Tuesday

---

141 *TA*, vii, 7, 14–15.
142 M. MacLeod Banks, *British Calendar Customs: Scotland* (3 vols., Folklore Society, 1937, 1939, 1941), i, 123, 127. In 1532 Christiane Ray was queen of the bean and was given livery by the treasurer: *TA*, vi, 37.
143 See above and chapter 4.
144 Banks, *British Calendar Customs*, iii, 189–94, 200–1, 223. The only reference to a Robin Hood at court during the reign of James V was in April 1531, presumably at the Easter celebrations: *TA*, v, 432–3.
145 *TA*, v, 254, 316; vi, 186, 255; vii, 276. Mumming involved masked and silent 'guisers' entering the company in procession and starting games of dice: Enid Welsford, *The Court Masque: A Study in the Relationship between Poetry and the Revels* (Cambridge, 1927), 128.
146 Welsford, *The Court Masque*, 116–8; Stevens, *Early Tudor Court*, 252; Wulstan, *Tudor Music*, 72, 78; Baldwin, *The Chapel Royal*, 302.
147 SRO, Liber Domicili, E.31/8, fo. 126r.
148 E.g., at Aberdeen, *Abdn. Counc.*, vol. i, p.xxv, pp.445, 449–51. See Banks, *British Calendar Customs*, ii, 163–4.

(Fastern's eve) and Ash Wednesday, the beginning of Lent. Lent was strictly observed as a meat-free season at the Scottish court and seems to have been something of a holiday for the king's butcher.[149] Holy Week and Easter were usually celebrated at Stirling, although not with a royal retreat, as we have seen.[150] We have no evidence of any special ceremonies on Palm Sunday, although the day is noted in the records.[151] James distributed alms on Maundy Thursday (Skire Thursday) to a group of bedesmen whose number represented the age of the king. As James was born on 10 April, his birthday sometimes fell just before Easter and sometimes just after, but the number of bedesmen seems to have been increased by one every year regardless. They received gifts of blue gowns, bonnets, shoes and a sum of cash and were expected to remember the king in their prayers but there is no indication that he washed their feet, as was done at the English court.[152] Following Easter, Ascension day is noted in the household accounts but does not seem to have been marked by any particular events at court, but the court did go maying, often at St. Andrews, where jousts and feasts were held.[153] Whitsun was the second time in the year when liveries were distributed to the royal household and after this feast James would often travel beyond his usual circuit. Summer jaunts included pilgrimages, hunting parties, justice ayres and two voyages to the Northern and Western Isles. Summer festivals which are noted in the accounts but do not seem to have been especially marked at court include the feast of Corpus Christi, St. John the Baptist (24 June), St. Peter and St. Paul (29 June), St. Laurence (10 August) and the Assumption of the Virgin Mary (15 August).[154] Surprisingly, there is no indication in the accounts that St. Andrew's day (30 November) was celebrated in any way, even though he was both a national saint and the patron of the Order of the Golden Fleece, and other saints with Scottish connections such as St. Giles, St. Ninian and St. Mungo seem to

---

149 Robert Henderson completely disappears from the accounts during Lent and fish dominates the menu, e.g., in 1532; SRO, Liber Emptorum, E.32/2, fos. 66v.-84r.

150 See above. Easter was another occasion for gifts of game to the royal kitchens: e.g. from the abbots of Iona and Lindores and the earl of Argyll in 1533: SRO, Liber Domicili, E.31/4, fo. 66r.

151 E.g. SRO, Liber Emptorum, E.32/2, fo. 81v. (1532); Liber Domicili, E.31/4, fo. 64r. (1533).

152 *TA*, v, 387, 429–30; vi, 32–3, 89, 200; Hutton, *Merry England*, 21–2, 57.

153 SRO, Liber Emptorum, E.32/2, fo. 99r.; *MW*, i, 36; *TA*, vii, 168.

154 SRO, Libri Domicilii et Emptorum, E.31/4, fo. 82v.; E.32/2, fo. 115v.; E.31/6, fo. 77v.; E.32/4, fo, 125v.; E.32/5, fo. 120v.

have been rather neglected too. However, Bishop Leslie believed that the feasts of the chivalric saints (Andrew, George and Michael) were celebrated at James V's court but he did not give any specific examples.[155]

James V and many of his courtiers were clearly enthusiastic about music, and adopted a largely conventional approach to religious observance. The patronage of minstrels, singers, composers, clerics, religious orders and shrines by the court was, on the whole, both generous and discerning, and indicates an awareness of contemporary practices in England, France, the Netherlands and, to a lesser extent, Italy. Clearly there was a willingness to borrow fashionable styles and customs from other courts, to adapt them to Scottish purposes, and to integrate musical and liturgical novelties into the routines of daily life. Furthermore, James V was largely successful in keeping up to date with such developments: the *chanson* form and the consort of viols appeared at the Scottish court at about the same time as they became popular in France, nor was there any appreciable delay in encouraging the composers of sacred works to adopt a simpler more homophonic style in response to evangelical pressure, as we have seen. James's pragmatic and somewhat ambiguous response to the rising tide of the European Reformation was not unlike the policy of his father-in-law, Francis I, who could glory in his title of Most Christian King and suppress evangelicals and Protestants within his own lands, whilst simultaneously encouraging German Lutherans to make life difficult for his Habsburg rival.[156] Thus the musical and liturgical aspects of the culture of the Scottish court were areas in which the honour, prestige and magnificence of the Scottish realm and its resurgent monarch could be upheld in a manner which built upon the achievements of earlier generations and which accorded closely with the practice at other princely courts of the period.

155 SRO, Liber Domicili, E.31/7, fo. 20r.; Leslie, *Historie*, ii (STS), ii, 230.
156 Knecht, *Renaissance Warrior and Patron*, 306–28.

FOUR

'Notabill Storeis': Learning and Literature

James V is not usually regarded as one of the most learned of sixteenth-century princes; indeed, Lindsay's lament that 'Imprudentlie, lyk wytles fullis,/Thay tuke that young prince frome the sculis' is probably one of the most oft-quoted comments on the king.[1] He was certainly neither a polyglot nor a polymath, in the mould of Henry VIII or Isabella d'Este, yet nor was his court devoid of scholarship and literary endeavour. Had his minority not been so politically chaotic, he might have experienced an education similar to that provided for his Tudor kin.[2] By the late-fifteenth century, the established pattern at the English court was that the royal infants would be provided with a miniature household including chaplains, physicians, minstrels and menial servants but would spend their earliest years primarily in the care of a team of nurses and rockers, under the supervision of an aristocratic 'lady mistress.' At the age of five to seven years, boys would graduate from the care of governesses into the hands of masters to begin a more formal education, which would have two main spheres: the literary and intellectual exercises of the schoolroom and the physical and social exercises necessary to acquire the skills of chivalry and courtesy. The first part of the curriculum would be taught by the grammar master or tutor, who would often be a university-trained household cleric. The medieval practice had been for the second field to be taught by a noble master or governor, well versed in horsemanship, hunting, jousting, sword-play and courtly manners, but by the 1480s and 1490s such training was expected to be provided within the prince's household in general. It is thus impossible to tell who taught Henry VIII the boisterous knightly games at which he excelled, but his academic training was in the hands of the poet, John Skelton, John Holt (a former schoolmaster at Magdalen College School, Oxford and at Chichester), William Hone (also a former master of Chichester School) and Giles

---

1 Lindsay, *Works*, i, 43 (*Complaynt*).
2 For the education of Francis I and Charles V see Knecht, *Warrior and Patron*, 6–8, 149–54, 306–307; Karl Brandi, *The Emperor Charles V*, trans. C. V. Wedgewood (London, 1965), 47–8; Thomas, 'Renaissance Culture', 178 n.2.

D'Ewes (a Fleming, who taught the future king French and later became his librarian). The result was a prince who knew Latin and French well (with a smattering of Italian, Spanish and Greek) and who had an abiding interest in mathematics, theology, astronomy, geometry, poetry and music.[3] Although he undoubtedly had assistance in writing his *Assertio Septem Sacramentorum* (1521), his primary authorship of the core of this orthodox theological tract is usually accepted.[4] However, Henry's sister Margaret, although a product of the same Tudor nursery, was not a particularly erudite lady. This may have been for temperamental reasons, or because her marriage at the age of thirteen effectively ended her formal education, but was probably largely because the education of aristocratic women in England would not really be taken seriously for another generation.[5] Whatever the reasons, it is clear that she could neither write nor spell well and her apparent lack of interest in scholarship possibly had some impact on the education of her son.[6]

In his earliest years James V was provided with a household appropriate to a prince of Scotland, some of whom were appointed to their posts before his father's death. He had the usual complement of chaplains, nurses and other servants and care was taken to ensure his security.[7] However, it is with the next stage of his development that problems have been identified. The king's tutor or preceptor was Master Gavin Dunbar (c.1490–1547), who appears in the household lists from February 1517, when James was nearly five years old, and was last recorded as such in September 1525, when his pupil was thirteen. Dunbar was a nephew of the bishop of Aberdeen of the same name and had graduated in arts from the university of Paris and in law from the university of Angers before returning to Scotland

3 Nicholas Orme, *From Childhood to Chivalry: the Education of the English Kings and Aristocracy, 1066–1530* (London, 1984), 12–24; Firth Green, *Poets and Princepleasers*, 73–6, 97; A. A. MacDonald, 'The Renaissance Household as Centre of Learning', in Drivers and MacDonald (eds.), *Centres of Learning*, 289–98; Scarisbrick, *Henry VIII*, 14–15.

4 The fact that it is a short, pedestrian and unremarkable work suggests that the king's personal contribution may well have been significant: Scarisbrick, *Henry VIII*, 110–13.

5 Juan Luis Vives's *De Institutione Foeminae Christianae* (Antwerp, 1527, English translation, 1529) was influential. It was dedicated to Katherine of Aragon, and advocated that women should be well educated. Mary I and Elizabeth I both benefited from the new opportunities championed by Vives: Orme, *Childhood to Chivalry*, 231–5.

6 Orme, *Childhood to Chivalry*, 159.

7 See chapter 1.

to assume his royal duties. He was appointed to the metropolitan see of Glasgow in July 1524 but was ousted from his post as royal tutor during the regime of the earl of Angus. When the king asserted his authority in the summer of 1528, he chose not to restore the office of tutor and Dunbar was appointed chancellor instead, in which post he replaced the deposed earl. George Buchanan remarked on his learning and he had links with the scholarly and literary elite of his day but the contemporary sources shed very little light on his personal qualities.[8] There is no surviving indication of the curriculum he delivered to his pupil and certainly no suggestion that he ever produced a manual for the king's instruction which might resemble the *Speculum Principis* (1501) produced by John Skelton for princes Arthur and Henry of England.[9] Among the known contents of his library is nothing which might have appealed to the interest and imagination of a child.[10] In later years the deficiencies of James's education would be remarked upon but if, as seems to have been the case, the king had no formal academic tuition beyond the age of thirteen for political reasons, it may not be fair to blame Dunbar entirely for the problem.[11] However, the king does seem to have been able to express himself effectively in the Scots language. The poems *Peblis to the Play*, *Chrystis Kirk on the Grene*, *The Gaberlunzie Man* and *The Jolly Beggar* have all been attributed to him, although without any convincing evidence being presented,[12] but if Lindsay's *Answer to the*

---

8 *TA*, v, 111; Major, *History*, 445; *DSCHT*, 260–61; D. E. Easson, *Gavin Dunbar: Chancellor of Scotland, Archbishop of Glasgow* (Edinburgh and London, 1947), 7, 25–40; Buchanan, *History*, ii, 239.

9 Orme, *Childhood to Chivalry*, 103. In 1522 James's schoolmaster was directed to teach him to read, write and speak Latin and French and to instruct him in 'the virtues', nothing more specific is noted: *HMC Mar and Kellie*, 11.

10 The list is almost certainly only a fraction of the whole and consists of theological and legal works: J. Durkan and A. Ross, *Early Scottish Libraries* (Glasgow, 1961), 30–31.

11 'The kingis grace I knaw is nocht perfite/ In Latyn toung, and nemelie in sic dyte/ It wilbe tedious, that dar I tak on hand,/ To reid the thing he can nocht understand': William Stewart, *The Buik of the Croniclis of Scotland*, ed. W. B. Turnbull (3 vols., Rolls Series, 1858), i, 4. For his inability to reply to a speech made in French during his royal entry into Paris, 31 December 1536, see Teulet, *Relations*, i, 107–8 and chapter 6.

12 George Eyre-Todd, *Scottish Poetry of the Sixteenth Century* (Glasgow, 1892), 159–82. *The Jolly Beggar* and *The Gaberlunzie Man* are probably **about** James rather than **by** him. *Peblis to the Play* is attributed to James I by John Major, *History*, 366, and *Chrystis Kirk on the Grene* to the same king by George Bannatyne, *The Bannatyne Manuscript Writtin in Tyme of Pest, 1568*, ed. W. Tod Ritchie, (4 vols., STS, 1934 & 1928 & 1930), ii, 268.

Kingis Flyting is a genuine reply to a piece of royal invective he must have made at least one attempt at writing verse which has not survived.[13] Furthermore, John Bellenden's *Proloug apoun the traductioun of Titus Livius* (1533) also suggests that the king was a poet in his own right:

> And ye, my soverane, be lyne continewall
> Ay cumin of kingis youre progenitouris,
> And writis in ornate stile poeticall
> Qwik flowand verss of rethorik cullouris,
> Sa freschlie springand in youre lusty flouris,
> To the grete comforte of all trew Scottismen;
> Be now my muse and ledare of my pen.[14]

James seems to have been a much more able pupil in the field of courtesy and chivalry than in the schoolroom. Here the poet, Lindsay, in his role as the king's master usher, claimed some credit for teaching the boy music, dancing, games and tales.[15] The king also had a mule from 1517, when he was four years old, and his yeoman of the stable at that time, Robert Purves, must have had a hand in teaching him to ride.[16] The ordinance for the keeping of the king which was drawn up in August 1522 (shortly before Albany left for France for the second time during his regency) placed the king in the custody of John, Lord Erskine, at Stirling Castle and named as his closest servants not only Erskine but also Alan Stewart (captain of the guard), Andrew Towers (Stewart's lieutenant) and Robert Borthwick (master gunner) as well. These men would almost certainly have contributed to the king's love of riding, shooting, archery, sword play and other chivalric pursuits. Furthermore, the ordinance implies that at ten years old the king was already very keen to ride out into the

13 Lindsay, *Works*, i, 101–4.
14 Bellenden's *Livy*, i, 1.
15 The master usher to an adult king would be responsible for regulating entry to the king's chambers and ensuring orderly conduct within these apartments. However, as a child James V had a much smaller household establishment than as an adult and it is likely that Lindsay's duties were therefore more wide-ranging. The poet himself claimed to have acted as the king's sewer, carver, cupbearer, pursemaster, chief 'cubiculare', usher and playmate rolled into one: *Works*, i, 4–5 (*The Dreme*). In one revealing entry of 1517 he was accorded the technically incorrect, but perhaps functionally accurate, title of master of household: *TA*, v, 160. See also chapter 1.
16 *TA*, v, 130.

countryside on a regular basis and it made elaborate arrangements for his security on such jaunts.[17] In 1524 when the household was re-organised under Queen Margaret's second regency, Lindsay was replaced as master usher by Andrew, Lord Avandale, and the king's guard, previously dominated by men loyal to the duke of Albany, was re-constituted and staffed by men loyal to Margaret and Henry VIII (who was paying their wages).[18] Prominent among these new attendants was Henry Stewart, soon to become Margaret's third husband, Lord Methven, and master of the king's artillery. Avandale and Methven are likely to have taken over the king's knightly training as well and to have been followed in their turn, during Angus's rule, by Archibald Douglas of Kilspindie, whom the king apparently nicknamed Greysteil.[19]

During this period in his development, it is highly unlikely that the king would have been kept in complete isolation from other children but it is very difficult to discover who might have been his classmates and sparring partners. In 1540–41 James's short-lived son and heir would have had the companionship of his half-sister, Lady Jane, and several French page-boys who were attendant on the queen. The childhood friends of his successor, the four Marys, are legendary[20] but the youthful companions of James V (if there were any) are shrouded in mystery. The death of his younger brother, Alexander, duke of Ross, in December 1515 deprived him of the company of a sibling, but there is one reference which suggests that one of his half-sisters, the Lady Margaret, may have been at court in the mid-1520s.[21] Beyond this we are in the realms of supposition and speculation. It is possible that James found some companionship in the children and wards of his senior household officers. In later life, almost all of his mistresses were the daughters of such men, and he seems to have been close to the earl of Huntly, who for a while shared the same guardian, the earl of Angus.[22] Moreover, in the records of the household of the

---

17 *HMC Mar and Kellie*, 11–12. Neither Dunbar nor Lindsay are mentioned by name in the ordinance but the posts of master and usher are listed as part of the household establishment.

18 Wood, *Letters*, i, 341–5; Strickland, *Lives*, i, 196–8; *L&P Henry VIII*, iv, I, 600, 637, 656, 657, 658, 674, 767, 797, 803, 805, 806, 809, 811, 813, 817, 823, 835, 889, 1026.

19 John Purser, 'Greysteil', in Hadley Williams (ed.), *Stewart Style*, 150–51.

20 Rosalind K. Marshall, *Queen of Scots* (Edinburgh, 1988), 27.

21 *TA*, v, 314. This is probably a reference to Lady Margaret Douglas, the daughter of Margaret Tudor and Angus.

22 See chapter 1 and Cameron, *James V*, 37.

minority appear the names of several 'henchmen' who may have been boys from good families sent to court to be brought up alongside the king. In the English court the role of henchman was clearly defined along these lines,[23] but the surviving records shed no light on their position in the Scottish court. None of the names on the list are particularly distinguished and several of them seem to have obtained subsequent employment in the royal stables so their role at the Scottish court may not have been as prestigious as their English counterparts.[24]

However hazy the details of the king's education and upbringing may be, it is quite clear that as he grew older he increasingly became the focus of literary offerings by Scottish scholars and writers hoping to obtain his patronage and approval, and also to influence his beliefs and attitudes. By the early sixteenth century the tradition of the advice-to-princes genre was well established; there were several Scottish examples. His father, James IV, had been the dedicatee of John Ireland's *Meroure of Wyssdome* (1490) and in 1456 Sir Gilbert Hay had translated into Scots (from a French translation of the Latin) one of the standard texts on the subject, the *Secreta Secretorum*, which purported to be the advice offered to Alexander the Great by Aristotle.[25] In addition to such works from the past, James V was presented with a series of new volumes instructing him on how to live the life of a virtuous, vigorous and successful ruler. Among the earliest were two monumental tracts on Scottish history produced by two of the most respected scholars of the day, John Major or Mair (c.1467–1550) and Hector Boece (c.1470–1536). Much ink has already been spilled in analysing these masterful yet contrasting texts (Major's *Historia Majoris Britanniae tam Angliae quam Scotiae* [Paris, 1521] and Boece's *Scotorum Historiae a prima gentis origine cum aliarum et rerum et gentium illustratione non vulgari* [Paris,

---

23 Orme, *Childhood to Chivalry*, 50–53; Firth Green, *Poets and Princepleasers*, 72, 80–81, 84–85. See also Thomas, 'Renaissance Culture', 184 n.31.

24 The names were James Edmonston, Patrick Bruce (possibly a son of Sir David Bruce of Clackmannan), Robert Ormiston, the laird of Many and Troilus. See Thomas, 'Renaissance Culture,' App. A.

25 John Ireland, *The Meroure of Wyssdome*, ed. C. Macpherson, F. Quinn and C. McDonald (3 vols, STS, 1926, 1965, 1990); Gilbert of the Haye, *Prose Manuscript (A.D. 1456)*, ii: *The Buke of Knychthede and The Buke of the Governaunce of Princis*, ed. J. H. Stevenson (STS, 1914); J. H. Burns, 'John Ireland and "The Meroure of Wyssdome"', *IR*, vi (1955), 77–98; Burns, *The True Law of Kingship: Concepts of Monarchy in Early-Modern Scotland* (Oxford, 1996), 19–39. Haye's translation was dedicated to the earl of Caithness, chancellor of Scotland, rather than to the king.

1527]),[26] and it is not necessary to repeat the details here, but it is important to stress that whatever other motives may have spurred the writers into action, both works were dedicated to the king and explicitly intended for his edification.

Major had not published any historical works prior to 1521 but rather, during the course of a long career at the university of Paris, he had become renowned as a scholastic logician and theologian.[27] It is therefore worth considering why he should make his sole foray into history at this point. In 1518 he returned from Paris to Scotland where he was briefly principal of Glasgow University and treasurer of the chapel royal at Stirling. He had originally been offered the chapel royal prebend in 1509 but he was named in the post only in documents of 1520, 1522 and 1525.[28] In 1520 he designated Andrew Durie as his

26 For **Major**: John Major, *A History of Greater Britain as well England as Scotland compiled from the Ancient Authorities 1521*, ed. and trans. A. Constable with a *Life of the Author* by Æ. J. G. Mackay (STS, 1892); J. Durkan, 'John Major: After 400 Years', *IR*, i (1950), 131–9; Durkan, 'The School of John Major: A Bibliography', ibid., i, 140–57; J. H. Burns, 'The Scotland of John Major', ibid., ii (1951), 65–76; Burns, 'New Light on John Major', ibid., v (1954), 83–100; Roger A. Mason, 'Kingship, Nobility and Anglo-Scottish Union: John Mair's *History of Greater Britain* (1521)', ibid., xli (1990), 182–222; *DSCHT*, 540–41.

For **Boece**: Hector Boece, *The Chronicles of Scotland*, trans. John Bellenden (1531), eds. R. W. Chambers, E. C. Batho and H. W. Husbands (2 vols., STS, 1938 & 1941); L. J. MacFarlane, 'Hector Boece and Early Scottish Humanism', *The Deeside Field*, xviii (1984), 65–9; *DSCHT*, 82–3; Nicola Royan, 'The *Scotorum Historia* of Hector Boece: A Study' (University of Oxford DPhil, 1996); Nicola Royan, 'The Relationship between the *Scotorum Historia* of Hector Boece and John Bellenden's *Chronicles of Scotland*' in Mapstone and Wood (eds.), *The Rose and the Thistle*, 136–57.

For **both**: A. Ross, 'Some Scottish Catholic Historians', *IR*, i (1950), 5–21; J. Durkan, 'The Beginnings of Humanism in Scotland', ibid., iv (1953), 5–24; John and Winifred MacQueen, 'Latin Prose Literature', in R. S. Jack (ed.), *The History of Scottish Literature Volume One: Origins to 1660* (Aberdeen, 1988), 227–43; John MacQueen, 'Aspects of Humanism in Sixteenth- and Seventeenth-Century Literature', in MacQueen (ed.), *Humanism in Renaissance Scotland* (Edinburgh, 1990), 19–26; Burns, *True Law of Kingship*, 39–92; William Ferguson, *The Identity of the Scottish Nation: An Historic Quest* (Edinburgh, 1998), 56–75.

27 A. Broadie, *The Circle of John Mair: Logic and Logicians in Pre-Reformation Scotland* (Oxford, 1985); Broadie, 'Philosophy in Renaissance Scotland: Loss and Gain', in MacQueen (ed.), *Humanism in Renaissance Scotland*, 75–93; Broadie, *The Shadow of Scotus: Philosophy and Faith in Pre-Reformation Scotland* (Edinburgh, 1995).

28 Durkan, 'John Major', 132; *RSS*, i, 1977: Burns, 'New Light', 88–91. Burns thinks that he rejected the offer in 1509 but he may have accepted the prebend as an absentee. *RSS*, i, 3067; Major, *History*, Appendix, p. cxvii.

successor in the post, but the next holder actually seems to have been Robert Galbraith, between 1528 and 1532.[29] It is not possible to detect Major's presence in the court circle during the years when he was at least nominally a canon of the chapel royal and he may never have taken up residence in Stirling, but it seems almost certain that his *Historia Majoris Britanniae* was written in the years 1518–20 and perhaps it was his brief association with a royal college which inspired him to write it. The young king himself was certainly in residence in Stirling between 1522 and 1524 and Major explicitly stated in his preamble that he intended the work for the king.[30] He hoped to educate James in the nature of his realm and of his subjects and he provided a dispassionate and even rather clinical critique of the poorly-educated, chivalry-obsessed Scottish nobility, who were failing to maintain peace and civil order. Like so many other writers of the period, he stressed that a king should rule for the common good (*bonum commune*) rather than for singular profit, but he was quite original in his definition of what this meant. For Major, stability and prosperity would be most effectively gained by the union of the two realms of England and Scotland and James V, the son of a Stewart king and a Tudor princess, would be the person most likely to achieve it. Major's constitutional views were also note-worthy: drawing on his knowledge of Aristotle, Marsilius of Padua and Jean Gerson, he considered sovereignty to reside in the will of the people (or the 'worthier part' thereof), who therefore had the collective right to depose tyrants.[31] Considering his difficulties with Latin, it is unlikely that the king ever read the book, although his tutor or one of his clerks may have explained it to him. However, John Major

---

29 *RSS*, i, 3067; *RMS*, iii, 605; *RSS*, ii, 1104. Durie had studied at the university of Montpellier, was later abbot of Melrose and (from 1541) bishop of Galloway and dean of the chapel royal. He was also named as a poet by John Rolland, *The Seuin Seages*, ed. G. Black, (STS, 1932), 1–2; and by Knox, *Works*, i, 261–2. Galbraith was, like Major, a scholastic philosopher at Paris before his royal preferment in Scotland: John Durkan, 'The Cultural Background', in D. McRoberts (ed.), *Essays on the Scottish Reformation, 1513–1625* (Glasgow, 1962), 282, 295, and he may have been the 'Galbreith' listed as one of the poets of the court of James V by Lindsay, *Works*, i, 57 (*Papyngo*).

30 Burns, 'New Light', 91; Emond, 'Minority', 313, 416; Major, *History*, 41–2, 186, 217–19, 289.

31 Mason, 'Kingship, Nobility', 183–222; John and Winifred MacQueen, 'Latin Prose Literature', 235–6. Major's views directly influenced George Buchanan's *De jure regni apud Scotos* (1579) and (through him) resistance theories of the seventeenth and eighteenth centuries: Mason, 'Kingship, Nobility', 213. Buchanan was a pupil of Major's.

does not appear to have received any further royal patronage after its publication. Indeed, he moved away from the Glasgow/Stirling orbit to St. Andrews in 1523 (perhaps in the train of Archbishop James Beaton who was translated from the see of Glasgow to the primacy in that year) and spent the years 1526–31 in Paris again. However, from 1533 until his death in 1550 he was provost of St. Salvator's College at St. Andrews, where his patrons would probably have been the two Beaton archbishops rather than the crown.[32] His vision of a united kingdom never aroused the enthusiasm of the king who was rather more interested in renewing the auld alliance with France, and one can imagine Major being bitterly disappointed with the course of events after 1542. However, the archbishops of St. Andrews were significant figures in the court and government of the realm, from 1538 the prior of St. Andrews was a son of the king, and the court was frequently in residence there between 1538 and 1542, so even if his views were unpopular, Major was never very far from the orbit of the royal court.

In contrast to Major's work, Hector Boece's *Scotorum Historia* was well received at court. Like Major, Boece had also taught at the university of Paris but he returned to Scotland c.1503 and from 1505 he served as the first principal of the university of Aberdeen, a post he held until his death in 1536.[33] He was a humanist admirer of Erasmus and had written an earlier historical work, *Murthlacensium et Aberdonensium Episcoporum Vitae* (Paris, 1522), which consisted largely of a panegyric of William Elphinstone, bishop of Aberdeen between 1483 and 1514, who had founded Boece's university in 1495.[34] Boece's *Scotorum Historia* may well have been intended as a response to Major's work, since it discusses much of the same material with a very different style and emphasis. Although Major is usually categorised as a scholastic, he was aware of humanist developments and took his inspiration at least partially from Sallust and Livy (but also Bede). His work was

---

32 Burns, 'New Light', 92–100; Durkan, 'John Major', 132.

33 J. & W. MacQueen, 'Latin Prose Literature', 236–7.

34 Hector Boece, *Murthlacensium et Aberdonensium Episcoporum Vitae*, ed. and trans. James Moir (New Spalding Club, 1894). Boece may have been inspired by a similar work produced a few years earlier by another learned Scot, Alexander Mylne (c.1474–c.1549), who later became abbot of Cambuskenneth, president of the college of justice and administrator of the priory of St. Andrews for the underage commendator, Lord James Stewart. Mylne's *Vitae Episcoporum Dunkeldensium* (1515), was essentially a panegyric on bishop George Brown, written when the author was Official of Dunkeld: see Alexander Mylne, *Vitae Episcoporum Dunkeldensium*, ed. T. Thomson (Bannatyne Club, 1823) and a partial translation in *Rentale Dunkeldense*, ed. and trans. R. K. Hannay (SHS, 1915), 302–34.

intended primarily as a piece of didactic literature and he was critical of his sources and sceptical about some of the origin-myths of the Scots.[35] Boece, on the other hand, took Tacitus, Livy and Cicero as his models, presented his history as a piece of rhetorical literature, and was rather cavalier in his use of sources: relying largely on Fordun and Bower's *Scotichronicon*, citing a mysterious medieval writer called Veremund (whose work has since been lost) and adopting uncritically the traditional stories of ancient Greek and Egyptian refugees and a long line of Celtic kings.[36] In this he was writing history in a similar style to Jean Lemaire de Belges's *Illustrations de Gaule* (1510–13), in which the myth of the Trojan origins of the French kings and the legend of the Gallic Hercules were popularised.[37] More importantly for Boece, the history of the Scots was one of persistent and noble resistance to repeated assaults from aggressively expansionist English kings and, far from advocating a union of the realms, he saw the king of Scots as the most important focus of heroic national independence.[38] Before his history was published in 1527 Boece does not appear to have been the recipient of any royal patronage, but his work was also dedicated to the young James V in the hope that he would profit from the lessons contained therein, and the author did subsequently receive royal recognition. In July 1527 he was granted an annual pension of £50 to be paid from the casualties of the sheriffdom of Aberdeen. In July 1529 the same pension was assigned to the Aberdeen customs revenues and was to be paid until the king could allocate him a benefice worth a hundred merks per annum. In 1533 and 1534 the pension was paid jointly by the treasurer and comptroller and in 1535–36 it ceased upon Boece's appointment to the rectory of Tyrie.[39]

Boece's history was so appealing to James V that he commissioned one of his clerks, John Bellenden, to translate it into Scots for him. Bellenden (c.1495–1548) was a graduate of St. Salvator's College, St.

---

35 Major, *History*, pp. cxxxiii – cxxxv & pp. 4, 64; Mason, 'Kingship, Nobility', 183–9.

36 Veremund may have been Richard Vairement, a culdee of St. Andrews in the 1250s: MacQueen, 'Aspects of Humanism', 20–25; J. & W. MacQueen, 'Latin Prose Literature', 236–7; MacFarlane, 'Hector Boece', 68.

37 I. D. McFarlane, *A Literary History of France: The Renaissance, 1470–1589* (London, 1974), 49–50.

38 J. & W. MacQueen, 'Latin Prose Literature', 238; MacFarlane, 'Hector Boece', 68. For Leslie, Boece's *History* was 'so eloquent stile, so truelie and diligentlie collected, that none of all the wreittaris at that tyme wreitt better': Lesley, *History* (Bann. Club), 144.

39 *RSS*, i, 3841; *ER*, xvi, 42, 63; *RSS*, ii, 251; *TA*, vi, 102, 213; *RSS*, ii, 2192.

Andrews, served as a clerk of the expenses to James V between 1515 and 1522, was archdeacon of Moray between 1533 and 1538, precentor of Glasgow from 1538 to his death, and rector of Glasgow University between 1542 and 1544. His family was prominent in royal service: his father, Patrick, was Queen Margaret's steward until his death in 1514; his mother, Mariota or Marion Douglas, was probably one of the king's childhood nurses; his sister, Katherine, was a seamstress in the royal wardrobe from 1537 and the wife of a royal favourite, Oliver Sinclair of Pitcairn; his brother, Master Thomas Bellenden of Auchnoul, was a senator of the college of justice from 1535, director of chancery from 1538 and justice clerk from 1539.[40] It was probably this family tradition of loyal service which saved him from reprisals by the king when, in September 1528 he appeared before the parliament to register a formal protest against the charges of treason levied at the earl of Angus and his adherents. The following April Bellenden and his servant, William Fleming, received a precept of remission for treasonably assisting the Douglases, and the commission to translate Boece was probably granted in 1530. In 1531 he received three payments totalling £66 for 'translating of the cronykill' and his work was later printed by Thomas Davidson and read 'to the greit furderaunce and common weille of the hole natione.'[41] In his preface to the translation, Bellenden re-iterated Boece's dedication to James V and stressed the advisory purpose of the work:

> I, that bene thi native and humyll servitour sen thi first infance, be impulsioun of luff and vehement affeccioun quhilk I bere unto the samyn, has translatit 'The History of Scotland' . . . in quhilkis ar contenit nocht only the nobill feetis of thi vailyeannt anticessouris, bot als be quhat industry and wisedome this realme bene governit thir xviii c. & lx yeris, quhilk was nevir subdewitt to uncouth empire, bot onlye to the native princis thairof, howbeit the samyn had sustenit grete afflicioun be Romanis, Inglis & Danys.[42]

---

40 *ER*, xiv, 55, 119, 228, 321, 466; xv, 88, 89, 200; *TA*, v, 435, 438; *RMS*, iii, 1877; *RSS*, ii, 2368; E. A. Sheppard, 'John Bellenden', in Bellenden, *Chronicles*, ii, 411–35; Theo van Heijnsbergen, 'The Interaction Between Literature and History in Queen Mary's Edinburgh; The Bannatyne Manuscript and its Prosopographical Context', in A. A. MacDonald, M. Lynch and I. B. Cowan (eds.), *The Renaissance in Scotland: Studies in Literature, Religion, History and Culture Offered to John Durkan* (Leiden, New York, Köln, 1994), 185, 191–94.
41 *APS*, ii, 322, 324; *RSS*, ii, 56; *TA*, v, 434; vi, 36; Lesley, *History* (Bann. Club), 144.
42 Bellenden, *Chronicles*, i, 16.

and in the *Ballat apone the Translatione*, otherwise known as the *Proheme of the Historie*:

> Thocht thow pass furtht as bird implume to licht,
>   His gracious eiris to my werk implore,
> Quhair he may se, as in ane mirrour bricht,
> Sa notabill storeis baith of vice and glore,
> Quhilk nevir was sene into his toung afore;
> Quhairthrow he may be prudent governyng
> Als wele his honoure as his realme decore,
> And be ane vertuous and ane nobill king.[43]

Bellenden's work was a rather free translation and he took the opportunity to inject some of his own ideas into Boece's narrative: the loyal and energetic services of past generations of the Douglases are stressed in a subtle piece of special pleading, and the unity of Scotland under the leadership of its kings is highlighted in a manner that plays down Boece's awareness of the ethnic diversity of the nation. Whilst Boece's *Historia* was dedicated to the king, it was nevertheless written with an eye to a European humanist readership, whereas Bellenden's work was aimed more narrowly at the Scottish king and court.[44]

In 1533 Bellenden was paid £12 for 'ane new cornikle' [sic] which may have been a revision of his Boece or may have been a reference to his translation into Scots of the first five books of Livy's *History of Rome*, which he produced between July 1533 and January 1534. This translation was also a royal commission, dedicated to James V, and again Bellenden seems to have intended it to educate the king in politics and government, for he draws many direct parallels between ancient Rome and sixteenth-century Scotland.[45] In particular he hopes that the king will emulate the moral virtue and military prowess of the Romans:

> Of awfull batalllis the crafty governance,
>   The wise array, the manlie jeoperdie,
> Ye may fynd here, with mony doutsum chance,
>   Als quyk as thai war led afore your ee.
>   Ye may also be mony stories see

---

43 Bellenden, *Chronicles*, ii, 408.
44 Royan, 'The Relationship between Boece and Bellenden', 138–9, 152.
45 £36 was also paid specifically for the Livy translation: *TA*, vi, 97–8, 206; *Livy's History of Rome: The First Five Books translated into Scots by John Bellenden, 1533*, ed. W. A. Craigie (2 vols., STS, 1901 & 1903); MacQueen, 'Aspects of Humanism', 11–19.

> Quhat besynes may proffitt or avance
> Youre princely state with ferme continuance . . .

> . . . ffor in quhat sorte youre hienes will delite,
> Ye may gett stories to youre appetite

> Richt proffittabill till undermynde youre fais
> And for to lere the arte of chevelrie[46]

Bellenden was not only a Latin scholar of some stature but also a vernacular poet of renown. In 1530 David Lindsay, surveying the literary scene at court, considered him one of the foremost poets of the day:

> Bot, now, of lait, is starte upe, haistelie,
> One cunnyng clerk, quhilk wrytith craftelie,
> One plant of poetis, callit Ballentyne,
> Quhose ornat workis my wytt can nocht defyne:
> Gett he in to the courte auctoritie,
> He wyll precell Quintyng and Kennetie.[47]

Likewise, in 1560 John Rolland looked back upon the court of James V and listed Bellenden as one of the greatest poets there, alongside David Lindsay, Andrew Durie and William Stewart.[48] Each of his translations was accompanied by prefatory verses: *The Proheme of the Historie*, *The Proheme of the Cosmographie* (both 1531) and *The Proloug apoun the traduction of Titus Livius* (1533) and the printed edition of his *Boece* additionally contained *The Excusation of the Prentar*, which is usually attributed to Davidson, but was claimed as Bellenden's work by one commentator.[49] However, all of these verses post-date Lindsay's encomium in *Papyngo* (c.1530). We have only one other Bellenden piece which is undated, *The Benner of Peetie*, and therefore if Lindsay's praises were ever justified there must have been many more poems which have since been lost. All of Bellenden's known poems are addressed, whether directly or indirectly, to the king. *The Proheme of the Cosmographie* reminds James of the poet's service and his loss of office under Albany's second regency:

---

46 Bellenden's *Livy*, i, 4–5.
47 Lindsay, *Works*, i, 57 (*Papyngo*). Quintin and Kennedy were both poets of the court of James IV: ibid., iii, 68–70.
48 Rolland, *Seuin Seages*, 1–2.
49 Bellenden, *Chronicles*, ii, 403–9; *Bann. MS*, iv, 313–6; ibid., ii, 9–20; Bellenden's *Livy*, i, 1–5; Eyre-Tod, *Scottish Poetry*, 134–5.

And first occurrit to my remmembring
How that I wes in service witht the king,
Put to his Grace in yeiris tendirest.
Clerk of his comptis thocht I wes inding
Witht hart and hand and every uthir thing
That micht him pleiss in ony maner best.
Quhill hie invy me frome his service kest.
Be thame that had the court in governing
As bird but plumes heryit of hir nest.[50]

It then proceeds to describe a dream-vision in which the allegorical ladies, 'Delyt' and 'Vertew' contend for the affections of a crowned king who, like the nineteen-year-old James, has 'tender downis rysand on his beird.' The poet does his best to recommend the ultimate rewards of virtue and to decry the disgrace brought by self-indulgence but the poem ends before the choice has been made. Considering that by 1531 James had already sired the first two of his eight recorded illegitimate children, it is hardly surprising that Bellenden does not seem to have been confident of his advice being heeded.[51] *The Proheme of the Historie* is more explicitly an advice-to-princes poem, suggesting that true nobility arises from virtuous deeds rather than exalted pedigree and that a successful king should be prudent, courageous, generous and fair.[52] As we have seen, *The Proloug apoun the traduction* is also addressed directly to James V, urging him to accomplishments of which the ancient Romans would have been proud. The *Benner of Peetie* is not obviously in the same mould, for it is essentially a pious meditation upon the incarnation and crucifixion, but Bellenden borrowed his theme and structure from book two of John Ireland's *Meroure of Wyssdome* and this association with a work intended for the instruction of James IV, as well as the morality it preaches, places *The Benner of Peetie* firmly within the *speculum principis* tradition.[53]

John Bellenden was not the only vernacular poet of the court of James V to make a translation of Boece's *History* and address advisory verses to the king. The other was William Stewart (c.1476–1548), also a graduate of St. Andrews, possibly related to Lord Methven, who was in royal service

50 *Bann. MS*, ii, 10.
51 Ibid., ii, 11. See chapter 1.
52 Bellenden, *Chronicles*, ii, 403–9.
53 Sally Mapstone, 'A Mirror for a Divine Prince: John Ireland and the Four Daughters of God', in J. Derrick McClure and Michael R. G. Spiller (eds.), *Bryght Lanternis: Essays on the Language and Literature of Medieval Scotland* (Aberdeen, 1986), 308–23.

from 1526. It is possible that he was also vicar of Pencaitland (East Lothian) and rector of Quothquan (Lanarkshire) and he may have continued in service with Mary of Guise after the death of the king.[54] His verse translation of Boece's *History* was written between April 1531 and September 1535 and was undertaken on the orders of a lady, who has been identified as Queen Margaret, but who may have been just an imaginary allegorical muse.[55] It is also dedicated to James V (although no specific payments for it can be traced in the surviving accounts) and prefaced with a verse prologue in which Stewart makes it clear that he hopes the stories of his royal ancestors will inspire the king to great deeds comparable to those of the 'nine worthies' of chivalric lore:

> Thair sall he find als nobill and als fyne,
> As evir wes ony of the nobill nyne.
> And fra his grace considder weill sic thing
> How that he wes predestinat to ring,
> Siclike as tha, into thair settis suir,
> I traist he suld do diligence and cuir,
> To follow thame with possibilitie,
> So like with poettis for to prysit be.[56]

At about the same time there was a third (prose) translation of Boece's *History* undertaken by an anonymous clerk of the diocese of Dunkeld, which is named after the house in which the manuscript was discovered in 1928, Mar Lodge. Perhaps a suitable candidate for the vacant post of translator would be Laurence Telfer, who was treasurer of Dunkeld between 1532 and his death in 1545. Telfer was described as the king's familiar and as a faithful servant of James IV and James V; he was employed by James V as one of the collectors of the ecclesiastical taxes of 1531 and he moved in scholarly and literary circles since he

---

54 A. A. MacDonald, 'William Stewart and the Court Poetry of James V', in Hadley Williams (ed.), *Stewart Style*, 187; J. M. Sanderson, 'Two Stewarts of the Sixteenth Century: Mr William Stewart, Poet, and William Stewart, Elder, Depute Clerk of Edinburgh', *The Stewarts*, xvii (1984), 25–46; Lindsay, *Works*, iii, 76–7. One commentator considers the author of the metrical translation of Boece to have been the William Stewart who was bishop of Aberdeen and lord high treasurer but this view has not been widely accepted: M. P. McDiarmid, 'The Metrical Chronicles and Non-alliterative Romances', in Jack (ed.), *History of Scottish Literature*, i, 36.

55 Stewart, *The Croniclis*, vol. i, p. vii & pp.1–5; MacDonald, 'William Stewart', 190.

56 Stewart, *The Croniclis*, i, 2.

was, along with Henry Balnaves, a godfather to James Bannatyne's eldest son in 1539.[57]

Many of William Stewart's other known poems also offer advice to James V on the traditional themes of leading an upright and noble personal life, respecting good counsel and ruling justly and wisely.[58] None of these poems are dated but internal evidence, such as comments on the king's youth or references to his mother and regency council, suggests that some were written during the minority (*Precelland prince, Rolling in my remembrance, Schir, sen of men* and *This hindir nycht*). As one might expect, they complain of injustices and misrule and exhort the king to cultivate the virtues he will need in order to give redress to his subjects. *This hindir nycht* in particular depicts the allegorical figure of 'Dame Verite,' who catalogues the vices which will need to be driven from the court if James is to rule well ('yung counsale,' 'singular proffeit,' 'dissimulance,' 'flattery,' 'falsheid,' and others) and recommends their replacement by virtues (such as 'justice,' 'prudens,' 'forss,' 'temperans,' 'commounweill,' and the like). In this analysis of the ills of the minority of James V, Stewart seems to be anticipating the more famous representation of the ills of the minority of Mary by Lindsay in his *Satyre of the Thrie Estaitis*.[59] Other poems appear to date from the adult reign: *O man remember* is a religious lyric, focused on the Passion of Christ, which has a tone very similar to Bellenden's *Benner of Peete* in that it is apparently addressing all sinners but also makes a direct appeal to the king ('Thow lykis in lust & ryalte to ring,' line 108). *First lerges,* is more obviously a poem of the court in that it makes a sardonic comment on the lack of generosity displayed by a series of courtiers at the annual ritual of the distribution of new year gifts.[60]

---

57 *The Mar Lodge Translation of the History of Scotland by Hector Boece*, ed. George Watson (STS, 1946); Watt, *Fasti*, 114; *James V Letters*, 67, 247–8; *TA*, v, 454, 156–58, 461; *Bann. MS*, i, p. cxlii.

58 The full list of attributions and a detailed anatomy of the poems is given by MacDonald, 'William Stewart', 188–200.

59 Ibid., 189.

60 MacDonald makes a convincing case for dating this poem to January 1542 rather than 1527 and provides identifications for the figures who appear: 'William Stewart', 195–7. However, he does not appreciate the full extent of the joke in the reference to the earl of Bothwell 'The quhilk in fredome dois excell.' He notes that Bothwell seemed to be banished from the court at the time. This was certainly the case but moreover, he had spent most of the 1530s in ward, first in Edinburgh Castle and later at Inverness under (justifiable) suspicion of treasonable dealings with Henry VIII. From 1539 Bothwell was not only banished from court but also from the realm and by 1541 he had travelled as far as Venice. His 'freedom' was therefore that of the exiled felon: Cameron, *James V*, 86–91.

Other minor poets of the period also wrote in a similar vein to Stewart. Three anonymous poems of the minority also make complaints of unjust rule by regency lords who are only interested in their own profit: *Suppoiss I war in court most he, Jesu chryst that deit on tre* and *Now is our king in tendir aige*. The latter, in its representation of 'Johne uponland' also anticipates one of the heroes of Lindsay's *Satyre* and *Jesu chryst* has the refrain, 'Allace our king is nocht of eild.'[61] Two other anonymous poems which used to be attributed to William Dunbar discuss similar problems: *Quhen the Governor Past in France* (c.1517) and *We Lordis hes chosin a Chiftane Mervellous* (c.1520) have the respective refrains 'For, but thy [Christ's] help, this kynrick is forlorne,' and 'In lak of justice this realme is schent allace.'[62] Similarly, *The rich fontane of hailfull sapience* by Alexander Kyd discusses the familiar advice-to-princes *topoi* and, in its direct appeal to a 'rycht potent prince preclair,' seems to be addressed to the adult James V. Conventionally, it recommends that the king cultivate virtue, abhor vice and rule wisely and justly, but it takes an unusual twist in the penultimate stanza:

> Eftir thi meit of instrumentis muisicall
> Thow suld be fed witht plesand armony
> quhilk is exercitioun most regall
> Lichtis the mynd plesand to heir & se
> attour all thing in musick cunnand be
> quhilk ornat Homeir decoir of discepling
> ane kendill of curage off rankour inneme
> musik callit wirthy for ony king.[63]

Kyd's particular concern with the musical education of the king is probably explained by his own occupation: he was a prebendary of the chapel royal at Stirling (holding the canonry of Strathbrawn *primo* until 1531, when he was promoted to the canonry of Ayr *sexto*) and from 1533/4 he was succentor of Aberdeen, which was a post involving musical responsibilities.[64] It is therefore likely that Kyd was not entirely disinterested when he sought to encourage the king to take an interest in music.

Of course, the most famous court poet of the reign was Sir David

---

61 *Bann. MS*, ii, 233–4, 245–7, 247–9; MacDonald, 'William Stewart', 198.
62 *The Poems of William Dunbar*, ed. J. Small (3 vols., STS, 1893), ii, 235–6, 237–8.
63 *Bann. MS*, ii, 245.
64 *RSS*, ii, 786, 787; *ER*, xvi, 370.

Lindsay of the Mount, James V's senior herald and former master usher, and many of his works were clearly intended for the entertainment and edification of the king. Lindsay's career and oeuvre have been thoroughly and effectively examined by Carol Edington and it is not necessary to rehearse her findings here.[65] However, it is important to stress the extent to which Lindsay's pre-1542 output is grounded in his experience as a courtier and confidante of the king. It has been suggested that Lindsay wrote *Gyre Carling* to entertain the young James V but this is difficult to establish with any certainty.[66] However, Lindsay's first acknowledged surviving work, *The Dreme of Schir David Lyndesay of the Mount, Familiar Servitour to our Soverane Lord Kyng James the Fyft* (c.1526), is 'topped and tailed' by direct appeals to the young monarch, *The Epistil* and *The Exhortatioun to the Kyngis Grace*, in which the poet makes a conventional examination of the qualities necessary for good kingship and exhorts James V to cultivate them. In between are *The ProlOug* and *The Complaynt of the Comoun Weill of Scotland* in which the allegorical figures of 'Dame Rememberance' and 'John the Commonweal' consider the plight of Scotland under the misrule of the minority and look forward to the reign of 'ane gude auld prudent kyng.' All of Lindsay's next seven poems dating from c.1530 to c.1542 are explicitly set at court and discuss the lives and concerns of courtiers. *The Complaynt of Schir David Lindsay* (c.1530) is a combination of two traditional genres: the begging poem, appealing for preferment or reward for loyal service, and the advice-to-princes poem, in which Lindsay relates how he personally, and the realm generally, suffered under the immoral and irresponsible minority regimes and seeks better government from the new king. *The Testament and Complaynt of our Soverane Lordis Papyngo* (c.1530) is also an advice-to-princes poem combined with a morality tale of how 'pride goeth before a fall' and a beast-fable satirising the avarice and corruption of the clergy.[67] The 'papyngo' of the title is the king's pet parrot, who after a foolish and useless life of luxury and vanity is inspired on her deathbed to offer sage advice to others (not just the king, but also the courtiers). There is clear evidence that James V actually did possess a pet parrot,[68] but

---

65 Edington, *Court and Culture*.

66 J. E. H. Williams, 'James V, David Lyndsay, and the Bannatyne Manuscript Poem of the *Gyre Carling*', *Studies in Scottish Literature*, xxvi (1991), 164–71.

67 Lindsay, *Works*, i, 3–38, 39–53, 55–90.

68 In April 1537 captain Lundy purchased one for the king and in 1538 Thomas Kells was paid as the keeper of the king's parrots: *TA*, vii, 22; vi, 390, 429. The dating of these entries might suggest that the poem was written slightly later than is generally thought.

Lindsay may also have had in mind two earlier courtly poems which utilised the same device: the *Première epistre de l'amant vert* of Jean Lemaire de Belges (the court poet and historiographer to Margaret of Austria at Mechlin) and *Speke Parott* (1521) of John Skelton.[69]

The Complaint and Publict Confessioun of the Kingis Auld Hound, callit Bagsche is very similar to *Papyngo* in that it is another beast-fable offering moral advice to the king and court. This time the speaker is the king's pet dog who discourses upon the vices indulged in by many influential courtiers and the fickleness of favour and fortune. Again, Lindsay was using the names of real pets, known to have been owned by the king, for both Bagsche and Bawte (the young dog to whom he addresses his advice) appear in the records.[70] *The Answer quhilk Schir David Lindesay maid to the Kingis Flyting*, as we have seen, was Lindsay's response to a poetic challenge from the king himself. The flyting genre was a popular one in middle-Scots verse and involved a verbal duel between two competitors, fought with the weapons of poetical and rhetorical invective. Since the literary gauntlet had been thrown down by the king, Lindsay had to be somewhat circumspect in his response; nevertheless he made a stinging attack upon James's sexual promiscuity and expressed the wish that the eagerly-anticipated French wife would curb his excesses. *The Deploratioun of the Deith of Quene Magdalene* (1537) is a poem commemorating this first French wife, in which Lindsay describes in detail the joyful preparations made by the town of Edinburgh to welcome their new queen and how all was turned to sorrow upon her sudden and early death. *The Iusting betuix James Watsoun and Jhone Barbour, servitouris to King James the Fyft* (1538–42) is a comic poem describing a parody of a chivalric tournament in which the combatants are not accomplished knights but rather humble, clumsy and cowardly household servants. *Ane Suplication Directit frome Schir David Lyndesay, Knycht, to the Kyngis Grace, in Contemptioun of Syde Tallis* (1537–42) is a comic petition to the king in which the poet requests

69 Picker, 'The Habsburg Courts', 229; McFarlane, *Literary History*, 41–3; Janet M. Smith, *The French Background to Middle Scots Literature* (Edinburgh, 1934), 135–6; John Skelton, *The Complete English Poems*, ed. John Scattergood (Harmondsworth, 1983), 230–46. It may be significant that Lindsay had made visits to the courts of the Netherlands and England, in 1531, 1532 and 1535: *James V Letters*, 191, 193–4, 204; *TA*, vi, 44, 46; *L&P Henry VIII*, ix, 151; Edington, *Court and Culture*, 32–3.

70 Lindsay, *Works*, i, 91–99; *TA*, vii, 96: payment to John Campbell 'for mending of the kingis dog callit Begsche'; Murray, 'Accounts of King's Pursemaster', 40: payment to a smith of Stirling for a chain for a dog called Bawte.

the proscription of fashionably over-long ladies' gowns, which he presents ironically as a source of great wickedness within the realm.[71]

These poems are the only surviving examples of Lindsay's work from the reign of James V but two other pieces of his are noted in contemporary sources. One was a collaborative effort between him, Sir Adam Otterburn (the king's advocate) and Sir James Foulis (the clerk register) to produce a suitably dignified oration to welcome Queen Mary of Guise on her entry into Edinburgh in July 1538, and the other was a court entertainment or interlude, which seems to have been a prototype of his play *Ane Satyre of the Thrie Estaitis* (1552), staged at the palace of Linlithgow on twelfth night 1540, in the presence of the king, queen and court dignitaries. We know of the Edinburgh oration only from a brief entry in the *Burgh Records*, but the Linlithgow entertainment was described in some detail in an English espionage report because it was thought to indicate the king's willingness to respond to Henry VIII's demands that the Scottish church should be reformed in line with English practice. Sir Thomas Bellenden (justice clerk), apparently told Sir William Eure at Berwick that James had specifically asked for the interlude to be staged because he was minded to curb the power of his prelates and that at the end of the performance 'the king of Scotts dide call upon the busshope of Glascoe being chancelour and diverse other busshops exorting thaym to reform thair facions and maners of lyving, saying that oneles thay soe did he wold sende sex of the proudeste of thaym unto his uncle of England and as thoes were ordoured soe he wold ordour all the reste that wolde not a mende.'[72] However, such hopes proved to be ill-founded, for James well understood the distinction between enjoying in private some ribald anti-clerical humour and publicly throwing himself into the arms of his heretic uncle. Indeed, it is possible that Bellenden was engaged in a campaign of disinformation to keep Henry VIII at bay.

It is worth noting that in writing *Ane Satyre* and, to a lesser extent, the Linlithgow interlude, Lindsay seems to have been influenced by the work of John Skelton for a second time. There are many parallels between Skelton's *Magnyfycence* (written in 1519 but published in 1532) and the first part of *Ane Satyre*. Both plays depict a young and impressionable king ('Magnyfycence' in Skelton, 'Rex Humanitas' in

71 Lindsay, *Works*, i, 101–04, 105–12, 113–16, 117–22. See also chapters 1 and 6.

72 *Edin. Recs.*, ii, 91; *L&P Henry VIII*, xv, 114; Lindsay, *Works*, ii, 1–6; R. J. Lyall, 'The Linlithgow Interlude of 1540' in *Actes du 2e. Colloque de Langue et du Littérature Ecossaises*, ed. J.-J. Blanchot & C. Graf (Strasbourg, 1978), 409–21. See also Burns, *True Law of Kingship*, 98–112.

Lindsay) swayed by the persuasive tongues of allegorised vices into a life of luxury and profligacy, which results in the neglect of good government. Justice is eventually restored by the intervention of virtues offering good counsel, and reforms which benefit the whole realm are ultimately instituted. The 1540 interlude does not follow quite the same pattern but even here the king is influenced by 'Placebo,' 'Pikthanke' and 'Flaterye,' (who bear some resemblance to Skelton's 'Fansy,' 'Foly,' 'Crafty Conveyaunce,' and others) and is rescued by 'Experience' brandishing a vernacular New Testament (who is not unrelated to Skelton's 'Good Hope,' 'Perseveraunce' and 'Redresse').[73] In dispensing such strong medicine to James V, it might be imagined that Lindsay was rashly provoking the royal wrath, but some comments by Greg Walker on the Skelton play may make the position clearer. He suggests that within the enclosed world of the royal or noble court, a household retainer had a certain licence, even a duty, to speak his mind. 'The notion of "good counsel" provided both the stimulus for offering harsh advice and a framework which partially neutralised its harmful implications,' he states, and proceeds to explain how a play which was overtly critical of royal policy was, by its very existence, imposing the role of virtuous prince upon the patron, by assuming that he would be willing to accept unpalatable advice. This view would have been thoroughly endorsed by Castiglione, as we have seen.[74]

Lindsay's association with Foulis and Otterburn in 1538 connects him with the neo-Latin culture of the humanists at the Scottish court, for both of these men were authors of Latin verses. Some verses by James Foulis of Colinton were published in Robert Galbraith's *Quadrapertium* (Paris, 1510), and whilst he was a student at the university of Orléans in 1512, Foulis also published a volume of poetry on Scottish themes dedicated to Alexander Stewart, archbishop of St. Andrews (who was a half-brother of James V and a former pupil of Erasmus in Siena): *Iacobi Follisii Edinburgensis Calamitose pestis Elega deploratio. Eiusdem ad divam Margaritam reginam Sapphicum carmen. De mercatorum*

---

73 Skelton, *Complete English Poems*, 140–214; Gregory Kratzmann, *Anglo-Scottish Literary Relations, 1430–1550* (Cambridge, 1980), 168, 196, 204–19; Greg Walker, *Plays of Persuasion: Drama and Politics at the Court of Henry VIII* (Cambridge, 1991), 61–89. Lindsay's *Satyre* was also possibly influenced by two French plays, Pierre Gingore's *Jeu du Prince des Sotz* (1511) and André de la Vigne's *La Mystère de Saint Martin* (1496): Kratzmann, *Anglo-Scottish Literary Relations*, 196; Smith, *French Background*, 124–37. See also A. A. MacDonald, 'Anglo-Scottish Literary Relations: Problems and Possibilities,' *Studies in Scottish Literature*, xxvi (1991), 172–84.

74 Walker, *Plays of Persuasion*, 58; Castiglione, *Courtier*, 284–5.

facilitate aesclepiadeum item et alia quedam carmina. In the same year he was elected procurator of the Scottish nation at the university of Orléans and he inserted his *Carmen elegum* into its *Register*.[75] In 1516 Foulis returned from France to Scotland and set himself up as a lawyer in Edinburgh; from 1529 he was employed as an auditor of some of the royal accounts; in 1530 he was acting king's advocate in the absence of Otterburn and in March 1532 he was appointed clerk of the rolls, register and council.[76] His only known work to address the king directly was the *Strena ad Jacobum V. Scotorum Regem de Suscepto Regni Regimine*, which was probably printed in Edinburgh by Thomas Davidson c.1528. The poem celebrates the king's assumption of authority and predicts the dawning of a new golden age for Scotland in Ovidian terms. Fradenburg speculates that his motive may have been to stress the loyalty of himself personally and the town of Edinburgh corporately to the new regime, because both had co-operated with the minority regime of the earl of Angus.[77] His Edinburgh associate, Sir Adam Otterburn of Oldham and Redhall, was also suspected of Douglas sympathies, was warded for a year from September 1538 and only released on payment of a £2,000 fine. However, before this he had served for fourteen years as king's advocate and had also been a provost of Edinburgh, lord of session, royal councillor and ambassador to England. None of his poetry survives but it was praised by George Buchanan, who may be considered a competent judge.[78] Foulis and Otterburn not only collaborated on the oration for Mary of Guise's Edinburgh entry but also worked together with Adam Mure on *Laudes Gulielmi Elphinstoni*, which Durkan considers to be an outstanding example of Renaissance Latin.[79]

The Latin culture of the Scottish court was given a boost with the

---

75 J. Ijsewijn and D. F. Thomson, 'The Latin Poems of Jacobus Follisius or James Foullis of Edinburgh', *Humanistica Lovaniensia*, xxiv (1975), 102–32, 133–4, 134–5; Durkan, 'Beginnings of Humanism', 8; MacQueen, 'Scottish Latin Poetry', in Jack (ed.), *History of Scottish Literature*, i, 214; John Kirkpatrick (ed.), 'The Scottish Nation in the University of Orléans, 1336–1538', in *SHS Misc.*, ii (1904), 82, 97.

76 *MW*, i, 8; *ADCP*, 335, 338; *RSS*, ii, 1189; L. O. Fradenburg, *City, Marriage, Tournament: Arts of Rule in Late Medieval Scotland* (Wisconsin, 1991), 47–64. See also Durkan and Ross, *Early Scottish Libraries*, 99–100.

77 *Bann. Club Misc.*, ii, (1836), 3–8; Ijsewijn and Thomson, 'Latin Poems', 135–7; Fradenburg, *City, Marriage, Tournament*, 57–64.

78 See the Introduction. *ADCP*, 479–80; Inglis, *Sir Adam Otterburn*; McFarlane, *Buchanan*, 50.

79 J. Durkan, 'Adam Mure's "Laudes Gulielmi Elphinstoni,"' and 'Adam Mure: a biography', *Humanistica Lovaniensia*, xviii (1979), 199–231, 232–3.

residence there of Giovanni Ferrerio (1502–1579) between 1528 and 1531. Ferrerio was a Piedmontese scholar who had met Robert Reid, abbot of Kinloss, at the university of Paris and been persuaded by him to spend some years living and working in Scotland. He spent most of his time at the abbey of Kinloss (1531–37 and 1540–45), teaching the monks and expanding the library, but whilst at the royal court he established friendships with Sir Walter Lindsay, Sir John Campbell of Lundy, Sir Thomas Scot of Pitgormo, Laurence Telfer and Foulis of Colinton. In 1531 he wrote *De vera cometae significatione* for James V, to persuade him that his interest in astrology was superstitious and irrational and that he should put all his trust in God. Ferrerio had a long and distinguished academic career after he left Scotland, but his sojourn there obviously had quite an impact upon him and he later undertook a continuation of Boece's *Scotorum Historia* (Lausanne, 1574). He was an admirer of Jacques Lefèvre d'Etaples and a humanist in the Erasmian mould, which was reflected in the curriculum he devised for Kinloss. Before he left he wrote a history of the abbey and a life of Thomas Crystal, Reid's predecessor as abbot.[80]

The most distinguished Scottish neo-Latinist of the day was George Buchanan (1506–82) and, although most of his output was produced after the death of James V, he was briefly a member of the court circle and wrote poetry for the king. He had studied under John Major at the universities of St. Andrews and Paris in the 1520s, had served as a regent at the college of Sainte Barbe between 1528 and 1531 and was employed as tutor to Gilbert Kennedy, earl of Cassillis between 1531 and 1535. At this period in his development he seems to have come under the influence of Lefèvre d'Etaples, Guillaume Budé and Erasmus: his biographer describes him as 'a vanguard humanist susceptible to evangelical currents' but he had so far published only translations of Linacre's *Rudimenta* and of Vives' *De ratione studii puerilis*.[81] In 1535 he returned to Scotland in the train of his noble pupil and found employment as the tutor of one of the king's illegitimate sons, Lord James

80 Durkan, 'The Beginnings of Humanism', 14–16; Durkan, 'Giovanni Ferrerio, Humanist: His Influence in Sixteenth-Century Scotland', in K. Robbins (ed.), *Studies in Church History*, xvii (Oxford, 1981), 181–94; Durkan, 'Education: The Laying of the Foundations', in MacQueen (ed.), *Humanism*, 125–6, 153; Ferrerii, *Historia Abbatum de Kynlos* (Bannatyne Club, 1839).

81 McFarlane, *Buchanan*, 22–47; J. Durkan, S. Rawles and N. Thorpe, *George Buchanan (1506–1582) Renaissance Scholar* (Exhibition Catalogue, Glasgow University Library, 1982); J. Durkan, *Bibliography of George Buchanan* (Glasgow, 1994), p. ix-xiii; Durkan, 'George Buchanan: New Light on the Poems', *The Bibliothek*, x (1990), 1–9.

9. James V's presence chamber, Stirling Castle, a conjectural restoration. (Courtesy of the Royal Commission on the Ancient and Historical Monuments of Scotland)

10. Two of the Stirling Heads. Above: Hercules; below; Jester. The roundels decorated the ceiling of James V's presence chamber at Stirling. (Courtesy of Historic Scotland)

11. Blackness Castle, south tower, c.1540. The wide-mouthed gun ports were designed to accommodate the latest artillery. (Courtesy of Historic Scotland)

12. The royal arms from the title page of the printed edition of John Bellenden's translation of Hector Boece's *History of Scotland* (c.1540). This stressed that the book was produced under royal patronage. (Courtesy of the trustees of the National Museum of Scotland)

13. A dirge for a king of Scots. From the Book of Hours of James IV and Margaret Tudor. (Courtesy of the National Library of Austria, Vienna)

14. Falkland Palace, the chapel, looking west. The panelled ceiling and spindle-screen were made for James V but the painted decoration dates from the reign of Charles I. (Courtesy of the National Trust of Scotland.)

15. Falkland Palace, the chapel, looking east. (Courtesy of the National Trust for Scotland)

16. Above: a gold bonnet piece of 1539 with a portrait of James V. Below: a billon bawbee of 1538 showing the arched, imperial crown. (Courtesy of the trustees of the National Museums of Scotland)

Stewart, between 1536 and 1539.[82] In 1535 he wrote a poem, the *Somnium*, which was partially a translation of the first four stanzas of William Dunbar's *The Dreme*, but which then developed a life of its own and became a satirical attack on the order of St. Francis. This was followed by his *Franciscanus*, written at the behest of the king,[83] which is a lengthier and even more savage consideration of the same theme, and the *Pallinodiae* (both c.1536/7) which purport to be recantations and apologies but actually reinforce the earlier criticisms.[84] None of these poems was published before 1566 and they were almost certainly subject to later revision, so it is not possible to be sure how much of the invective actually dates from the reign of James V. However, the poems as they were written in the 1530s (they probably circulated in manuscript) seem to have been sufficiently strident to attract the enmity of the Scottish clergy. Since it was clearly possible for other poets, such as Lindsay, to write in an anti-clerical vein without being pursued on a charge of heresy and driven into exile (as happened to Buchanan in 1539), perhaps the most significant enemy he made during his brief residence at the Scottish court was not a friar but the king's favourite mistress, Margaret Erskine. James V had three natural sons named James and Buchanan seems to have been engaged to educate the eldest, who was produced by Elizabeth Shaw of Sauchie in 1529. Margaret Erskine's son was the second Lord James (born 1531) and she may have been jealous of the special provision made for another woman's child. In any event, Buchanan himself identifies her as one of the people behind his persecution, and one of the men appointed to examine him was Sir Thomas Erskine of Brechin, the king's secretary and possibly a kinsman of the Lady Margaret.[85] Buchanan managed to escape his captivity, apparently with the connivance of the king, and did not return to Scotland until after the Reformation, when he was to become classical tutor to Mary, queen of Scots and then her son, King James VI, rather than to a royal bastard.

---

82 McFarlance, *Buchanan*, 48–51; *TA*, vi, 289, 353, 430; vii, 59; *RSS*, ii, 384; *ER*, xvii, 169.

83 Buchanan tells us this himself (Buchanan, *History*, i, p. xii-xiii see also Moir Bryce, *The Scottish Greyfriars*, i, 111f.) but the king was, at least publicly, very supportive of the order: see chapter 3.

84 John MacQueen, 'Scottish Latin Poetry', in Jack (ed.), *History of Scottish Literature*, i, 214–5. MacQueen identifies the classical influences on Buchanan's style as Catullus and Horace (*Somnium*), Juvenal (*Franciscanus*) and Ovid (*Pallinodiae*). Buchanan may also have been inspired by Erasmus: Durkan, 'Beginnings of Humanism', 9–10.

85 Buchanan, *History*, i, p. xii, pp. 4–8; McFarlane, *Buchanan*, 67.

The doctrinal disputes of the Renaissance humanists had already impinged on the court of James V even before Buchanan became the object of a heresy enquiry. The debate was opened by Alexander Allan, known as Alesius (1500–1565). He had been an Augustinian canon of St. Andrews and an admirer of Patrick Hamilton, who fled to Germany after the latter's execution and became a follower of Melanchthon. In 1533 he published his *Epistola contra Decretum quoddam Episcoporum in Scotia*, which attacked the Scottish proscription of evangelical texts (in particular, the vernacular Bible) and wrote to James V on the same subject. The gauntlet was taken up by John Dobneck, known as Cochlaeus, a Catholic controversialist and friend of Erasmus. He replied with *Pro Scotiae Regno Apologia Iohannis Cochlaei Adversus Personatum Alexandrum Alesuim Scotum*, which he wished to dedicate to James V. Since the king of Scots had never had any previous contact with him, Cochlaeus sought recommendations from his friend, Erasmus, and his sovereign, Ferdinand, king of the Romans. They both wrote to James on behalf of Cochlaeus in December 1533 and January 1534 and the king replied a few months later thanking them for their interest and graciously accepting the book. Erasmus's letter is of interest in that he presumes upon his Scottish royal connections, established by his former role as tutor to the king's half-brothers (the late Alexander Stewart, archbishop of St. Andrews, and James Stewart, earl of Moray), in order to urge Cochlaeus's case and he obviously remembers his erstwhile pupils with some affection.[86]

As with other aspects of Scottish cultural development, the literary life of the court was considerably affected by James V's visit to France in 1536–37. James may well have taken his presentation copy of Davidson's edition of Bellenden's translation of Boece with him, because the binding is apparently of Parisian workmanship.[87] If this was so, it could also have been the source for a French description of Scotland, list of its kings and brief history which was written in the final months of 1536 for Princess Madeleine, to inform her about her new realm. The book, *Summaire de l'origine description & mervilles Descosse. Avec une petite cronique des roys du dict pays jusques a ce temps*, was clearly based upon Boece and Bellenden's work and was written by Jean Démontiers, a learned gentleman in the household of Francis I, who had possibly

---

86 *James V Letters*, 241, 252, 271; *TA*, vi, 236; R. J. Lyall, 'The Literature of Lowland Scotland, 1350–1700', in Paul H. Scott (ed.) *Scotland: A Concise Cultural History* (Edinburgh, 1993), 89; Durkan, 'Beginnings of Humanism', 10.

87 D. W. Doughty, 'Renaissance books, bindings and owners in St. Andrews and elsewhere: the humanists', *The Bibliothek*, vii (1974–5), 119.

served the duke of Albany. It was not printed until the spring of 1538, by which time Madeleine was already dead, so the book was extended to include a description of her marriage, voyage and death and was dedicated to the dauphine, Catherine de Medici. The printed edition also included four Latin epitaphs for the dead queen; one was anonymous (perhaps by Démontiers himself) and the other three were by Etienne Dolet, Jean Visagier and Nicolas Desfrenes.[88] The inclusion of Dolet's name on the list may indicate that there was possibly some substance to Buchanan's view that Madeleine was inclined to evangelicalism, since Dolet's advanced opinions brought him under suspicion of heresy in the late 1530s and he was eventually burned at the stake in 1546. Desfrenes, a Louvain theologian and follower of Lefèvre d'Etaples, was also in the evangelical camp. Visagier produced two other neo-Latin poems to commemorate Madeleine's death, which were also published in Paris in 1538.[89] French verses commemorating the late queen were penned by Giles Corrozet (*Vers funèbres sur la mort de très noble dame madame Magdalaine de France, Roynne d'Escosse*) and Pierre Ronsard, who was in her train, would later write about her death and James's grief in *Le Tombeau de Marguerite de France, Duchesse de Savoye*.[90] It may be significant that the only surviving Scottish poem commemorating the death of Queen Madeleine, Lindsay's *Deploratioun*, was written in a French genre and it was certainly the case that the French *chanson*-form became very popular with Scottish poets.[91] More joyful poetry had been written earlier at the French court to celebrate the wedding of James and Madeleine in January 1537: Clément Marot offered a *Chant nuptial du Roy d'Escoce & de Madame Magdelene Premiere Fille de France* and Jean Leblond, seigneur de Branville, produced a broadsheet edition of his *Nuptiaulx Virelayz du mariage du roy Descoce: et de madame magdaleine premiere fille de France*. Two anonymous poems were also presented to the happy couple on the morning after their

88 A. H. Millar, 'Scotland described for Queen Magdalene: A Curious Volume', *SHR*, i (1903–4), 27–38; Bentley-Cranch and Marshall, 'Iconography and Literature', 282.

89 Buchanan, *History*, i, p. xii; ibid., ii, p. 256; Knecht, *Warrior and Patron*, 467, 508, 510; McFarlane, *Literary History*, 151–2; Henri Weber, 'Etienne Dolet: l'énigme d'une pensée et le sens d'un combat', in Pauline M. Smith & I. D. McFarlane (eds.), *Literature and the Arts in the Reign of Francis I* (Lexington, 1985), 237–48; Millar, 'Scotland described', 37; Bentley-Cranch and Marshall, 'Iconography and Literature', 282.

90 *Cronique du Roy*, 217–20; Pierre Ronsard, *Oeuvres complètes*, ed. G. Cohen (20 vols., Paris, 1950), ii, 480–91. See also McFarlane, *Literary History*, 104–15.

91 Lindsay, *Works*, i, 105–12. See chapter 3.

wedding: *Epithalame ou vers nuptiaulz pour les nopces du serenissime roy d'Escosse et Madame Magdaleine de France fille aisnee du Roy son espouse* and *Elegie nuptiale presentee a Madame Magdaleine, premiere fille de France, le lendemain de ces nopces et mariage celebre avec le Roy d'Escoce.*[92] All of these poets were lavish in their praise of the royal couple and several classical allusions were drawn, such as the comparison of Madeleine with Helen of Troy, and of James with the sun-god, Phoebus.[93]

At the English court there was a post of king's printer, which was held by Richard Pynson before his death in 1530 and by Thomas Berthelet thereafter. Likewise, Francis I appointed several specialist printers, such as Robert Estienne, who was the king's printer of Latin, Hebrew and Greek texts from 1539.[94] James V had only one king's printer, Thomas Davidson of Edinburgh, who received his official appointment in August 1536 but had been working for the king since at least 1534–35 and possibly earlier. He seems to have been a native of Aberdeen and may have learned his trade in Louvain in the 1520s.[95] There does not seem to have been any obvious connection or continuity between Davidson's press, set up in Edinburgh in the mid-1520s, and the earlier venture of Chepman and Millar (1507–10), although in March 1542 the king granted him the tenancy of the tavern and booth previously held by Walter Chepman. Davidson does not appear to have done very much to foster a native Scottish printing trade: he bought type and woodcuts from the Netherlands, paper from France, and hired labour from both countries.[96] Scottish printers clearly found it very difficult to compete with the more skilful, numerous and economical editions from the continental presses but royal patronage

92 Clément Marot, *Oeuvres complètes*, ed. C. A. Mayer (6 vols, London, 1958–80), iii, 314–18; Bentley-Cranch and Marshall, 'Iconography and Literature', 280–1. See also McFarlane, *Literary History*, 297–327. Extracts from several of these poems are printed in Lindsay, *Works*, iii, 127–30.

93 E.g. 'De beaulté d'homme avoit plus grande part/ Que le Troyen qui fut espris d'Helene' (Marot, *Chant Nuptial*, lines 19–20) and 'Ton blond Phebus' (*Elegie nuptiale*, line 28).

94 H. G. Aldis, J. Carter and B. Crutchley, *The Printed Book* (Cambridge, 1951), 27–8, 34.

95 *RSS*, ii, 2141, 4275; *ER*, xvi, 398; Habakkuk Bisset, *Rolment of Courtis (1626)*, ed. Sir Philip J. Hamilton-Grierson (3 vols, STS, 1920, 1922, 1926), i, 71–2 describes him as 'ane northland man borne on the wattirsyde of die', and suggests that he was designated king's printer as early as 1532. See also Durkan, 'Cultural Background', 275, 277.

96 *RSS*, ii, 4521; *RMS*, iii, 2612; P. B. Watry, 'Sixteenth-Century Printing Types and Ornaments of Scotland with an Introductory Survey of the Scottish Book Trade' (University of Oxford, DPhil thesis, 1993), 20.

at least ensured the survival of the Davidson press during the lifetime of the king. Davidson's known output consists of only Foulis's *Strena* (c.1528), Douglas's *Palice of Honour* (1530s), Bellenden's Boece (c.1536) and *The New Actis and Constitutions of Parliament maid be the Rycht Excellent Prince James the Fift Kyng of Scottis*, for which he received a commission in December 1541. In addition, he may have printed some lost editions of Lindsay's poetry[97] and a little tract called *The Trompet of Honour* (c.1537), the title page of which apparently accorded James V the style Defender of the Christian Faith. The book itself has not survived but its existence was noted in an undated letter from an English minister to a Scottish prelate (probably Thomas Cromwell to David Beaton in June or July of 1537), which indicated how angry Henry VIII was with this usurpation by his nephew of the title he considered to be his alone.[98] In his patronage of Davidson, James V seems to have had in mind the same reasons of state which motivated his father's establishment of the Chepman and Millar press in 1507 (Bishop Elphinstone was also very influential): that is, the creation of a native print shop, under crown control, which would produce editions of the laws, liturgy and the 'official' history of Scotland.[99]

James IV is also praised frequently for his enlightened patronage of Scottish educational developments such as the new university of Aberdeen, founded in 1495, or the education act of 1496, which required all property holders to ensure that their heirs were given at least the basic rudiments of literacy and numeracy, as well as a familiarity with the laws of the realm. However, benign and gracious though the king's role may have been in such projects, it is clear that the real initiative (as with the printing press) was taken by Bishop Elphinstone of Aberdeen.[100] This being the case, there seems little reason to deny James V the same aura of sanctity, since new educational initiatives, driven by ecclesiastics, were taken in his reign as well. We

---

97 *RSS*, ii, 4335. Watry, 'Printing Types and Ornaments', 19–20.

98 *L&P Henry VIII*, xvi, 1301; John Durkan, 'The Trompet of Honour (Edinburgh? 1537)', *The Bibliothek*, xi (1982), 1–2. Durkan has linked the use of the title to the papal gift of the blessed cap and sword, bestowed upon James V in February of that year: see chapter 6.

99 The royal patent of 15 Sept. 1507 authorised Chepman and Millar 'for imprenting within our realme of the bukis of our lawis, actis of parliament, croniclis, mess bukis and potuus efter the use of our realme . . . and al utheris bukis that sal be sene necessare': *RSS*, i, 1546.

100 Macdougall, *James IV*, 114–5, 174–5, 218, 284–5; L. J. MacFarlane, *William Elphinstone and the Kingdom of Scotland, 1431–1514* (Aberdeen, 1995), 236–7, 245, 290–402.

have already seen how Robert Reid recruited Giovanni Ferrerio to establish a humanist academy at the abbey of Kinloss and another new project was the foundation of St. Mary's College by the two Beaton archbishops at the university of St. Andrews. James Beaton seems to have been toying with the idea of a new college during the 1520s and 1530s, spurred on by the schemes of Archibald Hay, who published *Ad Reverendissimum in Christo patrem D. Iacobum Betoun, pro Collegii erectione* in Paris in 1538.[101] Hay, like David Beaton, was a nephew of Archbishop James and he had made his mark teaching at the college of Montaigu in the university of Paris. His plan for the new foundation was to include the teaching of Latin, Greek, Hebrew and, if possible, Chaldaic as well as the more usual curriculum. He also hoped to establish an extensive library and printing press. When David Beaton succeeded his uncle as primate in 1538, he went ahead with the scheme, and Hay eventually moved from Paris in 1545 to become the first principal of the new college, just as the political fabric of Scotland was rent by the 'Rough Wooing.' In May 1546 David Beaton was murdered at St. Andrews by his political and religious enemies and in September 1547 Hay died at the battle of Pinkie. However, St. Mary's College survived this inauspicious start and was reconstituted by Archbishop John Hamilton in the 1550s. Likewise, the ghost of the intellectual patronage of the court of James V can be detected in the establishment of three royal lecturers (in Law, Greek, and Latin and Philosophy) in Edinburgh in the 1550s. The inspiration probably came from Francis I's *lecteurs royaux* of 1530 and the initiative was driven by Robert Reid (by that time promoted from Kinloss to the see of Orkney) and patronised by Mary of Guise. This project also served as a basis for the 'Toun College' of Edinburgh, opened in 1583 and partly funded from Reid's legacy, which later developed into the University of Edinburgh.[102]

---

101 John Durkan, 'Education: The Laying of Fresh Foundations', in MacQueen (ed.), *Humanism*, 154–55; James K. Cameron, 'Humanism and Religious Life', in ibid., 165–67; Durkan, 'Beginnings of Humanism', 14; J. K. Cameron, 'A Trilingual College for Scotland: The Founding of St Mary's College', in D. W. D. Shaw (ed.), *In Divers Manners: A St Mary's Miscellany* (St Andrews, 1990), 29–42. See also Euan Cameron, 'Archibald Hay's *Elegantiae*: Writings of a Scots Humanist at the College de Montaigu in the Time of Budé and Beza', in J.-C. Margolin (ed.) *Acta Conventus Neo-Latini Turonensis* (Paris, 1980), 277–301. I am grateful to Dr. Roger Mason for drawing my attention to the last two articles.

102 John Durkan, 'The Royal Lectureships under Mary of Lorraine', *SHR*, lxii (1983), 73–8; D. B. Horn, 'The Origins of the University of Edinburgh', *University of Edinburgh Journal*, xxii (1966), 213–25, 297–312; M. Lynch, 'The Origins of Edinburgh's "Toun College": a Revision Article', *IR*, xxxiii (1982), 3–14.

The early death of the king in December 1542 was undoubtedly a blow to the literary and scholarly culture which had evolved at the royal court, and some creative momentum was almost certainly lost in the ensuing minority. There is no indication of any significant cultural activity within the circle of the Regent Arran, who does not seem to have had much interest in such matters, and the production of poetry and prose by many of the figures discussed above seems to have ceased after 1542. None of Thomas Davidson's editions can be dated later than 1541; no poems by John Bellenden or William Stewart can be traced to Mary's minority; Giovanni Ferrerio departed from his haven at Kinloss in 1545 to return to work in France; and George Buchanan remained in exile on the continent until after the Reformation. However, talent and creativity cannot just be turned off like a tap, and the 1540s and 1550s is a period of Scottish cultural history which has received little attention so far. Further research into this area may well yield interesting results and two areas which probably merit closer inspection would be the francophile court which coalesced around Mary of Guise at Stirling Castle and the patronage wielded by some of the Scottish burghs of the period. Indeed, Theo van Heijnsbergen has identified the circle around the dowager queen as an important focus for the poetic talents of the young Alexander Scott (who also spent some time in France during the 1540s);[103] whilst the burgh of Cupar was the scene of the first full-scale performance of Sir David Lindsay's *Satyre* in 1552. Certainly, Lindsay retreated from the royal court after the death of James V to settle on his Fifeshire estates and his later poems, whilst still concerned with the issues of monarchy and high politics have, according to Carol Edington, a broad socio-political vision concerned with the community of the realm and the commonweal, which he developed out of his more courtly works of the 1530s.[104]

As was the case with other monarchs of the period, James V both as a minor and an adult attracted the attention of writers and scholars who wished to offer him advice and encouragement, much of which was framed in the traditions of the medieval *speculum principis* genre. The literary output of the minority stressed the vulnerability and confusion

103 van Heijnsbergen, 'The Scottish Chapel Royal', 307–08; van Heijnsbergen, 'Interaction', 222–23. See also MacQueen (ed.), *Ballattis of Luve*, pp xxxvi–lix; MacQueen, 'The Biography of Alexander Scot and the Authorship of *Lo, quhat it is to lufe*', in J. Derrick McClure (ed.), *Scotland and the Lowland Tongue: Studies in the Language and Literature of Lowland Scotland in honour of David D. Murison* (Aberdeen, 1983), 52–8; Shire, *Song, Dance and Poetry*, 49–55.

104 Edington, *Court and Culture*, 115–41.

of the realm in the absence of a strong adult male ruler and called upon the king to be a vigorous, assertive and just monarch. If writers such as Bellenden, Stewart and Lindsay were expressing views that were widely held by others within the Scottish realm (which admittedly is a moot point, since they were all courtiers), it would appear that far from being wary of a 'predatory' Stewart king, there was some longing for firm leadership – a desire that the *dominus* should dominate. As we have already seen, even if he disappointed the moralists with his sexual promiscuity, James V seems to have made every effort to live up to the political ideals of Renaissance kingship. As the adult reign progressed he sought to enforce his authority and to enhance his prestige, and the writers of this period, whilst engaging in theological and moral debates, also celebrate the glories of a resurgent monarchy. Foulis's *Strena* marks James's assumption of regal powers; Lindsay's *Deploratioun* is more a celebration of the national and personal triumph of James V's first marriage than a lament for a dead queen; and the French *chansons* and *élégies* of 1537 present the king as a classical or chivalric hero. James's revival of a Scottish press also had a clear political purpose, since Davidson succeeded (where Chepman and Millar had failed) in issuing the first printed edition of the acts of the Scottish parliament, a clear signal that the king intended his laws to be observed. James even seems to have been open to the constructive criticism and wise counsel offered by men such as Boece and Lindsay. Yet as his diplomacy demonstrates, he was clearly more attracted to his image as a valiant defender of the Scottish nation within the context of the 'auld alliance', than to Major's vision of Anglo-Scottish union. Cameron considered the adult James V to be capable of commanding the loyalty and co-operation of the majority of his nobles in his attempt to enforce and extend royal authority,[105] and judging by the surviving literary output of the court, the king was also able to rely on the services of writers and scholars in Latin, Scots and French to support these aims.

---

105 Cameron, *James V*, 328–35.

FIVE

Strength and Status:
Technological Developments

The possession of a fleet of ships armed with the latest artillery was a matter of strategic importance and also of some prestige to sixteenth-century monarchs. For instance, Henry VII of England began to develop a navy in the latter years of his reign and this concern was taken up enthusiastically by his son who built new dockyards at Deptford and Woolwich, expanded the facilities at Portsmouth and appointed a council 'for marine causes' to administer the commissioning and maintenance of the royal ships. By 1520 he possessed a standing navy of about thirty ships and by the end of his reign this number had increased to seventy.[1] James IV was also obsessed with developing a royal navy and, with French financial and technical aid, he had built up a fleet of about a dozen ships by 1513 and created a modern shipyard at Newhaven, not far from Leith. The pride of Scotland was the *Great Michael*, a ship of a thousand tons launched at Newhaven in October 1511. This was a vessel larger than those at the command of the king of England and Henry's response was to commission the equally large *Henry Grâce à Dieu*, which was laid down in December 1512 and launched in June 1514. By then however, the *Great Michael* had been sold to the French king following the defeat at Flodden.[2] James IV's leading captains were Andrew Wood of Largo and Andrew Barton of Leith, and kinsmen of both these men were prominent in the service of James V who resurrected his father's naval ambitions in the latter part of his adult reign.[3]

It is not clear what ships, if any, were owned by the Scottish crown in

---

1 David Loades, *The Tudor Navy: An Administrative, Political and Military History* (Aldershot, 1992), 2–5, 72; David Loades, 'Henry VIII: the Real Founder of the Royal Navy?' in Starkey (ed.), *European Court*, 172. See also E. H. Jenkins, *A History of the French Navy from its Beginnings to the Present Day* (London, 1973), 10–11.

2 Norman Macdougall, '"The greatest scheip that ewer saillit in Ingland or France": James IV's "Great Michael"', in Macdougall (ed.), *Scotland and War, AD 79–1918* (Edinburgh, 1991), 36–60; Macdougall, *James IV*, 223–43; Loades, 'Henry VIII', 174; Loades, *Tudor Navy*, 65–6.

3 See W. Stanford Reid, *Skipper from Leith: The History of Robert Barton of Over Barnton* (Oxford, 1962) and Mowat, *The Port of Leith*, 83–98.

1528 and when James V was planning his pacification of the Western and Northern Isles in 1531 it is entirely possible that he was intending to use ships hired from his captains (Robert Wood, John Barton and George Wallace) alongside four boats from Anstruther and Crail which were pressed into service for a month. The Isles raid did not take place as it had originally been planned because the troublesome MacDonald chief, Alexander Johncanochson of Islay, submitted to the king at Stirling at the last minute but the expenses of ships, men, victuals and artillery listed in the accounts, and enigmatic references to 'the raid of Caithness' suggest that some sort of expedition was mounted at this time by the earl of Moray acting as lieutenant of the north.[4] The first definite mention of ships owned by the king occurs in 1533 when vessels were captured from the English during a period of hostility. In February 1533 Chapuys reported that Henry VIII had sent four ships to 'stop the trade' of the Scots[5] and in April 1533 messengers were being sent to all parts of the Scottish realm to order the strengthening of coastal defences.[6] At this point Hector Maclean of Duart seems to have raided Ireland and the Isle of Man and captured an English ship which he presented to James V. The king was in correspondence with him over this ship in July 1533 and in September and October he went into Argyll to take possession in person.[7] One of the king's captains, Robert Fogo, was also involved in the capture of an English ship at this time.[8] Neither the ship captured in the Isles nor that taken by Fogo are named in the 1533 accounts but the likelihood is that one was the *Mary Willoughby* and the other the *Lion*, since both appear in later records.[9] The ship taken in the Isles was given a thorough refit at Dumbarton between December 1533 and August 1534 under the supervision of her skipper, George Wallace, and in 1535 he sailed her to Dieppe and Bordeaux, perhaps to buy wines for the king.[10]

4 *TA*, v, 450–62; *ADCP*, 348, 358; Cameron, *James V*, 75, 229–32.
5 *L&P Henry VIII*, vi, 142. Chapuys was the Imperial ambassador to the court of Henry VIII.
6 *TA*, vi, 129–30.
7 SRO, Libri Domicilii et Emptorum, E.31/4, fos. 99v.-105v.; E.31/5, fos. 1r.-5v.; E.32/3, fos. 7r. & v.; *ER*, xvi, 90; *TA*, vi, 87, 136, 216; *RSS*, ii, 1560; *James V Letters*, 249.
8 *TA*, vi, 163–4; Reid, *Skipper from Leith*, 194–8.
9 For the *Mary Willoughby* and the *Lion* in English service see *L&P Henry VIII*, iii, II, 2014; Loades, *Tudor Navy*, 91, 142, 153, 228; M. Oppenheim, *A History of the Administration of the Royal Navy* (London, 1896), 50. See also Thomas, 'Renaissance Culture', 216 n.15.
10 *TA*, vi, 233–6, 262. Again the king's ship is unnamed in 1534–35 but in July 1537 George Wallace was skipper of the *Mary Willoughby*: ibid., vi, 330.

In 1536 the king made two major voyages and expanded his fleet of ships. Firstly, he set sail from Pittenweem on Sunday 23 July, sailed north to the Pentland Firth and back down the west coast landing at Whithorn on Friday 4 August.[11] The names of the ships used in this voyage are not recorded but the king seems to have been accompanied by the earl of Atholl, the earl of Rothes, Walter Lundy of that ilk, Robert Barton of Overbarnton, Andrew Wood of Largo and his brothers, John and Robert, all of whom were granted remission from legal actions against them whilst they were away.[12] The sources are very confused about the purposes of this trip and it may have been the case that the king deliberately shrouded it in a cloud of disinformation. The household book simply states that he was sailing to the Northern Isles (*versus boriales insulas*) but Queen Margaret had assured Henry VIII that James was coming to visit the English court and had been driven north by contrary winds.[13] However, Leslie, Pitscottie and Buchanan relate the story that James was intending to sail to France by a westerly route (to avoid the possibility of interception by the English) but, encountering stormy weather, took shelter in Whithorn. It is even suggested that the ships were turned back when the king was asleep, on the orders of Hamilton of Finnart, who thereafter fell from royal favour.[14] The chroniclers also assert that the king undertook this voyage without consulting his council and without making proper arrangements for the government of the realm in his absence, but the council records show that they knew of his departure from at least 27 July and that a council of regency was acting on 2 August.[15]

On Friday 1 September he set sail again from Kirkcaldy. This time France was definitely his destination and the proper arrangements for a council of regency were certainly made.[16] He landed at the Newhaven

11 SRO, Liber Emptorum, E.32/5, fos. 112r.-118v.
12 *RSS*, ii, 2108, 2113, 2114; *ADCP*, 455-6. It is also possible that James was accompanied on his voyage by the bishop of Aberdeen and the earl Marischal, both of whom were with him in Pittenweem just before he sailed and witnessed a charter: ibid., 458.
13 SRO, Liber Emptorum, E.32/5, fo. 112v.; Wood, *Letters*, ii, 278-80. See also Cameron, *James V*, 206.
14 Lesley, *History* (Bann. Club), 150; Pitscottie, *Historie* (STS), i, 355; Buchanan, *History*, ii, 311-14. For more on the Finnart story see Thomas, 'Renaissance Culture', 217 n.20 and *L&P Henry VIII*, xi, 916.
15 *ADCP*, 455, 458. The lords regent were named as the chancellor and the earls of Huntly, Argyll, Eglinton and Montrose.
16 SRO, Liber Emptorum, E.32/6 fo. 1r. The council of regency consisted of the chancellor, the archbishop of St. Andrews, Lord Maxwell and the earls of Huntly, Montrose and Eglinton: *RMS*, iii, 1618. Respites   *cont'd over/*

of Dieppe on 9 September and spent the next nine months as a guest of the French king, whose daughter he married on 1 January 1537. James must have made the outward voyage with several ships but only the *Mary Willoughby* is named in the accounts, whilst Pitscottie claims that the *Lion* went too.[17] However, payments are also recorded for the ships of Thomas Richardson, Patrick Barcar and John Lawson, but these vessels were probably hired by the king rather than owned by him.[18] Almost as soon as he had landed in France, James sent two men off to purchase a new ship for him, but since Francis I later decided to cover his guest's expenses the purchase became a gift. This acquisition was probably the *Moriset*, which was provided with some new fittings in October 1536 and set sail for Scotland on 15 November carrying powder, guns and some of the king's gentlemen. By March 1537 the *Moriset* was back in France and was one of the ships used to bring the king and queen home in May.[19] The French king also presented James with a second ship, the *Salamander*, which appears in the records from March 1537, when it was provided with a mast at Honfleur. There was a reward of twenty crowns paid to 'the maister tymmerman quhilk maid the Salamander' in May, which seems to suggest that the vessel was commissioned especially for the king of Scots, but since Francis had had no warning of James's visit, and the construction of a new ship often took a year or two at this period, this is unlikely.[20] The ship was presumably destined for James's fleet as it neared completion, having been originally intended for the French king (the salamander was his personal badge). When James and Madeleine returned to Scotland in May, their ships were escorted by two French galleys, *Perforce* and *Monsieur de Roy*, but these ships did not stay in Scotland.[21]

Ships were also prepared in May 1538 to sail to France to collect Mary of Guise, although the king himself did not travel on this occasion. The accounts specifically mention the *Salamander*, the *Moriset*, the *Mary*

cont'd from legal actions were granted to several men who accompanied the king: the earl of Argyll, James Gordon of Lochinver, David Beaton, Lord Fleming, the earl of Arran. Probably John Hamilton of Colmskeith and Thomas Doughtie (the hermit of Loretto) went too: *RSS*, ii, 2150, 2151, 2155, 2158, 2162, 2166, 2167, 2173, 2165, 2175.

17 *TA*, vi, 451–2, 462–5; Pitscottie, *Historie* (STS), i, 367. See also *L&P Henry VIII*, xi, 400, 631.

18 *TA*, vi, 453, 464–5; vii, 15, 22.

19 Ibid., vi, 451, 453, 454, 463, 466.

20 Ibid., vi, 463; vii, 24. The *Salamander*, along with another royal ship, the *Unicorn*, was captured by the English at Leith in 1544: Oppenheim, *Royal Navy*, 50.

21 *TA*, vii, 25.

Willoughby and 'the French challop' but others may have been hired from the two Leith captains who received payments at this time (John Barton and Robert Wood) and crewed by men summoned into service from across Scotland. Like Madeleine, Mary received an escort of French galleys (one was called the *Riall*) under the command of 'Captain Marmoling', and to reduce the risk of interception the English coast was reconnoitred by Archibald Pennecuik.[22]

By this time it is clear that the king was building his own ships in Scotland. In March two ships were sent to Lochaber to collect timber for building galleys, and from July Walter Howieson, with his two assistants, was employed as the 'master timberman' (i.e. wright) of the king's ships.[23] At the same time John Barton provided timber, labour, painted sails and other supplies for the king's 'row boit' and the *Moriset* was repaired.[24] It is interesting that James was building 'galleys' (or probably galleases) rather than sailing ships; perhaps he was inspired by his visit to the Western Isles in 1536, for galleys were the mainstay of Gaelic seafaring, or perhaps he was hoping to imitate the French Mediterranean fleet, which also relied on such vessels.[25] The English navy also contained galleys/galleases but not in any large number.[26] In January 1539 workmen were still constructing the king's new ships at Leith and by July the *Unicorn* was launched, armed with artillery, given sea trials in the Forth (with the *Mary Willoughby* in attendance), and sent to seek pirates off the east coast.[27] By August the 'litill new bark' was ready for launch and sea-trials (when she 'previt salage'). The ship, which was named the *Little Unicorn* to distinguish her from the *Great Unicorn*, was furnished with colourful banners, flags and pennants, richly carved chambers for the king and queen, and masts, sails and oars that were painted and gilded with arms and 'faces' (possibly grotesques).[28] The *Little Unicorn*'s maiden voyage (accompanied by the *Great Unicorn* and the *Mary Willoughby*) was a four day trip in which she took the king and queen on pilgrimage to the Isle of May and then

22 Ibid., vi, 390–1, 400–1, 406; vii, 59–60; viii, 157–62. Monsieur Marmoling had also escorted Madeleine in 1537: ibid., vii, 24.

23 Ibid., vi, 381; vii, 257.

24 Ibid., vi, 381, 421; vii, 257. The reference to sails being provided for a rowing boat suggests that it was a gallease rather than a galley. Galleys were driven by oars alone, whilst galleases had the option of using oars or sails.

25 Jenkins, *French Navy*, 10–11.

26 Loades, *Tudor Navy*, 95.

27 *TA*, vii, 190, 224–5, 228.

28 Ibid., vii, 140, 189–90, 229.

on to Dundee for the queen's royal entry and the wedding of the earl of
Errol, before returning to Leith.[29] In celebration of the successful
launches, the master shipwright, Walter Howieson, now titled the
'patroun' of the king's ships, was presented with a silver whistle on
a long chain. Howieson continued to receive payments for some years
and ship-building obviously continued, for later in the year more
timber was supplied along with ropes and pulleys. Another ship which
may have been the result of his operations was the *Lychtar*, recorded as
a king's vessel in July 1542.[30]

In June 1540 the king made his second major voyage to the Western
and Northern Isles, shortly after the birth and baptism of Prince James
at St. Andrews.[31] Unfortunately, the household accounts of this period
have not survived to help construct his itinerary, but it is clear that his
fleet set sail from somewhere in Fife on Saturday 12 June and on
Tuesday 6 July a letter was written from Edinburgh in the king's name,
so he was probably back by then. However, 6 July was also the date on
which the ships of Dumbarton, Ayr and Irvine had been ordered to
meet the king in the Isles with provisions, but these stores were
probably intended to supply the king's ships for the return voyage
around the entire Scottish coastline and back to Leith, whilst James
himself travelled back overland from Dumbarton to Edinburgh.[32] The
ships named for the voyage were the *Lion*, the *Great Unicorn*, the *Little
Unicorn*, the *Salamander* and the *Mary Willoughby*, a stone-boat from
Burntisland (perhaps a barge for carrying stores and baggage) and
ships owned by Alexander Wallace and Peter Falconer may also have
taken part.[33] The king's cabin was provided with bedding, curtains and
hangings and all the ships were furnished with flags, tents and guns.
The king's goldsmith even supplied some silver plate for the royal
table, and a gold whistle for the royal costume, symbolic of naval
command.[34] English espionage reports suggest that the 'raid' was

29 SRO, Liber Domicili, E.31/8, fos. 99v.-102r.
30 *TA*, vii, 197, 204, 207; viii, 94, 148, 169. Timber was also obtained for ship-
      building in 1541: ibid., vii, 474. Howieson was still in royal service in May
      1546, when he was described as the 'patroun' of the *Lion*: ibid., viii, 458.
31 In the absence of the king Matthew, earl of Lennox, William, earl of
      Montrose and John, lord Erskine were jointly appointed 'tutouris,
      testamentouris, gydaris and governors' to the baby prince: *HMC Mar and
      Kellie*, 14.
32 *TA*, vii, 317, 353; *James V Letters*, 402.
33 *TA*, vii, 353–5, 314.
34 Ibid., vii, 309–14, 353–7. This is very reminiscent of Henry VIII decking
      himself out as a sailor and blowing a golden whistle at the launch of the
      Great Galley in 1515: Loades, *Tudor Navy*, 71; *L&P Henry VIII*, ii, 1113.

made by sixteen ships carrying between two and four thousand men and that the earls of Argyll, Huntly, Arran, Atholl, Errol, Moray, Cassillis and the earl Marischal, as well as Lord Maxwell (the lord admiral) and Cardinal Beaton were in attendance. However, the same reports also suggested that James was bound for France or Ireland so their accuracy may be questioned.[35] According to Leslie, the fleet sailed up the east coast as far as Caithness and then made the crossing to Orkney, where the king visited the bishop, Robert Maxwell, and replenished supplies. The voyage proceeded to Lewis, Skye and then down the coast of Ross past Knapdale and Kintyre to land at Dumbarton.[36] Leslie states that the king landed regularly to receive the submissions of the clan chiefs and to take hostages or pledges from the Macleods, McConnells, MacDonalds and MacLeans, whom he retained in ward thus ensuring obedience and payment of crown revenues for the rest of the reign.[37] This explanation for the voyage is perfectly credible and in character, and indeed there is a record of Highland men being warded at Dunbar, Tantallon and the Bass shortly afterwards.[38] A recent commentator has suggested that the king was also concerned to survey the lands of the MacIans which he purchased from the earl of Argyll in August 1541.[39] Another significant factor in the general crackdown may have been that the crown earldoms of Orkney and Ross and the lordships of Ardmannach and the Isles formed a part of the jointure of the recently-crowned queen.[40] Furthermore, the newly-born Prince James of Scotland was also styled duke of Rothesay and the construction of the forework at Rothesay Castle, which had been started by James IV was resumed at this time and completed in 1541–42.[41] Shortly after the voyage Archibald Stewart was paid for the expenses of three gunners in the castles of 'Dunnewik and Iland, Lochbrum in Ilay' (probably Dunivaig and Port Ellen on Islay) of which the king seems to have taken possession, and in October, a ship called

35 *L&P Henry VIII*, xv, 632, 634, 709, 710.
36 Lesley, *History* (Bann. Club), 156–7.
37 There is a Macleod tradition that James V visited Dunvegan Castle in 1536 and 1540 and that on the first visit he was feasted in the open air by the chief, Alasdair Crotach: W. Douglas Simpson, 'A Chronicle History of Dunvegan Castle', *Transactions of the Gaelic Society of Inverness*, xxxvii (1934–6), 377.
38 *TA*, vii, 323.
39 Cameron, *James V*, 240–42.
40 *James V Letters*, 340–1.
41 Denys Pringle, *Rothesay Castle and St. Mary's Church* (Edinburgh, 1995), 2, 9, 19; Pitscottie, *Historie* (STS), i, 389.

the *Little Forfar*, captained by Colin Porterfield, was sent with supplies to the master of Kilmaurs in the Isles.[42] Another highland fortress, Dunaverty Castle in Kintyre, also received attention at this period: £200 was spent on building work there and the castle was manned by two or three gunners under the captaincy of the master of Glencairn.[43]

Another consequence of the king's 'circumnavigation' of Scotland in 1540 (or perhaps of the 1536 voyage) was the production of the first comprehensive rutter of the Scottish seas by the pilot, Alexander Lindsay.[44] For a king who was concerned to create a royal navy and to enforce his authority on the more distant parts of his realm by visiting them in person, such a project would have been a natural extension of his activities. A rutter was a list of instructions for navigating coastal waters by sailing from one headland to the next using only a compass, sand-glass, traverse-board and lead-line as navigational aids. In north-western Europe the use of rutters preceded the use of charts by about a century and the rutters usually included information on tides, currents, winds and soundings as well as descriptions of the main landmarks, harbours and dangers to be encountered.[45] Courses were set by compass points and the distances to be covered were calculated very roughly in miles or 'kennings'.[46] The earliest English rutters and French *routiers* in manuscript date from the late-fifteenth century and they were available in print from the 1520s.[47] Lindsay's rutter gives directions for voyages from Leith south to the Humber, from Leith north to Duncansby Head, from Duncansby Head

42 *TA*, vii, 328, 400. Porterfield was paid again for a voyage to the Isles in March 1541: ibid., vii, 438.

43 *MW*, i, 269; *TA*, vii, 444, 482; viii, 106; *RCAHMS Argyll (Kintyre)*, 157.

44 Alexander Lindsay, *A Rutter of the Scottish Seas, c.1540*, eds. A. B. Taylor, I. H. Adams and G. Fortune (Maritime Monographs and Reports, no. 44, 1980); Alexander Lindsay, 'The Navigation of King James V Round Scotland, the Orkney Isles and the Hebrides or Western Isles', ed. Nicholas d'Arfeville, trans. Robert Chapman, in *Miscellanea Scotica: A Collection of Tracts Relating to the History, Antiquities, Topography and Literature of Scotland* (3 vols., Glasgow, 1820), iii, 100–122.

45 Lindsay, *A Rutter*, 5, 23–6.

46 A 'kenning' was a variable unit of distance extending as far as the eye could see. In Lindsay's rutter it is taken to be approximately 14 miles: Angelo Forte, 'Kenning be Kenning and Course be Course': Maritime Jurimetrics in Fifteenth and Sixteenth Century Northern Europe with Particular Reference to Scottish Maritime Law' (unpublished paper delivered to the 39th Conference of the Colloquium for Scottish Medieval and Renaissance Studies, Pitlochry, 7 January, 1996).

47 See D. W. Waters (ed.), *The Rutters of the Sea* (New Haven and London, 1967). In the Mediterranean world these documents were called 'portolans'.

to the Mull of Kintyre (taking in Orkney) and from the Mull of Kintyre to the Solway. He seems to have drawn upon information from earlier local or regional rutters but he made no record of his sources. His original manuscript has not survived but we know of its existence from English versions derived from the one made to assist the 'Rough Wooing' (c.1546)[48] and a translation by Nicholas de Nicolay, sieur d'Arfeville, and chief cosmographer royal at the French court (c.1547 but published in 1559 and 1583).[49] Indeed, it is from d'Arfeville's edition that we learn that the rutter was compiled at the command of James V, since there is no record of expenditure on such an item in the surviving royal accounts, and Lindsay himself hardly features in the Scottish sources either.[50]

The final indication of the king's interest in naval matters was his construction of a new harbour at Burntisland, Fife, between August 1540 and 1542, where Robert Orrock of that ilk was master of works. Over £2,300 was spent in these two years on the new haven, renamed 'Our Lady Porte', which seems to have been located just below Rossend Castle.[51] The castle was a property belonging to the abbey of Dunfermline, which was officially made over to the king in 1542 by the commendator, George Durie, in a deal involving an exchange of lands. James V also founded the royal burgh of Burntisland in 1541.[52] Alongside the fortifications at Kinghorn, Ravenscraig and Inchgarvie and the

48 In 1546 the admiral of England, John Dudley, lord Lisle, possessed a copy of the rutter, perhaps acquired from one of the 'assured Scots' taken at Solway Moss. The best of the later English versions is NLS, Adv. MS, 33.2.27: see Lindsay, *A Rutter*, 6, 7, 9, 33, 34, 38.

49 D'Arfeville took his copy from a Scots text lent to him by Dudley and then had it translated into French with assistance from Ferrerio: see Lindsay, 'The Navigation', 103 and Lindsay, *A Rutter*, 6, 28, 30, 31, 36.

50 An Alexander Lindsay was recorded as an usher of the queen's outer chamber between July 1539 and July 1542 but this may not have been the same man: *TA*, vii, 182; viii, 101. A man of the same name (who was possibly from Kinghorn) made a clock ('orlage') for Falkland Palace in 1540/1 and he may well have been the compiler of the rutter: *MW*, i, 275. An Alexander Lindsay was also recorded as one of the crew on James IV's *Great Michael* in 1513: *TA*, iv, 504. For the Tudor king's interest in cartography see Peter Barber, 'Henry VIII and Mapmaking', in Starkey (ed.), *European Court*, 145–51.

51 *TA*, vii, 331, 429, 474, 494, 500; viii, 94–5, 114; Gifford, *Buildings of Scotland: Fife*, 108.

52 *RMS*, iii, 2383, 2731. Even before this, in February 1541, some sort of arrangement had been reached with the abbey since the laird of Sillebawbe (Alexander Orrok, brother of Robert) was given £33 to be paid to the monks for sealing a charter relating to Burntisland: *TA*, vii, 429.

harbours at Leith and Blackness, the new port seems to have been part of a system for defending the Firth of Forth from English seaborne assault. An English account of 1544 described the harbour at Burntisland as having three blockhouses furnished with guns and a pier 'wher the gret schips comonly doth lye in a dokk' and recommended that English vessels should avoid getting too close.[53]

James V clearly took the defence of his realm seriously. Having ascended the throne after the battle of Flodden, he was brought up to be aware of the destructive potential of war with England, and he twice had to defend his kingdom from English incursions, in 1532–33 and in 1542. During his adult reign he not only spent heavily on naval developments but also on fortifications.[54] It used to be thought that the years between 1480 and 1560 constituted a barren period in the building of Scottish castles and fortifications, but Zeune's recent examination of the archaeological and architectural record, which produced a revised chronology for many Scottish castles, has shown this to be a misconception. Indeed the reigns of James IV and James V may have seen the peak of Scottish castle building.[55] An investigation of the documentary sources also suggests considerable activity and development at this period. James V followed the precedent of his immediate forbears by legislating to encourage the propertied classes of Scotland to contribute to the defence of the kingdom. In 1426 James I had ensured that all holders of castles beyond the Mounth were obliged to restore and maintain their properties, and in 1481 James III had ordered all coastal and border fortresses to be repaired and supplied with men, provisions and artillery in readiness to resist English incursions. As we have seen already, James V issued similar instructions for the fortification of coastal towns and castles during the hostilities with England of 1533, and in 1535 he followed this up with another act of parliament 'for bigging of strenthis on the bordouris.' In addition, Zeune's analysis of the feu charters recorded in the *Register of the Great Seal* indicates that the Stewart monarchs were encouraging and licensing their subjects to build fortified residences, and that James V was the most active in this respect.[56]

53 *Hamilton Papers*, ii, App. II, nos. 714–5.

54 The naval expenditure in the two years 1538–40 alone amounted to at least £3,600: *TA*, vi, 381, 421, 438, 450–4, 463; vii, 19, 24, 140, 169, 189–90, 204, 207, 257–8, 281, 297, 310–14, 322.

55 Joachim Zeune, *The Last Scottish Castles: Investigations with particular reference to domestic architecture from the 15th to 17th centuries* trans. Silke Böger (Internationale Archäologie, Band 12, Erlbach, 1992), 310. See also Stewart Cruden, *The Scottish Castle* (Edinburgh and London, 1960), 144–5.

56 *APS*, ii, 13, 133, 346; *TA*, vi, 129; Zeune, *Last Scottish Castles*, 109–11.

In upgrading the defensive capabilities of royal castles, James V had been set an example by his regent, John, duke of Albany, for whom a new blockhouse had been constructed at his castle of Dunbar between 1515 and 1523. No accounts of the building work survive and we know that the blockhouse was in existence by June 1523 only because of an espionage report from Lord Dacre, which is corroborated by Pitscottie. Dacre describes the Dunbar blockhouse as 'in manner imprenable' and according to Pitscottie Albany furnished it with 'artaillye pulder and bullatis.'[57] Perhaps the fortification was planned by Antoine d'Arces, sieur de la Bastie, who was Albany's captain of Dunbar until his murder in September 1517, or maybe the scheme was devised by Moses/Mogin Martin, the master mason, who subsequently worked for James V at Falkland.[58] The French gunners at Dunbar, under the command of master Wolf, may have contributed to the design as well, for the blockhouse contains the first dateable Scottish examples of the wide-mouthed gun-port of the period, and was clearly intended to exploit the defensive possibilities of heavy artillery and smaller fire-arms.[59] The squat shape, with massively thick walls, also indicates that it was designed to withstand the pounding of attacking gunfire, and its layout is somewhat reminiscent of the most up-to-date Italian angle-bastioned fortifications; although this may have been serendipitous rather than deliberate, for it is largely dictated by the shape of the rock on which it stands.[60] However, Albany had had experience of Italian campaigns and had close Italian connections through the marriage of his sister-in-law, Madeleine de la Tour Auvergne, to Lorenzo de Medici in 1518.[61] After Albany's death without legitimate issue in June 1536, Dunbar Castle reverted to the crown and the blockhouse may have served as the inspiration for some of James V's subsequent fortifications at Blackness, Tantallon and elsewhere.

Blackness Castle, near Linlithgow, was originally built in the 1440s

57 *L&P Henry VIII*, iii, 3134; Pitscottie, *Historie* (STS), i, 303.
58 See chapter 2.
59 For a detailed description see Iain MacIvor, 'Artillery and Major Places of Strength in the Lothians and the East Border, 1513–1542', in David H. Caldwell (ed.), *Scottish Weapons and Fortifications, 1100–1800* (Edinburgh, 1981), 107–19.
60 For Italian developments see David Eltis, *The Military Revolution in Sixteenth-Century Europe* (London, 1995), 76–85 and Geoffrey Stell, 'Late Medieval Defences in Scotland', in Caldwell (ed.), *Scottish Weapons and Fortifications*, 43. For the Dunbar layout see MacIvor, 'Artillery and Major Places', 112–13.
61 Stuart, *Scot who was a Frenchman*, 96–9.

for Sir George Crichton but was annexed by James II (along with other Crichton properties) on his death in 1454. Improvements to the fortifications there seem to have been planned by Sir James Hamilton of Finnart, as captain of Linlithgow, from August 1536, just as the works at the palace approached completion,[62] and were concluded (after Finnart's execution in August 1540) under the rector of Dysart, John Denniston, in 1542.[63] Well over £1,000 was spent during this period in thickening the walls of the southern and eastern defences to a depth of five and a half metres, constructing vaulted gun-emplacements and raising the south tower.[64] The bulwark thereby constructed at the southern approach to the castle bears some resemblance to the blockhouse at Dunbar in its polygonal plan and deep casemates opening at wide-mouthed gun ports. Furthermore, the south tower, which contained the principal accommodation, probably also had the capability to house a great gun at the hall window and small arms on the parapet.[65]

A similar concern for the use of masonry on a massive scale and the provision of gun emplacements was a feature of the works carried out for James V at Tantallon. With its massive curtain wall and extensive outer earthworks, the castle of the earl of Angus was sufficiently well-fortified to withstand the besieging forces of the king in October and November 1528. By April 1529 the castle (and other Douglas property) was in the king's hands following a deal with England which sent Angus into exile. Although the castle was manned and supplied at an early date, there is no evidence of any major construction work there until 1538 and 1539, when nearly £1,300 was spent.[66] The master mason was George Semple and the accounts were handled by the king's secretary, Sir Thomas Erskine, and his cupbearer, Oliver Sinclair, who was listed as the captain of Tantallon from September 1539 to August 1542.[67] The works involved filling in the mural stairs and chambers, which had created weak-spots in the curtain wall, attaching a forework to the central gate-tower, constructing a crenellated parapet

---

62 See chapter 2.
63 *TA*, viii, 73. In 1540 John Bog, a yeoman of the king's stable, was named as the keeper of Blackness Castle and he may have contributed to the works as well: *ER*, xvii, 289.
64 *ADCP*, 453; *TA*, vi, 304; vii, 91, 302, 474; viii, 73.
65 Zeune, *Last Scottish Castles*, 278–9; MacIvor, 'Artillery and Major Places',128–32; Iain MacIvor, *Blackness Castle* (Historic Scotland, 1993), 4–20.
66 *Diurnal of Occurrents*, 12; Cameron, *James V*, 47–68; *TA*, v, 434; *MW*, i, 198, 200, 228, 236, 241; *TA*, vii, 256; *ER*, xvii, 120.
67 *MW*, i, 236, 241; *ER*, xvii, 120, 601; *TA*, vii, 256.

along the top of the curtain wall, and improving the defences of the towers. The bases of the east and mid towers were reinforced with heavy masonry and had wide-mouthed gun-ports inserted on a pattern related to that of the Dunbar blockhouse, and it is likely that the Douglas (north) tower was treated in a similar way, but most of this structure has been lost.[68] By 1543, as a result of the works undertaken for James V, Sir Ralph Sadler could report that both Blackness and Tantallon castles were impregnable.[69]

The combination of these works at Burntisland, Dunbar, Blackness and Tantallon considerably strengthened the defences of the approach to Edinburgh from England by land or sea and this seems to have been a quite deliberate policy, for other strategic sites also received attention at this period. James IV had appointed John Dundas to fortify the island of Inchgarvie in the Forth in 1491 and these works were still being completed in 1515–16 when Charles Denniston, captain of Inchgarvie, was paid for a large staff, the majority of whom were masons. His account also shows that the castle was armed with two serpentines (large, breech-loading, forged-iron guns) which were supplied with five chambers (canisters containing shot and powder to be loaded at the breech).[70] In 1529–30 Patrick Wemyss of Pittencrieff (later a master household depute) had been keeper of Inchgarvie for four years and was protesting to the council that he had not been paid. In February 1533, in the midst of the hostilities with England, James Dundas of Dundas was appointed keeper for a year and was paid £33 6s. 8d. for minor repairs. However, by 1535 Wemyss was in charge again, although it is not stated in the sources why the post of keeper was alternated in this way. In May 1544 the English forces reported the capture and slighting of the 'blockhouse' on the island of Inchgarvie. The assault was swift, so presumably the fortifications here were not particularly effective. Another Forth tower on which some work was done for James V was Kinghorn Tower in Fife, but no details survive.[71]

Further south, work was undertaken on several of the towers and castles of the eastern, middle and western marches. A little way to the south of Peebles, beneath the waters of the Meggat reservoir, lies the site of Cramalt Tower, which James V used regularly as a hunting

---

68 MacIvor, 'Artillery and Major Places', 132–3; Zeune, *Last Scottish Castles*, 278.

69 *L&P Henry VIII*, xviii, I, 897; xviii, II, 343.

70 *APS*, ii, 270; *RMS*, ii, 2038; *TA*, iv, 445, 529; v, 20–26. See also William M. Mackenzie, *The Medieval Castle in Scotland* (1972), 219, 225.

71 *ADCP*, 314, 322, 397; *TA*, vi, 125, 161, 262; *Hamilton Papers*, ii, 366; *MW*, i, 228.

lodge. The limited archaeological evidence surviving from a dig undertaken before the site was flooded suggests that one of the two towers on
the site dates from c.1500 and the other from the latter half of the
century, but some minor work must have been done there in 1533–4
when 36s. was paid to a mason called Bickerton *per edificatione domorum
in Cramald*.[72] Unfortunately there are no further references to works
there in any of the surviving sources, and this reference need not
necessarily have had defensive implications. However, further west, at
Crawfordjohn, Upper Ward of Lanarkshire, fortification was almost
certainly carried out for James V, even though no traces now remain. In
1513 James Hamilton of Finnart had been granted half of the lordship of
Crawfordjohn by his father, the earl of Arran, and in 1529 he obtained
the other half by exchange. In February 1536 the lands of Crawfordjohn
were in turn exchanged with the king for the rents of Kilmarnock and
by March the king was able to announce his intention to build a
'fortalice' in Crawfordmuir (which is probably a reference to the
subsequent work at Crawfordjohn) to the council.[73] Payments totalling
£423 2s. for works at Crawfordjohn are recorded between 1535 and
1541 involving the mason, Thomas Cadder, the master wright, John
Drummond, and the glasswright, Thomas Peebles.[74] Although it is
impossible to say exactly what was done at Crawfordjohn at this time, a
report sent to the earl of Hertford in 1547 suggested that the site
contained a tower and barmkin on a rather small scale: 'the hous is wele
ludgit within, bot it is of na strynth, for the barmekyn beand wyne, the
hous is gottin.'[75] The tower of Cockburnspath, held by Queen Margaret, was also reinforced at this period.[76]

Hermitage Castle in Liddesdale was another border fortress where
work may have been carried out for James V. This key stronghold had
been the property of the earl of Bothwell, who was convicted of
treasonable dealings with the English in 1531, warded for some years
and eventually exiled in 1539. Hermitage (along with the property
formerly belonging to other forfeited lords such as Angus, Glamis and

72 Alastair M. T. Maxwell-Irving, 'Cramalt Tower: A Historical Survey and
   Excavations, 1977–9', *PSAS*, cxi (1981), 421–3 suggests dates in the 1460s or
   1470s, but this date is revised by Zeune's reappraisal of Maxwell-Irving's
   findings: Zeune, *Last Scottish Castles*, 223–4. The first documentary record
   of a building on the site is in 1530: *ADCP*, 329. For Bickerton: SRO, Liber
   Emptorum, E.32/3, 127r., 128v.
73 *RMS*, ii, 3803; iii, 768, 769, 1543; *ADCP*, 451.
74 *MW*, i, 192, 198, 228; *TA*, vi, 364; vii, 495–7; *ER*, xvii, 128.
75 *CSP Scot*, i, no.67.
76 *ADCP*, 450.

Finnart) was annexed to the crown in the parliament of December 1540. The castle was initially entrusted to the care of James Sandilands of Calder and later transferred to that of Lord Maxwell. In August 1542 two gunners, James Law and John Byres were posted to Hermitage and provided with munitions, just as tensions with England were reaching boiling point.[77] It looks as if some work was done there at this period which involved blocking up the western entrance and replacing it with a smaller, better defended one. Wide-mouthed gun-ports were inserted at strategic points, to facilitate the work of the artillery men, and an outer earthwork or ravelin may also have been constructed at the same time.[78]

Another castle annexed in 1540 was Finnart's seat at Craignethan in Lanarkshire. The king installed his own staff to keep Craignethan from September 1540, that is immediately after Finnart's execution and before the parliament sat in December. The keeper, who seems to have had a staff of five or six men, was initially David Orrok and after a year he was replaced by Gavin Gifford. There is a record of stables being built there for the king in 1542 and if David Orrok was any relation to the Robert Orrok who was master of works at Burntisland, there may have been work on the fortifications undertaken there too.[79] The surviving defences at Craignethan, which are usually ascribed to Hamilton of Finnart in the 1530s, are certainly remarkable, and it is at least possible that some of the work was done for the king after Finnart's fall. The promontory on which the castle stands is defended by a deep, stone-lined ditch in which was constructed a caponier. This structure is an enclosed, vaulted, stone gun-gallery (entered from a staircase leading to the castle itself), with wide-mouthed and angled gun ports, capable of raking the entire ditch and thus turning it into a killing-field. This is the only known Scottish example of a caponier until the eighteenth century and suggests some familiarity with Italian developments, since caponiers were in use in Italy from the late-fifteenth century. The western rampart, which lies immediately beyond the ditch and caponier, is a massive masonry barrier, similar to the south wall at Blackness. The loops in the caponier and enceinte were suitable for small firearms whilst the parapets atop the western rampart and tower house could mount larger guns.[80] Craignethan's spell as a

77 Cameron, *James V*, 86–91, 213–4, 271–2; *APS*, ii, 360–1; *ADCP*, 382, 410, 455; *TA*, vi, 165, 204, 237, 281; viii, 110, 111.
78 Nick Bridgland, *Hermitage Castle* (Historic Scotland, 1996), 23.
79 *TA*, vii, 393, 480–1; viii, 37, 55; *ER*, xvii, 582–3.
80 Charles McKean, 'Craignethan Castle', *PSAS*, cxxv (1995), 1069–90; MacIvor, 'Artillery and Major Places', 124–5; Zeune, *Last Scottish Castles*, 281–2.

royal castle was a brief twenty-eight months and is therefore often
overlooked (on James V's death it passed to the second earl of Arran),
but given the king's enthusiasm for defence work elsewhere, and that
he is known to have built stables at the castle, it is possible that the
fortifications there were completed for the crown rather than for
Finnart. Even if this were not the case, the speed with which the king
moved to take possession of the castle may indicate that he was well
aware of its importance.

All the ships in James V's navy and all the strategic fortifications
which attracted his attention were at some point provided with
artillery, shot and gunners. Again, James V was following a precedent
in this respect, for his great-grandfather, James II, was the king for
whom *Mons Meg* was sent to Scotland, and who perished at the siege of
Roxburgh in 1460 when he stationed himself too close to one of his own
guns, which exploded and killed him.[81] James III and James IV had also
been enthusiastic collectors of artillery pieces: the manufacture of cast
iron guns was undertaken in Edinburgh in the 1470s and 1480s, and
forged iron guns were made at Stirling Castle at the same period.[82]
From about 1505 James IV was employing French workmen to cast
bronze guns, which were more accurate, reliable and had a longer
range than their iron predecessors and could fire iron shot instead of
stone.[83] The fifteenth-century iron guns were bombards (great siege
guns, such as *Mons Meg*) and serpentines (medium-sized weapons for
mounting on fortifications) and were usually loaded at the breech by
the insertion of a 'chamber' or canister containing shot and powder.
They were cheaper than the cast bronze guns and continued to be used
in blockhouses and on ships, where there was not enough room behind
the gun-ports to retract a muzzle-loading piece. The muzzle-loading
cast bronze guns of the sixteenth century ranged in size from the large
cannon and culverins (which were battering guns), through the smaller
culverins and larger falcons (which were carriage-mounted field guns),
down to the smaller falcons and hagbuts of crock, which were mounted
on wooden rails at gun loops and parapets. There were also even
smaller culverins and hagbuts which could be used as hand-guns.[84] By

81 Claude Gaier, 'The Origins of Mons Meg', *Journal of the Arms and Armour
   Society*, v (1965–7), 425–52; David Caldwell, 'Royal Patronage of Arms and
   Armour Making in Fifteenth and Sixteenth-Century Scotland', in Caldwell
   (ed.), *Scottish Weapons and Fortifications*, 74; McGladdery, *James II*, 111, 156.
82 *TA*, i, 48–9, 54, 68, 69, 74; *ER*, viii, 234, 275; ix, 218, 286, 291, 416, 434. See
   also Caldwell 'Royal Patronage', 75.
83 *TA*, iii, 139; iv, 109–13, 116–7, 127, 132–6, 139, 276–7, 372, 378.
84 MacIvor, 'Artillery and Major Places', 97–9.

the end of James IV's reign Edinburgh Castle had become the centre of Scottish artillery manufacture under Robert Borthwick and John Drummond, both of whom continued to serve James V.[85]

The Scottish army at Flodden was well supplied with artillery, much of which had been purchased abroad, but some was likely to have been of native manufacture. These pieces were captured by the English.[86] Consequently the Scottish royal arsenal had to be restocked after 1513 and there is some evidence of this work being undertaken for the duke of Albany. When Albany landed at Dumbarton on 26 May 1515, he arrived with a fleet of ships including the *Margaret* and the *James*, which had accompanied the *Great Michael* to France in the summer of 1513, and guns from these ships were immediately retrieved and returned to Edinburgh. Albany's castle of Dunbar was manned by a group of French gunners and craftsmen and a new blockhouse built there, as we have seen.[87] At the main royal arsenal in Edinburgh Castle, a new furnace was built and Borthwick (with his French assistant, Piers Rouen) and Drummond were instructed to re-arm under the supervision of a Frenchman, captain Jean Bouskat, who was described as commissioner of the artillery.[88] Two Dutch culverin-makers (George Keppin and his servant, Kasper Lepus), who had worked for James IV, also continued in service at this time.[89] Much of the ordnance used by Albany in his campaigns against Carlisle (1522) and Wark (1523) may well have been imported from France and returned there afterwards.[90] Despite the efforts made in 1515–17 to replenish the Scottish royal arsenal, by 1528 there was little serviceable artillery available. Indeed, the adult James V seems to have started a re-armament programme virtually from scratch.[91]

The inadequacies of the arsenal taken over by James V in the summer 1528 were amply demonstrated by the failure of the siege of Tantallon in October and November of that year. Angus and his

---

85 Borthwick was master melter of the king's guns from 1512 (*RSS*, i, 2374; *TA*, iv, 261, 515) and died in 1531–2 (*ADCP*, 354, 390). Drummond was employed as a wright from 1506 (*TA*, iii, 114), was appointed the king's principal carpenter and founder or melter of his artillery on 18 June 1532 (*RSS*, ii, 1304). He was still receiving livery at Christmas 1550 (*TA*, ix, 461).

86 Caldwell, 'Royal Patronage', 76–7.

87 *TA*, v, 16–17; Pitscottie, *Historie* (STS), i, 288; *TA*, v, 161–2.

88 *TA*, v, 17–19, 30, 32, 36, 37, 41, 52, 66–7, 69, 71, 93.

89 Ibid., iv, 276, 333, 374, 379, 439; v, 32–3, 69.

90 *See L&P Henry VIII*, iii, II, 3403.

91 This predicament is echoed in Buchanan's comment that the king's guardians had plundered his palaces and squandered his revenue during the minority: *History*, ii, 324.

adherents had been forfeited in the September parliament and the king was eager to enforce his authority by seizing control of this key Douglas stronghold. The host was called to muster on 20 October, but the master of the king's artillery, Sir Alexander Jardine of Applegarth, immediately protested to the council that he was insufficiently supplied and should not be held responsible for the outcome. The experienced gunners and armourers of James IV, Robert Borthwick and John Drummond, were called upon to solve the problem and they advised the council about how to make the best use of what little ordnance it possessed. Only four cannons and a culverin battard, with enough shot to fire thirty-rounds a piece, seem to have been available at Edinburgh Castle and they suggested the best way of transporting these guns to the siege. They also recommended purchasing munitions abroad and seeking help from the French garrison of Albany's castle at Dunbar.[92] According to one account, the captain of Dunbar supplied the king with two great cannon, two great battards, two medium-sized pieces, two double-falcons, four quarter-falcons, plus powder, shot and gunners, but only upon receipt of pledges for their safe return. Another report suggested that James also made use of munitions belonging to the exiled king of Denmark, Christian II, which had been entrusted to Robert Barton of Leith as security for credit.[93] The siege probably took place between 18 October and 4 November and ended with humiliation for the royal forces.[94] The artillery that the council had managed to scrape together was unable to make any significant impression on the fortress because the outer earthworks forced the guns out of range of the castle walls; the king therefore ordered the siege to be lifted, at which point Angus's force made a sally, attacked the rearguard, killed two royal soldiers (Henry Borthwick, a gunner, and David Falconer, the captain of the footband) and captured many of the remaining guns and their captain, Robert Borthwick. Borthwick and the ordnance were returned to the king soon afterwards but the humiliation rankled.[95]

Following this embarrassing episode, the king made strenuous efforts to improve his ordnance. In January 1529 he wrote to King Frederick of Denmark asking for supplies of ships and armaments and in 1530 he turned to the duke of Albany for French and Italian supplies

---

92 *ADCP*, 284–5.
93 Pitscottie, *Historie* (STS), i, 330–1; Reid, *Skipper from Leith*, 223, 226.
94 Fraser, *Douglas*, iv, 137–8. Another account dates it to 20 Oct. to 5 Nov.: *Diurnal*, 12.
95 Cameron, *James V*, 48–9; Fraser, *Douglas*, iv, 137–8.

and expertise. In 1531 powder was purchased from Robert Barton in Leith, Thomas Stewart, laird of Gawston, was sent to France to purchase munitions and by that summer the arsenal at Edinburgh Castle was sufficiently well-stocked to supply artillery for the Isles raid.[96] Men in the king's service at this period who were probably involved in the manufacture of guns included John Drummond, George Ormiston, Robert Borthwick and his French assistant, Piers Rouen.[97] In addition there were several men described as smiths and armourers, who were probably making swords, helmets and items of plate and chain-mail armour, but who may also have been involved in the manufacture of artillery.[98] There seems to have been a royal armoury on quite a large scale established at Holyrood in 1532, where 'Ewo' (perhaps Yves), a French wright from the castle of Dunbar, set up a new horse-mill for the armourers, which operated in conjunction with an armoury, forge, harness-house, melting-house and coining-house. The Holyrood horse-mill had cogged wheels of oak, grinding stones, 'polysouris' (polishers) covered with leather and a wooden axle thirty-two feet long, which passed through the mill and the building in which it was housed; it was driven by two horses.[99] This development echoes the establishment of the English royal armouries at Greenwich in 1511 and 1515, which were staffed mainly by Flemings, Italians and Germans.[100] Also in 1532 James despatched his master almoner, Master James Scrymgeour, to Flanders with over £2,000 to spend on munitions and tapestries. Unfortunately Scrymgeour died in Flanders but seven and a half tons of copper, powder and saltpetre, which he had purchased, made their way back to Scotland.[101] It was just as well that the king moved quickly on this matter, for by December 1532

96 *James V Letters*, 150, 171–2, 176, 189–90; *TA*, v, 439, 458, 461; vi, 48, 372–3.
97 For Drummond and Borthwick see above n.85; also *RSS*, ii, 1213, 1304; *ER*, xvi, 152–3. Rouen was serving as Borthwick's assistant from 1515: *TA*, v, 18. Ormiston was described as a gunner in 1532 but by 1535 he was listed as an engineer (*machinator*): *TA*, vi, 39; *ER*, xvi, 398.
98 E.g. William Hill, a smith, who is recorded throughout the 1530s and 1540s (and received regular wages as one of the staff of the Edinburgh arsenal until 1561: *TA*, xi, 104) was usually paid for making iron window frames, locks etc. (*MW*, i, 3f.-259) but in September 1536 was employed to make falcons (*TA*, vi, 303).
99 *MW*, i, 96, 101–2, 242, 290; *TA*, vi, 34. A wright from Dunbar called Evone (presumably the same man) had also given assistance at the siege of Tantallon: *ADCP*, 285.
100 Karen Watts, 'Henry VIII and the Founding of the Greenwich Armouries', in Starkey (ed.), *European Court*, 42–6.
101 *TA*, vi, 151, 158; *ADCP*, 249.

artillery from Edinburgh Castle was needed on the borders to help
resist the English incursions. Guns were retrieved from Ross (following
the raid of Caithness), timber was transported from Lochaber to make
gun-stocks and a series of expeditions were armed from the arsenals at
Edinburgh, Dunbar and Tantallon. At Haddington in December 1532
the king's forces were supplied with eighty hagbuts and their 'trestis'
(the forked staves on which they were propped for firing), forty-four
culverins, seven falcons, their attendant pioneers and a large force of
footsoldiers. In January 1533 more artillery was despatched from
Edinburgh Castle and in March four falcons were sent to the lieutenant,
the earl of Moray, at Jedburgh.[102]

Even after this crisis was resolved by a peace treaty (which was
intended to last for the rest of the reign), James continued his campaign
to expand the crown's military capability. Indeed, the English ambassadors who visited Edinburgh for the ratification of the treaty in June
1534 were treated to a demonstration of the capabilities of the Scottish
royal arsenal when a salute was fired from the castle.[103] In 1534 James
sent a request to Stuart of Aubigny for two or three expert armourers to
be despatched to Scotland, along with 'Lorge Montgomery' as a
military adviser, and an expedition to Denmark was launched to
purchase war horses and gunmetal.[104] The newly refitted *Mary Willoughby* was armed with cannon sent from 'Ilingreg' (probably Eilean
Craig) by the earl of Argyll and three cannon were brought to Edinburgh from Dumfries by John Drummond. In November 1535 munitions worth £80 were purchased from Katherine Hamilton and in
September 1536 the smith, William Hill, was supplied with iron and
lead to make falcons.[105] In October 1536, with the king away in France,
the lords regent summoned the royal artillery to the siege of Edgerston
house, a relatively minor border incident which they seem to have
handled competently.[106] At this period James V also legislated for the
use and provision of armaments. In February 1531 the use of small
arms (culverins or 'lime wands') in hunting wild fowl or great fish was
forbidden (presumably to conserve stocks), a measure which suggests
that these modern weapons were becoming more popular in Scot-

---

102 *TA*, vi, 155–7, 158–60, 161; *ADCP*, 395.
103 *TA*, vi, 215.
104 *James V Letters*, 262, 272. Jacques de Montgommery, seigneur de Lorges,
     was related to the earls of Eglinton and in the service of Francis I. It is not
     clear if he responded to the invitation at this time but he made an
     expedition to Scotland in 1545: see *Balcarres Papers*, i, 119.
105 *TA*, vi, 223, 237, 261, 303.
106 *TA*, vi, 303, 308; *MW*, i, 193; Cameron, *James V*, 178–9.

land.[107] However, in the parliament of 1535 acts were passed suggesting that there was a shortage of ordnance in Scotland and instituting regulations to address the problem. One act obliged all landowners (both temporal and spiritual) and the burghs to furnish themselves with hagbuts of crock, culverins, powder, shot and skilled gunners according to their degree. A second statute required merchants travelling abroad to return with as much artillery, powder or gunmetal as they could carry. These two statutes were repeated in the parliament of 1540.[108]

However, the greatest expansion of the royal arsenal took place after the king's visit to France, when gifts from his father-in-law and the purchasing power of two French dowries allowed him to indulge his enthusiasm for artillery and other arms. The earliest purchases of guns and powder bought in France in September and October 1536 were shipped to Scotland in November on the *Moriset* (as we have seen) and acquisitions continued. In November the king obtained two stands of harness (one in the style of Francis I and one in the style of the dauphin); armour, blades, spears and crossbows were bought in Paris in January 1537; culverin powder was bought in Rouen in February; in March artillery was being sent to the Newhaven of Dieppe (probably gifts from the French king), crossbows and spears were bought in Rouen, and in April the master mason of Dunbar (who had accompanied James to France) was preparing munitions for the Scottish fleet.[109] Apart from the mason of Dunbar (Moses or Mogin Martin), William Smibert and Piers Rouen were also present on this trip and put in charge of the new guns and munitions.[110] The munitions staff was also expanded since seven new names appear in the records at this time, some of whom were obviously foreigners.[111] From March 1538 into the 1560s there were regular payments to a team of gunners in the crown's service, many with foreign names, whose number fluctuated over time but was

---

107 *ADCP*, 350–1; *TA*, vii, 422. The king himself had used hagbuts at a hunt in 1530–1: *TA*, v, 435–6.

108 *APS*, ii, 345–6, 371–2. Hagbuts of crock were handguns intended to be used from parapets, and were therefore supported by wooden rails in the embrasures rather than by 'trestis'.

109 *TA*, vi, 453, 460, 462–4; vii, 8, 13–14. It is not clear whether the stands of harness were trappings for the king's horses or body-armour for James himself, or both.

110 *TA*, vi, 315–16, 462–3; vii, 16, 23.

111 Nicholas Burdit, Hollay, Gavin Hamilton, David McPherson, Christopher Grand Morsen, Robert Hector, William Agradane/Agagarant: *TA*, vi, 438, 464, 466, 334; vii, 16, 20, 25, 194, 428, 205. For further details see Thomas, 'Renaissance Culture,' 241 and Appendix A.

not usually less than three.[112] In May 1538 John Drummond and William Hill were members of the party sent to France to escort Mary of Guise to Scotland and at the same time the two sons of Piers Rouen were sent into apprenticeships in France and munitions were purchased there for the king by John Barton.[113] From the middle of 1538 until the end of the reign, guns, powder, shot, spears, bows and war-horses were imported in large quantities from Denmark, Flanders and France at a total cost of over £7,000.[114] Furthermore, the production of guns both large and small, forged and cast, at Edinburgh Castle was also carried out on a grand scale.[115] To facilitate these operations a new munitions house and powder mill were constructed at the castle, and, as if for good measure, a new register house was built there as well to store the crown archives. The munitions house was built in the converted chapel of St. Mary, which had old doors and windows blocked and a new great door struck out; also, a new passage was blasted out of the rock to allow access for cannon. The powder mill was operational by February 1541 and by August 1542 the five workmen employed there had produced eighteen barrels of powder (each barrel weighing fifteen stones).[116] It was the Edinburgh arsenal which supplied arms to the king's expanding navy and he seems to have taken a close interest in its operation, making a personal visit there in June 1539, when the guns were laid out for him to inspect.[117] Alongside his enthusiasm for the latest artillery pieces, James V also maintained supplies of traditional weapons (swords, knives, pikes, halberds, crossbows and bolts, longbows and arrows) and employed staff to manufacture and maintain them, such as a cutler, a sword-slipper, a crossbow-maker and an English bow-maker (i.e. he made longbows).[118] Much of this interest in traditional arms was stimulated by the king's chivalric obsession with

---

112 E.g. in March 1538, Christopher, William Agradane, Jacques Leschender and John Cunningham: *TA*, vi, 382. For details of this establishment in later years see Thomas, 'Renaissance Culture', 241 and Appendix A.

113 *TA*, vi, 401–2, 413–14. One of the sons, David, later joined his father as a principal maker and melter of the king's guns: *RSS*, ii, 4964 (27 Oct. 1542).

114 *TA*, vi, 441; vii, 48, 51, 59, 184, 257, 405, 438, 498; viii, 46–7, 59, 72, 94, 118–20, 123, 151–5.

115 *TA*, vi, 438, 441; vii, 123, 195, 209–10, 213, 217, 348–51, 359–60, 428, 489, 501; viii, 124–7; *MW*, i, 229–34.

116 *TA*, vii, 214–15, 220, 224, 226–31, 337, 341–5, 349, 359, 489–91, 499; viii, 130, 132–3. See also *RCAHMS Edinburgh*, 4; Thomas, 'Renaissance Culture', 242 n.163.

117 *TA*, vii, 222, 225–6.

118 William Rae, Thomas Softlaw, Adrian Abel, John Bower: see Thomas, 'Renaissance Culture,' Appendix A.

tournaments but many were also stockpiled for military campaigns.[119]

Another aspect of technological development in Scotland in which James V had a particular interest was the exploitation of the gold deposits in Crawfordmuir. It seems likely that silver deposits had been worked in Scotland since the thirteenth century and in 1424 parliament reserved rights to all precious metals to the crown.[120] The gold mines of Crawfordmuir had first been worked in the reign of James IV, who appointed Sir James Pettigrew as overseer of the Flemish or Dutch miners.[121] Interest in the mines was also sustained by the duke of Albany, who commissioned John Campbell, bishop-elect of the Isles, accompanied by a French finer and melter of gold, John Drane, to supervise the workings at Crawfordmuir in 1515.[122] The Albany medal of 1524 was probably made from Scottish gold.[123] Under the earl of Angus in 1526, a forty-three year lease of all the Scottish gold and silver mines was granted to a group of Dutchmen and/or Germans and the same men received a ten-year contract in 1527 for minting the Scottish coinage.[124] However, neither the lease nor the contract ran to full-term, for in 1529 it was suggested that the foreign miners had failed to honour the contract and in 1531 they left Scotland, leaving James Atkinson (or Acheson) operating as the master coiner.[125] In 1532 a new sixteen-year

---

119 E.g. *TA*, viii, 122–3. See also Gladys Dickinson, 'Some Notes on the Scottish Army in the first half of the Sixteenth Century', *SHR*, xxviii (1949), 133–45. James V's interest in tournaments is considered in the following chapter.

120 R. W. Cochran-Patrick, *Early Records relating to Mining in Scotland* (Edinburgh, 1878), pp xiii & xxxv; *APS*, ii, 5. See also J. Moir Porteous, *God's Treasure-House in Scotland* (London, 1876) and Stephen Atkinson, *The Discoverie and Historie of the Gold Mynes in Scotland (1619)*, ed. Gilbert Laing Meason (Bannatyne Club, 1825).

121 The foreign miners were Sebald Northberge (master finer), Andrew Ireland (finer) and Gerald Essemer (melter). In 1513 John Damien, alchemist and commendator of Tongland inspected the mines at Crawfordmuir: *TA*, iv, 273, 396, 408, 442; *HMC 4th Rep.*, 517.

122 *TA*, v, 19–20, 154–9.

123 Cochran-Patrick, *Early Records*, p. xiv; *Angels, Nobles and Unicorns*, 101–2.

124 The men were Joachim Hochstetter, Quintin de Lawitz, Gerard Sterk, Erasmus Sohets and Anthony de Nikets: *HMC, 4th Report*, 517; *ADCP*, 247, 350; *James V Letters*, 146–7.

125 *James V Letters*, 160; *TA*, v, 387, 406, 437, 441. Atkinson had held this post since 1526 (*APS*, ii, 310) and continued until 1538 when he was succeeded by Alexander Orrok, who was listed as master of the mint until June 1542. In 1531, 1538, 1539 and 1540, Richard Wardlaw was recorded dealing with the coinage. In 1541–3 Atkinson resumed a role in the 'cunyehous'. In 1540 William Galbraith was paid compensation for relinquishing his hereditary interest in the mint: *ADCP*, 508; *TA*, vii, 315, 338–9.

contract was made with men of Hamburg to mine for lead, copper, tin, gold and silver in Scotland. The Germans were to pay £1,500 a year for their rights which gave them a monopoly in Scotland and were requested to allow Richard Wardlaw and James King (of the royal coining-house) to work alongside them.[126] In 1535 officers were appointed to search for and prevent specie being exported at Scottish ports and a commission was set up to consider the working of the gold deposits and to offer a contract to foreign miners. By 1537 and 1538, gold from the mines of Crawfordmuir was being delivered to the royal treasury.[127] After Mary of Guise arrived in Scotland her family were asked to send experienced miners to help with the operations and they arrived in 1539 and worked at Crawfordmuir between July and October, where interpreters had to be provided for them. As a token of gratitude, a nugget of Crawfordmuir gold was sent to the duke of Guise in February 1540.[128] In the same year the export of bullion from Scotland was prohibited and another foreign miner, Balthasar Rusler or Howster, arrived from Norway or Germany seeking employment with James V.[129] Much of the metal mined at this time seems to have been used in the royal regalia, which was extensively re-fashioned, but a new issue of coins made from native gold, the most prestigious and regal of metals, was also struck between 1539 and 1542: the distinctive 'bonnet pieces'.[130]

The coinage of James V's reign follows the contemporary fashion, and the precedent set by James III, for using the motif of the arched 'imperial' or 'closed' crown, rather than the open fillet of medieval tradition. Such crowns imitated the diadem of the Holy Roman Empire and symbolised the notion that the king was a sovereign ruler (*rex in regno suo est imperator*), who acknowledged no superior authority before God (*rex qui superiorem non recognoscit*). The use of such images was therefore a gesture of defiance towards the long-standing pretensions of popes and emperors to temporal suzerainty in

126 *ADCP*, 350, 360–1. The men of Hamburg were named as Nicholas Troist, Nicholas Tryle, James Huelp and John Hose, who were acting as agents of John Huelp, Matthew Wackin, Henry Heulk, John Helbarth and Frederick Schomakre. One result of these operations may have been the order for the minting of new gold and billion coins in March 1532: ibid., 398–9.

127 *APS*, ii, 343; *James V Letters*, 287–8; *TA*, vi, 332, 393.

128 *Balcarres Papers*, i, 17–18, 19–20, 23, 25, 26, 27, 32–3; *TA*, vii, 182, 193–4, 256, 289.

129 *TA*, vii, 440, 307; *James V Letters*, 412, 415.

130 For the regalia, see chapter 6. For the 'bonnet pieces' see I. H. Stewart, *The Scottish Coinage* (London, 1955), 75, 78, 146.

other realms.[131] Kings of England and France had increasingly promoted images of themselves wearing closed crowns throughout the
fifteenth century and this became a widespread trend in European
coins of the period. The gold *enriques* of Henry IV of Castile (1454–74) is
thought to have been the first coin to place an arched crown above a
heraldic shield and on the king's head. This probably inspired Maximilian's Flemish *réal d'or* of 1487, which in turn was imitated by Henry
VII's gold 'sovereign' of 1489 (and the very name of this coin underlines
the political significance of its iconography).[132] James III's silver groats
and half groats were first issued c.1485 and the inspiration in this case
may well have been Italian since the king was shown not only wearing
an arched crown but in a realistic three-quarter face portrait: 'probably
the earliest Renaissance coin portrait outside Italy'.[133] The initiative
was not pursued by his son, since James IV's coinage reverted to the use
of the stereotyped king's head wearing an open crown, of medieval
tradition, although he did adopt Roman rather than old English
lettering on his later coins.[134] However, by the 1530s the symbolism
of sovereign kingship had become a commonplace feature of political
discourse. It acquired its most direct expression in Henry VIII's *Act in
Restraint of Appeals* of 1533 in which it was stated that

> . . . this Realme of Englond is an Impire, and so hath ben accepted
> in the worlde, governed by oon supreme heede and King having
> the dignitie and roiall estate of the Imperial crown of the same.[135]

As we have seen, James V maintained regular diplomatic contacts
with England and even came under pressure from his uncle to declare
himself supreme head of the church in Scotland, so he was well aware

---

131 John Robertson, 'Empire and Union: Two Concepts of the Early Modern
   European Political Order' in David Armitage (ed.), *Theories of Empire, 1450–
   1800* (Aldershot, 1998), 11–44.
132 Dale Hoak, 'The Iconography of the Crown Imperial' in Hoak (ed.), *Tudor
   Political Culture* (Cambridge, 1995), 55–70; Philip Grierson, 'The Origins of
   the English Sovereign and the Symbolism of the Closed Crown', *The British
   Numismatic Journal*, xxxiii (1964), 118–34. See also Roger A. Mason, '*Regnum
   et Imperium*: Humanism and the Political Culture of Early Renaissance
   Scotland' in Mason, *Kingship and the Commonweal: Political Thought in
   Renaissance and Reformation Scotland* (East Linton, 1998), 126–31. I would
   like to thank Dr. Mason for allowing me to read a draft of this paper prior
   to publication.
133 Stewart, *Scottish Coinage*, 67. See also Peter Seaby and P. Frank Purvey,
   Coins of Scotland, Ireland and the Islands (London, 1984), 34.
134 Stewart, *Scottish Coinage*, 68–74; Seaby and Purvey, *Coins of Scotland*, 36–40.
135 *Statutes of the Realm* (11 vols., 1810–28), iii, 427.

of the significance of the arched crown motif. Nevertheless, it was perfectly possible for him to claim imperial and sovereign status within his realm without renouncing spiritual allegiance to Rome (like Francis I).[136] Furthermore, there was an earlier Scottish precedent for him to follow since the parliament of 1469 had declared that James III possessed 'ful jurisdictione and free impire within his realm' and it is in this sense in which the symbolism of James V's coinage should be understood.[137] The arched 'imperial' crown appears on the king's head and above Stewart heraldic badges on the billon 'bawbees', silver groats and gold 'bonnet pieces' (or ducats, current at forty shillings) of James V's reign. Furthermore, the bonnet pieces and groats echo the coinage of James III in that the image of the king presented thereon is a realistic profile portrait. The gold ducat of James V is also the first Scottish coin to bear a date, although the mint did not necessarily change it every year. The chronology of James V's coinage is a difficult one to establish with any certainty but the numismatic consensus would appear to be that the first coinage of the reign (1513–26), which was struck during the minority, did not include any imperial crowns or images. The imperial crown appears first on the silver groats of the second coinage (1526–39), just as the young king was beginning to assert himself politically, and is developed most vigorously on the bawbees and ducats of the third coinage (1538–42), when James was at the height of his powers.[138] The symbolism of the coins would therefore appear to reflect the political developments of the period and also, as we shall see in the next chapter, the actual form taken by the royal regalia.

It seems to have been the case that in the field of technological advancement, as in so many other areas, James V was determined to maintain his royal dignity and status as far as his means allowed. His systematic programmes of naval expansion, fortification and re-armament were clearly designed to strengthen Scottish defences against the English threat, but his schemes also increased the ability of the crown to enforce its will on potentially troublesome regions such as the Borders and the Highlands, which James took care to visit in person. Cameron's study of the politics of the adult reign concluded that James V was largely successful in imposing his authority in these areas and that he

136 Knecht, *Renaissance Warrior and Patron*, 519–25, 537–40.
137 *APS*, ii, 95.
138 Robert K. B. Stevenson, 'The Bawbee Issues of James V and Mary', *The British Numismatic Journal*, lix (1989), 120–27; Stevenson, 'The Groat Coinage of James V, 1526–38', *The British Numismatic Journal*, lxi (1991), 37–56; Stewart, *Scottish Coinage*, 75–9; Seaby and Purvey, *Coins of Scotland*, 41–44.

won the co-operation of the majority of his magnates in doing so.[139] By the end of the reign, the likelihood that very few (if any) of the Scots nobles could command as much fire-power as the king might well have helped James in this task, but more detailed research on the military capabilities of the magnates of this period is needed to confirm this. In the matter of unearthing the mineral wealth of his kingdom, James seems to have been well aware that exploiting the gold deposits of Crawfordmuir could boost his financial position considerably. Since he used the 'gold of the mine' primarily for a new and prestigious issue of coins, and for embellishing the royal regalia, the king also seems to have been keen to propagate a regal image that would stand comparison with the grander princes of other European realms. This issue of the ceremonial and symbolic panoply of Renaissance kingship received a lot of attention from other monarchs of the age and the activities of James V in this area are examined in the following chapter.

---

139 Cameron, *James V*, 70–97, 228–54. See also Thomas I. Rae, *The Administration of the Scottish Frontier, 1513–1603* (Edinburgh, 1966), 167–78.

SIX

'Laud and Glorie': Pageantry and Ceremonial

In the sixteenth century it seemed natural to utilise grand state occasions such as royal entries, coronations, weddings and funerals as opportunities for making public statements of power and prestige.[1] At such events the monarch would be presented in all his splendour, accompanied by great nobles, prelates and other dignitaries, all of whom would be paraded before the populace. Even the poor would be included in the ceremonies, not just as onlookers but also as the recipients of alms and largesse. The image of the monarch could be portrayed in several ways stressing his genealogy, his Christian piety, his sovereignty, his wisdom, or the popular loyalty and obedience he commanded, for example. All of these concepts were familiar features of medieval royal and ecclesiastical pageantry, which persisted into the sixteenth and seventeenth centuries. In addition, the Renaissance spirit brought a tendency to compare kings to the Roman emperors of old, through the use of the closed 'imperial' crown and triumphal arches. Monarchs were also likened to the heroes of classical mythology, such as Hercules, a character who was of supreme importance in the iconography of both Charles V and Henry II.[2] Furthermore, the cult of chivalry was developed to glorify the prince as a valiant knight and the heraldic devices and chivalric orders could also be used to develop a sense of national identity.[3] Such tendencies have already been detected in France, England and the Habsburg lands, as well as in the Scotland of

1 Roy Strong, *Splendour at Court: Renaissance Spectacle and Illusion* (London, 1973), 23–44, 87–99; Roy Strong, *Art and Power: Renaissance Festivals, 1450–1650* (Woodbridge, 1984), 7–11, 65–9, 75–85; Sydney Anglo, *Spectacle and Pageantry and Early Tudor Policy* (Oxford, 1969), 100–23.

2 Marcel Bataillon, 'Plus Oultre: La Cour découvre le nouveau monde', in Jean Jacquot (ed.), *Les Fêtes de la Renaissance* (3 vols, Paris, 1956, 1960, 1975), ii, 13–27; Lawrence M. Bryant, 'Politics, Ceremonies, and Embodiments of Majesty in Henry II's France', in Heinz Duchhardt, Richard A. Jackson and David Sturdy (eds.), *European Monarchy, its Evolution and Practice from Roman Antiquity to Modern Times* (Stuttgart, 1992), 127–54.

3 Steven Gunn, 'Chivalry and the Politics of the Early Tudor Court', in Sydney Anglo (ed.), *Chivalry in the Renaissance* (Woodbridge, 1990), 107–28.

James II, III and IV[4] but very little attention has been paid hitherto to the court ceremonial of James V, who, despite a long and turbulent minority was to prove a vigorous and ambitious ruler during his brief adult reign.[5] Since James maintained connections with all of his neighbouring monarchs, and made a personal visit to the court of France in 1536–37, as we have seen, it would be surprising if he had not attempted to utilise state occasions in the contemporary manner. An examination of the relevant events of his majority appears to indicate that he wished to participate fully in the courtly developments of the day.

There is some poetic justice in the fact that the first major state ceremony of the reign, James V's marriage to Madeleine de Valois, was held in France and paid for by the French king.[6] James had first been promised the hand of one of Francis I's daughters under the treaty of Rouen, a grudging and conditional agreement extracted from a half-hearted ally by the personal and forceful attention of the Regent Albany in August 1517.[7] At that time and for most of his reign, Francis I's foreign ambitions were largely directed to pursuing his claims to the duchy of Milan and he would make and break alliances with the papacy, the empire and England as circumstances dictated in order to maintain his Italian interests. The role he expected his Scottish allies to play in this scheme was to threaten the English borders when Henry VIII was planning campaigns in northern France (as he was in 1522–3) and to participate meekly as junior partners in peace treaties with England when this suited French diplomacy: such a deal was forced on the Scots without consultation in May 1515 and August 1525 and French envoys brokered the Anglo-Scottish peace of 1533–4.[8] Once James V began to rule in his own right in 1528 he started to pursue actively a marriage that would bring him personal prestige and political

---

4 Jenny Wormald, 'The House of Stewart and its Realm'; Norman Macdougall, 'The Kingship of James IV of Scotland: "The Glory of All Princely Governing"?'; Roderick Lyall, 'The Court as a Cultural Centre', all in Jenny Wormald (ed.), *Scotland Revisited* (London, 1991), 12–24, 25–35, 36–48.

5 See Cameron, *James V*, for the politics of the adult reign. The most successful exploration of the culture of the court so far is in Edington, *Court and Culture*, but see also Hadley Williams (ed.), *Stewart Style*.

6 Francis paid for the expenses of James V, Madeleine and 'Madame Marguerite' (Madeleine's younger sister) from 13 October 1536. By 31 January, the bill had reached £14,615 10d. tournois (almost £6,500 Scots): Teulet, *Relations*, 108–9; see also Knecht, *Warrior and Patron*, 343 and Thomas, 'Renaissance Culture', 247 n.6.

7 *James V Letters*, 51–2; Teulet, *Papiers*, i, 39–43. The treaty was not ratified until 1521–2: Donaldson, *James V-James VII*, 19–20.

8 Knecht, *Warrior and Patron*, 195, 200–1, 244; Head, 'Henry VIII's Scottish Policy', 1–24; *TA*, vi, 124 131, 133–5, 151–3.

advantage and he naturally turned first to France. However, in the aftermath of defeat and capture at Pavia (1525) and a peace treaty with the emperor (Cambrai, 1529) which acknowledged Habsburg supremacy in Italy for the time being, Francis had to be careful not to antagonise Henry VIII. Henry was becoming increasingly alienated from both the papacy and the empire by his quest for a divorce from Katherine of Aragon and therefore an Anglo-French rapprochement would suit both monarchs for a few years but a Franco-Scottish marriage might jeopardise the delicate relationship. Thus the Scottish king's marriage became an issue for international diplomacy and James found himself negotiating with Francis, Henry and Charles simultaneously; but as the years passed and no conclusion was reached, it became clear that each king was offering potential brides not so much out of enthusiasm for a Scottish match as from a desire to disrupt negotiations with a rival power if they looked too promising.[9] Therefore by March 1536 James found himself engaged not to one of Francis's own daughters but to a less prestigious and more diplomatically acceptable alternative, Marie de Bourbon, daughter of the duke of Vendôme. Her father was the first prince of the blood royal after the king's own sons and Francis offered to give her the title of an adopted daughter of France as a sop to Scottish sensibilities.[10]

Once James actually reached France in the Autumn of 1536 he was able to persuade Francis to revert to the original arrangement of the treaty of Rouen. It is unclear exactly how this was achieved but James seems to have categorically refused to marry Marie after visiting her at St. Quentin and perhaps he took advantage of Francis's desire to appear as a gracious host.[11] His arrival in France coincided with a retreat of imperial forces from campaigns in Provence and Picardy and it was widely reported that the one event had precipitated the other because James had arrived with troops and artillery to assist his ally in an hour of need.[12] There is no

9 Bapst, *Mariages*, 7–281; *James V Letters*, 170–2, 181, 199–201, 212–3, 215–6, 237, 245–6, 255, 257–8, 277, 280–3, 289, 294–5, 297–9, 302–7, 314–5. A total of seventeen different ladies from eight states were considered as potential brides of James V between 1517 and 1537: see Cameron, *James V*, 132–3; McNeill and MacQueen (eds.), *Atlas*, 123.
10 Teulet, *Papiers*, 109–21. See chapter 1 for her dowry and jointure.
11 Bapst, *Mariages*, 289–90; Pitscottie, *Historie* (STS), i, 357–63.
12 The same reason was later given for James being accorded a Parisian royal entry as if he had been the dauphin; see below. For varying versions of the story see Pitscottie, *Historie* (STS), i, 357–8; Bapst, *Mariages*, 288; Francisque-Michel, *Les Ecossais en France les Français en Ecosse* (London, 1862), i, 400–1; Bentley-Cranch and Marshall, 'Iconography and Literature', 275. The real reasons for the retreat were more prosaic – famine and disease amongst the imperial troops: Knecht, *Warrior and Patron*, 337–8.

evidence that James had really intended to engage in battle with the emperor's forces (he had brought courtiers with him not soldiers) but the story was a useful piece of propaganda to explain honourably Francis's sudden change of heart toward the Scottish king. It is also possible that James played upon the moral debt owed by France to Scotland after Flodden and that the Princess Madeleine's own wishes may have added to the pressure. The poet Ronsard was a page in Madeleine's service and later told Brantôme that Madeleine had been determined to become a queen but found life in Scotland very hard.[13] Whatever the strategy, it is clear that Francis hesitated from giving his consent until he had gauged the likely English reaction and discovered that Henry was far too preoccupied with domestic problems to do more than write a few letters of complaint; the pope was also consulted.[14] Even then, Francis strenuously tried to substitute his younger daughter, Marguerite (who was only thirteen), for Madeleine (aged sixteen). Francis pleaded Madeleine's frailty as an impediment to marriage (with good cause, as events were to show) but marriage to the eldest daughter of a king traditionally carried more prestige than a union with a younger sister and James would not be deterred. The marriage contract with Madeleine was duly signed at Blois on 26 November, in the presence of the English ambassadors.[15] The date of the wedding was set for 1 January 1537 in Paris and Francis ordered the reluctant city to accord James the singular honour of a Parisian royal entry, as if he had been the dauphin, the day before. This was a triumph of international significance not only for the Scottish king but also for the political standing of his realm.[16]

Accordingly, at 2pm on Sunday 31 December 1536, a mounted procession of civic and clerical dignitaries and the members of the Paris parlement in their scarlet robes of office made their way to greet James V at St. Anthoine des Champs, just outside the city's bounds.

13 Francisque-Michel, Les Ecossais, 419–20; Bapst, Mariages, 302; Pierre de Bourdeilles, Abbé et seigneur de Brantôme, Oeuvres Complètes (13 vols, Paris, 1890), ix, 298–9. The Bishop of Faenza, papal emissary to the French court, reported a similar story: L&P Henry VIII, xi, 1183.

14 Bapst, Mariages, 295–303; L&P Henry VIII, xi, 848, 984, 1012. See also Scarisbrick, Henry VIII, 339–45.

15 L&P Henry VIII, xi, 1183; James V Letters, 325–6. See also chapter 1.

16 Teulet, Relations, i, 106–7. James was also treated as if he were the dauphin in one other respect: the household of Dauphin Francis, which had not yet been disbanded after the latter's death in August 1536, was transferred to James's service whilst he was in France: L&P Henry VIII, xi, 916. The maitre d'hôtel of this establishment was given a new year's gift of 300 crowns: TA, vii, 15.

There they found the king of Scots accompanied by the dauphin, the king of Navarre and other princes and nobles of the realm, and official speeches of welcome were made by the chancellor, the first president of the parlement and other senior figures. According to an English report, James had suffered a head injury that morning during some sort of martial sport and this may explain his reluctance to respond to the *harangues* with a speech of his own; the *Register of the Parlement* records that he simply embraced the orators without a word because his command of the French language was very poor. James was provided with a canopy of estate of cloth of gold and the assembled company then paraded through the streets of Paris which were hung with tapestries and decorated with the arms of France, Scotland, the French queen and the dauphin.[17] Sir David Lindsay of the Mount compared the procession to a Roman triumph complete with triumphal arches:

> O Paris, of all citeis principall,
> Quhilk did resave our prince with laud and glorie,
> Solempnitlie, throw arkis truimphall,
> Quhilk day bene digne to put in memorie.
> For as Pompey, efter his victorie,
> Was in to Rome resavit with greit joy,
> So thou resavit our richt redoutit roy.[18]

A service of thanksgiving was held at the cathedral of Nôtre Dame, where King Francis joined his guest, and James was then escorted to his lodgings where he was feasted by the citizens. Probably as part of the same event James also exercised the *droit de grâce*: the granting of pardons to prisoners.[19] No account exists of the details of the entry procession but it almost certainly followed a traditional route through the streets of Paris punctuated by *tableaux vivants* at 'stations' along the way celebrating the 'auld alliance' and the impending marriage using biblical, classical and heraldic allusions, since this was how Parisian entries were customarily conducted. Indeed, something very similar was staged at the Parisian royal entry given for the Emperor Charles V on 1 January 1540, which included imperial imagery (triumphal arches, eagles, figures of Hercules and decorations *à l'antique*). It could even be suggested that, since this was only the

---

17 *L&P Henry VIII*, xii, I, 12;Teulet, *Relations*, i, 107–8; *Cronique de Roy*, 201–5.
18 Lindsay, *Works*, i, 108 (*Deploratioun*).
19 Bentley-Cranch and Marshall, 'Iconography and Literature', 278; *Diurnal of Occurrents*, 21.

second occasion ever on which a foreign prince was accorded such an honour, the entry of Charles V may have followed precedents set by that of James V.[20] The fact that a Parisian royal entry was a civic ritual, offered by the burgesses and the parlement as a compliment to their sovereigns (usually) meant that James was bound not only to the French royal family by ties of blood but also, symbolically, to the community of the French realm.

At ten o'clock the following morning the royal party processed along a specially constructed platform, which raised them above the heads of the crowd, from the palace of the bishop of Paris to a stage at the west door of Nôtre Dame. First came many musicians, guards, heralds and prelates, then followed Dauphin Henry with his younger brother (Charles, duke of Orléans), Francis I and James V arm-in-arm, the English ambassadors (Stephen Gardiner, bishop of Winchester, and Master John Wallop), then the Princess Madeleine escorted by the king of Navarre, the queens of France and Navarre, the dauphine and other royal and noble ladies. At the door of the cathedral James and Madeleine were married by the cardinal of Bourbon and then the bridal party entered the church for the nuptial mass celebrated by the bishop of Paris, whilst largesse was cried and distributed to the crowd by the heralds. After the service a sumptuous dinner was held in the *grande salle* of the bishop's palace and that evening another feast was hosted by the parlement at the Palais de Justice. Both banqueting halls were hung with rich cloths and tapestries, buffets displayed gold and silver plate and musicians played throughout. In addition, the evening feast was notable for being held at a marble-topped table and was followed by dancing and masques, led by James, the dauphin and the cardinal of Lorraine. There followed a fortnight of celebrations and tournaments at the palaces of the Louvre and Tournelles.[21] According to Pitscottie, James had secured the attendance at his marriage of many Scottish magnates: six earls, six lords, six bishops and twenty great barons of the realm.[22] They are not named but the abbot of Arbroath, earl of Lennox and Lord Darnley were certainly present and the congregation possibly included the earls of Argyll, Arran and Moray,

20 Lawrence M. Bryant, *The King and the City in the Parisian Royal Entry Ceremony: Politics, Ritual and Art in the Renaissance* (Geneva, 1986); Bryant, 'Politics, Ceremonies, and Embodiments of Majesty in Henry II's France' in Duchhardt, Jackson and Sturdy (eds.), *European Monarchy*, 127–54. For Charles V's entry see Jean Jacquot, 'Panorama des fêtes et cérémonies du règne', in Jacquot (ed.), *Fêtes de la Renaissance*, iii, 437–9.

21 *L&P Henry VIII*, xii, I, 12; *Cronique du Roy*, 202–5; Teulet, *Relations*, i, 107–8.

22 Pitscottie, *Historie* (STS), i, 364.

Lords Fleming and Erskine, Sir James Kirkcaldy of Grange and Sir David Lindsay of the Mount.[23] Pitscottie also suggests that the celebrations were so splendid as to recall the golden age of Charlemagne. He mentions jousts and tournaments both on horse and on foot, artillery salutes, feasts, triumphs and plays involving elaborate special effects such as fire-breathing dragons flying in the air, or mock naval battles conducted in the flooded streets.[24] The pageantry of this marriage was to be repeated almost exactly for James V's daughter, Mary, queen of Scots, on 24 April 1558, when she processed along a walkway from the bishop's palace to her wedding to Dauphin Francis at the door of Nôtre Dame. The locations and protocol correspond to those used in 1537 down to the marriage being performed by the cardinal of Bourbon and the evening feast being held at the marble table of the Palais de Justice. We have more information about the evening's entertainment in 1558, which included figures dressed as the seven planetary deities, artificial horses ridden around the hall by young princes and artificial ships 'sailed' around the floor by the guests (the ship was the emblem of the city of Paris).[25]

Just as James had been honoured by his Parisian entry, so Madeleine was to receive a royal entry into Edinburgh at the time of her coronation as queen of Scots. The provost and officers of the burgh began preparations on 17 March 1537 with a decision to offer her a 'propine' (formal gift) of forty tuns of wine and to raise a tax of £1,000 to cover the expenses of this event and other (unspecified) public works. The lord treasurer spent £100 on 'cottis of armour' (armorial tabards) for the heralds who would be involved in the entry, and a convention of lords was called to Edinburgh to coincide with the ceremony.[26] Unfortunately, these fragments of information are the only surviving official records of the plans and it is clear from the royal household books that the entry and coronation never actually took place.[27] Madeleine was

---

23 For Arbroath, Lennox and Darnley see Teulet, *Inventaire*, 81, 83; *TA*, vii, 2; Pitscottie, *Historie* (STS), i, 366. The other lords are known to have been in France with James at some stage during his visit but cannot be specifically located there at the time of the wedding.

24 Pitscottie, *Historie* (STS), i, 365–6.

25 Teulet, *Papiers*, i, 292–303; *Ceremonial at the Marriage of Mary, Queen of Scots, with the Dauphin of France*, ed. W. Bentham (London, Roxburghe Club, 1818); Gabriel de Pimodan, *La Mère des Guises* (Paris, 1925), 157–64.

26 *Edin. Recs.*, ii, 74; *TA*, vi, 303, 313.

27 SRO, Liber Emptorum, E.32/6, fos. 61v.-88r. This shows that the king and queen landed at Leith, moved to Holyrood and stayed there until the day of the queen's death.

almost certainly consumptive; the newlyweds' return to Scotland had been delayed until May 1537 to allow her to gather her strength but nevertheless the voyage took its toll. They landed at Leith on Saturday 19 May, rested there (presumably in the King's Wark) on Sunday 20 (Whitsun) and moved to Holyrood Palace on Monday 21. Madeleine did not stir from Holyrood for the next seven weeks and died there on the morning of Saturday 7 July, mourned by two kingdoms. The only evidence we have of the pageantry that should have been staged in Edinburgh for Queen Madeleine is in Lindsay's poem, *The Deploratioun*.[28] He describes fountains ready to flow with wine and stages prepared with colourful scenery on which 'disagysit folkis' would have acted out stories of 'creaturis devyne'. He lists the categories of civic dignitaries that would have taken part in the procession: the craftsmen in green; the burgesses in scarlet and 'grane'; the provost, baillies and lords of the town with the senators of the college of justice in purple, black and brown silk; the lords of parliament, barons and 'banrents' in silk and gold; the clergy in their vestments; the musicians playing tabors, trumpets, shawms and clarions; the heralds in their tabards and macers with their batons and finally the new queen herself, bedecked in silks and jewels, under a pall of cloth of gold, escorted by the ladies of the realm and the king's guards. The company would have paraded through the burgh to the cheers of the populace and eloquent speeches of the dignitaries until the queen reached her coronation at the abbey of Holyrood, which would have been followed by banquets, tournaments and other celebrations. As Snowdon Herald and acting Lord Lyon, Lindsay would have been in charge of the arrangements for this event and the picture he paints in his poem is therefore not only vivid but authentic.

Lindsay's account corresponds well to the more detailed record of the previous entry, marriage and coronation of a new queen of Scots, that of Margaret Tudor on 7 and 8 August 1503, which was recorded by the English herald, John Young.[29] However, Young refers to holy crosses and relics being offered to the king and queen for them to kiss: a ritual that is not mentioned in Lindsay's poem, perhaps because of his own scepticism about such matters.[30] Young also notes the details of the *tableaux vivants* presented at intervals along the route and it is highly likely that similar scenes would have greeted Madeleine, with suitable adjustments made to replace English badges and heraldic

28 Lindsay, *Works*, i, 105–12.
29 Leland, *Collectanea*, iv, 287–96.
30 See Edington, *Court and Culture*, 145–62.

devices with French ones. The scenes in 1503 were as follows: just outside the town two knights pretended to be in dispute over a lady, thus according the king an excuse for arranging a chivalrous combat to be held later. At the burgh gate (probably the West Port) Margaret was met by the greyfriars carrying relics and was then presented with the symbolic keys to the burgh by angels in a tower (a tower is still the emblem of the burgh). As she moved through the town she was met by the college of St. Giles (also with relics), passed a fountain flowing with wine and scenes depicting the judgement of Paris, the annunciation, the marriage of the Virgin Mary and Joseph, the four cardinal virtues trampling on their corresponding vices and a representation of a unicorn with a greyhound and a thistle with a rose (Stewart and Tudor badges). With the exception of the heraldic emblems, all of these images would have been equally suitable for Madeleine's entry as for Margaret's and indeed the presentation of keys (by angels in 1590 but by boys in 1561 and 1579), the personification of four virtues (not necessarily the same ones), fountains of wine and biblical and mythological allusions continued to feature in Edinburgh entries later in the century, suggesting a strong element of tradition in the arrangements.[31]

An Edinburgh entry was performed for the reception of James's second French wife, Mary of Guise, on Saturday 20 July, 1538. She had spent the previous night at Dunfermline as a guest of the abbot and made a stop at Costorphine before entering Edinburgh.[32] The burgh records note that the streets were to be cleaned of all refuse, beggars were to be expelled, the mercat cross was newly painted and scaffold-

31 *Documents Relative to the Reception at Edinburgh of the Kings and Queens of Scotland, 1561–1650*, ed. Sir Patrick Walker (Edinburgh, 1822); Douglas Grey, 'The Royal Entry in Sixteenth-Century Scotland', in Mapstone and Wood (eds.), *The Rose and the Thistle*, 10–37; Ian Campbell, 'James IV and Edinburgh's First Triumphal Arches', in D. Mays (ed.), *The Architecture of Scottish Cities: Essays in Honour of David Walker* (East Linton, 1997); 26–33; A. A. MacDonald, 'Mary Stewart's Entry to Edinburgh: an Ambiguous Triumph', *IR*, xlii (1991), 101–10; Michael Lynch, 'Court Ceremony and Ritual during the Personal Reign of James VI' in Julian Goodare and Michael Lynch (eds.), *The Reign of James VI* (East Linton, 2000), 71–92. I am very grateful to Professor Lynch for allowing me to see the this article prior to publication. See also David Stevenson, *Scotland's Last Royal Wedding: The Marriage of James VI and Anne of Denmark* (Edinburgh, 1997), 57–62, 107–20, and John Burel's description of the royal entry of Anna of Denmark in May 1590 in James Watson, *Choice Collection of Comic and Serious Scots Poems*, ed. H. H. Wood (STS, 1977), i, 1–15.
32 SRO, Liber Domicili, E.31/7, fo. 79v.; *TA*, vi, 431–2.

ing for the pageants was to be erected at the West Port, the Overbow, the tolbooth, the mercat cross, the tron and the Netherbow. Each station was assigned to two or three prominent burgesses as their specific responsibility under the overall control of Sir David Lindsay. Lindsay, Adam Otterburn and James Foulis wrote a French oration of welcome which was to be delivered by Master Henry Lauder[33] and the order of the civic procession was set: twelve burgesses in three relays of four were appointed to carry the queen's pall and were to be dressed in velvet gowns of purple (for the first quartet), tanny (for the second) and black (for the third). An escort of sixteen footmen wearing the burgh's livery of a black coat with the town's arms on the sleeve was also appointed, along with a mounted escort of thirty-seven burgh dignitaries dressed in silk with their horses trapped in velvet. The clothing and conduct of the lesser inhabitants of the burgh was also regulated for the occasion.[34] No contemporary narrative account has survived to impart any more details of the imagery and allusion displayed at this event but it is again reasonable to assume that it would have been similar to that staged for Queen Margaret in 1503 and planned for Queen Madeleine in 1537. The *Diurnal of Occurrents* notes only that

> sho maid her entres in Edinburgh with greit triumphe, and als with ordour of the haill nobillis; hir grace come in first at the West Port, and raid doun the hie gait to the abbay of Halyrudhous, with greit sportis playit to hir grace throuw all the pairtis of the toun.

Similarly Pitscottie states that

> the king and the quen was weill ressavit witht great treumph in the castell and toun and in the palice and thair he was honestlie and richlie propynit witht the provost and communitie of the toun baitht witht spyce and wyne, gold and sillver and also greit triumph phraissis maid and playis wnto the queins grace on the expenssis of the said toun.[35]

Perhaps the Edinburgh entry involved some sort of mechanical device for moving scenery as apparently happened at Mary's earlier entry to St. Andrews on 16 June 1538.[36] According to Pitscottie, David Lindsay arranged for her to be met at the new abbey gate by a cloud descending from heaven from which stepped a lady dressed as an angel to present

---

33 For Lindsay, Otterburn, Foulis and Lauder see chapter 4.
34 *Edin. Recs.*, ii, 89–91.
35 *Diurnal of Occurents*, 22; Pitscottie, *Historie* (STS), i, 381.
36 Pitscottie, *Historie* (STS), i, 379. SRO, Liber Domicili, E.31/7, fo. 70r.

her with the keys of Scotland 'in signe and taikin that all the heartis of
Scottland was opnit to the ressaving of hir grace'. Lindsay then made
'certane wriesouns and exortatiouns . . . quhilk teichit hir to serve her
god, obey hir husband, and keep hir body clene according to godis will
and commandement.' The following day her marriage to James, which
had already been performed in France with Lord Maxwell as the king's
proxy, was confirmed in the abbey kirk and three weeks of celebrations
followed involving feasts, music, dancing, plays, 'farces', tournaments
and hunting.[37] Queen Mary also made ceremonial entries into the
burghs of Dundee (28 August 1539), Perth and Old Aberdeen (both in
the autumn of 1541), although no descriptions of the first two survive.
For the Aberdeen event we have only a brief entry in the burgh records
and Leslie's comment that

> she was ressavit thair with diverse triumphes and playes maid be
> the town, and be the university and scules thairof, and remanit
> thair the space of fiftein dayes, weill intertenit be the bischop,
> quhair their wes excersise and disputationes in all kind of
> sciences, in the colledge and scules, with diverse oratiouns maid
> in Greke, Latine and uther languages, quhilk wes mickell com-
> mendit be the king and quene, and all thair company.[38]

The Aberdeen entry may have resembled the processions staged by the
burgh for major feast days such as Candlemas (2 February) or Corpus
Christi (a moveable feast in May or June), which involved each guild
taking responsibility for staging a pageant depicting the life of a saint or
biblical story. The burgh employed an organist and corps of minstrels
to provide music for these and other civic occasions.[39] It is also possible
that the entry of Mary of Guise to Aberdeen resembled that of Margaret
Tudor, which was staged in 1511 and of which the poet, Dunbar has left
an account.[40] In this event Margaret was met at the burgh gates by
artillery salutes and the burgesses in their finest clothes, who arranged
for four young men clad in velvet to carry the crimson pall over her
head. The streets were hung with tapestries, the crowds cheered,
minstrels played and a fountain of wine was set at the mercat cross.
Pageants were presented depicting the annunciation, the adoration of
the magi, the expulsion of Adam and Eve from the garden of Eden, and

37 Pitscottie, *Historie* (STS), i, 378–81.
38 SRO, Liber Domicili, E.31/8 fo. 101r.; *TA*, vii, 202; *Abdn. Counc.*, i, 179;
   Lesley, *History* (Bann. Club), 159.
39 *Abdn. Counc.*, i, 95, 105, 450–51.
40 Dunbar, *Poems*, ii, 251–3 (*Blyth Aberdein*).

the Stewart family tree descending from King Robert Bruce (perhaps making a comparison with the traditional depiction of the ancestry of Christ in the 'tree of Jesse'). Finally, when the queen reached her lodgings, she was presented with a gold cup filled with coins as a 'propine.' The emphasis on nativity and genealogy would have been entirely suitable for the entry of a queen who, after eight years of marriage and four pregnancies, had hitherto failed to produce a healthy heir. A similar anxiety would also have surrounded the entry of 1541, which occurred only a few months after the deaths of two baby princes, and this coincidence may have suggested to the burgesses that it would be appropriate to re-produce some of the 1511 scenes, quite apart from the natural tendency to rely on precedence and tradition.

These ceremonial entries for the new queen were financed and organised by the burghs concerned, with the assistance of the king's senior herald, and were intended not only to welcome and honour her but also to serve as an opportunity for the burgesses to engage in a ritualised form of political dialogue with the crown. The use of allegorical figures of virtues, representations of biblical scenes and classical heroes was designed to emphasise the peace, justice, prosperity and good rule that the people sought from their sovereign lord and lady. The expressions of loyalty and devotion were accompanied by symbolic reminders of the responsibilities and duties of monarchs to secure the welfare of their subjects and to uphold the church. In fact it is possible to interpret the royal entries of this period as a visual equivalent of the traditional *speculum principis* literary genre. The receptions of Mary of Guise at St. Andrews and Edinburgh also had an international dimension. As with the earlier marriage to Madeleine, the wedding of 1538 was accompanied by diplomatic manoeuvres designed to delay and disrupt. James requested a replacement bride from Francis with what would be considered today as indecent haste but at the time was an indication of political and dynastic necessity. However, having lost one princess to the rigours of the Scottish climate, Francis could hardly be expected to offer the hand of his sole surviving daughter, Marguerite, and in any case James had now acquired the dignity and prestige that marriage to the eldest daughter of the king of France could bestow and was more concerned with finding a bride capable of bearing sons (Marguerite was still only fourteen). Yet there was no question of him reverting to the jilted Marie de Vendôme, for this would have been a slight to his honour, and so Francis quickly suggested the recently widowed duchess of Longueville, who had borne her first husband two sons, was twenty-two and healthy. The marriage was delayed for a few months whilst the details of the dowry and jointure were negotiated (and perhaps to allow Mary to complete a full year's mourning for her first husband) and this allowed Henry VIII to enter the fray. His third wife, Jane Seymour, died in October 1537 after giving birth to Prince Edward and immediately Henry instructed his ambassadors to sue for the hand of the duchess of Longueville, asserting that he would accept no one else as his fourth queen.[41] This was such a blatant attempt to prevent a renewed Franco-Scottish match that Francis found little difficulty in dispensing with it, especially as his relationship with the English king was less important than formerly because he was becoming increasingly friendly with the emperor. The marriage therefore went ahead in June 1538 as a means of binding Scotland into the new Catholic alliance that was developing in Europe and which was threatening to launch a crusade against the heretic king of England.[42] Henry naturally took it as a personal and political slight by his nephew and embarked upon a diplomatic campaign to detach him from his French alliance by other means.[43] So the ceremonial and pageantry attending Mary of Guise's receptions at St. Andrews and Edinburgh, which was witnessed by the French delegation escorting her to Scotland, was also significant as a sign of Scotland's commitment to her foreign allies and an expression of respect and reverence for France.

The ceremonial entry of Mary of Guise into Edinburgh in 1538 differed in one major respect from that of Margaret Tudor in 1503: it was not a prelude to the queen's coronation. As she was not a king's daughter, Mary was not of sufficient status to expect this as a matter of course and the timing of her eventual coronation at the abbey of Holyrood (22 February 1540) was calculated to stress the importance of her child-bearing duties. The plans for her coronation were laid only from October 1539, when she would have been roughly two months pregnant, and by February 1540 the fact that she was expecting a baby would have been clearly visible.[44] Her coronation was the most solemn ritual acknowledgement of her status as one chosen by God as an instrument of international alliance and as a means of perpetuating a line of kings. We have no narrative of the event but there are clear indications in the *Treasurer's Accounts* that James V intended the

---

41 Bapst, *Mariages*, 311–17; *Balcarres Papers*, i, 2–5; Pimodan, *La Mère des Guises*, 65–6; *L&P Henry VIII*, xii, 1004, 1201, 1285, 1292 & 1293.

42 Knecht, *Warrior and Patron*, 385–9; Head, 'Henry VIII's Scottish Policy', 14–5; Scarisbrick, *Henry VIII*, 355–63.

43 Sir Ralph Sadler's embassies of 1540 and 1541 were aimed at securing a meeting between Henry VIII and James V and persuading the Scots to reject papal authority: *Sadler's Papers*, i, 3–55.

44 *TA*, vii, 254.

occasion to enhance the dignity of the Scottish monarchy. His own coronation as a child in the aftermath of Flodden had been a muted and hurried affair, a political act that had to be accomplished swiftly so that the more urgent business of securing the Scottish realm from the English threat could be attended to.[45] In preparation for his marriage to Madeleine he had ordered some embellishments and alterations to the royal regalia and further work was undertaken in 1539 and 1540 as the queen's coronation approached.

Most work was concentrated on the king's crown: it was repaired and remodelled in May 1532, repaired again in October 1533 and remodelled January-February 1540.[46] In May 1532 seven and a quarter ounces, plus a half unicorn of gold were bought from a goldsmith called Thomas Wood, along with an ounce of gold bought from James Acheson, the coiner, to mend the king's crown. In August 1532 payment was made to Acheson for a further three-ounce ingot of gold which may also have gone into the crown, since it was listed in the accounts at the same time as the fee to the goldsmith who had done the work, Adam Leys. He was paid £6 for mending the crown 'and making of the spryngis thairto.' The exact meaning of the word 'springs' in this context is unclear but it is possible that 'arches' were meant. If this were the case it would mean that this was the date on which the Scottish crown was closed with 'imperial' arches for the first time, bringing it into line with the image that had been used on coins and portraits since the reign of James III. May 1532 was also the date of the inauguration of the college of justice and it may have been the case that the new, arched crown would have been given its first public airing on this occasion. In the same account of May 1532 payments were recorded for a purple velvet bonnet lined with buckram and black which was made for the crown and £23 worth of gold was purchased to make a small chain for the king: these expenses were perhaps associated with the same event. Recent commentators on the royal regalia certainly agree that the Scottish crown was closed before 1540 but have so far not identified the point at which this occurred.[47] As we have already seen in relation

45 The coronation took place at the chapel royal, Stirling, 21 September, 1513: *ADCP*, 1.

46 *TA*, vi, 25–6, 73, 179; vii, 278.

47 C. J. Burnett and C. J. Tabraham, *The Honours of Scotland* (Edinburgh, 1993), 24; Charles J. Burnett, Ross Herald of Arms, 'Outward Signs of Majesty, 1535–1540' in Hadley Williams (ed.), *Stewart Style*, 293–4; A. J. S. Brook, 'Technical Description of the Regalia of Scotland', *PSAS*, xxiv (1889–90), 82–7. See also *Papers Relative to the Regalia of Scotland*, ed. William Bell (Bannatyne Club, 1829) and above, chapter five, for the coinage.

to the coinage, James V was keen to exploit the political symbolism attached to a 'closed' rather than an 'open' crown, which stressed his status as a sovereign prince, acknowledging no superior authority before God. The closed crown appears in the *Wardrobe Inventory* of 25 March 1539, where it is described as made of gold, set with twenty diamonds and sixty-eight oriental pearls and lacking one golden fleur de lys.[48] In the remodelling of 1540 John Mossman added 41 oz of gold from the mine of Crawfordmuir and twenty-three stones including three great garnets and a great amethyst. This is the version of the royal crown that still survives today on display in Edinburgh Castle. An analysis of the gold and the construction suggests that at this point Mossman melted down and recast the gold fillet with the additional metal but then simply re-attached the arches as they had been made in 1532.[49] The mound and cross which is set at the point where the arches intersect and the enamelled oak-leaf decorations applied to them are of French manufacture and were possibly purchased by Mossman when he was sent to France in September 1539 with £50 to spend on gold work. He delivered the new crown to James V at Holyrood on 8 February 1540 at which point a new purple velvet cap, lined with purple satin, and a new case were provided for it.[50]

Other items of the royal regalia also received attention. James V had two swords of state, both of which were papal gifts. The first had been sent to his father by Pope Julius II in 1507 and in July 1536 Adam Leys was employed to mend and gild it. In March 1539 a new case was made for the sword of honour, and since the sword of 1507 (which is also on display in Edinburgh Castle) still has its original scabbard this was probably for the second one which was sent by Paul III and presented to James V at Compiègne in February 1537.[51] The gift signified papal approval of the marriage alliance and the hope that the Scottish king would act as a defender of the true faith in the face of pressure from his English uncle to defect.[52] The royal sceptre was yet another papal gift, sent by Alexander VI to James IV in 1494, and at the same time that Leys was working on the sword he was also commissioned to extend and gild the sceptre. On 10 May 1537, whilst James was on his way home from France, Leys was again employed to gild 'the knoppis of the kingis stule' (possibly his throne) with £3 worth of

48 SRO, Wardrobe Inventory, E.35/1, fo. 21r.
49 *TA*, vii, 278; Brook, 'Technical Description', 59–62, 82–92.
50 *TA*, vii, 204, 285.
51 Ibid., vi, 285; vii, 142.
52 C. Burns, 'Papal Gifts to Scottish Monarch: The Golden Rose and the Blessed Sword', *IR*, xx, (1969), 180–3; *James V Letters*, 328.

gold ducats and at the same time the 'stule' was lined with red leather, covered with green velvet and fringed with silk and gold.[53] As the coronation approached the preparations became more intense. The refashioning of the king's crown was accompanied by many other purchases. On 5 October 1539 Mossman was provided with thirty-five ounces of gold from the mine with which to fashion the queen's crown. He also provided the stones and pearls for its decoration but unfortunately we have no information on the exact form it took.[54] On 21 January 1540 payments are recorded for the king's 'robe royal' made of thirty-eight ells of purple velvet, lined with forty dozen skins of spotted ermine and for the queen's robe made of twenty-two and a half ells of purple velvet and lined with ten ells of white taffeta. At the same time a gold belt set with a sapphire, and a turquoise ring were purchased, perhaps also for the coronation.[55] On 6 February, John Mossman was given four rose nobles (worth £10 12s.) to gild the queen's sceptre which he had fashioned from thirty-one and a half ounces of silver and which was topped with 'ane quhyt hand'. This description suggests that the queen's sceptre was made in the French style and therefore is not the unidentified wand which was recovered with the rest of the royal regalia in 1818.[56]

All this work on the royal regalia suggests that the coronation of February 1540 would have been a magnificent occasion but unfortunately we have no narratives of the event. We are still reliant on snippets of information from the financial accounts to paint the picture. Nineteen cart-loads of timber boards and spars were used to construct the tiered stands erected in the abbey kirk to seat the congregation. The ladies of the great families of Scotland were summoned to attend the queen, as we know from the payments made for sending letters to them, but we have no specific details of which ladies responded to the call nor of the roles they played in the ceremonial. Presumably they would have supplemented Mary's staff of ladies-in-waiting and maids of honour to give her an expanded train. Eleven chaplains from the chapel royal were present in Edinburgh from 14 February to 22 March

53 *TA*, vi, 285–6, 299; Brook, 'Technical Description', 101–4.
54 *TA*, vii, 254.
55 Ibid., vii, 277–8.
56 Ibid., vii, 285–6. SRO, Wardrobe Inventory, E.35/4 fo. 41r. For the French *main de justice* see Danielle Gaborit-Chopin, *Regalia: les instruments de sacre des rois de France et les 'honneurs de Charlemagne'* (Paris, 1987), 76–7. For the suggestion that the wand traditionally known as 'the Lord Treasurer's Rod' might have been the queen's sceptre see J. J. Reid, 'The Scottish Regalia, Anciently Styled the Honours of Scotland', *PSAS*, xxiv (1889–90), 27.

and were paid an allowance of two shillings a day each but we have no information on the duties they performed. Presumably they would have assisted in the religious rites attending the coronation, thus enhancing the dignity and solemnity of the occasion simply by expanding the number of clergy present. At the same time thirty guns were placed at the head of David's Tower in Edinburgh Castle, probably to fire salutes, but no more details are recorded.[57] There are no documents of established authenticity recording the pre-Reformation Scottish coronation service and the first Scottish order of service which has survived, that for the coronation of Charles I at Holyrood in 1633, makes no mention of the procedure for crowning a queen consort.[58] At the coronation of Anna of Denmark in May 1590 she was invested with a crown, sceptre and robe at a ceremony in the abbey kirk of Holyrood which involved a procession, acclamation, unction and sermon. Anna gave an oath to support the church and realm of Scotland and received the homage of the Scottish estates. There was no recitation of the royal genealogy which was traditional for the investiture of a reigning monarch. Mary of Guise's coronation may well have been very similar to Anna's, with the addition of a solemn Mass and without the references to stamping out popery.[59]

The celebrations surrounding the queen's coronation were followed swiftly by rejoicing for the birth of a male heir, Prince James, at St. Andrews on 22 May. Again we have no detailed narrative but since the child was baptised within a few days of his birth (on Wednesday 26 May) the pageantry could not have been as elaborate as that attending the baptism of Prince Charles James, the future James VI, at Stirling in December 1566, which took six months to prepare.[60] The godparents in 1540 were Margaret Tudor, the queen dowager, Cardinal David Beaton, archbishop of St. Andrews and Gavin Dunbar, archbishop of Glasgow.[61] Fifteen ells of white Genoese taffeta were used as serviettes

57 *TA*, vii, 297, 302, 346–7, 487.
58 R. J. Lyall, 'The Medieval Scottish Coronation Service: Some Seventeenth-Century Evidence', *IR*, xxviii (1977), 3–21.
59 *TA*, vii, 282, 302; *Papers Relative to the Marriage of James VI*, 52; Stevenson, *Scotland's Last Royal Wedding*, 58–9, 104–7; Lyall, 'Scottish Coronation Service', 19; Sir Thomas Innes of Learney, 'The Style and Title of "Lord Lyon King of Arms," *JR*, xliv (1932), 200. Cardinal Beaton celebrated the Mass according to one account: *Diurnal of Occurrents*, 23.
60 SRO, Despence de la Maison Royale, E.33/1, Lib. 7, fo. 13v.; Michael Lynch, 'Queen Mary's Triumph: the Baptismal Celebrations at Stirling in December 1566', *SHR*, lxix (1990), 1–21.
61 *Diurnal of Occurrents*, 23. In Lesley, *History* (Bann. Club), 157 the archbishop of Glasgow is replaced by the earl of Arran.

to hold the torches at the baptism and the child was provided with a cradle carved by a French craftsman (Andrew Manson) and a canopy for his bed of state. Members of the nobility were again summoned to attend and coats of arms were painted. Some of the king's silver plate was sent from Edinburgh for the occasion and a payment of £666 13s 4d (one thousand merks) was made to Sir David Lindsay of the Mount and his wife, Janet Douglas, for services which are not specified but were possibly connected with the baptism.[62] James V could not have been in St. Andrews at the time of the birth since a messenger was sent to him with the news and was rewarded with a fine suit of clothes.[63] The news of the birth was also sent to James V's uncle, Henry VIII, and father-in-law, Francis I.[64] It is possible that the birth was celebrated with a fireworks display as the munitions accounts of May 1540 reveal that some French gunners were paid for dealing with 'fyre werk schot devisit be the kingis grace'. As fireworks were certainly used in France to celebrate the Field of Cloth of Gold in 1520, and may have been used to mark the wedding of James and Madeleine in 1537, this is perhaps another example of French influence on the Scottish court.[65] The following April the birth and baptism of James and Mary's second son, Robert, duke of Albany, was celebrated at Stirling. He must have been born on or shortly before 24 April, for on this date payments were entered for eight ells of white taffeta for serviettes to hold the candles at his baptism and for guns to be hauled on to the wall-head at Edinburgh Castle to fire a salute. However, any celebrations on this occasion were short-lived for the baby died within a few days and was joined in the grave by his elder brother at about the same time. The boys were buried at Holyrood.[66]

All of the events considered above were accompanied by jousts and tournaments as part of the traditional celebrations.[67] Both James II and James IV had achieved international fame for the splendid tournaments

---

62 *TA*, vii, 304, 307, 308–9, 314, 315.
63 Ibid., vii, 322. The king may have been in Leith making preparations for his voyage to the Northern and Western Isles: *RSS*, ii, 3508. However, Murray, 'Pursemaster's Accounts', 50 suggest that the king was in St. Andrews on 22 May 1540.
64 *TA*, vii, 307, 328.
65 *TA*, vii, 357; J. C. Russell, *The Field of Cloth of Gold* (London, 1969), 176; Pitscottie, *Historie* (STS), i, 365–6.
66 *TA*, vii, 442, 495; *Diurnal of Occurrents*, 24. For the confusion surrounding the name of the new prince see Thomas, 'Renaissance Culture', 267 n.94.
67 *L & P Henry VIII*, xii, I, 12; *Cronique du Roy*, 204–5; Lindsay, *Works*, i, 111 (*The Deploratioun*); *TA*, vi, 402, 412–3; vii, 278, 292–3, 317; *MW*, i, 288.

they staged in Scotland and, although the chivalric exploits of James V's reign have not acquired the same legendary status, it is likely that they were also quite spectacular.[68] James was a keen participant from an early age. When he was only thirteen years old, English envoys were reporting to Henry VIII that he relished his martial training and particularly desired a full-sized adult sword, rather than the smaller version usually given to children, and early in his adult reign references to lists appear in the accounts, such as those erected at Holyrood in May 1530 or at Stirling in January 1531.[69] James seems to have regarded jousts and tournaments as a necessary part of celebrating such festivals as Christmas, Easter and May Day[70] and his wardrobe accounts are scattered with purchases of spears, swords, horse harness and riding jackets throughout the reign, although it is not always specifically stated that such items were for use in martial sports (they would also have been used for hunting and for judicial progresses such as the border raids of 1529 and 1530). However, it is also apparent from the accounts that the jousts and tournaments staged to celebrate the marriages, coronation and baptisms of the years 1537 to 1541 were on a much grander scale than the earlier, seasonal events. For example, at the jousts of Christmas 1530 and New Year of 1531 the wardrobe purchased three dozen spears and several swords but for the celebrations of the marriage to Madeleine over four hundred spears were acquired and 181 French crowns were spent just on the feathers to decorate the caps and caparisons of the king and his knights. According to Pitscottie, James himself along with the earl of Lennox and his brother, Lord Darnley, particularly distinguished themselves in these tournaments. This is hardly surprising as James seems to have spent most of the time between his betrothal and marriage either hunting or jousting with the dauphin.[71] Considerable expense was also undertaken for the jousting at St. Andrews in June 1538 to celebrate Mary of Guise's arrival in Scotland: lists and counter-lists were erected under the supervision of George Elphinstone, five hundred spears were imported from France, cataphract horses were imported from Denmark, and the king had three new sets of velvet harness and jousting outfits, one red, one blue, and one multi-coloured, all embroidered with gold. Similarly, for the queen's coronation, more horses were sought

---

68 McGladdery, *James II*, 41–2; P. Hume Brown (ed.), *Early Travellers in Scotland* (Edinburgh 1891), 30–8; Macdougall, *James IV*, 294–5.

69 Wood, *Letters*, ii, 19–20; *MW*, i, 36; *TA*, v, 411–2.

70 E.g. *TA*, vii, 168.

71 *TA*, v, 411–12; vii, 8, 16; Pitscottie, *Historie* (STS), i, 366; *Cronique de Roy*, 201, 204–5; Bapst, *Mariages*, 304–5.

abroad, lists were erected at Holyrood and James had three more jousting outfits, this time of black silk and tanny velvet, embroidered with gold crowns, thistles, fleurs de lys and mottoes, whilst his harness was hung with gilt badges.[72]

Lindsay's poem, *The Iusting*, describes a comic parody of a chivalrous combat held between two distinctly un-knightly figures: James Watson and John Barber. Watson was a barber-surgeon and servant in the king's chamber, whilst Barber was a groom in the wardrobe, working under John Tennent. Lindsay sets their exploits at St. Andrews on Whitmonday, which is where the court really was in 1539 and 1542, and describes their incompetent progress from riding at one another with spears to a sword fight on foot and finally resorting to fisticuffs. However, their blundering ensured that 'that day was sched no blude.'[73] In *The Historie of Squyer William Meldrum* a single combat is described where the champion and his challenger meet formally in the lists attended by heralds, trumpeters and a crowd of onlookers to defend their honour. The two knights run several courses at the lists, breaking each other's spears and unseating one another. Meldrum wins the contest when his opponent is seriously wounded in a fall but chivalrously declines to accept his prize of his opponent's horse and armour; thus winning even more fame and honour for himself with the knights of three nations (France, Scotland and England).[74] These stories, together with the snippets of information from the financial accounts, suggest that James was staging in Scotland the same sort of chivalrous combat that was popular at all the European courts of the period. This included mounted knights tilting with lances and sword-play, often on foot, at the barriers. The tournament would usually be fought by teams of knights responding to a challenge, which arose from a fictitious scenario taken from Arthurian Romance or something similar, but most of the action concentrated on a series of single-combats, where the knights would attempt to break their spears or unseat their opponents.[75] The most famous Scottish example is James IV's tournament of the wild knight and the black lady, staged in 1507 and again in 1508 but, sadly, there is very little information on the themes adopted for James V's tournaments. The tournaments of 1507 and 1508 had involved an artificial 'tree

---

72 *James V Letters*, 345, 388; *MW*, i, 221–2, 288; *TA*, vi, 402, 412–3; vii, 48, 278, 292–3, 295.

73 Lindsay, *Works*, i, 113–6; SRO, Liber Domicili, E.31/8 fo. 74v. & Despence de la Maison, E.33/1, Lib. 12, fo. 38v.

74 Lindsay, *Works*, i, 156–61.

75 Richard Barber and Juliet Barker, *Tournaments: Jousts, Chivalry and Pageants in the Middle Ages* (Woodbridge, 1989), 107–37.

of esperance,' a group of 'wild men' and a 'black lady.'[76] Such features had already been developed at the obsessively chivalric court of the Valois dukes of Burgundy in the fifteenth century, to which the Scottish court had links through James II's marriage to Mary of Guelders. For example, the tournament held to celebrate the marriage of Duke Charles to Margaret of York in Bruges, 1468, was staged as the *Pas d'armes de l'arbre d'or*, and the *Pas d'armes de la dame sauvage* was staged at Ghent in 1470.[77] The fashions set by the Burgundian court continued to influence the chivalric exploits of the sixteenth century and perhaps the most famous example of the use of a tree of honour was that constructed for the lists at the Field of Cloth of Gold in 1520.[78] There is no indication that James ever used 'savages' in his tournaments but a French account of his Paris wedding of 1537 suggests that the lists were decorated with a heraldic tableau of a similar nature to a 'tree of honour.' At one end of the lists there was a sumptuous stage on which were displayed all the arms of the combatants, surmounted by two mannequins dressed as knights carrying lances with pennons in one hand and the escutcheons of Scotland and France in the other.[79] A hint that the servants of James V were familiar with chivalric imagery is also to be found in the pages of the household account books: in 1534, the clerk writing the accounts of the spice-house, wine cellar and avery opened his work with some sketches. The first shows a unicorn, a thistle and a rose, as well as the figure of a lady who appears to be stabbing herself with a small sword or dagger (perhaps a representation of Lucretia). The second is of a tree in blossom from which hangs an escutcheon depicting the head of a man wearing a curious headband. The third seems to be of a pavilion, such as was often used by knights at tournaments (although it also resembles a tree, wound around with ribbons), with an impish figure in a feathered cap alongside and surmounted by the motto *Spes Fove*. A later sketch in the kitchen accounts of 1538 depicts the arms of the king and queen perched upon a thistle branch.[80] These pieces of graffiti can hardly be taken as conclusive evidence of a pervasive chivalric culture at

76 *TA*, iii, 393–7; iv, 117–25; Pitscottie, *Historie* (STS), i, 241–4; Lesley, *History* (Bann. Club), 78; Macdougall, *James IV*, 294–5.

77 Barber and Barker, *Tournaments*, 121–4.

78 Russell, *The Field of Cloth of Gold*, 112–3. See also Sydney Anglo, 'L'arbre de chevalerie et le perron dans les tournois', in Jacquot (ed.), *Fêtes de la Renaissance*, iii, 283–98.

79 *Cronique du Roy*, 205.

80 SRO, Libri Domicilii, E.31/6, fos. 97r., 103r. & 105r.; E.31/8, fo. 3r. The motto *Spes Fove* also occurs on the back cover of a book which was once owned by John Denniston, rector of Dysart, and an extraordinary member of the king's household: see Durkan & Ross, *Early Scottish Libraries*, 87–8.

the court of James V but the fact that a scribe turned to such material for his doodles is certainly suggestive. Equally tantalising is the one mention in Lindsay's poems of a 'tabyll rounde' at Stirling and the fact that a member of the Dunbar garrison went by the name of Lancelot de Lake.[81]

There was no office of the revels at the Stewart court, as there was south of the border,[82] so the responsibility for planning and staging the entries, weddings, coronations, baptisms and tournaments fell across several departments of the royal household, including the office of arms, the stable, the wardrobe and the musicians. However, it seems clear that the senior officers at each of these events were the heralds. James had an establishment of six heralds (Albany, Islay, Marchmont, Ross, Rothesay and Snowden), six pursuivants (Bute, Carrick, Dingwall, Kintyre, Ormond and Unicorn), with two extraordinary pursuivants instituted if necessary (Falkland and Stirling), up to a dozen macers and many messengers-at-arms. The entire department was under the control of the Lyon king of arms. This title was held for most of the adult reign by Thomas Pettigrew of Magdalensyde, but the functions were actually performed by Sir David Lindsay of the Mount, who succeeded to the full title on Pettigrew's death in 1542. Lyon had the status of a great officer of state as well as a senior figure within the household and between them the heralds acted as the priesthood of the cult of chivalry.[83] Their duties included organising and policing all the public events discussed above; adjudicating in disputes over precedence, genealogy and armorial bearings; making public the royal proclamations; carrying royal letters and messages and accompanying foreign embassies.[84] In all their functions they represented the person of the monarch and in the case of the Lyon this aspect of his role was stressed to the extent that he was crowned at his inauguration and to deforce him was an act of treason.[85] The heralds of James V's reign clearly took their responsibilities seriously: Sir David Lindsay's *Armor-*

81 Lindsay, *Works*, i, 75 (*Papyngo*); *TA*, vii, 256. For more on the round table see Thomas, 'Renaissance Culture', 272 n.119.

82 Anglo, *Spectacle and Pageantry*, 261; Loades, *Tudor Court*, 113.

83 *RSS*, ii, 4910; Innes of Learney, 'Lyon King of Arms', 198; Sir Francis James Grant, *Court of the Lord Lyon, 1318–1945* (SRS, 1945), p. i. See also Edington, *Court and Culture*, 27.

84 Sir James Balfour Paul, *Heraldry in Relation to Scottish History and Art* (Edinburgh, 1900), 90–1, 98–103; J. H. Stevenson, *Heraldry in Scotland* (2 vols, Glasgow, 1914), ii, 421–35; Charles J. Burnett, 'Early Officers of Arms in Scotland', *ROSC*, ix (1995–6), 3–13; Burnett, 'Outward Signs of Majesty', 289–90, 299–301.

85 Balfour Paul, *Heraldry*, 91; George Seton, *The Law and Practice of Heraldry in Scotland* (Edinburgh, 1863), 29–31.

ial (c.1542) is one of the earliest known Scottish heraldic registers and
there are several other heraldic manuscripts surviving from the libraries of his immediate subordinates. These are the manuscripts which
once belonged to John Scrymgeour of Myres (the hereditary macer),
Peter Thomson (Bute pursuivant and Islay herald), John Meldrum
(Marchmont herald) and Robert Forman (Ross herald and Lindsay's
successor as Lyon after 1555).[86]

Lindsay's *Armorial* was intended as a work of reference recording all
the heraldic bearings of the Scottish royal family from the accession of
the Stewarts as well as the arms of one hundred and fourteen noble and
over three hundred lairdly families. However, the work opens with
depictions of the fictitious arms accorded to Prester John, the biblical
three kings, and the nine worthies of chivalric lore, followed by the
arms of the monarchs of all the main European states.[87] Thus Lindsay
was placing the Scottish armigerous community firmly within the
context of the heroes of chivalric legend as well as among the leading
European exponents of the cult of chivalry of his own day. In addition,
the references to Prester John and Godfrey of Bouillon also suggest the
lingering importance of the crusading ideal for the code of honour of
the period. Lindsay may have been inspired by the heraldic ceiling of
St. Machar's Cathedral, Aberdeen (1520–21), which includes many of
the same arms and appears to have been designed for a similar
purpose.[88] The arms of the only Scottish royal saint, St. Margaret,
are also given a prominent position both at Aberdeen and in the
Armorial, perhaps suggesting an attempt to acquire the same type of
prestige that the French kings gained from their descent from St. Louis,
and the English from their connections with St. Edward. The main
difference between the manuscript and the ceiling is that the Aberdeen
scheme includes the arms of all the Scottish bishops, whilst Lindsay

86 NLS, Adv. MS, 31.4.3 and *Facsimile of an Ancient Heraldic Manuscript
   Emblazoned by Sir David Lyndsay of the Mount, Lyon King of Arms, 1542*, ed.
   W. D. Laing (Edinburgh, 1822); NLS, Adv. MSS, 31.5.2, 31.7.22, 31.6.5,
   31.4.2.
87 H. A. B. Lawson, 'The Armorial Register of Sir David Lindsay of the
   Mount', *The Scottish Genealogist*, iv (1957), 12–19; Edington, *Court and
   Culture*, 37–9; Burnett, 'Outward Signs of Majesty', 297–8. The nine
   worthies were King David, Joshua, Judas Maccabeus, Julius Caesar,
   Alexander the Great, Hector of Troy, Charlemagne, King Arthur and
   Godfrey of Bouillon (the crusader king of Jerusalem).
88 Helena M. Shire, 'The Heraldic Ceiling of St. Machar's Cathedral, Old
   Aberdeen, c.1520', in Hadley Williams (ed.) *Stewart Style*, 63–72. See also,
   David McRoberts, *The Heraldic Ceiling of St. Machar's Cathedral, Aberdeen*
   (Aberdeen, 1976).

includes the arms of only one prelate (one who was so eminent that it would have been almost impossible to ignore him), David Beaton, cardinal of St. Stephen's, archbishop of St. Andrews, primate of Scotland, chancellor, legate, bishop of Mirepoix and commendator of Arbroath. The absence of other ecclesiastical arms may be another indication of Lindsay's own anti-clerical prejudices.[89] Scrymgeour's manuscript is a version of a heraldic treatise copied in 1494 by Adam Loutfut, Kintyre pursuivant, from a mid-fifteenth-century original by Sir Gilbert Hay.[90] It includes instructions on how to run a tournament and how to cry largesse, as well as comments on the offices of constable and marshal, the technicalities of blazon and a chivalric code of conduct. Thomson's manuscript includes similar material with information on the coronation of an emperor or king and an account of the jousting which took place at the wedding of Katherine of Aragon to Arthur, prince of Wales, in 1501. Meldrum's manuscript includes copies of two popular heraldic treatises, Bartolus de Saxoferato's *De insignis armis* and Nicholas Upton's *De studio militari*. Forman's manuscript is another armorial, not as fine as Lindsay's but probably compiled for the same purpose, as a work of reference. The survival of these manuscripts (and many others) is a considerable testament to the antiquarian enthusiasms of a seventeenth-century Lord Lyon, Sir James Balfour of Denmilne, from whose collection they passed to the Advocates' Library and were thus preserved. However, given that so many records from the reign of James V have not survived the centuries, it may well have been the case that there were many more like these in circulation among the heralds of the 1530s and 1540s and if this were indeed the case it would indicate the officers' erudition, dedication and cosmopolitan outlook.

One of the distinctive features of European chivalry from the fourteenth century onwards was the foundation by sovereign princes of

---

89 Edington, *Court and Culture*, 145–62; The fact that Beaton is given the title of chancellor in the manuscript, to which office he was appointed in January 1543, suggests that the *Armorial* was not fully completed before the death of James V. The *Armorial* is dated 1542 but by the reckoning of the period the year 1543 did not begin until 25 March. However, the absence of any reference to Mary, queen of Scots, suggests that it was largely a work of James V's reign.

90 For Loutfut's work see *Gilbert of the Haye's Prose Manuscript*, ed. J. H. Stevenson (2 vols, STS, 1914), vol. ii, pp. xxi–xxxiii and *The Buk of the Ordre of Chyvalry*, ed. Alfred T. P. Bayles (EETS, Original Series, 168, London, 1926), pp. xxvi–xxix. Hay was an author known to Lindsay see Lindsay, *Works*, i, 56 (*Papyngo*).

chivalric orders. These were exclusive knightly brotherhoods who would swear to obey the statutes of their order, wear distinctive insignia and/or robes of membership and who were expected to maintain the highest standards of honourable deportment. Societies such as the Order of the Garter in England (founded in 1349 by Edward III) or the Order of St. Michael in France (founded in 1469 by Louis XI) added lustre to kings who sought to present an image of knightly dignity and prowess, and at the same time bound their nobles to them in ties of fellowship, loyalty and patriotism. They also perpetuated the crusading ideal in knightly circles, which (along with the veneration of patron saints and the provision of masses and prayers for the souls of departed brethren) added a veneer of piety to the pursuit of martial glory. It soon became customary for the princely heads of these fraternities to admit one other to their own orders on the clear understanding that such membership was intended as a mark of esteem and that any oaths of obedience would be given to the head of an order only in that capacity and not as a sovereign lord.[91] James V who, as we have already seen, was enthusiastic about all things chivalric was eager to be admitted to each of the most prestigious European orders and used the diplomatic leverage of his tangled marriage negotiations to obtain his wishes. The first honour to be acquired was membership of the Burgundian Order of the Golden Fleece, conferred upon him on 26 April 1532 when Charles V was trying to tempt him into an imperial marriage. Charles sent his chamberlain, Sieur Pierre de Rosimboz, accompanied by Burgundy king of arms to invest James with the collar and mantle at Edinburgh. Possibly as part of the events surrounding the embassy James gave the imperial envoys a demonstration of his adherence to the Catholic church when a heresy trial was staged at Holyrood Abbey; he showed his commitment to chivalry when a judicial duel was fought at the palace between the lairds of Drumlanrig and Hempsfield. The king's admission to the order also coincided with the preparations for the institution of the college of justice, another prestigious public occasion, which took place a few weeks later on 27 May.[92]

Having thus obtained one chivalric status symbol, James would be able to exert increased pressure upon the kings of France and England

91 D'Arcy Jonathan Dacre Boulton, *The Knights of the Crown: The Monarchical Orders of Knighthood in Later Medieval Europe, 1325–1520* (Woodbridge, 1987).

92 *James V Letters*, 221–2; MW, i, 100, 102; ADCP, 373–8. *Diurnal of Occurrents*, 15–16. There is no detailed narrative of the ceremonial at the institution of the college of justice.

to present him with others if they wished their diplomatic missions in Scotland to succeed. Accordingly James was elected a knight companion of the Order of the Garter in January 1535,[93] a few months after a peace treaty had been sealed between Scotland and England which was supposed to endure for one year beyond the lifetime of whichever king died first.[94] On 21 February the English ambassador, Lord William Howard, accompanied by Garter king of arms, administered the oath of the order to James V, attached the garter to his left leg and invested him with the gown, mantle and collar of the order at a solemn mass in Holyrood Abbey. This was followed by a great feast, noted in the household books. The statutes of the order, which were also presented at the ceremony, still survive in the National Library of Scotland. Lord Erskine, accompanied by Sir David Lindsay, was sent to England in July to act as the king's proxy at his formal installation in the chapel of the order at Windsor on 22 August.[95] The last European order to offer membership to the king was that of St. Michael, and James was driven to demanding that he be admitted as a condition for his acceptance of Marie de Vendôme as a bride instead of Madeleine de Valois. The marriage was agreed in March 1536 and in May a *valet de chambre* of Francis I, Monsieur d'Izernay, arrived in Scotland with the collar of the order, accompanied by the earl of Moray, who had been in France negotiating the match and who was already a member of the order.[96]

Although not strictly an order of chivalry, it is possible to view the papal gift of the blessed cap and sword as a similar distinction conferred upon James as part of the diplomatic routine of the 1530s, and this again underlines the religious connotations of the distribution of honours at this period. Traditionally the decision as to which prince should become the recipient of the gift was made by the pontiff each Christmas and the papal chamberlain, Giovanni Antonio

93 *James V Letters*, 285; *L&P Henry VIII*, viii, 69; G Holmes, *The Order of the Garter: its Knights and Stall Plates 1348 to 1984* (Windsor, 1984), 74.

94 Peace was signed on 11 May 1534: *L&P Henry VIII*, vii, 647. The English ambassadors, were received into Edinburgh for the confirmation of the peace on 30 June 1534: SRO, Liber Domicili, E.31/5, fo.62v.; Liber Emptorum, E.32/3 fo.84v.; *L&P Henry VIII*, vii, 911. It was ratified in England on 2 Aug: ibid., vii, 1031 & 1032.

95 *Diurnal of Occurrents*, 19; *L&P Henry VIII*, viii, 70, 429; Brook, 'Technical Description', 126–9; SRO, Liber Domicili, E.31/6, fo. 42v.; Liber Emptorum, E.32/4, fo. 55v.; NLS, MS 7143; *James V Letters*, 297; *TA*, vi, 303, 315; *L&P Henry VIII*, viii, 1009; ix, 7, 178, 233.

96 Teulet, *Papiers*, i, 109–21; *James V Letters*, 318; Burnett, 'Outward Signs of Majesty', 290.

di Campeggio, made the ceremonial presentation at Compiègne on 19
February 1537. It was intended to reward James for eluding the
summit meeting with Henry VIII that had been planned for September 1536, to congratulate him on his marital alliance with the Most
Christian King and to encourage him to be a firm upholder of the
Catholic church.[97] Henry VIII thought that the pope was intending to
rescind his title of *Fidei Defensor* and award it to James instead but
James never used this style publicly.[98] According to Leslie, James was
very proud of these honours and used to mark the feasts of the patron
saints of each order with great pomp, wearing his insignia at court.
The feast day of the Order of the Garter is St. George's day, 23 April;
that of the French order was Michaelmas, 29 September; and that of
the Order of the Golden Fleece was St. Andrew's day, 30 November.
None of these dates receives any special attention in the household
accounts to indicate that a feast was being marked and, even though
St. Andrew was also the patron saint of Scotland, his day is noted only
once, in the account book for 1537. Leslie may have been mistaken on
this point but he was certainly correct to state that James had the arms
and collars of his orders carved above the outer gate of Linlithgow
Palace. On this site, alongside the insignia of the Garter, Golden Fleece
and St. Michael, was set the arms and collar of the Scottish Order of
the Thistle, which Leslie calls 'the ornamentis of St Andro quilkes ar
the proper armes of our natioune.'[99]

The exact status of the Order of the Thistle at this date is something of
a puzzle. It was not founded as a properly constituted order of chivalry
until the reign of James VII, yet the thistle collar, or collar of St. Andrew,
appears on a portrait of James III and surrounds the royal arms on
books and official documents from the reigns of James IV to Charles
II.[100] For example, in March 1540 James V ordered the manufacture of

97 C. Burns, 'Papal Gifts to Scottish Monarchs: The Golden Rose and the
    Blessed Sword', *IR*, xx (1969), 180–3; *James V Letters*, 316, 328.
98 *L & P Henry VIII*, xii, I, 665. For one possible instance of the unofficial use
    of the title see Durkan, 'Trompet of Honour', 1–2, and chapter 4.
99 Leslie, *Historie* (STS), ii, 230; SRO, Liber Domicili, E.31/7, fo. 20r. The
    bishop of Aberdeen writing to Cromwell stated that James intended to
    wear his Garter insignia on St. George's day: *L&P Henry VIII*, ix, 7. For
    Linlithgow see chapter 2.
100 R. J. Malloch, 'The Order of the Thistle', *Journal of the Heraldry Society of
    Scotland*, i (1977–8), 35–46; Charles Burnett, 'Reflections on the Order of the
    Thistle', *The Double Tressure: Journal of the Heraldry Society of Scotland*, v
    (1983), 39–42; C. J. Burnett, 'The Development of the Royal Arms to 1603',
    Journal of the Heraldry Society of Scotland, i (1977–8), 7–19; Burnett, 'Outward
    Signs of Majesty', 291; Edington, *Court and Culture*, 104–7.

new matrices for the great and privy seals and the images they were to bear were specified. Each was to carry the royal arms surmounted by a 'clos crown' and, in addition, the great seal was to show 'the kingis grace ordour of the mollettis and thrissillis about the scheld fra the nukis of the croun'.[101] One commentator has classified the Order of the Thistle as a 'cliential pseudo-order' and suggested that it was little more than a Stewart livery badge or collar, awarded to royal familiars from the reign of James III onwards, just as the same king had rewarded Anselm Adornes (an Italo-Flemish knight who frequented his court) with the 'ordre de la Licorne.'[102] However, if this were the case one would expect to find contemporary evidence that the 'order' was bestowed upon key nobles and servants and so far nothing of this nature (such as a portrait of a noble wearing the collar or badge) has come to light. There is one comment in Leslie's *History* that James IV awarded 'his ordour of Scotland' to the lord of Campveere in 1507, and Chapuys's report that James V delayed taking the Garter oath until he was in a position to offer Henry VIII a reciprocal honour.[103] There are also a few oblique references to chivalric orders in the Scottish records for the reign of James V. In the accounts of the French trip of 1536–37 there is a goldsmith's bill for a hundred crowns for a chain from which was hung 'the king of Frauncis ordour' and twenty and a half crowns for a chain from which was hung another order which is not named. More hopefully, in April 1538 the Edinburgh goldsmith, John Mossman, was paid for mending 'the kingis ordour and targat': this may be a reference to the Thistle collar and pendant but as April is the month in which the feast of St. George falls, it is probably the Garter. Finally, in January 1539 there was a purchase of ten ells of black ribbon from which to hang the 'tabillatis' which the king gave away during the New Year's Mass. There is no corresponding bill for the purchase or manufacture of these 'tablets' (medals or pendants). This entry might mean that James was presenting his favourites with the badge of St. Andrew but it is so ambiguous as to be open to other interpretations too.[104] Perhaps the most telling evidence for the non-existence of the Order of the Thistle at this period is the *Wardrobe Inventory* in which the robes and insignia of the English, French and Burgundian orders, and the papal swords and hat, are clearly listed but no mention is made of a

101 *ADCP*, 485.
102 Boulton, *Knights of the Crown*, 399.
103 Lesley, *History* (Bann. Club), 75; *L&P Henry VIII*, viii, 429, 430. James has to 'dressé son ordre.'
104 *TA*, vii, 39; vi, 394; vii, 123.

Scottish order.[105] James may have found it useful to have a Thistle collar portrayed on his arms, portraits and seals but there is no firm evidence that he actually possessed such an item of regalia.

The final instance of a rite of passage which could also be a public occasion full of pageantry and ceremonial but not celebration, was the royal funeral, and the court of James V staged several: those of Queen Madeleine in July 1537, of Princes James and Robert in April 1541, of Queen Margaret in October 1541 and the king's own in January 1543, after which his household establishment was disbanded. Madeleine died on 7 July 1537 at the palace of Holyrood and was buried in the abbey, probably on the 14th.[106] She had brought a large and eminent entourage with her to Scotland which included Jean de Langeac, bishop of Limoges and Anne de Boissy, dame de Montreuil, and James seems to have been determined to give her a funeral which would impress them. Many of the leading Scottish clerics were summoned to Edinburgh to attend the obsequies and there was considerable expense on mourning clothes ('dule') and funerary trappings. Four French ladies were provided with mourning garb 'of the fassone of preistis gounis,' two ladies of honour were given fur-lined gowns and hoods, and the queen's nine pages were dressed in black. A French tailor, organist, apothecary, cook and priest were also given new outfits and the king wore a 'dule coit and hude.' The coffin and bier were draped with purple and black velvet palls which were fringed in black and embroidered with white crosses, armorial bearings and 'knoppis and fassis.'[107] The choir of the abbey church was hung with black velvet and four hundred arms, and there was such a shortage of black cloth in Edinburgh that the burgh of Dundee was ordered to bring its supplies to the capital.[108] A *castrum doloris* or *chapelle ardente* was constructed at the abbey holding two hundred and ten great candles, and smaller candles were kept burning at her tomb for at least two years after her death.[109] Every year whilst James was still living, the anniversary of her death was marked by a ceremony at Holyrood which is variously described in the accounts as her 'suffrage' or her 'soul mass and dirge.' This seems to have involved between 150 and 215 chaplains saying prayers for her soul in a solemn service for which a bell was tolled and the church was again decorated with arms, candles and black hangings.

105 SRO, Wardrobe Inventories, E.35/1, fos. 21r. & 41r.
106 SRO, Liber Emptorum, E.32/6, fo. 88r. Funeral expenses are listed up to, but not beyond, 14 July: *TA*, vi, 354.
107 *TA*, vi, 313–4, 354, 334, 342–3, 350, 339, 332, 350–2.
108 *TA*, vi, 352, 334, 330. See also Thomas, 'Renaissance Culture', 281 n.170.
109 SRO, Libri Domicilii, E.31/7, fos. 98v., 102v.; E.31/8, fos. 126v., 131r.

In July 1538 a 'powpenny' (an offering made on behalf of the deceased) of twenty shillings was paid by Sir David Lindsay as 'Lyoun herald.' In 1539 the earl of Moray made the offering and in 1541 it was given by the earl of Buchan but the persons performing this office in 1540 and 1542 are not recorded.[110]

George Buchanan considered Madeleine's obsequies to be the first occasion on which public mourning was undertaken in this manner in Scotland:

Her death occasioned such a general sorrow to the whole country besides, that then first, I believe, mourning dresses were worn by the Scots, which even now, after forty years, are not very frequent, although public fashions have greatly increased for the worse.[111]

Whether he was correct or not, the king's devotion to the memory of Madeleine suggests that James regarded his first marriage as an event of supreme importance not just for himself but also for the Scottish realm. In comparison, the arrangements made for the funerals of his two young sons must have been very low-key and private for the only trace of them to emerge in the records is the purchase of a lead capsule to enclose one of the tiny bodies. We know that the boys were buried at Holyrood, probably in a joint funeral, but there is no evidence of public mourning or anniversary services as for Madeleine.[112] The bereaved parents were naturally greatly distressed at the double loss and it may have been the case that neither had the heart to undertake an elaborate rite to mark their sons' passing. There are not even any entries for the purchase of 'dule' for the king and queen and the mourning gown that was provided for the countess of Errol, one of the queen's ladies, was for the death of the earl, which also occurred in April 1541.[113] However, the death of the king's mother, Queen Margaret, in October 1541 was followed by a state funeral. The great earls, lords and abbots were summoned to attend her burial at the charterhouse of Perth and dule clothes were provided for the king, queen, Lady Jane Stewart and many of the ladies of the court as well as for David Blyth, Dingwall pursuivant, who was sent to the English court. Leslie considered that she was interred 'with greit honour and pompe funerall' and the following Christmas feast seems to have been a solemn occasion since the king's

110 *TA*, vi, 422–3; vii, 181, 321, 446; viii, 90–1.
111 Buchanan, *History*, ii, 315.
112 *TA*, vii, 442; *Diurnal of Occurrents*, 24.
113 *TA*, vii, 449.

and queen's chambers and the chapel were entirely hung with black.[114] The following summer the queen and her ladies were again in mourning, this time for the death of her sister, Louise de Lorraine, who had been married to the prince de Chimay for only one year before her death.[115]

The death of James V at Falkland Palace on 14 December 1542 precipitated the grandest state funeral of them all. Leslie describes the occasion thus:

> Not lang efter [James's death] his buriall with publik processioune was brocht frome Ffalkland till Edinburgh, quhair quhat evir culd be devysed in solemne pompe, or honourable decore, or duilful dolour and dule, sturt and kair, heirall was done fillit with all dew ceremonies and all diligence: torches lychtet, places spred with tapestrie, with notable claith, and weil paincted, lamentable trumpetis, qwisselis of dule, cardinalis al in sadnes, as thair heidis shew. The erles of Argyle, Arran, Rothese, and Merchal, and otheris in gret number of the nobilitie, filthie in dule weid, war al in the meine tyme sa drest, that albeit ye may mervel mekle of thair pompe in ordour, in colour nochttheles esilie dule ye mycht sie (for al war in dule weid), quhen in Edinburgh in the abbay of Haly rudhous, in the samyn sepulchre quhair Magdalen his sueit wyfe was buriit, was he layd.[116]

The surviving pages of the financial accounts suggest that Leslie's depiction of pomp and splendour is quite plausible. Sir David Lindsay was clearly in charge of the arrangements and most of the accounts are in his name as Lyon king of arms. It was certainly a heraldic funeral, fit for a knight of three major chivalric orders, and all the Scottish heralds and pursuivants and four macers were in attendance, dressed in dule habits and bonnets. A black velvet cloth of state with a white satin cross on it, a black velvet pall, black hangings for the bier and a crimson and gold banner of arms were the first purchases made. The banner was supplemented by 1,648 great and small arms and a black 'Dolorus Chapell' was constructed to hold candles, clubs, spears and arms. As at the queen's coronation three years earlier, the abbey church was provided with timber stands in which to seat the notables attending the service. An effigy of the king was constructed, laid on a canvas mattress and provided with a replica crown, sceptre and shield. The

114 *TA*, viii, 26, 34–7, 39–40, 42–3, 47–8; Lesley, *History* (Bann. Club), 157.
115 *TA*, viii, 83–4, 93; *Balcarres Papers*, i, p. xii.
116 Leslie, *Historie* (STS), ii, 259–60.

body was encased in lead and a stone tomb was erected on which were carved a lion, a crown and an inscription in Roman letters. At this point, infuriatingly, two pages of the accounts have been lost and they resume with payment for the king's soul-mass and dirge, which was usually observed thirty days after the death and thereafter on the anniversary. For this a bellman was employed (as for Madeleine's services) and the lord governor, the earl of Arran, offered the 'powpenny.' Alms were distributed to the poor and to the chaplains who performed the service by the king's master almoner, sir George Clapperton, and one of his clerks, Master George Cook. We also have the payments made for mourning clothes for the queen, her ladies and their horses and litters, to messengers to summon the Scottish lords to attend the funeral and to order the men of Fife to convey the body from Falkland to the Forth ferry at Kinghorn, which they did on Sunday 7 January, immediately after the festive season of Christmas, New Year and Epiphany had ended.[117]

The funeral took place on Monday 8 January at Holyrood[118] and for the details of the sort of chivalric ceremony that probably took place we need to turn again to the poetry of Lindsay. In *The Testament of Squyer William Meldrum* the hero explains at great length the type of heraldic funeral which he would like his executors to arrange for him and he specifies that Sir David Lindsay is to be in charge of the ceremonial, as he was in fact for the funeral of James V.[119] This poem was probably written in 1550, when the pageantry of 1543 would still have been quite fresh in Lindsay's memory, and the grand scale of the demands made by Meldrum suggests a funeral for a king rather than a Fife laird. First of all the body was to be embalmed and enclosed in a finely carved coffin of cedar or cypress wood. The heart and tongue were to be enclosed separately in golden, jewelled caskets. The tomb for his body was to be of sculpted marble, designed to honour Mars, the god of war; whilst his tongue was to be offered to Mercury, the god of eloquence, and his heart to Venus, the goddess of love. (Lindsay presents these pagan elements in a Christian ceremony in a 'deadpan' manner but the reader is clearly intended to notice, and be amused by, the incongruity.) The funeral procession was to be headed by a champion carrying Meldrum's 'pensil' (pennon) and accompanied by a thousand hagbutters instead of the monks or friars that would conventionally enter a funeral cortège at this point. There would then

117 *TA*, viii, 141–7.
118 *Diurnal of Occurrents*, 25.
119 Lindsay, *Works*, i, 190–4.

follow a thousand foot soldiers in livery carrying spears, bows and shields; then a hundred mounted noble men-at-arms, escorting their captain who should ride a 'bardit' (caparisoned) horse and carry Meldrum's standard. The banner was also to be borne by the same band, who were to be accompanied by musicians playing the instruments of war: the tabor, trumpet, clarion and horn. Next should ride the champion of honour, carrying Meldrum's helm, and followed by knights bearing his sword, gauntlets, shield and coat of arms. Then, just before the bier, would come the 'corspresent' (an offering to the church on behalf of the deceased) of Meldrum's caparisoned horse, spear, harness, armour and an altar cloth. The horse was to be ridden or led by a knight impersonating the dead man and wearing his armour. Here Meldrum specifies that no black 'dule' is to be worn but only his livery colours because he considers mourning garb to be a form of hypocrisy (Lindsay is being rather sardonic here). The bier is to be escorted by earls, lords, knights and other men of good pedigree, all bearing laurel branches 'in signe of victorie/ Becaus I fled never out of the feild/ Nor yit, as presoner, unto my fois me yeild.' This could well be a sly comment on the battle of Solway Moss, appropriate to an account of James V's funeral but not to one of Meldrum's. The squire specifies that no priest should be allowed to take part in the proceedings 'without he be of Venus professioun' and all who were 'most exercit in hir warkis' were to be specially summoned to attend. Here, Lindsay is clearly being ironic again since, as a reading of *Ane Satyre of the Thrie Estatis* makes clear, in his opinion virtually all clerics met this qualification.[120] A bishop of the same persuasion was to say the soul mass with more (joyful) music being played and after a gospel reading and the offertory, a eulogy was to be given from the pulpit, followed by prayers. Then the interment was to be made, not to the tolling of bells but to the firing of cannon and the thousand hagbuts. The funeral achievements (Meldrum's harness, shield, spear, coat of arms, banner, helm and crest) were to be hung over the tomb. An epitaph was to be inscribed on the grave in letters of gold telling of his fame and prowess. Meldrum expected that the ladies of France, England and Ireland would be distraught when they heard of his death and would wear mourning in his honour.

If this account of a heraldic funeral bears any relation to what actually happened at the burial of James V in January 1543, it would accord well with what was common practice in France and other countries at the time. It was certainly necessary to embalm the body if the coffin were to

---

120 Lindsay, *Works*, ii.

be kept lying in state for several weeks before the burial and the process would have required the removal of the entrails, which would be buried separately. This was the case in the funerals of Francis I and Henry VIII (both in 1547) and seems to have happened for James V too.[121] The account of Meldrum's funeral makes no mention of an effigy but, as we have seen, one was certainly made for James V. If it followed royal funerary customs in other countries, this would have been a life-size and life-like recumbent image of the king as he had been in his prime (as if he were just sleeping with his eyes open), dressed in the royal robes of state and invested with replica royal regalia.[122] In France, the royal effigy was imbued with mystical significance as the embodiment of the maxim *le roi ne meurt jamais* for the period between the death of the old king and the coronation of the new, during which time the new king's exact status was somewhat ambiguous because he held all the powers of a king but the effigy possessed the regal dignity. Thus it was that in the French funeral procession through the streets of Paris, the coffin and the effigy were separated so that the former could be attended by signs of mourning, whilst the latter was paraded in triumph and regal splendour.[123] There is a faint hint that something similar may have happened for James V in Meldrum's insistence that at his funeral no dule should be worn and that the music should be joyful and triumphant but the evidence is insufficient to determine conclusively the symbolic significance of the Scottish effigy. If the English practice were followed, the effigy served the practical purpose of substituting for the corpse when the body was too old to be displayed, thus allowing preparations for an elaborate funeral to be made without undue haste. However, Kantorowicz has argued that the English effigy represented the enduring royal dignity and that in a monarch's funeral there was an element of symbolic role-reversal: whilst the king was alive it was the 'body natural' that was visible and the 'body politic' that was hidden, but the opposite was the case in a monarch's funeral.[124]

121 Ralph E. Giesey, *The Royal Funeral Ceremony in Renaissance France* (Geneva, 1960), 2; Clare Gittings, *Death, Burial and the Individual in Early Modern England* (London, 1984), 216. An account for packets of spices rendered on 9 Jan 1543 may have been for this purpose: SRO, Liber Emptorum, E.32/8, fo. 127v.

122 Julian Litten, 'The Funeral Effigy: Its Function and Purpose', in Anthony Harvey and Richard Mortimer (eds.), *The Funeral Effigies of Westminster Abbey* (Woodbridge, 1994), 3–19. I am grateful to Dr Alison Rosie for drawing my attention to this volume.

123 Giesey, *The Royal Funeral*, 119–23, 174–92.

124 Gittings, *Death, Burial and the Individual*, 223–4; Ernst Kantorowicz, *The King's Two Bodies: A Study in Medieval Political Theology* (Princeton, 1957), 423.

The 'dolorus chapell' of James V's accounts was a feature of royal funerals that would have been familiar to the French court as a *chapelle ardente* and to the English as a 'hearse' or 'tabernacle'. It was a raised wooden stand, shaped like an elongated pyramid, draped in black and decorated with arms and hundreds of candles. The coffin would be placed underneath it and chaplains would be employed to say prayers for the soul of the departed alongside. A depiction of how a Flemish artist imagined a Scottish dolorous chapel would look appears in the *Book of Hours* of James IV and Margaret Tudor and is usually identified as a picture of the funeral of James III. That prepared for James V may well have resembled this portrayal.[125] James V's accounts suggest that heraldic achievements were prepared and these also feature in Meldrum's instructions. They were also used in French and English customs and consisted of symbols of knighthood such as replicas of the dead man's escutcheon, helmet and other accoutrements which would be paraded in the funeral and deposited at the grave, just as Meldrum describes (in France they were known as the *pièces d'honneur*).[126] Heraldic funerals abroad might also include the display of a standard, banner and pennon, a champion, a knight impersonating the deceased and making offerings on his behalf and a eulogy (in French, *oraison funèbre*). In addition, at royal and noble funerals, the household officers of the deceased would continue in their posts until the moment of burial, at which point they would break their wands of office and throw them into the grave.[127] This may well have happened at Holyrood in January 1543 and it was certainly the case that the household of James V was disbanded at about this time: hardly any of his servants were retained in the service of the lord governor, who preferred to use his own staff. The funeral of January 1543 was thus the last service these men provided for their sovereign lord.

The pageantry and ceremonial of the court of James V was clearly intended to emulate the most fashionable aspects of such events as staged by Francis I, Henry VIII and Charles V, as well as drawing on

---

125 Giesey, *The Royal Funeral*, 10; Gittings, *Death, Burial and the Individual*, 216, 219; Leslie MacFarlane, 'The Book of Hours of James IV and Margaret Tudor', *IR*, xi (1960), plate vii.

126 *TA*, viii, 142; Giesey, *The Royal Funeral*, 9; Gittings, *Death, Burial and the Individual*, 172, 220. The original funeral achievements of the Black Prince (d. 1376) are still on display near his tomb in Canterbury Cathedral: D. Ingram Hill, *Canterbury Cathedral* (London, 1986), 133–4.

127 Giesey, *The Royal Funeral*, 12–17, 90, 119; Gittings, *Death, Burial and the Individual*, 171–9, 219–20. The *Oraison Funèbre* for Mary of Guise by Claude d'Espence was published in Paris in 1561.

the taste for princely magnificence developed by earlier Stewart kings. James V's marriages, his Parisian royal entry and his membership of the premier European chivalric orders gave him an international profile at least as high as, and arguably higher than, any of his predecessors. His devotion to the cult of chivalry and his love of the joust, tilt and tourney was probably as enthusiastic as that displayed by other princes of the period and may well have equalled the famous exploits of his father's court. Yet, largely because of a lack of detailed narrative sources, his activities in this sphere remain somewhat obscure. What is clear is that James made considerable efforts to utilise the political symbolism of imperial or sovereign monarchy, in the manner of the age. As we have seen, in many aspects of his cultural patronage James V was inspired (and enriched) by his visit to the court of Francis I, yet the construction of an arched or 'closed' crown probably predates the French 'holiday' by some four years. At a relatively early stage of his adult reign James V seems to have decided to turn the imaginary regal images on coins and pictures into reality in the royal regalia. Furthermore, this development coincided with his admission to the Order of the Golden Fleece (26 April) and the institution of the college of justice (27 May). Thus, in the spring of 1532 James seems to have set the agenda for the subsequent development of pageantry and ceremonial at his court. The Scottish king signalled publicly in his utilisation of symbolism and ritual that he was determined to be taken seriously as a modern monarch both on the international stage and at home. Had he lived to pursue his aims beyond 1542, his funeral might eventually have been even more lavish than the grand heraldic event which marked the passing of this ambitious Renaissance prince.

Conclusion

The adult James V did not develop the image of Scottish kingship and courtliness within a cultural vacuum. As we have seen, contacts with the courts of England, France, the Netherlands, Italy, Denmark and other countries were well established and regular.[1] Furthermore, his predecessors and namesakes, the first four Jameses were all noted for their interest in art, architecture, literature, music, the cult of chivalry, state ceremonial and so forth and the ways in which these pursuits could be utilised to bolster the authority of the king.[2] Some of the most significant examples of this focus in earlier reigns include the Burgundian and Flemish influences that shaped the cultural life of the Scottish court following James II's marriage to Mary of Guelders in 1449 and the splendid tournaments of the wild knight and the black lady staged by James IV in 1507 and 1508.[3] Certainly, James IV was in touch with the English court through his marriage to a Tudor princess; with the French court through the contacts with Bernard Stewart, Sieur d'Aubigny; with the Low Countries through trading links; with the Spanish kingdoms through Pedro de Ayala; and with the pope, from whom he received a gift of the blessed cap and sword in 1507.[4] This cosmopolitan and sophisticated outlook could not simply vanish after the battle of

1 The king's correspondents included all the popes of the period, Francis I, Henry VIII, Christian II and Frederick I of Denmark, Charles V, Margaret of Austria, Mary of Hungary, Ferdinand, king of the Romans, John III of Portugal and many other European princes and dignitaries: *Letters of James V*, 146–446.
2 See Alastair Cherry, *Princes, Poets and Patrons: The Stewarts and Scotland* (Edinburgh, 1987), 9–37; Michael Lynch, 'Scottish Culture in its Historical Perspective', Roderick Lyall, 'The Literature of Lowland Scotland, 1350–1700', Duncan Macmillan, 'Scottish Art', and Charles McKean, 'The Scottishness of Scottish Architecture', all in Paul H. Scott (ed.), *Scotland: A Concise Cultural History* (Edinburgh, 1993), 17–39, 77–94, 207–11, 235–37.
3 McRoberts, 'Scoto-Flemish Contacts', 91–96; Macdougall, *James IV*, 294–5.
4 Macdougall, *James IV*, 146–47, 155, 196–97, 218, 254–55, 282–87. See also Barbara E. Crawford, 'Scotland's Foreign Relations: Scandinavia', and Norman A. T. Macdougall, 'Scotland's Foreign Relations: England and France', both in Jennifer M. Brown (ed.), *Scottish Society in the Fifteenth Century* (London, 1977), 85–100, 101–11.

Flodden, especially since the regent for the young James V between 1515 and 1524 was a French nobleman, with Scottish royal ancestry, John Stewart, duke of Albany. However, the political upheavals of the minority certainly would have made cultural patronage very difficult to develop consistently and there is no evidence that Albany was responsible for the creation of anything more culturally significant than a new blockhouse at the castle of Dunbar during his time in Scotland.[5] From the poetry of the minority one might obtain the impression of the court almost holding its breath until the young king should come of age.[6]

It would appear that the first rôle-model James sought to emulate was his own father. The new departure of the years immediately after 1528 attempted to wipe out the unhappy memories of the minority regimes and to recall the golden age of King James IV. Of course, James V would not have remembered very much (if anything) about his father but he still had men within his household and government who had served his father and who would be able to inform him about the 'good old days'. These men included the king's senior chaplain and almoner, sir James Haswell; another chaplain and keeper of Holyrood Palace, sir John Sharp; Sir John Campbell of Lundy, who was the justice depute and a former lord treasurer; and most notably, Sir David Lindsay of the Mount.[7] Lindsay's depiction of James IV in his poem *The Testament of the Papyngo* (c.1530) provides a recipe for good kingship which James V seems to have made every effort to follow.

> Allace, quhare bene that rycht redoutit roye,
> That potent prince, gentyll king James the feird?
> I pray to Christe his saule for to convoye;
> Ane greater nobyll rang nocht in to the eird.
> O Atropus, warye we maye thy weird,
> For he wes myrrour of humylitie,
> Lode sterne and lampe of libiralytie.

> Duryng his tyme so justice did prevaill,
> The savage Iles trymblit for terrour;
> Eskdale, Euisdale, Liddisdale, and Annerdale
> Durste nocht rebell, doutyng his dyntis dour,

---

5 MacIvor, 'Artillery and Major Places', 107–19.
6 MacDonald, 'William Stewart', 184–94. See also chapter 4.
7 *James V Letters*, 155; SRO, Bill of Household, 1507/08, E.34/1, fo. 6r.; *TA*, v, 13, 70, 438, 463; vi, 36, 403; Edington, *Court and Culture*, 13–25.

And of his lordis had sic perfyte favour:
So, for to schaw that he aferit no sone,
Out throuch his realme he wald ryde hym alone.

And, of his court, throuch Europe sprang the fame
　　Off lustie lordis and lufesum ladyis ying,
Tryumphand tornayis, justyng, & knychtly game,
　　With all pastyme accordyng for one kyng.
He wes the glore of princelie governyng,
Quhilk, throuch the ardent lufe he had to France,
Agane Ingland did move his ordinance.[8]

Setting aside the reference to Flodden in the last two lines of this extract, Lindsay's description of Scottish kingship would appear to be equally applicable to James V as to James IV. James V's pursuit of firm governance in the Isles and Borders was discussed in chapter five and, as we saw there, his concern was accompanied by an enthusiasm just like his father's for ship-building and one even more pronounced than his father's for artillery manufacture and fortification. Lindsay's mention of humility is presumably a reference to James IV wearing an iron belt as a life-long penance for his part in the overthrow and murder of his father, James III, in 1488: an example which James V did not need to follow.[9] However, the patterns of religious observance and conventional acts of piety, which also seem to have been virtually identical in the adult reigns of James IV and James V, were discussed in chapter three. James V's reputation for making incognito excursions among his humble subjects was similar to that of his father, and this also receives some corroboration in the household accounts (where the food and other supplies provided for him when he was away from the main household establishment are listed separately) and in the itinerary which plots his relentless perambulations across the realm.[10] For the other items on Lindsay's 'shopping-list' we can turn to the household accounts and the records, narratives and cultural artefacts of the court considered in this study. Here we have found considerable evidence of the king's liberality, not just in his lavish expenditure (by Scottish standards) on palaces, furnishings, clothes, ceremonial and so forth but also in his presentations of gifts of suits of clothes, swords, items of

8 Lindsay, *Works*, i, 70–71.
9 Macdougall, *James IV*, 52–3.
10 See chapter 1 and Thomas, 'Renaissance Culture', Appendix C, pp. 386–423.

plate and jewellery and purses of money to courtiers and visitors to his court.[11] The same sources also note purchases and arrangements made for tournaments and jousts, which (as we saw in chapter six) were staged seasonally throughout the reign and in greater splendour for special occasions such as a wedding, coronation or peace treaty.

James V also seems to have drawn upon the example of his grandfather, James III, in developing the symbolism and iconography of imperial kingship. James III's parliament of 1469 may have announced his possession of 'ful jurisdictione and free impire within his realm' but James V appears to have been more successful than his ancestor in pursuing this claim.[12] He imitated the realistic portraiture of James III's silver groats of c.1485 on his groats and 'bonnet pieces' of the 1530s and adopted the symbol of the 'closed' crown for his coins, seals and documents. Moreover, he was the first Stewart king to possess an arched imperial crown as a part of the royal regalia. This seems to have been constructed for the king in the spring of 1532 just before the public ceremony to mark the establishment of the college of justice in Edinburgh.[13]

For Lindsay, the lavish chivalric display pioneered by James IV and developed by James V was a magnet drawing 'lustie lordis and lufesum ladyis' into the royal affinity, reflecting glory on all concerned, and ensuring that 'throuch Europe sprang the fame' of the Scottish court. Lindsay's view would seem to confirm the opinion of many scholars of the early modern period that the Renaissance court was a tool used by assertive and centralising monarchs to 'tame' potentially 'over-mighty' magnates to the royal will by turning them from warriors into courtiers. Geoffrey Elton and David Starkey have postulated such a role for the court of Henry VIII of England and Norbert Elias has painted a similar picture on the broader canvas of Germany and France, culminating in the court of Louis XIV.[14] The essential contention is that Renaissance monarchs drew their nobles to courts from which emanated all political patronage and influence, and that this process effectively neutralised the capacity of the greater magnates to act independently (and especially in defiance) of the crown, which was in any case (mainly for reasons of cost) beginning to monopolise the most up-to-date aspects of

11 See chapter 2.
12 *APS*, ii, 95.
13 See chapters five and six.
14 Elton, 'The Court', 211–28; Starkey (ed.), *English Court*, 1–24, 71–117; Starkey, 'From Feud to Faction: English Politics c.1450–1550', *History Today*, xxxii, (Nov. 1982), 16–22; N. Elias, *The Process of Civilization* (2 vols., Oxford, 1978–82); Elias, *The Court Society* (Oxford, 1983).

military technology. The medieval model of kingship exercised by a monarch who ruled as a *primus inter pares* was to be transformed into a more autocratic pattern of government by a sovereign prince wielding imperial power over his subjects and presiding over a more standardised, centralised, bureaucratic machine. The use of imperial imagery in the coinage, regalia and heraldry, and the iconography of court pageantry and ceremonial were designed to enhance the political pretensions of the Renaissance prince, whilst the Renaissance nobleman-turned-courtier was encouraged to view attendance at court and personal service to the king (even of a rather menial nature) as an honourable sphere of activity. This adjustment was sweetened by the attractions of the chivalric and heraldic displays of the tournaments, festivals and ceremonies in which the Renaissance court specialised.[15]

This vision of the civilising tendency and propaganda role of the Renaissance court certainly provides a coherent and compelling framework into which to place the disparate aspects of courtly culture of James V's reign. Indeed, the exploration of classical (or neo-classical) models, imperial imagery, and humanist concerns, which has been detected in the developing culture of the Scottish court of the 1530s, seems to fit very neatly into this wider framework. However, as is so often the case in history, developments which may appear to be novel need not necessarily be so, and it may well have been the case that there was rather more evolution than revolution, more adaptation than innovation, in the cultural and political activities of the sixteenth-century royal court. We have already seen how Castiglione's *Book of the Courtier* mined a deep vein of medieval moral discourse about courts and courtiers in order to expound his vision of the Renaissance ideal.[16] Clearly the perception of the court as a location where urbanity, courtesy and chivalric honour could be acquired (and where the vices of flattery, deceit, and greed also thrived) has a very long pedigree. Such views were held of the knightly companions of Richard II, of some of the German courts of the thirteenth century, and of the courtly culture of the

---

15 Starkey, 'Court History in Perspective', in Starkey (ed.), *English Court*, 1–24; Prevenier and Blockmans, *Burgundian Netherlands*, 214–41; R. G. Asch, 'Court and Household from the Fifteenth to the Seventeenth Centuries' and David Starkey, 'Court, Council and Nobility in Tudor England' both in Ronald G. Asch and Adolf M. Birke (eds.), *Princes, Patronage and the Nobility: The Court at the Beginning of the Modern Age, c.1450–1650* (Oxford, 1991), 1–38, 175–203; Starkey, 'Representation through Intimacy', 212–13; Strong, *Splendour at Court*, 19–76; Strong, *Art and Power*, 21–26, 42–62, 65–69, 76–85.

16 See the introduction.

reign of Henry II.[17] Indeed, the very term 'courtesy' (*curialitas*) would appear to have entered the Latin language at the turn of the eleventh and twelfth centuries,[18] at about the same time that the knightly values of the cult of chivalry began to be formulated.[19] In a recent consideration of the courtly culture of the Valois dukes of Burgundy (a court which is generally considered to have been the prototype for the Renaissance courts of northern Europe) Werner Paravicini suggests that there was little that was demonstrably original in the phenomenon. Rather, the Burgundian court of the mid-fifteenth century harked back to the traditions and customs of Charles VI of France and Richard II of England. Yet there clearly were things that had changed over time, and Paravicini argues that the Valois dukes (and their sixteenth-century imitators) created a courtly culture that was grander, more flamboyant, and more costly than anything seen before: 'a quantitative excess that led to a qualitative difference'. To this one might add the self-conscious and single-minded pursuit of worldly fame and glory, such as to leave a great impression on posterity, which Jacob Burckhardt long ago identified as one of the abiding characteristics of Renaissance culture.[20]

It is difficult to be precise about exactly where the Scottish experience fits into this analysis of late medieval and early modern European courts and kingship. For many years it was taken as almost self-evident that the adult reigns of the first five Jameses were essentially aimed at reducing their 'over-mighty', factious and violent nobles to a state of peaceful, law-abiding subjection; and that with every turbulent minority the initiative was lost and had to be revived when the next king came of age.[21] In this scenario, the glittering chivalric court with its pageantry and protocol could be useful as a vehicle for stressing the power and

---

17 Gevase Mathew, *The Court of Richard II* (London, 1968), 1–52, 106–28; Given Wilson, *Royal Household and King's Affinity*, 160–74, 187–88; Joachim Bumke, *Courtly Culture: Literature and Society in the High Middle Ages*, trans. Thomas Dunlap (Berkeley, 1991), 275–413; Jaeger, *Origins of Courtliness*, 55, 113–75. See also A. G. Dickens, 'Monarchy and Cultural Revival: Courts in the Middle Ages', in Dickens (ed.), *Courts of Europe*, 8–31 and Greg Walker, 'Henry VIII and the Invention of the Royal Court', *History Today*, xlvii (February 1997), 13–20.

18 R. E. Latham (ed.), *Revised Medieval Latin Word-List from British and Irish Sources* (London, 1965), 126.

19 Anglo (ed.), *Chivalry in the Renaissance*, pp xi–xvi.

20 Werner Paravicini, 'The Court of the Dukes of Burgundy,' in Asch and Birke, *Princes, Patronage and the Nobility*, 69–102; Jacob Burckhardt, *The Civilization of the Renaissance in Italy*, trans. S. G. C. Middlemore (Oxford and London, 1945; originally Basel, 1860), 87–93.

21 For example, P. Hume Brown, *History of Scotland* (3 vols., Cambridge, 1909–12), i, 184–401.

dignity of the king as part of a campaign to overawe potentially unruly lords. However, in the last twenty years, a very different explanation of the relationship between the crown and the magnates has been developed by Alexander Grant and Jenny Wormald, which stresses the co-operation and inter-dependence of the king and the nobles in a realm which successfully maintained a decentralised, *laissez-faire* tradition of government.[22] For Grant and Wormald, violence and political crisis were the exceptions rather than the rule, and when kings found it necessary to crush an individual noble or noble faction, it was undertaken with the compliance and support of the remainder of the second estate. In this scenario, the court was a broadly based community which united the monarch and his lords in political, religious and cultural activities reflecting their mutual interests in stability, hierarchy and honour. More recently still the 'new orthodoxy' has been challenged by Michael Brown; he re-emphasises the significance of the murders of the duke of Rothesay, James I and James III and the clashes between James II and the Black Douglases and between James IV and the rebels of 1489 as serious crises in a lengthy power-struggle between Scottish nobles and the assertive Stewart kings.[23] The tussle between James V and the sixth earl of Angus in 1528–29 might well be seen in the same light. Certainly the king was disappointed with the outcome of the siege of Tantallon and was prepared to wait years for a suitable moment to take his revenge on those who he thought had let him down in his moment of need, as Cameron acknowledges. Yet Cameron's study of the politics of the adult reign also concluded that there was much more co-operation and goodwill between James V and his nobility than had previously been acknowledged, and that magnate participation in the administration was quite broadly-based and effective.[24] Perhaps one might square the circle by suggesting that the nobles of late fifteenth- and early sixteenth-century Scotland were probably keen to serve an assertive and vigorous monarch in principle, in the hope that they might prosper in the process; but that if in practice the ambitions of a particular king threatened the personal interests of an individual magnate (as in the case

---

22 A. Grant, *Independence and Nationhood: Scotland 1306–1469* (London, 1984), 153–97; J. Wormald, 'Taming the Magnates?' in K. J. Stringer (ed.), *Essays on the Nobility of Medieval Scotland* (Edinburgh, 1985), 270–80; Jennifer M. Brown, 'Introduction', in Brown (ed.), *Scottish Society*, 1–9; Wormald, *Court, Kirk and Community*), 3–26.

23 M. H. Brown, 'Scotland Tamed? Kings and Magnates in Late Medieval Scotland: a review of Recent work', *IR*, xlv (1994), 120–46. See also Brown, *The Black Douglases*, 321–332.

24 Cameron, *James V*, 328–35.

of the earl of Angus in 1528), defiance and rebellion would result, and in any such conflict a Stewart monarch could not be certain of victory.

As we have seen, the cultural activities of the court of James V seem to have developed from a combination of many influences and considerations and to have served multiple purposes. The chivalric code and national spirit which were cultivated in the literary and ceremonial life of the court could well have bound monarch and nobility together rather than stressed the distinction between them. The surviving contemporary sources are such that (as we saw in chapter one) it is very difficult to know just how many of the Scottish nobles actually attended court functions on a regular basis. Yet a magnate presence at the coronation, baptisms, royal entries and funerals would probably have been significant, and it is highly likely that they willingly participated in the celebrations of religious feasts, hunts, jousts, pilgrimages, sailing-trips and other events as well. Certainly, the king's itinerary indicates that he made regular excursions into areas of Scotland beyond the Lothian-Fife-Perthshire-Stirlingshire heartlands, and so if the nobles did not frequently come to court, it occasionally came to them. Yet James V could also be ambitious and aggressive. In the use of imperial symbolism and classical allusion, many of the images of kingship cultivated within the court could indeed be used to glorify the unique dignity and status of the monarch, in emulation of the grander princes of other realms.

James V emerged defiantly from a long and turbulent minority, and in the fourteen years of his adult reign managed to create an exuberant and cosmopolitan court, of some cultural significance. Historiographically, interest in his reign has traditionally been overshadowed by the romantically tragic figures of his father and daughter, but in dissecting the domestic structure and many-sided cultural patronage of his court this book aims to demonstrate that such neglect is unwarranted. Indeed, the most notable cultural developments of the court of James IV took place after 1503, the year in which he celebrated his thirtieth birthday and fifteen years on the throne, whilst his son's court had already attained considerable distinction before the king's thirtieth year (and James V did not live to see his thirty-first birthday). Although we are lacking detailed accounts of the tournaments and jousts of the 1530s which might enable some comparison to be made with those of 1507 and 1508, James V's membership of the most prestigious orders of knighthood suggests that his chivalric credentials probably did justice to his father's memory. Certainly, the architectural, musical, religious, literary, military and ceremonial developments of his court equalled, and in some areas excelled, the cultural achievements of his forbears and are worthy of greater interest than they have attracted hitherto.

The Royal Household in 1539

This appendix is a reduction from the full list of James V's recorded household officers which can be found in Andrea Thomas 'Renaissance Culture at the Court of James V, 1528–1542' (University of Edinburgh Ph.D. thesis, 1997), 299–375. The full list is divided into two sections: part two lists the subjects by department (as in this reduction), whilst part one lists the people alphabetically and also cites the references locating them in the records of the period. The year 1539 has been taken to provide a picture of the household of James V when he was at the height of his powers, and also to illustrate the personnel of the household of Mary of Guise, which is most fully documented in this year. The appendix strays outside the year 1539 with the recorded servants of Prince James of Scotland (1540–41) to illustrate the nature of the service provided for a royal child.

The dates given for each person on the list are not necessarily the dates of their appointment and dismissal/retirement from a particular position (although they might be), but are the dates of the first and last reference to them in that particular post. The symbol '+' after a date indicates that further references to the person concerned may be found in the records of the reign of Mary. The symbol '†' after a date indicates that the person was dead on or before that date. The order in which the departmental table is laid out is one which has been suggested by the livery lists and rates of pay of the period, but should not be taken to be a definitive statement of the structure of the royal household. The household accounts are very ambiguous and contradictory on such matters, and the reality might well have been much more untidy than this table would appear to imply.

Office	Name		
Master of the Household	Archibald Campbell, 4th earl of Argyll	29 Oct 1529	27 Apr 1541
Great Constable of Scotland	William Hay, 6th earl of Errol	10 Dec 1540	11 Sep 1541 †
Great Chamberlain of Scotland	Malcolm, Lord Fleming	26 Jun 1528	11 Aug 1546
Master of the Household Depute	Patrick Wemyss of Pittencrieff	Sep 1537	Jul 1542
Master of the Household Depute	James Learmonth of Dairsie	29 Aug 1537	Dec 1542
Of the bedchamber/cubicular	John Denniston, rector of Dysart	Jul 1539	Nov 1542
Principal/Master Sewer	Sir James Hamilton of Finnart	1526	22 Sep 1539
Steward/Sewer of the King	Sir James Kirkcaldy of Grange	1538	Dec 1542
Steward/Sewer of the King	John Leslie of Cleish, the younger	Dec 1538	Jul 1542
Carver to the King	David Wood of Craig	Dec 1538	Jul 1542
Carver to the King	Andrew Wood of Largo	Dec 1538	Dec 1542
King's Cupbearer	Henry Kemp of Thomaston	1538	Aug 1542
King's Cupbearer	Oliver Sinclair of Pitcairn	Dec 1538	Aug 1542
King's Pursemaster	John Tennent of Listonshiels	1532	1540
Clerk of the Closet	Master David Hamilton	1 Jun 1527	5 Mar 1540
Clerk of the Closet	Master William Meldrum, vicar of Strabrook	20 Apr 1537	Jul 1542
Usher of the Inner Chamber Door	William Wood of Bonnington	1525	Jul 1542
Principal Usher/Guard of the Inner Door	John Ross of Craigy	14 Sep 1537	13 Sep 1541
Usher of the Outer Chamber Door	William Bard	1525	Dec 1542
Usher of the Outer Chamber Door	James Wood	1531	Dec 1542
Barber-Surgeon/Yeoman of the Chamber	James Watson	11 Aug 1538	Jul 1542
Yeoman of Chamber	John Guthrie	1529	Dec 1542
Yeoman of Chamber	Patrick Kirkcaldy	1535	Dec 1542
Yeoman of Chamber	Norman Leslie, Master of Rothes	Dec 1538	3 Sep 1542
Yeoman of Chamber	John Murray	Dec 1538	Mar 1541 †
Groom/Valet of Chamber/feeds the king's dogs	Patrick Stirling	1525	Feb 1540
Groom/Valet of Chamber	Alexander Kemp	1526	1 Dec 1542
Groom/Valet of Chamber	Andrew Drummond	1532	Dec 1542
Groom/Valet of Chamber	Murdo Mackenzie	Dec 1538	Dec 1542
Groom/Valet of Chamber	Alexander Whitelaw	Dec 1538	Dec 1542
Cleans & makes fires in Chamber	Guillaume	May 1539	Jul 1542
Keeper of the King's Parrots & Cachpules	Thomas Kells	Jul 1538	15 Mar 1540

Role	Name		
Musician	sir John Fethy		
Trumpeter	Ninian Brown, Italian?	1529	Jan 1542
Trumpeter/Trumpeter of War	John Kemp	1529	30 Dec 1542
Taborer	Anthony Taburner, Frenchman	1534	Jul 1539
Taborers	the 2 Todds, old & young	1525	1546
Taborer	Jacques, Frenchman?	1538	Jul 1542
Viols player	Jakis Columbell & his 3 fellows	Jul 1539	Feb 1540
Fiddler	John/Thomas Cabroch	9 Jul 1538	1 Jul 1542
Lutenist	Urre/Hare Schennek, foreigner?	1530	31 Dec 1540
Lutenist	Duncan Cunningham	1526	3 Mar 1540
Supplier of Organs	William Calderwood	Jun 1539	Dec 1541
Dwarf	Jane Frenchwoman	1537	Jan 1542
Fool	John Maccrery	Mar 1539	Mar 1539
Fool	John Lowes	1525	Dec 1540
Juggler	James Atkinson	Dec 1539	Apr 1543
Esquire of Stable	Robert Gibb of Carriber	Sep 1538	Dec 1542
Keeper of the king's great horse	John Charteris of Cuthilgurdy	Jun 1538	1 Dec 1542
Horse Marshal	Nicholas Arth	Dec 1538	1 Jul 1542
Master of the king's mares	Charles Murray	Mar 1539	Aug 1541
Keeper of the Dutch horses	Thomas Richardson	Oct 1539	Jul 1542
Yeoman/groom of Stable	Robert Purves	1516	1 Dec 1542
Yeoman/groom of Stable	Andrew Michelson	1525	Dec 1542
Yeoman of Stable	John Bog of Burnhouse	1525	Dec 1542
Yeoman of Stable	Arthur Sinclair	Apr 1538	Mar 1540
Henchman	Robert (Hob) Ormiston	1526	Jul 1542
Henchman	James Kincaid	1532	Dec 1539
Groom of Stable	James Purves	Sep 1536	May 1540
Sumpterman	Templeton	1532	Mar 1542+
Sumpterman	David Hay	Mar 1539	Dec 1542
Yeoman of Avery	John Purves	1532	Jul 1542
Master Saddler	Patrick Slater	Jun 1534	Apr 1543

Role	Name		
Saddler	Andrew Lorimer	Jul 1532	Dec 1542
Lorimer/bucklemaker	William Forest	Nov 1538	Apr 1543
Blacksmith (Farrier)	John Sprotty	1525	Dec 1542
Smith (Farrier)	Thomas Sprotty	Sep 1538	Aug 1541
Master Falconer	James Lindsay	1529	Dec 1542
Falconer	David Spens	1525	16 Nov 1539
Falconer	Edward Stewart	1529	Jul 1542+
Falconer	John Caldwell	1532	May 1543
Falconer	John Park	1537	1540
Falconer	Chesman	Jul 1538	Jul 1542
Falconer	William Mann	8 Nov 1539	8 Nov 1539
King's Chief Herdsman	Robert Liddel	1538	1540
Master Tailor	Thomas Arthur, burgess of Edinburgh	1529	1 Dec 1542
Tailor	Malcolm Gourlay	1522	Jul 1542
Tailor, servant to Tom Arthur	Thomas Hannay	1535	Dec 1541
Tailor	John Daniel	Aug 1539	Aug 1539
Yeoman of the Wardrobe	John Tennent of Listonshiels	1534	Dec 1542
Groom of the Wardrobe	David Bonar	1525	Jul 1542
Groom of the Wardrobe	John Barbour	Jul 1537	Jul 1542
Groom in the Wardrobe	Thomas Tulloch	Sep 1536	Jul 1542
Master Cordiner	Arthur Littlejohn	15 Aug 1536	Aug 1540
King's Furrier	David Ferry	1531	Aug 1541
Furrier	James Scrymgeour	Dec 1538	Jul 1542
Broudstar/Embroiderer	John Young	24 Jun 1535	1 Mar 1543
Goldsmith	Patrick Lindsay	1531	Apr 1543
Goldsmith	Thomas Rhind	Feb 1532	Feb 1542
Goldsmith	John Mosman	Feb 1534	Dec 1542
Goldsmith	Hotman, Frenchman	1538	1539
Case-maker	John Paterson	Jan 1539	Jul 1542+
Sword-slipper	Thomas Softlaw	Dec 1538	Jul 1542
Seamstress	Janet Douglas	1522	Jun 1540

Seamstress/embroiderer	Helene Ross	1529	Jun 1542+
King's Laundress	Mavis Acheson	1517	1 Jul 1542
Laundress	Margaret/Madge Tulloch	1538	Dec 1541
Laundress	Bessie Drupis	Dec 1539	Feb 1543
Court laundress	Katherine Maccorran	Jun 1539	Jun 1539
Tapiser	William Edbe	1536	1540
Tapiser	Jacques Habet, Frenchman	Aug 1539	Jul 1542
Carter	John Gogar	1532	Jun 1540
Carter	John Balglavy	Aug 1538	Jan 1541
Carter	Thomas Braidwood	Dec 1538	Aug 1541
Carter	Thomas Miller	Jun 1530	Apr 1541
Carter	William Miller	Mar 1539	May 1541
Carter	Robert Stewart	Dec 1538	Oct 1540
Carter	David Sibbald	Oct 1538	Jan 1542
Of the Wardrobe	Katherine Bellenden	Feb 1537	Jul 1542
Of the Wardrobe	Mackesson	1531	1542
Of the Wardrobe	Alexander Cochran	Dec 1539	Dec 1541
Steward of the Household	sir David Christison	1535	Dec 1542
Master of the silver vessels	Thomas Duddingston of Kilduncan	20 Jan 1531	Dec 1542
Under keeper of the silver vessels	Gavin Wann	1532	Jul 1542
Carter of the silver vessels	sir John Affleck	1539	1 Mar 1542
Keeper of the pewter/tin vessels	James Dempster	1518	Aug 1540
Keeper of the pewter/tin vessels	Henry Dempster	1536	Jan 1543
Keeper of the pewter vessels/household plate	Thomas Kells	Dec 1538	Jul 1542
In the Cuphouse	Thomas Touch	Nov 1538	Mar 1542+
Cupbearer	John Menteith	1536	Jul 1542
Cupbearer/Server	John Richardson	Dec 1538	Jul 1542
Groom/Server/Dichter in Hall	John Murray	1526	Jul 1542
Groom/Server in Hall	Troilus	Dec 1538	Jul 1542
Groom/Server in Hall	Patrick Clerk	Dec 1538	Jul 1542
Usher of the hall door	John Lawson of Bowanshaw	1525	Aug 1541

Position	Name		
King's Porter/Janitor	George Inglis	1524	1539
Master of Entry & Principal Porter	John Crammy	5 Feb 1536	Aug 1540
Porter	Patrick Crammy	5 Feb 1536	Jul 1542
Porter	William Crammy	Dec 1538	Jul 1542
Porter	James Bog	May 1539	12 Sep 1542
Coalman	Duncan Dawson	r. James III	6 Mar 1540
Coalman	John Lawson of Bowanshaw	10 Feb 1531	Jan 1544
Dichter of the king's palaces	Andrew Angus	1538	1 Jul 1542
Caterer/Purveyor	sir John Macall, dean of Lismore	1532	Jan 1544
Poultryman	John Macall	Sep 1538	Jul 1542
Master cook	Thomas Marshall	1533	Dec 1542
Groom in Kitchen	David Kirkcaldy	Jul 1538	Jul 1542
Groom in Kitchen	John Angus	Dec 1538	Jul 1542
Under groom in Kitchen	Inverugie	Aug 1539	Jul 1542
Usher of the Kitchen Door	William Galbraith	1538	Jul 1542
Principal Cook in Hall Kitchen	Peter Hamilton	1536	Jun 1544
Yeoman/Groom of Hall Kitchen	John Mount	1531	Aug 1541
Groom in Hall Kitchen	William Nichol	1538	Jul 1542
Groom in Hall Kitchen	James Duncan	Dec 1538	Jul 1542
Yeoman in Wine Cellar	James Aikenhead	1531	1 Aug 1541
Yeoman in Wine Cellar	Archibald Campbell of Clauchan	24 Mar 1538	Aug 1541
Butler in Wine Cellar	William Duchale	1538	Aug 1541
Groom of Wine Cellar	Thomas Mushet	1532	Aug 1540
Master of Ale Cellar	James Murray	17 Jan 1539	8 Apr 1539
Principal Yeoman/Groom of Ale Cellar	James Murray	May 1532	Dec 1542
Groom in Ale Cellar	Thomas Murray	1538	Aug 1541
In the Ale Cellar	Patrick Henderson	Dec 1538	Aug 1541
Master Brewer in Buttery	Robert Wood	1525	Sep 1541
Principal Brewer in Buttery	Patrick Kincaid of Leith	1532	Jul 1542+
Master Baker	George Gibson of Goldenstone	12 Jul 1535	Jul 1542
Patisser/Baker	Murdoch Stirling	1537	Jul 1542

Office	Holder		
Baker	Alexander Scott	1534	Aug 1540
Master of the Pantry	John Hay	Dec 1538	Aug 1541
Yeoman of Pantry	Walter Moncur in Forgund	Dec 1538	Aug 1541
Groom in Pantry	Patrick Anderson	Dec 1538	Jul 1542
Groom in Pantry	John Gilchrist	Feb 1539	Dec 1541
Master Butcher	Robert Henderson, burgess of Edinburgh	12 Apr 1531	1 Dec 1543
Yeoman of Great Larder	David Blantyre	1529	Dec 1542
Groom of Larder, dichts the vessels	William Bell	Jul 1538	Jul 1542
Yeoman in the Petty Larder	James Richardson	Dec 1538	Aug 1541
Yeoman of the Spice-House	Thomas Hamilton	10 Oct 1524	Dec 1542
Groom in the Spice-House	John Clydesdale	Dec 1538	Jul 1542
King's Mediciner	Doctor Arbuthnot	16 Dec 1508	Jun 1541
King's Surgeon	George Leith	1523	1542
King's Principal Surgeon	Master/sir Duncan Omay	3 Jul 1526	31 Dec 1541
Apothecary	Francis Aikman, burgess of Edinburgh	13 Feb 1532	1543+
Master Almoner	sir George Clapperton	23 Jun 1535	Dec 1542
Almoner's priest/chaplain	sir John Jordan	1529	Jul 1542
Dean of Chapel Royal	Henry Wemyss, Bishop of Galloway	24 Jul 1526	1540
Treasurer of Chapel Royal	sir Walter Stewart, Precentor of Ross	16 Jun 1531	10 Feb 1541
Sacristan of Chapel Royal	sir Alexander Paterson	Dec 1533	Jan 1542
Prebendary & Canon of Chapel Royal	sir Michael Dysart	31 May 1531	1 Dec 1542
Prebendary & Canon of Chapel Royal	sir John Lambert	before 2 Jan 1531	
Prebendary of Chapel Royal (Ayr quarto)	sir William Drummond	26 Dec 1535	28 Feb 1539
Prebendary & Canon of Chapel Royal	Alexander Scott	28 Feb 1539	Aug 1541
Vicar of the Church in Stirling Castle	David Arnot	before 19 May 1539	28 Feb 1539
Vicar of the Church in Stirling Castle	sir James Nicholson	19 May 1539	19 May 1539
Chaplain of the Barres	sir James Alan (Ellem)	6 Jun 1508	1541
Chaplain of St Margaret's, Edinburgh Castle	sir David Young	28 Nov 1529	1542
			1541

Role	Name		
Chaplain/Prebendary of Leith/Restalrig	sir William Turner	6 Feb 1532	May 1541
Chaplain & Keeper of Holyrood Palace	Master Thomas Hay	20 May 1538	1542
Chaplain of James III at Cambuskenneth	sir James Inglis	1515	Jul 1542
Chaplain of St Thomas, Falkland Palace	sir Thomas Kilgour	2 Jan 1529	1542
Chaplain & Keeper of Linlithgow Palace	sir Thomas Johnson	Feb 1535	Aug 1541
Chaplain at Linlithgow	sir John Polwarth	1538	1540
Chaplain	sir John Marr	1529	Aug 1542
Chaplain	sir Henry Balfour	Sep 1536	May 1540
Secretary	Master/Sir Thomas Erskine of Brechin/Haltoun	15 Jun 1526	26 Oct 1542
Chancellor	Gavin Dunbar, Archbishop of Glasgow	26 Jun 1528	13 Sep 1543
Director of Chancery	Master Thomas Bellenden of Auchnoul	10 Sep 1538	12 Dec 1543
Clerk Register	Master James Foulis of Colinton	12 Mar 1532	11 Aug 1546
Clerk Register Depute	George Good	Nov 1526	13 Mar 1540
Writer in Chancery	William Ogill	1531	1540
Justice General	Archibald Campbell, 4th earl of Argyll	29 Oct 1529	27 Apr 1541
Justice Depute	Sir John Campbell of Lundy	1530	13 May 1542
Justice Clerk	Master Thomas Scott of Pitgormo	13 Apr 1536	24 Apr 1540
Justice Clerk	Master Thomas Bellenden of Auchnoul	27 Dec 1539	11 Aug 1546
Keeper of the Privy Seal	Cardinal David Beaton, Archbishop of St Andrews	3 Jan 1529	11 Aug 1542
Scribe of Privy Seal	Thomas Sinclair	Aug 1536	20 Dec 1539
Scribe of Privy Seal	Master George Cook	20 Apr 1539	Jan 1543
Writer of Signet (in criminal causes)	John Bellenden	1524	Jul 1542
Writer to Signet/Casualty	Master Thomas Kene	1534	Jul 1542
Writer of Signet, Exchequer & Treasury	James Bellenden	24 Jun 1538	Jul 1542
King's Advocate	Master Henry Lauder of St Germains	13 Sep 1538	Jul 1542+
Advocate for the Poor	Master John Williamson	Sep 1538	7 Jan 1540
Treasurer	Sir James Kirkcaldy of Grange	11 Sep 1536	Aug 1543
Clerk of Treasury/Exchequer	Master John Chisholm	1523	1539
Clerk of Treasury	Henry Balnaves of Halhill	Sep 1538	1542
Writer of the Casualty/Exchequer	Thomas Maben	1537	Aug 1540
Comptroller	David Wood of Craig	17 Jan 1539	8 Feb 1543

Role	Name		
Keeper of the Rolls	sir George Richardson	1526	Jul 1542
Comptroller's Clerk	George Ogilvy	Dec 1538	Dec 1542
Auditor & Dictator of the Rolls	sir James Kincraigie, dean of Aberdeen	1514	Sep 1539
Auditor & Clerk of Exchequer	sir Alexander Scott, provost of Corstorphine	1515	Sep 1541
Auditor of Exchequer	Master William Gibson, dean of Restalrig	1527	30 Jan 1541
Auditor	Master Thomas Scott of Pitgormo	4 Feb 1529	1 Dec 1539
Auditor	William Hamilton of Sanquhar & Macnairston	1530	Sep 1541
Auditor	Robert Reid, Abbot of Kinloss	1530	Sep 1541
Auditor/Clerk	John Denniston, Rector of Dysart	Mar 1531	Aug 1542+
Auditor	Alexander Mylne, Abbot of Cambuskenneth	Aug 1532	Sep 1541
Auditor, Councillor & Familiar	Henry Sinclair, Treasurer of Brechin	1532	Sep 1541
Auditor & Lord of Council	Master Henry Lauder of St Germains	Dec 1539	Sep 1541
Writer of the Rolls	George Good	1515	Jul 1542
Writer/keeper of the Rolls	Master James Scott	1526	Jul 1542+
Writer of the Rolls/Clerk of Accounts	John Wallace	1528	Jul 1542+
Writer in Exchequer	Master William Mobray	Mar 1534	Jul 1542
Writer in Exchequer	Thomas Sinclair	Sep 1539	Jul 1542
Labours in the Exchequer	John Pardovan	1538	Dec 1542+
Abbreviator of the Household Books	sir George Scott	1525	Dec 1542
Clerk of Expenses	Master John Colden	Sep 1538	Jul 1542
Master coiner/Master of the mint	James Atkinson	1529	30 Aug 1543
Master of the Mint	Alexander Orrok of Sillebawbie	May 1538	2 Jun 1542
Keeper of the King's Coin	John Mosman	24 Aug 1539	24 Aug 1539
Coiner	Richard Wardlaw	1531	May 1540
Ambassador to Flanders	Sir John Campbell of Lundy	28 Apr 1529	5 Oct 1540
Ambassador to the court of Rome	Master John Lauder	1531	Jul 1541
Ambassador to France	Cardinal David Beaton, archbishop	Feb 1533	10 Feb 1539
Sent abroad to buy wines, supplies & as envoy	John Barton	Jul 1537	Jul 1542
Tax Collector	Master John Williamson	1533	1540/41
Tax Collector	Master Thomas Gatherer	1533	1540/41
Tax Collector	Cuthbert George	1535	1540/41
Printer to the King	Thomas Davidson	1535	6 Mar 1542

Position	Name		
Squire and gentleman in the king's house	Patrick Hume	23 Jul 1526	Dec 1542
Householdman to the King	George Meldrum of Fyvie	6 Apr 1530	12 Mar 1541
Extraordinary household servant	John Hamilton of Colmskeith	Nov 1530	Aug 1544
King's familiar	Captain James Lundie	21 Dec 1516	8 May 1540
Familiar Servitour	George Steel of Houston	1527	20 Mar 1542
King's Familiar	Sir John Borthwick	27 Jul 1535	Feb 1540
Footman & Lackey	Weddell	1534	Jan 1543
Footman	George	8 Nov 1539	1 May 1540
Lackey/Footman	Mackesson	Mar 1538	11 May 1540
Lackey	George Robertson	Nov 1538	Jan 1543
Lackey	Snowdon	Mar 1539	May 1540
Page	Hallont	Sep 1538	Apr 1542
Page	Wandonay, Frenchboy	Jul 1539	Jul 1539
Page	Nicholas, Frenchboy	Oct 1539	Oct 1539
Servitour	William Douglas	1516	Sep 1541 (as Mr)
Servitor	James Grant of Freuchy	22 May 1529	19 Feb 1540
Servitour to King	William Gourlay of Kincraig	11 Oct 1531	28 Jul 1542
Servant of the King	Patrick Tennent	1537	Aug 1539
Servant to King	John Kirkcaldy	May 1534	Dec 1543
Captain & Keeper of Stirling Castle	John, Lord Erskine	1529	1540
Master of Works in Stirling Castle	sir James Nicholson	3 Jan 1530	Aug 1541
Carver & wright at Stirling	Robert Robertson	1531	32 Jun 1542
Upholding the Park Dykes at Stirling	Marion Douglas	1539	1539
Captain & Keeper of Edinburgh Castle	James Crichton of Cranston-Riddell	May 1523	1540
Glasswright/painter in Edinburgh Castle	Robert Binning	17 March 1504	Mar 1540
Keeper of Holyrood Palace	George Balglavy	Nov 1531	Dec 1542
Mason at Holyrood/Falkland	James Black	1536	1539
Gardener at Holyrood	John Auchter, citizen of Glasgow	31 Aug 1539	Jul 1542
Master Mason of Falkland	Mogin Martin the younger, Frenchman	1538	1540/41
Wright in Falkland	Richard Stewart	Jan 1539	Feb 1541
Gardener of Falkland	Thomas Melville	1535	1540

Forester of Falkland	Andrew Fernie	26 Apr 1515	19 Dec 1540
Carpenter at Linlithgow	Peter Johnson	5 Jan 1538	1540
Gardener at Linlithgow	Rankin/Rankel Morrison	31 May 1538	1540
Keeper of the Park of Linlithgow	Walter Loudon	Jun 1539	Mar 1540
Mason at Crawfordjohn	Thomas Cadder	1538	Aug 1541
Captain of Dunbar Castle	Sir John Melville of Raith	Jun 1528	Feb 1543
Sub Captain of Dunbar Castle	James Haldane of Gleneagles	1538	1539
Captain of Douglas Castle	John Gordon	1538	1542
Captain of Tantallon Castle	Oliver Sinclair of Pitcairn	Sep 1539	Aug 1542
Master Mason at Tantallon Castle	George Semple	Apr 1539	Apr 1539
Principal Master of Works	Sir James Hamilton of Finnart	9 Sep 1539	1 Apr 1540
Master of Works	Master John Scrymgeour of Myres, the younger	Aug 1529	May 1559+
Master Mason	John Brownhill	16 Jan 1532	Dec 1542
King's Master Mason	Thomas French	Mar 1534	1539
King's Master Mason	Nicholas Roy, Frenchman	22 Apr 1539	Jul 1541
Mason	William Cadislie	Aug 1529	Dec 1539
Mason	John Merliene	1535	Jul 1542
Mason	Peter Fleming, Dutchman	1538/9	1540/1
Quarrier	Thomas Towns	Aug 1529	Oct 1539
Quarrier	Constantine Clerk	Aug 1529	Feb 1540
Cutler to the King	William Ray, burgess of Edinburgh	Jan 1507	Jul 1542+
Glasswright	Thomas Peebles	1514	Nov 1542
Painter & Chaplain	sir John Kilgour	1527	Feb 1541
Painter	Robert Galbraith	Aug 1539	Aug 1539
Painter	Archibald Rule	Aug 1539	Feb 1540
Painter	Andrew Watson	Aug 1539	Jun 1543
Wright	William Lowrie	Nov 1538	Dec 1539
Wright	William Marshall	Nov 1538	Dec 1539
Wright	Thomas Lindsay	Nov 1538	Mar 1543

		before 6 Dec 1542	
Lyon King of Arms	Thomas Pettigrew	before 6 Dec 1542	6 Dec 1542
Albany Herald	William Brown	8 Nov 1516	18 Nov 1540
Islay Herald	Gilbert Lindsay	30 Oct 1538	15 Jun 1541
Ross Herald	John Dickson	1524	1540
Rothesay Herald	Robert Hart	1 Mar 1535	5 Nov 1542
Snowdon Herald	Sir David Lindsay of the Mount	1531	1542
Kintyre Pursuivant	Sir John Pettigrew	1536	1542
Stirling Pursuivant	John Paterson	Jun 1537	1539
Dingwall Pursuivant	David Blyth	1526	1 Dec 1541
Pursuivant, Messenger & Macer	Cuthbert George	1530	Nov 1542+
Pursuivant & Messenger	Peter Thomson	Oct 1536	Aug 1542+
Pursuivant & Messenger	John Paterson	Nov 1536	May 1542+
Macer	William Sheves	1515	Jul 1542
Macer	Andrew Purves	1522	29 Jul 1546
Macer & Pursuivant	Oliver Maxton of Drumgrene	17 Nov 1524	10 Dec 1540
Macer	John Pardovan	29 Oct 1524	Dec 1542+
Macer	James Johnson	1527	Jan 1543
Macer	Thomas Hamilton	1529	Dec 1542
Hereditary Macer	Master John Scrymgeour of Myres, the younger	15 Feb 1531	1542+
Macer	David Purves	1515	Dec 1542
Macer/Messenger	Adam Forman	1536	Jul 1542+
Macer	James Lindsay	Jul 1538	Jan 1543+
Macer	Robert Black, burgess of Edinburgh	7 Mar 1539	Dec 1542+
Messenger	John Langland	1515	1540/41
Messenger	Robert Hart	1515	Dec 1542+
Messenger & Pursuivant	Archibald Hogg	30 Jul 1517	27 Jul 1545
Messenger & Sergeant	John Gourlay	1522	19 Sep 1541
Messenger	Andrew Bonar	1522	1539
Messenger	Robert Champnay	1525	10 Dec 1540
Messenger	Andrew Murray	28 Jul 1529	Sep 1539
Messenger	James Bisset	1515	10 Dec 1540

Role	Name		
Messenger	Andrew Mercer	1514	Jan 1540
Messenger & Macer	William Mure	1529	6 Feb 1541
Messenger/Pursuivant	William Strathearn	1529	Dec 1542+
Messenger	Alexander Carmaig alias Hecht	1517	Dec 1542+
Messenger & Macer	John Cobb	1531	Dec 1542+
Messenger	James Geddes	1532	Nov 1543
Messenger	Andrew/Archibald Hardy	1535	Feb 1539
Messenger	Cuthbert Whiteford	Oct 1536	1540/41
Messenger	David Hardy	1536	Oct 1541
Messenger	Alexander Hutton	1536	Dec 1542+
Messenger	William Hardy	1537	Dec 1542+
Messenger	Archibald Heriot	1537	Dec 1542+
Messenger	James Moncur	8 Nov 1539	8 Nov 1539
Messenger	Alexander Melville	8 Mar 1533	24 Apr 1540
Messenger	David Norry	1538	1541
Royal Standard Bearer	James Scrymgeour of Dudop, constable of Dundee	31 Aug 1531	30 Apr 1540
Captain of ships/guns	Robert Fogo	1529	May 1542
Buys munitions in Denmark	James Anderson	1538	1542
Buys munitions	Master David Balfour	Aug 1539	Aug 1539
Master of Artillery	Henry Stewart, Lord Methven	Aug 1539	Dec 1542
Master Gunner	Master John/Hans Cochrane	Aug 1539	Aug 1541
Master Gunner of Dunbar Castle	John Wolf, Danish	Mar 1532	Sep 1541
Gunner in Dunbar	Michael Gardner	Jun 1538	Aug 1541+
Gunner	John Byres	Apr 1538	Aug 1542
Gunner	James Law	Apr 1538	Aug 1542
Gunner	John Cunningham	1518	21 Oct 1541
Gunner	Piers/Peris Rowan, Frenchman	1515	Dec 1542+
Gunner	William Agradane	Jul 1537	1 Sep 1539
Gunner	Christopher Grand Morsen, Frenchman	Apr 1537	Sep 1541
Gunner	Cornelius Braidhow, 'The Feir of Campveere'	Oct 1539	May 1541
Gunner	William Dalgleish	Oct 1539	Aug 1541

Office	Name		
Gunner	Thomas Liddel	Oct 1539	Aug 1541
Gunner	David Lumley	Dec 1539	Aug 1541
Master Armourer	William Smibert	1515	Mar 1542
Principal Carpenter & Founder of Artillery	John Drummond of Mylnab	6 Dec 1507	Dec 1542+
Smith	Robert Monypenny	1515	1540/41
Smith & Gunner	William Hill	8 Apr 1530	Dec 1542+
Engineer & Gunner	George Ormiston	Jan 1532	Jul 1542+
Gun maker	Robert Hector	Jun 1537	Feb 1541
Armourer & Gunner	Jacques Leschender	Mar 1538	Jul 1542
Wright & Gunner	John Crawford	Jul 1535	16 Jun 1542+
Armourer	Thomas Short	Apr 1539	12 May 1540
Wright, Carver & Gunner	Andrew Manson, Frenchman	Aug 1539	Dec 1542+
Plumber & Gunner	Robert Murray	1532	Dec 1542
Potter & Gunner	John Lang	1533	1542
Principal Jak Maker & Gunner	John Clerk	Apr 1539	Aug 1542+
Bow & Arrow Maker to the King	John Morris, English/Welshman	1530	Jan 1539
Bower/Arrowmaker to King	John Forrester	1538	Aug 1542+
Crossbowmaker	John Testard, French?	Dec 1538	Aug 1542+
Master Timmerman of Ships	Walter Howieson	1 Oct 1539	Dec 1542
Clerk of munitions of Ships	Florence Cornton in Leith	Dec 1539	Jul 1542
King's nurse	Marion Douglas	1518	1540
The King's Nurse	Margaret Kininmont	1541	1542
Servant of Queen Margaret & king	Marion Bunkle	1512	1542
Servant of Queen Margaret	Peter Allershaw	1531	1542
Queen Mary's Secretary and Comptroller	François du Fon/Fou/Feu	1538/9	1541
Queen Mary's Master of Household	Charles de la Haye, M. de Curel	1538/9	1538/9
Queen Mary's Esquire of the Household	Urban de la Touche	1538/9	1538/9
Queen Mary's Gentleman of the household	Gaspard de Villeneuve	1538/9	1538/9
Queen Mary's Gentleman of the household	Pierre de la Rainville	1538/9	1538/9

Position	Name		
Queen Mary's Master Almoner	Jean Fournier	1538/9	Sep 1541
Queen Mary's Almoner	sir Henry Littlejohn (Messire Henri Petit-Jehan)	1538/9	1538/9
Queen Mary's Chaplain	Messire Jean Guillet	1538/9	1538/9
Queen Mary's Doctor	Maître Michel Vial	1538/9	1538/9
Queen Mary's Apothecary	François Guestandt	1538/9	1538/9
Queen Mary's Lady in waiting	Mahaut des Essartz, Mlle. de Curel	1538/9	Nov 1541
Queen Mary's Lady	Renée d'Antigny, Mlle de la Touche	1538/9	Apr 1540
Queen Mary's Lady	Joanna Gresmor	May 1539	Aug 1540
Queen Mary's Lady	Madame Sowsy	1539	1542
Queen Mary's Maid of honour	Jeanne de la Rainville	1538/9	1538/9
Queen Mary's Maid of honour	Jeanne Pieddeser	1538/9	1538/9
Queen Mary's Maid of honour	Guillemine Dupont	1538/9	1538/9
Queen Mary's Maid of honour	Françoise de la Touche	1538/9	1538/9
Valet to Queen Mary's maids of honour	Nicolas du Moncel	1538/9	1538/9
Queen Mary's Jester	Ferat	Nov 1538	May 1542
Queen Mary's valet of the chamber	Jean Alloutet	1538/9	1538/9
Queen Mary's valet of the chamber	Jacques de la Grange	1538/9	1538/9
Master Usher/Groom of Queen Mary's Chamber	Walter Scrymgeour	Dec 1538	Aug 1542
Usher /Groom in Queen Mary's Chamber	Gilbert Moncrieff	Dec 1538	Jul 1542
Queen Mary's usher of the chamber	Pierre Quesnel	1538/9	1538/9
Usher /Groom in Queen Mary's Outer Chamber	John Moncrieff	Dec 1538	Jul 1542
Usher of Queen Mary's Outer Chamber	Alexander Lindsay	Jul 1539	Jul 1542
Queen Mary's gentlewoman of the chamber	Marguerite Pignon	1538/9	1538/9
Queen Mary's gentlewoman of the chamber	Jacquette Poiteville	1538/9	1538/9
Queen Mary's gentlewoman of the chamber	Marie Villeneuve	1538/9	1538/9
Queen Mary's gentlewoman of the chamber	Marguerite Roussine	1538/9	1538/9
Queen Mary's laundress	Jeanne Pasquiere	1538/9	1538/9
Queen Mary's usher of the hall	François de Chastillon	1538/9	1538/9
Queen Mary's esquire of the kitchen	Jacques Desongliers	1538/9	1538/9
Queen Mary's Master Cook	Tassin Duchesne	1538/9	1538/9
Queen Mary's groom of the kitchen	François Canin	1538/9	1538/9
Queen Mary's esquire of the hall kitchen	Lanveur le Coq	1538/9	1538/9

Office	Name	Date	Date
Queen Mary's master cook of the hall kitchen	Jean Bordais	1538/9	1538/9
Queen Mary's groom of the hall kitchen	Pierre Forest	1538/9	1538/9
Queen Mary's groom of the hall kitchen	Georges Angoux	1538/9	1538/9
Queen Mary's keeper of the vessels	Jean Grimanet	1538/9	1538/9
Queen Mary's Master of the Wine Cellar	Claude Autier	1538/9	1538/9
Butler of Queen Mary's wine cellar	Jean de Bimont	1538/9	1538/9
Butler of Queen Mary's wine cellar	Jean Meau	1538/9	1538/9
Groom of Queen Mary's wine cellar	Jean Nepuon	1538/9	1538/9
Groom of Queen Mary's wine cellar	Pierre Chastaignier	1538/9	Oct 1538
Patissier to Queen Mary & her Ladies	Thomas Lyon	Jan 1541	1538/9
Queen Mary's Patissier	Ambroise Bontel	1538/9	1538/9
Queen Mary's baker	Robert Fonain	1538/9	1538/9
Queen Mary's Master of the Pantry	Claude Autigny	1538/9	1538/9
Butler in Queen Mary's pantry	Jacques Danquetin	1538/9	1538/9
Butler in Queen Mary's pantry	Jean de Beausse	1538/9	1538/9
Groom in Queen Mary's pantry	Georges Huon	1538/9	Mar 1539
Doorman in Queen's Pantry	George Carpenter	Mar 1539	1538/9
Servant in Queen Mary's Spice House	Alexander Durham	Jan 1539	1538/9
Queen Mary's Esquire of the Stable	Philippe de Lainccth	1538/9	Apr 1539
In Queen Mary's Stable	Osay	Apr 1539	1538/9
Queen Mary's muleteer of the litter	Anthoine de Podir	1538/9	1538/9
Queen Mary's muleteer	Anthoine Villars	1538/9	1538/9
Queen Mary's groom of the mules	Jean Valle	1538/9	1538/9
Queen Mary's groom of the stable	Pierre Dubois	1538/9	1538/9
Queen Mary's assistant groom	Jacques Doret	1538/9	1538/9
Queen Mary's charioteer	Pierre Lay	1538/9	May 1538
Queen Mary's Master Avery	Walter Moncur in Forgund	Dec 1542	1538/9
Queen Mary's tailor	Jacob de la Grange	1538/9	1538/9
Queen Mary's yeoman of the wardrobe	Jacques de la Grange the younger	1538/9	1538/9
Queen Mary's embroiderer	Henri le Meine	1538/9	1538/9
Queen Mary's embroiderer	Jacques Herpon	1538/9	1538/9
Queen Mary's gardener	Louis Rialland	1538/9	1538/9

Role	Name		
Queen Mary's quartermaster	Alain Leboeuf	1538/9	1538/9
Groom of Queen Mary's quartermaster	David Sebec	1538/9	1538/9
Groom of Queen Mary's quartermaster	Jean Mirbeau	1538/9	1538/9
Queen Mary's carter	Simon Alexander	1538/9	1538/9
Queen Mary's carter	Jean de Choury	1538/9	1538/9
Servant of Queen Mary	Monsieur Acquys	Oct 1538	1 Aug 1539
Master of the Prince's Household	Thomas Duddingston of Kilduncan	Oct 1540	Aug 1541
The Prince's Master Almoner	sir William Laing	Jul 1541	Aug 1541
The Prince's Master Usher	the auld Laird	Aug 1541	1 Aug 1541
The Prince's Steward	Master Allan Lamont	Feb 1541	Aug 1541
Keeper of the Silver Vessels & Collier to the Prince	William Methven	Aug 1541	Aug 1541
The Prince's Master Cook	John Mount	Aug 1541	Aug 1541
Patissier in the Prince's Household	Patrick Marshall	Aug 1541	Aug 1541
In the Prince's Pantry	James Mackesson	Aug 1541	Aug 1541
The Prince's Tailor	sir Thomas Richardson	Dec 1540	Apr 1541
The Prince's Laundress	Margaret Maccombie	10 Jun 1540	10 Jun 1540
In the Prince's Service	Euphemia Strachan	Jan 1541	Jan 1541
In the Prince's Service	Katherine Ker	Feb 1541	Feb 1541
The Prince's Milkwife	Janet Macgee	Mar 1541	Mar 1541
In the Prince's Service	the wife of David Ramsay (unnamed)	Mar 1541	Mar 1541
In the Prince's Service	Margaret Scott	Apr 1541	Apr 1541
In the Prince's Household	William Crammy	Aug 1541	Aug 1541
In the Prince's Household	John Duchale	Aug 1540	Aug 1541
In the Prince's Household	Patrick Henderson	Aug 1541	Aug 1541
Lord James Stewart's Cook	Thomas Durie	May 1539	Mar 1542
Lord James's Laundress	Janet Ferguson	Aug 1539	Mar 1542
Page/Servant of the Abbot of Kelso	Walter Bell	Oct 1538	Aug 1539
Servant of Lord James	Angus Canochson	Nov 1538	Mar 1542
Servant of Lord James Stewart	Donald Begg	Aug 1539	Aug 1539
Servant to the King's 2 sons	John Cairns	Dec 1539	Dec 1539

Servant of Lord James	William Brown	Jun 1539	Mar 1541
Lady Jane Stewart's Nurse	Elizabeth Macall	1534	Aug 1542
Lady Jane Stewart's Nurse	Christina Baxter	Oct 1538	Jan 1542
Lady Jane Stewart's Tailor	Walter White	May 1538	Mar 1539
Lady Jane Stewart's Chamberlain/Servant	Thomas Troup	Mar 1539	Jul 1542
Paid with Livery	John Stewart	1526	Jan 1541
Paid for Misc Services	Thomas Kells	1532	3 May 1540
Gets Clothes	Robert Gourlay	Oct 1538	Jul 1541
Payments & Liveries to	the auld/the young Laird	Dec 1538	1 Aug 1541
Payments to	George Carmichael	Oct 1539	Jul 1541
Payments to	Master Andrew Whitelaw	Jan 1539	Dec 1542
Payments/Expenses	Master David Balfour	Aug 1539	Dec 1542
Servant to Thom Arthur	Robert Craig	Dec 1538	Jan 1542
Servitrix to Henry Kemp	Bessie Lundie	1538	19 May 1540
John Tennent's Falconer	Baxter	Jan 1539	25 Apr 1540
Servant to the Comptroller	Thomas Kay	1539	1539
John Lowes' Man	Murray	Dec 1539	Dec 1540

The King's Itinerary in 1538

This appendix lists the movements of the king and his household in the year 1538 as recorded in the household books of the period: SRO, Libri Domicilii, E.31/7–E.31/8 and SRO, Liber Emptorum, E.32/7. The individual folio references are not supplied since the records are written in chronological order anyway. This list is a reduction from the full itinerary which can be found in Andrea Thomas, 'Renaissance Culture at the Court of James V, 1528–1542' (University of Edinburgh Ph.D thesis, 1997), 386–423. Royal itineraries have previously been constructed using the evidence of documents issued under the great and privy seals (e.g. McGladdery, *James II*, 158–9; Macdougall, *James IV*, 313–15) but the reign of James V is the first one for which the daily accounts of the royal kitchen, pantry, buttery and cellar have survived in any quantity. The pattern of movements revealed in the household books does not always coincide with the itinerary suggested by the *Registers* of the great and privy seals, and it is likely that the record of where the king was fed would be a more accurate indication of his whereabouts than the record of where business was transacted in his name. Again, the sample year has been selected as one in which the king was at the peak of his powers, but 1539 (to match Appendix A) was not suitable because the household record is incomplete for this year.

The prefatory table indicates the pattern of the king's movements during the years of the adult reign by showing the percentage of nights in each year he spent in the given locations.

	Holyrood	Stirling	Linlithgow	Falkland	SE	SW	Fife, Perth	NE	Other
1528	67	17	3	9	0	4	0	0	0
1529	30	38	10	3	10	8	1	0	0
1530	17	41	5	9	6	6	15	1	0
1531	29	36	4	2	2	1	22	4	0
1532	27	41	5	8	4	4	11	0	0
1533	11	33	2	11	6	16	21	0	0
1534	8	27	1	2	11	4	46	1	0
1535	8	44	1	8	12	10	10	7	0
1536	1	29	1	13	4	8	8	0	36
1537	17	1	3	10	7	5	9	11	37
1538	15	17	12	14	3	10	28	0	1
1539	10	15	19	27	3	1	25	0	0
1540	30	8	15	15	3	1	26	1	1
1541	28	28	1	24	1	1	16	1	0
1542	40	10	4	19	9	1	17	0	0
Total	22	26	6	12	5	5	17	2	5

1538

Tue 1 – Sat 12 Jan............... Linlithgow (Lord James at Stirling)
Sun 13 Jan......................... Linlithgow to Glasgow
Mon 14 – Tue 15 Jan........... Glasgow (at archbishop's expense)
Wed 16 Jan .... Paisley (at abbot's expense)
Thu 17 – Fri 18 Jan .... Irvine (at earl of Eglinton's expense)
Sat 19 – Thu 31 Jan............. Ayr
Fri 1 Feb........................... Dumbarton to Glasgow
Sat 2 – Mon 4 Feb .... Glasgow (at archbishop's expense), Lord James
      still at Stirling
Tue 5 – Wed 20 Feb............ Stirling
Thu 21 Feb........................ Stirling to Falkland
Fri 22 Feb.......................... Falkland
Sat 23 Feb .... household at Falkland, king to Cupar
Sun 24 – Thu 28 Feb .... household at Falkland, king absent (Cupar?)
Fri 1 Mar .... household to Cupar, king to St. Andrews (at
      prior's expense)
Sat 2 – Tue 5 Mar............... king and household at St. Andrews, Lord James
      still at Stirling
Wed 6 Mar........................ king at St. Andrews, household to Dundee
Thu 7 Mar......................... household at Dundee, king absent
Fri 8 Mar .... king from Cupar to join household at Dundee
Sat 9 – Sat 16 Mar .... Dundee, king absent between 11th and 15th
      (Falkland, Glamis, Perth – *RSS, Letters*), Lord
      James still at Stirling
Sun 17 Mar .... Dundee to Perth
Mon 18 Mar .... Perth to Stirling
Tue 19 – Fri 22 Mar............. Stirling
Sat 23 Mar .... Stirling to Edinburgh
Sun 24 Mar – Thu 11 Apr .... Edinburgh (king absent on 11th)
Fri 12 Apr......................... household at Stirling, king at Perth/Cupar
Sat 13 – Tue 16 Apr............. household at Stirling, king at Perth
Wed 17 Apr .... household and Lord James at Stirling, king at
      Edinburgh
Thu 18 Apr .... king returns to Stirling
Fri 19 – Sun 28 Apr .... Stirling (Easter – 21st)
Mon 29 Apr – Wed 1 May ... Edinburgh
Thu 2 – Sun 5 May............. household at Edinburgh, king at Leith
Mon 6 – Wed 8 May........... household at Edinburgh, king on board ship (the
      Salamander) in the Forth
Thu 9 May .... household at Edinburgh, king sails to Isle of May
      and Dunbar
Fri 10 May .... household at Edinburgh, king lands at
      Pittenweem and heads for Perth for dinner
Sat 11 – Mon 13 May .... Perth
Tue 14 May........................ Perth to Falkland
Wed 15 – Thu 16 May......... Falkland
Fri 17 May .... Falkland to Stirling
Sat 18 – Thu 23 May............ Stirling
Fri 24 May .... Stirling to Falkland
Sat 25 May........................ Falkland to Perth
Sun 26 – Fri 31 May............ Perth
Sat 1 Jun........................... Perth to Cupar

Sun 2 – Fri 7 Jun .... Cupar
Sat 8 – Mon 10 Jun .... Perth
Tue 11 – Sat 15 Jun .... Pitlethie
Sun 16 Jun (Trinity Sun) ...... Mary of Guise arrives at St. Andrews
Mon 17 Jun – Thu 9 Jul .... king and queen at St. Andrews
Wed 10 Jul .... St. Andrews to Cupar
Thu 11 Jul .... Cupar to Falkland
Fri 12 – Mon 15 Jul .... Falkland
Tue 16 Jul .... Falkland to Dysart
Wed 17 – Thu 18 Jul .... Dysart
Fri 19 Jul .... Dunfermline (at abbot's expense)
Sat 20 Jul .... Dunfermline to Edinburgh (queen's royal entry)
Sun 21 – Wed 31 Jul .... Edinburgh
Thu 1 Aug .... Edinburgh to Linlithgow
Fri 2 – Thu 8 Aug .... Linlithgow
Fri 9 – Sun 11 Aug .... queen at Linlithgow, king to Stirling
Mon 12 – Sat 17 Aug .... king rejoins queen at Linlithgow
Sun 18 Aug .... king and queen to Stirling
Mon 19 Aug .... Stirling to Glenfinglas (hunting)
Tue 20 Aug .... queen returns to Stirling, king remains on hunt
Wed 21 – Sat 24 Aug .... queen at Stirling, king hunting in Glenfinglas
Sun 25 – Thu 29 Aug .... king and queen at Stirling
Fri 30 Aug .... Stirling to Linlithgow
Sat 31 Aug – Thu 5 Sep .... queen at Linlithgow, king hunting in Argyll
Fri 6 Sep .... king returns to Linlithgow
Sat 7 – Sun 14 Sep .... Linlithgow
Sun 15 Sep .... queen stays at Linlithgow, king to Peebles and
                                                 Cramalt for hunting
Mon 16 – Sat 21 Sep .... queen at Linlithgow, king at Peebles
Sun 22 – Sun 29 Sep .... king and queen at Linlithgow
Mon 30 Sep .... Linlithgow to Stirling
Tue 1 – Thu 3 Oct .... Stirling
Fri 4 – Sat 12 Oct .... queen at Stirling, king absent (Falkland, Cupar,
                                                 Montrose, Brechin)
Sun 13 – Mon 21 Oct .... Stirling
Tue 22 Oct .... Stirling to Falkland
Wed 23 Oct – Sat 23 Nov ..... Falkland
Sun 24 Nov – Tue 3 Dec ...... queen at Falkland, king to Dundee, Glamis,
                                                 Arbroath
Wed 4 – Sat 7 Dec .... king and queen at Falkland
Sun 8 – Sat 14 Dec .... queen at Falkland, king to Edinburgh
Sun 15 – Mon 16 Dec .... king and queen at Falkland
Tue 17 Dec .... Falkland to Dunfermline
Wed 18 – Fri 20 Dec .... king and queen at Dunfermline (at expense of
                                                 archbishop of St. Andrews)
Sat 21 Dec .... Dunfermline to Edinburgh
Sun 22 – Tue 31 Dec .... Edinburgh

Bibliography

1. MANUSCRIPTS

Scottish Record Office:

E.31/1–8	Libri Domicilii of James V	1525–26, 1528–29, 1529–30, 1532–33, 1533–34, 1534–35, 1537–38, 1538–39.
E.31/12	Liber Domicili of Prince James	1512
E.32/2–8	Libri Emptorum of James V	1531–32, 1533–34, 1534–35, 1535–36, 1536–37, 1537–38, 1542–43.
E.33/1–2	Despence de la Maison Royale of Mary of Guise (incomplete)	1538/9–41, 1541–43
E.34/1	Bill of Household of James IV	1507/08
E.34/2	Household fees and allowances of James IV and Margaret Tudor	1510
E.34/3	Bill of Robert Henderson, master butcher	May 1532
E.34/4	Fees of king's household	1537–38
E.34/5/1	Household liveries	1540–41
E.34/5/2	Household liveries	1541
E.34/6	Instructions for master of household	1528 x 1542
E.34/7	Job description of steward	c.1582
E.34/8/1–5	Household rolls of Mary of Guise (fragments)	1538/9–1541
E.35/1	Inventories of James V's Wardrobe	1539, 1542, 1543
RH.2/1/9	Transumpt of council sederunts	1518–53

National Library of Scotland:

MS 1746	Adam Abell's 'Roit or Quheill of Tyme'	1533–37
MS 7143	Statutes of the Order of the Garter	1535
Adv MS 29.2.5	Household papers of Mary of Guise (Balcarres Papers)	1530s and 1540s
Adv MS 31.4.2	Sir Robert Forman's armorial	c.1542
Adv MS 31.4.3	Sir David Lindsay's armorial	1542
Adv MS 31.5.2	John Scrymgeour's heraldic collection	early sixteenth century
Adv MS 31.6.5	John Meldrum's heraldic collection	early sixteenth century
Adv MS 31.7.22	Peter Thomson's heraldic collection	c.1547

2. PRINTED RECORD COLLECTIONS

'Accounts of the King's Pursemaster, 1539–40', ed. A. L. Murray, in *SHS Misc.*, x (1965), 13–51

Accounts of the Lord High Treasurer of Scotland, eds. Thomas Dickson and Sir James Balfour Paul (12 vols, Edinburgh, 1877–1916)

Accounts of the Master of Works, eds. Henry M. Paton et al. (Edinburgh, 1957–)

Acts of the Parliament of Scotland, eds. T. Thomson and C. Innes (12 vols, Edinburgh, 1814–75)

Acts of the Lords of Council in Public Affairs, 1501–54: Selections from the Acta Dominorum Concilii, ed. R. K. Hannay (Edinburgh, 1932)

Calendar of Letters and Papers, Foreign and Domestic of the reign of Henry VIII, eds. J. S. Brewer et al. (21 vols, London, 1864–1932)

Calendar of State Papers and Manuscripts relating to English affairs, existing in the Archives and Collections of Venice, eds. T. Brown et al., (London, 1864–)

Calendar of State Papers Relating to Scotland, 1509–1603, ed. M. J. Thorpe (2 vols, London, 1858)

Ceremonial at the Marriage of Mary, Queen of Scots, with the Dauphin of France, ed. W. Bentham (London, Roxburghe Club, 1818)

Charters and Documents relating to the Collegiate Church and Hospital of the Holy Trinity, and the Trinity Hospital, Edinburgh (SBRS, 1871)

Charters and other Documents relating to the City of Edinburgh, 1143–1540, ed. J. D. Marwick (SBRS, 1871)

Charters and other Documents relating to the City of Glasgow (2 vols, SBRS, 1894–1906)

Charters and other Documents relating to the Royal Burgh of Stirling, 1124–1705, ed. R. Renwick (SBRS, 1884)

Charters and other Writs illustrating the History of the Royal Burgh of Aberdeen, ed. P. J. Anderson (Aberdeen, 1890)

Charter Chest of the Earldom of Wigton, 1214–1681, ed. F. J. Grant (SRS, 1910)

Charters, Writs and Public Documents of the Royal Burgh of Dundee, ed. W. Hay (Dundee, 1880)

Cochran-Patrick, R. W. (ed.), *Early Records relating to Mining in Scotland* (Edinburgh, 1878)

A Collection of Inventories and other records of the royal Wardrobe and Jewelhouse; and of the Artillery and Munitioun in some of the Royal Castles, 1488–1606, ed. T. Thomson (Edinburgh, 1815)

Dunlop, James (ed.), *Papers Relative to the Royal Guard of Scottish Archers in France from Original Documents* (Maitland Club, 1835)

Excerpta e Libris Domicilii Domini Jacobi Quinti Regis Scotorum (Bannatyne Club, 1836)

Exchequer Rolls of Scotland, ed. G. Burnett et al., (23 vols, Edinburgh, 1878–1908)

Extracts from the Council Register of the Burgh of Aberdeen ed. John Stuart (2 vols, Spalding Club, 1844–48)

Extracts from the Records of the Burgh of Edinburgh ed. Sir James D. Marwick (14 vols, SBRS, 1869–92)

Extracts from the Records of the Royal Burgh of Lanark, ed. R. Renwick (SBRS, 1893)

Extracts from the Records of the Burgh of Stirling, ed. R. Renwick (2 vols, Glasgow, 1887–89)

Facsimile of an Ancient Heraldic Manuscript Emblazoned by Sir David Lyndsay of the Mount, Lyon King of Arms, 1542, ed. W. D. Laing (Edinburgh, 1822)

Facsimiles of the National Manuscripts of Scotland (3 vols, London, 1867–71)

Flodden Papers, 1507–17, ed. M. Wood (SHS, 1933)

Foreign Correspondence with Marie de Lorraine, Queen of Scotland, from the Originals in the Balcarres Papers, ed. M. Wood (2 vols, SHS, 1923–25)

Fraser, Sir William, *The Douglas Book* (4 vols, Edinburgh, 1885)
Fraser, Sir William, *The Elphinstone Family Book* (2 vols, Edinburgh, 1897)
Fraser, Sir William, *The Lennox* (2 vols, Edinburgh, 1874)
Fraser, Sir William, *The Red Book of Menteith* (Edinburgh, 1880)
The Hamilton Papers, ed. J. Bain (2 vols, Edinburgh, 1890–92)
Household Ordinances (Society of Antiquaries, 1790)
Hume Brown, P. (ed.), *Early Travellers in Scotland* (Edinburgh, 1891)
Inventaires de la Royne Descosse Douairière de France, ed. J. Robertson (Bannatyne Club, 1863)
'The Inventory of the Chapel Royal at Stirling, 1505', ed. F. C. Eeles, *TSES*, iii (1909–10), 310–25
The Knights of St. John of Jerusalem, eds. I. B. Cowan, P. H. R. MacKay and A. MacQuarrie (SHS, 1983)
Leland, John (ed.), *De Rebus Britannicis Collectanea* (6 vols, London, 1770)
'Letters of Cardinal Beaton, 1537–41' ed. A. Lang, *SHR*, vi (1909), 150–8
Letters of James IV, 1505–13, eds. R. K. Hannay and R. L. Mackie (SHS, 1953)
Letters of James V, eds. D. Hay and R. K. Hannay (Edinburgh, 1954)
Liber Cartarum Sancte Crucis (Bannatyne Club, 1860)
Liber Conventus S. Katherine Senensis prope Edinburgum ed. James Maidment (Abbotsford Club, 1841)
Lindsay, Alexander, 'The Navigation of King James V Round Scotland, the Orkney Isles and the Hebrides or Western Isles', ed. Nicholas d'Arfeville, trans. Robert Chapman, in *Miscellanea Scotica: A Collection of Tracts Relating to the History, Antiquities, Topography and Literature of Scotland* (3 vols, Glasgow, 1820), iii, 100–22
Lindsay, Alexander, *A Rutter of the Scottish Seas, c.1540*, eds. A. B. Taylor, I. H. Adams and G. Fortune (Maritime Monographs and Reports, no. 44, 1980)
Miscellaneous Papers Principally Illustrative of Events in the Reigns of Queen Mary and King James VI, ed. Andrew MacGeorge (Maitland Club, 1834)
'Muster-Roll of the French Garrison at Dunbar, 1553', ed. R. S. Rait, *SHS Misc.*, ii (1904), 103–114
Papers Relative to the Marriage of King James the Sixth of Scotland with the Princess Anna of Denmark, 1589, ed. J. T. Gibson Craig (Bannatyne Club, 1828)
Papers Relative to the Regalia of Scotland, ed. W. Bell (Bannatyne Club, 1829)
Pitcairn, R. (ed.), *Criminal Trials in Scotland from 1488 to 1624* (Edinburgh, 1833)
'Pitodrie Papers, 1524–1628', ed. J. Stuart, *Spalding Club Misc.*, ii (1842), 175–208
Privy Purse Expenses of Elizabeth of York and Wardrobe Accounts of Edward IV, ed. N. H. Nicolas, (London, 1830)
Protocol Books of Dominus Thomas Johnson, 1528–78, eds. J. Beveridge and F. Russell (SRS, 1920)
Registrum Magni Sigilli Regum Scotorum, eds. J. M. Thompson et al. (Edinburgh, 1882–)
Registrum Secreti Sigilli Regum Scotorum, eds. M. Livinstone et al. (Edinburgh, 1908–)
Rentale Dunkeldense, ed. R. K. Hannay (SHS, 1915)
Reports of the Royal Commission on Historical Manuscripts (London, 1870–)
'The Scottish King's Household', ed. M. Bateson, *SHS Misc.*, ii (1904), 3–43
'The Scottish Nation in the University of Orléans, 1336–1538', ed. J. Kirkpatrick, *SHS Misc.*, ii (1904), 45–102
Selected Cases from Acta Dominorum Concilii et Sessionis, 1532–33, ed. I. H. Shearer (Stair Society, 1951)
State Papers and Letters of Sir Ralph Sadler, ed. A. Clifford (3 vols, Edinburgh, 1809)
Teulet, A. (ed.), *Inventaire chronologique des documents relatifs à l'histoire d'Ecosse conservés aux archives du royaume à Paris* (Abbotsford Club, 1839)

Teulet, A. (ed.), *Papiers d'état, pièces et documents inédits ou peu connus rélatifs à l'histoire de l'Ecosse au XVIème siècle* (3 vols, Bannatyne Club, 1852–60)

Teulet, A. (ed.) *Rélations politique de la France et de L'Espagne avec L'Ecosse au XVIème siècle* (5 vols, Paris, 1862)

Walker, Sir Patrick (ed.), *Documents Relative to the Reception at Edinburgh of the Kings and Queens of Scotland, 1561–1650* (Edinburgh, 1822)

Wood, M. A. E. (ed.), *Letters of the Royal and Illustrious Ladies of Great Britain* (3 vols, London, 1846)

3. ORIGINAL WORKS

The Asloan Manuscript, ed. W. A. Craigie (2 vols, STS, 1923–25)

Atkinson, Stephen, *The Discoverie and Historie of the Gold Mynes in Scotland, 1619*, ed. Gilbert Laing Meason (Bannatyne Club, 1825)

The Bannatyne Manuscript, ed. W. Tod Ritchie (4 vols, STS, 1923–25)

Bisset, Habakkuk, *Rolment of Courtis*, ed. Sir Philip J. Hamilton-Grierson (3 vols, STS, 1920–26)

Boece, Hector, *The Chronicles of Scotland*, trans. John Bellenden (1531), eds. R. W. Chambers and E. C. Batho (2 vols, STS, 1938–41)

Boece, Hector, *The Mar Lodge Translation of the History of Scotland*, ed. G. Watson (STS, 1946)

Boece, Hector, *Murthlacensium et Aberdonensium Episcoporum Vitae*, ed. and trans. James Moir (New Spalding Club, 1894)

The Boke of the Ordre of Chyvalry translated and printed by William Caxton together with Adam Loutfut's Scottish Transcript, ed. A. T. P. Bayles (EETS, 1926)

Bower, Walter, *Scotichronicon*, ed. D. E. R. Watt (8 vols, Aberdeen, 1987–95)

Brantôme, Pierre de Bourdeilles, abbé et seigneur de, *Oeuvres Complètes* (13 vols, Paris, 1890)

Brosse, Jacques de la, *Two Missions: An Account of the Affairs of Scotland in the year 1543 and the Journal of the Seige of Leith, 1560*, ed. G. Dickinson (SHS, 1942)

Buchanan, George, *The History of Scotland from the Earliest Period to the Regency of the Earl of Moray*, ed. and trans. J. Aikman (4 vols, Glasgow, 1827)

Burel, John, 'The Description of the Queen's Majesties Maist Honorable Entry into the Toun of Edinburgh' in *James Watson's Choice Collection of Comic and Serious Scots Poems* ed. H. H. Wood (STS, 1977)

Calderwood, David, *History of the Kirk of Scotland*, eds. T. Thomson and D. Laing (8 vols, Woodrow Society, 1842–49)

Castiglione, Baldesar, *The Book of the Courtier*, ed. and trans. G. Bull (Harmondsworth, 1983)

Chalmers, David of Ormond, *A Chronicle of the Kings of Scotland* (Maitland Club, 1830)

'The Chronicle of Aberdeen', ed. J. Stuart, *Spalding Club Misc.*, ii (1842), 29–70

The Chronicle of Perth: A Register of Remarkable Occurences chiefly concerned with that city, 1210–1668 (Maitland Club, 1831)

Cronique du Roy Françoys Premier de ce nom publiée pour la première fois d'après un manuscrit de la Bibliothèque Impériale, ed. Georges Guiffrey (Paris, 1860)

'Discours particulier d'Escosse', ed. and trans. P. G. B. McNeill, *Stair Society Misc.*, ii, (1984), 86–131

A Diurnal of Remarkable Occurents that have passed within the country of Scotland since the death of King James the Fourth till the year 1575 (Bannatyne Club, 1833)

Douglas, Gavin, *The Poetical Works*, ed. J. Small (4 vols, Edinburgh and London, 1874)

Drummond, William, *The Genealogy of the Most Noble and Ancient House of Drummond, 1681* (Edinburgh, 1831)

Dunbar, William, *The Poems*, ed. J. Small (3 vols, STS, 1893)

Elliot, Kenneth (ed.) *Musica Scotica: Editions of Early Scottish Music*, (2 vols, Glasgow, 1996)

Elliot, K. and Shire, H. M. (eds.), 'Music of Scotland, 1500–1700', *Musica Britannica*, xv (1975)

d'Espence, Claude, *Oraison Funèbre es obseques de tres Haute, tres puissante & tres vertueuse Princesse, Marie par la grace de Dieu Royne douairiere d'Escoce. Prononcée à nostre Dame de Paris, le douzieme d'Aoust, mil cinq cens soixante* (Paris, 1561)

Extracta e Variis Cronicis Scocie, ed. W. B. D. Turnbull (Abbotsford Club, 1842)

Eyre-Todd, George (ed.), *Scottish Poetry of the Sixteenth Century* (Glasgow, 1892)

Ferrerius, Giovanni, *Historia Abbatum de Kynlos* (Bannatyne Club, 1839)

Foulis, Sir James, of Colinton, 'Strena ad Jacobum V. Scotorum Regem de Suscepto Regni Regimine', in *Bannatyne Club Misc.* ii (1836), 3–8

Das Gebetbuch Jakobs IV von Schottland und seiner Gemahlin Margaret Tudor ed. Franz Unterkircher (Graz, 1987)

Ireland, John, *The Meroure of Wyfsdome*, ed. C. Macpherson, F. Quinn and C. McDonald (3 vols, STS, 1926–1990)

Hall, E. *The Union of the Two Noble and Illustre Famelies of Lancastre and York* (London, 1809)

Hay, Sir Gilbert, *The Prose Manuscript, 1456*, ed. J. H. Stevenson (2 vols, STS, 1901–14)

Keith, Bishop Robert, *History of the Affairs of Church and State in Scotland* (3 vols, Spottiswoode Society, 1844)

Knox, John, *The Works*, ed. D. Laing (6 vols, Woodrow Society, 1846–64)

Leslie, Bishop John, *The History of Scotland from the Death of King James I in the year 1436 to the year 1561* (Bannatyne Club, 1830)

Leslie, John, *The Historie of Scotland*, trans. J. Dalrymple (1596), eds. E. G. Cody and W. Murison (STS, 1888–95)

Lindsay of the Mount, Sir David, *The Works, 1490–1555*, ed. D. Hamer (4 vols, STS, 1931–36)

Livius, Titus, *History of Rome: the First Five Books*, trans. John Bellenden (1533), ed. W. A. Craigie, (2 vols, STS, 1901–03)

MacQueen, John (ed.), *Ballattis of Luve* (Edinburgh, 1970)

Mair, John, *A History of Greater Britain as well England as Scotland, 1521*, ed. and trans. A. Constable with a *Life of the Author* by Æ. J. G. Mackay (SHS, 1892)

The Maitland Folio Manuscript, ed. W. A. Craigie (2 vols, STS, 1917–27)

The Maitland Quarto Manuscript, ed. W. A. Craigie (STS, 1920)

Maitland of Lethington, Sir Richard, *The Historie and Cronicle of the Hous and Surename of Seyton* (Maitland Club, 1829)

Marjoribanks, George, *Annals of Scotland from the yeir 1514 to the yeir 1591* (Edinburgh, 1814)

Marot, Clément, *Oeuvres complètes*, ed. C. A. Mayer (6 vols, London, 1958–80)

Myln, Alexander, *Vitae Episcoporum Dunkeldensium*, ed. T. Thomson (Bannatyne Club, 1823)

Pitscottie, Robert Lindsay of, *The Chronicles of Scotland*, ed. John Graham Dalyell (Edinburgh, 1814)

Pitscottie, Robert Lindsay of, *The Historie and Cronicles of Scotland*, ed. Æ. J. G. MacKay (3 vols, STS, 1899–1911)

Richardinus, Robert, *Commentary on the Rule of St. Augustine*, ed. G. G. Coulton (SHS, 1935)

Ronsard, Pierre, *Oeuvres complètes*, ed. G. Cohen (20 vols, Paris, 1950)

Rolland, John, *The Seuin Seages translatit out of prois in Scottis meter*, ed. G. F. Black (STS, 1932)

Seyssel, Claude de, *The Monarchy of France*, trans. J. H. Hexter and M. Sherman, ed. D. R. Kelley (New Haven and London, 1981)

Skelton, John, *The Complete English Poems*, ed. John Scattergood (Harmondsworth, 1983)

Stewart, William, *The Buik of the Croniclis of Scotland or A Metrical Version of the History of Hector Boece*, ed. W. B. Turnbull (3 vols, Rolls Series, 1858)

La tryumphante Entree de Charles Prince des Espagnes en Bruges, 1515: A Facsimile, ed. Sydney Anglo (Amsterdam, no date)

Wedderburn, Robert, *The Complaynt of Scotland c. 1550*, ed. A. M. Stewart (STS, 1979)

4. REFERENCE

Aldis, H. G., *A List of Books Published in Scotland before 1700* (Edinburgh, 1970)

Apted, M. R., and Hannabus, S., *Painters in Scotland, 1301–1700: A Biographical Dictionary* (SRS, 1978)

Baker, D. (ed.), *Bibliography of Reform* (Oxford, 1975)

Balfour Paul, Sir James, *The Scots Peerage* (9 vols, Edinburgh, 1904–14)

Biographie Nationale de Belgique (28 vols., Brussels, 1866–1944)

Black, G. F., *The Surnames of Scotland: Their Origin, Meaning, and History* (Edinburgh, 1993)

Brunton, G., and Haig, F., *An Historical Account of the Senators of The College of Justice* (Edinburgh, 1836)

Cameron, N. M. de S., Wright, D. F., Lachman, D. C., and Meek, D. E., (eds.), *Dictionary of Scottish Church History and Theology* (Edinburgh, 1993)

Cowan, I. B. and Easson, D. E., *Medieval Religious Houses* (London, 1976)

Cowan, S., *The Lord Chancellors of Scotland* (2 vols, Edinburgh and London, 1911)

Craigie, W. A., et al. (eds.), *A Dictionary of the Older Scottish Tongue: Twelfth Century to the end of the Seventeenth* (London and Aberdeen, 1937–)

Daiches, David (ed.), *The New Companion to Scottish Culture* (Edinburgh, 1993)

Dickinson, W. C., Donaldson, G., and Milne, I. A., (eds.), *A Source Book of Scottish History* (3 vols, Edinburgh, 1953)

Dictionary of National Biography (London and Oxford, 1885–1900)

Dowden, J., *The Bishops of Scotland* (Glasgow, 1912)

Dunbar, A. H., *Scottish Kings: A Revised Chronology of Scottish History, 1005–1625*, 2nd edition (Edinburgh, 1906)

Durkan, J. and Ross, A., *Early Scottish Libraries* (Glasgow, 1961)

Forbes, A. P., *Kalendars* [sic] *of Scottish Saints* (Edinburgh, 1872)

Forbes Leith, W., *Pre-Reformation Scholars in Scotland in the Sixteenth Century* (Glasgow, 1915)

Grant, Sir Francis James, *The Faculty of Advocates in Scotland, 1532–1943* (SRS, 1944)

Grant, Sir Francis James, *Court of the Lord Lyon, 1318–1945* (SRS, 1946)

Groome, F. H., *Ordnance Gazetteer of Scotland* (6 vols, Edinburgh, 1885–1901)

Henderson, J. M., *Scottish Reckonings of Time, Money, Weights and Measures* (Historical Association of Scotland, n.s. no. 4, 1926)

Imrie, J. et al., (eds.), *Guide to the National Archives of Scotland, Scottish Record Office* (Stair Society/HMSO, 1996)

Latham, R. E., *A Revised Medieval Latin Word-List from British and Irish Sources* (London, 1965)

Livingstone, M., *A Guide to the Public Records of Scotland* (Edinburgh, 1905)

McNeill, Peter G. B., and MacQueen, Hector L., *Atlas of Scottish History to 1707* (Edinburgh, 1996)

McNeill, Peter G. B., and Nicholson, R., *An Historical Atlas of Scotland, c.400–c.1600* (St, Andrews, 1975)

McRoberts, David, *Catalogue of Scottish Medieval Books and Fragments* (Glasgow, 1953)

Omond, G. W. T., *The Lords Advocate of Scotland* (3 vols, Edinburgh, 1883)

Powicke, F. M., and Fryde, E. B., *Handbook of British Chronology* (London, 1961)

Register of the Society of Writers to Her Majesty's Signet (Edinburgh, 1983)

Reports of the Royal Commission on Ancient and Historical Monuments of Scotland (Edinburgh, 1909–)

Sadie, S., (ed.), *The New Grove Dictionary of Music and Musicians* (20 vols, London, 1980)

Simpson, Grant G., *Scottish Handwriting, 1150–1650: An Introduction to the Reading of Documents* (Aberdeen, 1986)

Stevenson, David and Wendy B., *Scottish Texts and Calendars: an Analytical Guide to Serial Publications* (SHS, 1987)

Stevenson, J. H. and M. Wood, *Scottish Heraldic Seals* (Glasgow, 1940)

Thomson, J. M., *The Public Records of Scotland* (Edinburgh, 1922)

Watt, D. E. R., *Fasti Ecclesiae Scoticanae Medii Aevi ad annum 1638* (SRS, 1969)

Whitelaw, Charles E., *Scottish Arms Makers: A Biographical Dictionary of Makers of Firearms, edged weapons and armour working in Scotland from the fifteenth century to 1870* (London, 1977)

5. SECONDARY WORKS (MONOGRAPHS AND ARTICLES)

Adams, Simon, 'Faction, Clientage and Party: English Politics, 1550–1603', *History Today*, xxxii (Dec. 1982), 33–9

Aldis, H. G., Carter, J. and Crutchley, B., *The Printed Book* (Cambridge, 1951)

Anderson, J., *Ladies of the Reformation* (Glasgow, 1855)

Anderson, P. D., *Robert Stewart, Earl of Orkney, Lord of Shetland, 1533–1593* (Edinburgh, 1982)

Anderson, W. J. 'Rome and Scotland, 1513–1625', *IR*, x (1959), 173–93

Anderson, W. J. 'Three Sixteenth-Century Scottish Missals', *IR*, ix (1958), 204–9

Angels, Nobles and Unicorns: Art and Patronage in Medieval Scotland, NMS exhibition handbook (Edinburgh, 1982)

Anglo, Sydney, *Spectacle and Pageantry and Early Tudor Policy* (Oxford, 1969)

Anglo, Sydney (ed.), *Chivalry in the Renaissance* (Woodbridge, 1990)

Anon., 'The Life and Death of King James the Fifth of Scotland', *Miscellanea Scotica*, iv (1820), 81–164

Apted, M. R., *The Painted Ceilings of Scotland, 1550–1650* (Edinburgh, 1966)

Armitage, David (ed.), *Theories of Empire, 1450–1800* (Aldershot, 1998)

Asch, Ronald G. and Birke, Adolf M. (eds.), *Princes, Patronage and the Nobility: The Court at the Beginning of the Modern Age, c.1450–1650* (Oxford, 1991)

Babelon, Jean-Pierre, *Châteaux de France au siècle de la Renaissance* (Paris, 1989)

Baillie, Hugh Murray, 'Etiquette and the Planning of the State Apartments in Baroque Palaces', *Archaeologia*, ci (1967), 169–99

Baines, Anthony (ed.), *Musical Instruments Through the Ages* (London, 1973)

Baldwin, David, *The Chapel Royal, Ancient and Modern* (London, 1990)

Balfour Paul, Sir James, *Heraldry in Relation to Scottish History and Art* (Edinburgh, 1900)

Banks, M. MacLeod, *British Calendar Customs: Scotland* (3 vols., Folklore Society, 1937–41)

Bapst, Edmond, *Les Mariages de Jaques V* (Paris, 1889)

Barber, Richard and Barker, Juliet, *Tournaments: Jousts, Chivalry and Pageants in the Middle Ages* (Woodbridge, 1989)

Barrow, G. W. S. (ed.), *The Scottish Tradition: Essays in Honour of Ronald Gordon Cant* (Edinburgh, 1974)

Bawcutt, Priscilla, *Dunbar the Makar* (Oxford, 1992)

Bawcutt, Priscilla, *Gavin Douglas: A Critical Study* (Edinburgh, 1976)

Beard, Charles R., 'Early Stewart Portraits: A Discovery', *The Connoisseur*, lxxi (Jan.-Apr. 1925), 5–15

Bentley-Cranch, Dana, 'An early Sixteenth-century French Architectural source for the Palace of Falkland', *ROSC*, ii (1986), 85–95

Bentley-Cranch, Dana, 'Effigy and Portrait in Sixteenth Century Scotland', *ROSC*, iv (1988), 9–23

Bergen-Pantens, Christiane Van den (ed.), *L'ordre de la Toison d'or de Philippe le Bon à Philippe le Beau (1430–1505): idéal ou reflet d'une société?* (Brussels, 1996)

Bertelli, S., Cardini, F. and Zorzi, E. G. (eds.), *Italian Renaissance Courts* (London, 1986)

Bingham, Caroline, *James V, King of Scots, 1512–1542* (London, 1971)

Black Verschuur, Mary, 'The Perth Charterhouse in the Sixteenth Century', *IR*, xxxix (1988), 1–11

Blunt, A., *Art and Architecture in France, 1500–1700* (London, 1980)

Boardman, Stephen I., *The Early Stewart Kings: Robert II and Robert III, 1371–1406* (East Linton, 1996)

Boulton, D'Arcy Jonathan Dacre, *The Knights of the Crown: The Monarchical Orders of Knighthood in Later Medieval Europe, 1325–1520* (Woodbridge, 1987)

Brandi, Karl, *The Emperor Charles V*, trans. C. V. Wedgewood (London, 1965)

Breeze, D. J. (ed.), *Studies in Scottish Antiquity presented to Stewart Cruden* (Edinburgh, 1984)

Bridgland, Nick, *Hermitage Castle* (Historic Scotland, 1996)

Broadie, A., *The Circle of John Mair: Logic and Logicians in Pre-Reformation Scotland* (Oxford, 1985)

Broadie, A., *George Lokert: Late-Scholastic Logician* (Edinburgh, 1983)

Broadie, A., *The Shadow of Scotus: Philosophy and Faith in Pre-Reformation Scotland* (Edinburgh, 1995)

Brook, A. J. S., 'Technical Description of the Regalia of Scotland', *PSAS*, xxiv (1889–90), 49–141

Broun, Dauvit, Finlay, R. J. and Lynch, Michael (eds.), *Image and Identity: The Making and Re-making of Scotland Through the Ages* (Edinburgh, 1998)

Brown, Michael, *The Black Douglases: War and Lordship in Late Medieval Scotland, 1300–1455* (East Linton, 1998)

Brown, Michael, *James I* (Edinburgh, 1994)

Brown, M. H., 'Scotland Tamed? Kings and Magnates in Late Medieval Scotland: a review of Recent work', *IR*, xlv (1994), 120–46

Brown, Jennifer M. (ed.), *Scottish Society in the Fifteenth Century* (London, 1977)

Bryant, Lawrence M., *The King and the City in the Parisian Royal Entry Ceremony: Politics, Ritual and Art in the Renaissance* (Geneva, 1986)

Bryce, W. Moir, *The Scottish Greyfriars* (2 vols, Edinburgh and London, 1909)

Buchanan, Patricia H., *Margaret Tudor, Queen of Scots* (London and Edinburgh, 1985)

Bullock-Davies, Constance, *Minstrellorum Multitudo: Minstrels at a Royal Feast* (Cardiff, 1978)

Bumke, Joachim, *Courtly Culture: Literature and Society in the High Middle Ages*, trans. Thomas Dunlap (Berkeley, 1991)

Burckhardt, Jacob, *The Civilization of the Renaissance in Italy*, trans. S. G. C. Middlemore (Oxford and London, 1945; originally Basel, 1860)

Burke, Peter, *The Fortunes of the Courtier: The European Reception of Castiglione's Cortegiano* (Cambridge, 1995)

Burnett, Charles J. and Tabraham, C. J., *The Honours of Scotland* (Edinburgh, 1993)

Burnett, Charles J., 'The Act of 1471 and its effect on the Royal Arms of Scotland', *PSAS*, cv (1972–74), 312–15

Burnett, Charles J., 'Reflections on the Order of the Thistle', *The Double Tressure: Journal of the Heraldry Society of Scotland*, v (1983), 39–42

Burnett, Charles J., 'The Development of the Royal Arms to 1603', *Journal of the Heraldry Society of Scotland*, i (1977–8), 7–19

Burnett, Charles J., 'Early Officers of Arms in Scotland', *ROSC*, ix (1995–6), 3–13

Burns, C., 'Papal Gifts to Scottish Monarchs: The Golden Rose and the Blessed Sword', *IR*, xx (1969), 150–95

Burns, J., 'John Ireland and *The Meroure of Wyssdome*', *IR*, vi (1955), 77–98

Burns, J. H., 'The Scotland of John Major', *IR*, ii (1951), 65–76

Burns, J. H., 'New Light on John Major', *IR*, v (1954), 83–100

Burns, J. H., *The True Law of Kingship: Concepts of Monarchy in Early Modern Scotland* (Oxford, 1996)

Caldwell, D. H. (ed.), *Scottish Weapons and Fortifications, 1100–1800* (Edinburgh, 1981)

Cameron, Jamie, *James V: The Personal Rule, 1528–1542* (East Linton, 1998)

Campbell, Ian, 'Linlithgow's "Princely Palace" and its Influence in Europe', *Architectural Heritage*, v (1995), 1–20

Campbell, Ian, 'A Romanesque Revival and the Early Renaissance in Scotland, c.1380 – 1513', *Journal of the Society of Architectural Historians*, liv (1995), 302–25

Campbell, L., *The Early Flemish Pictures in the Collection of Her Majesty the Queen* (Cambridge, 1985)

Carmi Parsons, John (ed.), *Medieval Queenship* (Stroud, 1994)

Cavers, Keith, *A Vision of Scotland: The Nation Observed by John Slezer, 1671 to 1717* (Edinburgh, 1993)

Chambers, R., *Domestic Annals of Scotland from the Reformation to the Revolution* (3 vols, Edinburgh, 1874)

Champion, Pierre, *Ronsard et son temps* (Paris, 1925)

Chapman, Hester W., *The Sisters of Henry VIII* (Bath, 1974)

Cheape, Hugh (ed.), *Tools and Traditions: Studies in European Ethnology Presented to Alexander Fenton* (Edinburgh, 1993)

Cherry, Alastair, *Princes, Poets and Patrons: The Stewarts and Scotland* (Edinburgh, 1987)

Chrimes, S. B., *Henry VII* (London, 1987)

Clough, Cecil H., 'Francis I and the Courtiers of Castiglione's *Courtier*', in *European Studies Review*, xviii (1978), 23–50

Clowes, W. L., *The Royal Navy: A History from the Earliest Times to the Present* (7 vols, 1897–1903)

Colvin, H. M. et al. (eds.), *The History of the King's Works* (7 vols, London, 1963–73)

Constant, Jean-Marie, *Les Guises* (Paris, 1984)

Coventry, Martin, *The Castles of Scotland* (Edinburgh, 1995)

Cowan, I. B. and Shaw, D. (eds.), *The Renaissance and Reformation in Scotland: Essays in Honour of Gordon Donaldson* (Edinburgh, 1983)

Cox, E. H. M., *A History of Gardening in Scotland* (London, 1935)

Crawford, Henry J., *French Travellers in Scotland* (Stirling, 1939)

Cruden, Stewart, *The Scottish Castle* (Edinburgh and London, 1960)

Cust, Lady Elizabeth, *Some Account of the Stuarts of Aubigny in France, 1422–1672* (London, 1891)

Davidson, John and Gray, Alexander, *The Scottish Staple at Veere: A Study in the Economic History of Scotland* (London, 1909)

Davies, C. S. L., *Peace, Print and Protestantism, 1450–1558* (London, 1990)

Dickens, A. G. (ed.), *The Courts of Europe, 1400–1800* (New York, 1984)

Dickinson, Gladys, 'Some Notes on the Scottish Army in the first half of the Sixteenth Century', *SHR*, xxviii (1949), 133–145

Dilworth, Mark, 'Book of Hours of Mary of Guise', *IR*, xix (1968), 77–80

Dolmetsch, Mabel, *Dances of England and France from 1450 to 1600* (London, 1949)

Dolmetsch, Mabel, *Dances of Spain and Italy from 1400 to 1600* (London, 1954)

Donaldson, Gordon, *Scotland: James V-James VII* (Edinburgh, 1990)

Donaldson, Gordon, 'Stewart Builders: The Descendants of James V', *The Stewarts*, xiv (1974), 116–22

Donaldson, Gordon, 'The Bishops and Priors of Whithorn', *TDGAS*, 3rd Series, xxvii (1950), 147

Donaldson, Robert, 'The Cambuskenneth Books: the Norris of Speke Collection', *The Bibliothek*, xv (1988), 3–7

Doughty, D. W., 'The Library of James Stewart, Earl of Moray, 1531–70', *IR*, xxi (1970), 17–29

Doughty, D. W., 'Renaissance books, bindings and owners in St. Andrews and elsewhere: the humanists', *The Bibliothek*, vii (1974–5), 117–33

Dove, M., *The Perfect Age of Man's Life* (Cambridge, 1986)

Dowden, John, *The Medieval Church in Scotland* (Glasgow, 1910)

Drijvers, Jan Willem and MacDonald, A. A. (eds.), *Centres of Learning: Learning and Location in Pre-Modern Europe and the Near East* (Leiden, 1995)

Drummond, Humphrey, *Our Man in Scotland: Sir Ralph Sadleir [sic], 1507–1587* (London, 1969)

Duchhardt, Heinz, Jackson, Richard A. and Sturdy, David (eds.), *European Monarchy, its Evolution and Practice from Roman Antiquity to Modern Times* (Stuttgart, 1992)

Dunbar, John G., *The Historic Architecture of Scotland* (London, 1966)

Dunbar, John G., 'The Palace of Holyrood during the first half of the sixteenth century', *Arch. Journ. cxx* (1963), 242–254

Dunbar, John G., 'Some Aspects of the Planning of Scottish Royal Palaces in the sixteenth century', *Architect. Hist.* xxvii (1984), 15–24

Dunbar, John G., 'Some Sixteenth-century French Parallels for the Palace of Falkland', *ROSC*, vii (1991), 3–8

Dunbar, John G., *The Stirling Heads* (HMSO, 1975)

Dunbar, John G., 'Carved Heads to Adorn a Ceiling', *Country Life,* vol. cxxxii, no. 3418 (6 Sep. 1962), 528–9

Dunbar, John G., *Scottish Royal Palaces: The Architecture of the Royal Residences during the Late Medieval and Early Renaissance Periods* (East Linton, 1999)

Duncan, A. A. M., *James I, King of Scots* (Glasgow, 1984)

Duncan Gibb, Sir George, *The Life and Times of Robert Gib, Lord of Carriber, Familiar Servitor and Master of the Stables to King James V of Scotland* (2 vols, London, 1874)

Durkan, John, 'The Cultural Background in Sixteenth-Century Scotland', *IR*, x (1959), 382–439

Durkan, John, 'Education in the Century of the Reformation', *IR*, x (1959), 67–90

Durkan, John, 'The Library of Mary, Queen of Scots', *IR*, xxxviii (1987), 71–104

Durkan, John, 'The Observant Franciscan Province in Scotland', *IR*, xxxv (1984), 51–7

Durkan, John, 'The Sanctuary and College of Tain', *IR*, xiii (1962), 147–56

Durkan, John, 'John Major: After 400 Years', *IR*, i (1950), 131–39

Durkan, John, 'The School of John Major: A Bibliography', *IR*, i (1950), 140–57

Durkan, John, 'The Beginnings of Humanism in Scotland', *IR*, iv (1953), 5–24

Durkan, John, 'Chaplains in Scotland in the Late Middle Ages', *RSCHS*, xx (1979), 91–103

Durkan, John, '"Scottish Evangelicals" in the Patronage of Thomas Cromwell', *RSCHS*, xxi (1983), 127–56

Durkan, John, 'Scottish Reformers: the Less than Golden Legend', *IR*, xlv (1994), 1–28

Durkan, John, 'Adam Mure's "Laudes Gulielmi Elphinstoni,"' *Humanistica Lovaniensia*, xviii (1979), 199–231

Durkan, John, *Bibliography of George Buchanan* (Glasgow, 1994)

Durkan, John, 'George Buchanan: New Light on the Poems', *The Bibliothek*, x (1990), 1–9

Durkan, John, '*The Trompet of Honour* (Edinburgh? 1537)', *The Bibliothek*, xi (1982), 1–2

Durkan, John, 'The Royal Lectureships under Mary of Lorraine', *SHR*, lxii (1983), 73–8

Durkan, John, Rawles, S. and Thorpe, N., *George Buchanan (1506–1582) Renaissance Scholar* (Exhibition Catalogue, Glasgow University Library, 1982)

Dutton, Ralph, *English Court Life* (London, 1963)

Easson, D. E., *Gavin Dunbar, Chancellor of Scotland and Archbishop of Glasgow* (Edinburgh and London, 1947)

Eaves, R. G., *Henry VIII's Scottish Diplomacy, 1513–1524: England's Relations with the Regency Government of James V* (New York, 1971)

Eaves, R. G., *Henry VIII and James V's Regency, 1524–1528: A Study in Anglo-Scottish Diplomacy* (London, 1987)

Edington, Carol, *Court and Culture in Renaissance Scotland: Sir David Lindsay of the Mount* (East Linton, 1995)

Elias, Norbert, *The Process of Civilization* (2 vols., Oxford, 1978–82)

Elias, Norbert, *The Court Society* (Oxford, 1983)

Elliot, Kenneth, 'Another of Thomas Wood's Missing Parts', *IR*, xxxix (1988), 151–5

Elliot, Kenneth, 'The Carver Choir Book', *Music & Letters*, xli (1960), 349–57

Elliot, Kenneth and Rimmer, Frederick, *A History of Scottish Music* (London, 1973)

Ellis, Henry, 'Observations upon a Household Book of King James the Fifth of Scotland', *Archaeologia*, xxii (1829), 1–12

Eltis, David, *The Military Revolution in Sixteenth-Century Europe* (London, 1995)

Elton, G. R., 'Tudor Government: The Points of Contact, III: The Court', *TRHS*, xxvi (1976), 211–28

Emmerson, George S., *A Social History of Scottish Dance: Ane Celestial Recreatioun* (Montreal and London, 1972)

Evans, G. H., *French Connections: Scotland and the Arts of France* (Edinburgh, 1985)

Ewan, Elizabeth, 'Women's History in Scotland: Review Article', *IR*, xlvi (1995), 155–64

Ewan, Elizabeth, and Maureen M. Meikle (eds.), *Women in Scotland c.1100–c.1750*, (East Linton, 1999)

Farmer, Henry George , *A History of Music in Scotland* (London, 1947)

Fawcett, Richard, *Scottish Architecture from the Accession of the Stewarts to the Reformation, 1371–1560* (Edinburgh, 1994)

Fawcett, Richard, *Stirling Castle* (London, 1995)

Fenton, A. and Stell, G. (eds.), *Loads and Roads in Scotland and Beyond* (Edinburgh, 1984)

Fellowes, Edmund H., *The Knights of the Garter, 1348–1939* (London, 1939)

Feltch, Susan M., 'The Rhetoric of Biblical Authority: John Knox and the Question of Women', *The Sixteenth Century Journal*, xxvi (1995), 805–22

Fenlon, Iain (ed.), *The Renaissance* (London, 1989)

Ferguson, John, *Linlithgow Palace* (Edinburgh, 1910)

Ferguson, John, *Ecclesia Antiqua or the History of an Ancient Church (St. Michael's, Linlithgow) with an account of its chapels, chantries and endowments* (Edinburgh, 1905)

Ferguson, W., *Scotland's Relations with England: A Survey to 1707* (Edinburgh, 1994)

Ferguson, William, *The Identity of the Scottish Nation: An Historic Quest* (Edinburgh, 1998)

Findlay, I., *Scottish Gold and Silver Work* (London, 1956)

Firth Green, Richard, *Poets and Princepleasers: Literature and the English Court in the Late Middle Ages* (Toronto, 1980)

Fittis, R. S., *Sports and Pastimes of Scotland Historically Illustrated* (Wakefield, 1975)

Forrester, Duncan B. and Murray, Douglas M. (eds.), *Studies in the History of Worship in Scotland* (Edinburgh, 1984)

Forte, Angelo, 'Kenning be Kenning and Course be Course': Maritime Jurimetrics in Fifteenth and Sixteenth Century Northern Europe with Particular Reference to Scottish Maritime Law' (paper delivered to the 39th Conference of the Colloquium for Scottish Medieval and Renaissance Studies, Pitlochry, 7th January, 1996)

Fradenburg, L. O. (ed.), *Women and Sovereignty* (Edinburgh, 1992)

Fradenburg, L. O., *City, Marriage, Tournament: Arts of Rule in Late Medieval Scotland* (Wisconsin, 1991)

Frame, R., *The Political Development of the British Isles, 1100–1400* (Oxford, 1990)

Francisque-Michel, R., *Les Écossais en France, les Français en Écosse* (2 vols, London, 1862)

Gaborit-Chopin, Danielle, *Regalia: les instruments de sacre des rois de France et les 'honneurs de Charlemagne'* (Paris, 1987)

Gaier, Claude, 'The Origins of Mons Meg', *Journal of the Arms and Armour Society*, v (1965–7), 425–52

Gardner-Medwin, Alisoun and Williams, Janet Hadley(eds.), *A Day Estivall: Essays on the Music, Poetry and History of Scotland and England and Poems previously unpublished in Honour of Helena Mennie Shire* (Aberdeen, 1990)

Giesey, Ralph E., *The Royal Funeral Ceremony in Renaissance France* (Geneva, 1960)

Gifford, J., *The Buildings of Scotland: Fife* (London, 1988)

Gifford, J., et al., *The Buildings of Scotland: Edinburgh* (London, 1984)

Gilbert, John M., *Hunting and Hunting Reserves in Medieval Scotland* (Edinburgh, 1979)

Girouard, M., 'Falkland Palace, Fife I', *Country Life*, vol. cxxvi, no 3260 (27 Aug. 1959), 118–21

Girouard, M., 'Falkland Palace, Fife II', *Country Life*, vol cxxvi, no 3261 (3 Sep. 1959), 178–81

Gittings, Clare, *Death, Burial and the Individual in Early Modern England* (London, 1984)

Given Wilson, Chris, *The Royal Household and the King's Affinity: Service, Politics and Finance in England, 1360–1413* (New Haven and London, 1986)

Glendinning, Miles, MacInnes, Ranald, and MacKechnie, Aonghus, *A History of Scottish Architecture from the Renaissance to the Present Day* (Edinburgh, 1996)

Goodman, Anthony and MacKay, Angus (eds.), *The Impact of Humanism on Western Europe* (London, 1990)

Grant, Alexander, *Independence and Nationhood: Scotland 1306–1469* (London, 1984)

Green, M. A. E., *Lives of the Princesses of England from the Norman Conquest* (6 vols., London, 1849–55)

Grierson, Philip, 'The Origins of the English Sovereign and the Symbolism of the Closed Crown', *The British Numismatic Journal*, xxxiii (1964), 118–34

Gunn, S. J., *Charles Brandon, Duke of Suffolk c.1484–1545* (Oxford, 1988)

Guth, D. J. and McKenna, J. W. (eds.), *Tudor Rule & Revolution* (Cambridge, 1982)

Guy, John, *Tudor England* (Oxford, 1990)

Hale, J. R., *War and Society in Renaissance Europe, 1450–1620* (Leicester, 1985)

Hanawalt, Barbara A. (ed.), *Chaucer's England: Literature in Historical Context* (Minneapolis, 1992)

Hannay, R. K., *The College of Justice*, ed. Hector L. MacQueen (Stair Society, 1990)

Hannay, R. K., 'The Office of Justice Clerk', *Juridical Review*, xlvii (1935), 311–19

Harrison, John, *The History of the Monastery of the Holy-Rood and of the Palace of Holyrood House* (Edinburgh, 1919)

Harvey, Anthony and Mortimer, Richard (eds.), *The Funeral Effigies of Westminster Abbey* (Woodbridge, 1994)

Hay, G. 'The Late Medieval Development of the High Kirk of St. Giles, Edinburgh', *PSAS*, cvii (1975–76), 242–60

Hay Fleming, David, *The Reformation in Scotland; Causes, Characteristics, Consequences* (London, 1910)

Head, David M., 'Henry VIII's Scottish Policy: a Reassessment', *SHR*, lxi (1982), 1–24

Higgit, John (ed.), *Medieval Art and Architecture in the Diocese of St. Andrews* (London, 1994)

Hoak, D., 'The Secret History of the Tudor Court: The King's Coffers and the King's Purse, 1542–1553', in *Journal of British Studies*, xxvi (1987), 208–231

Hoak, Dale (ed.), *Tudor Political Culture* (Cambridge, 1995)

Hogwood, Christopher, *Music at Court* (London, 1977)

Hollstein, F. W. H., *German Engravings, Etchings and Woodcuts, c. 1400–1700* (Amsterdam, 1954 –)

Holmes, G., *The Order of the Garter: its Knights and Stall Plates 1348 to 1984* (Windsor, 1984)

Horn, D. B., 'The Origins of the University of Edinburgh', *University of Edinburgh Journal*, xxii (1966), 213–312

Hotle, C. Patrick, *Thorns and Thistles: Diplomacy between Henry VIII and James V, 1528–1542* (Lanham, 1996)

Houston, R. A., *Scottish Literacy and the Scottish Identity: Illiteracy and Society in Scotland and Northern England, 1600–1800* (Cambridge, 1985)

Howard, Deborah (ed.), *The Architecture of the Scottish Renaissance*, RIAS exhibition handbook (Edinburgh, 1990)

Howarth, David, *Images of Rule: Art and Politics in the English Renaissance, 1485–1649* (London, 1997)

Hughes, Joan and Ransom, W. S., *Poetry of the Stewart Court* (Canberra, 1982)

Hume Brown, P., *History of Scotland* (3 vols., Cambridge, 1909–12)

Hutton, Ronald, *The Rise and Fall of Merry England: The Ritual Year, 1400–1700* (Oxford, 1994)

Ijsewijn, J. and Thomson, D. F. S., 'The Latin Poems of Jacobus Follisius or James Foullis of Edinburgh', *Humanistica Lovaniensia*, xxiv (1975), 133–34

Inglis, J. A., *Sir Adam Otterburn of Redhall* (Glasgow, 1935)

Inglis, Jim, *The Organ in Scotland before 1700* (Schagen, 1991)

Ingram Hill, D., *Canterbury Cathedral* (London, 1986)

Innes of Learney, Sir Thomas, *Scots Heraldry* (Edinburgh, 1956)

Innes of Learney, Sir Thomas, 'The Style and Title of "Lord Lyon King of Arms", *Juridical Review*, xliv (1932), 197–220

Irving, George Vere and Murray, Alexander, *The Upper Ward of Lanarkshire Described and Delineated* (3 vols, Glasgow, 1864)

Ives, Eric, *Anne Boleyn* (London, 1988)

Jack, R. D. S. (ed.), *The History of Scottish Literature Volume One: Origins to 1660* (Aberdeen, 1988)

Jack, R. D. S., *The Italian Influence on Scottish Literature* (Edinburgh, 1972)

Jacquot, Jean et al. (eds.), *Les Fêtes de la Renaissance* (3 vols, Paris, 1956–65)

Jaeger, C. Stephen, *The Origins of Courtliness: Civilizing Trends and the Formation of Courtly Ideals, 939–1210* (Philadelphia, 1985)

Jenkins, E. H., *A History of the French Navy from its Beginnings to the Present Day* (London, 1973)

Jordan, Constance, 'Woman's Rule in Sixteenth-Century British Political Thought', *Renaissance Quarterly*, xl (1987), 421–51

Kantorowicz, Ernst, *The King's Two Bodies: A Study in Medieval Political Theology* (Princeton, 1957)

Kaufman, Peter Iver, 'Piety and Proprietary Rights: James IV of Scotland, 1488–1513', *The Sixteenth Century Journal*, xiii (1982), 83–99

Kerr, Andrew, 'Notes of Ancient tile paving in Linlithgow Palace', *PSAS*, xv (1880–81), 194–98

Kingsford, C. L., *English Historical Literature in the Fifteenth Century* (Oxford, 1913)

Kirk, J. (ed.), *Humanism and Reform: The Church in Europe, England, and Scotland, 1400–1634. Essays in Honour of James K. Cameron* (Oxford, 1991)

Knecht, R. J., *Renaissance Warrior and Patron: The Reign of Francis I* (Cambridge, 1994)

Knecht, R. J., 'The Court of Francis I', *European Studies Review*, viii (1978), 1–18

Knoop, Douglas and Jones, G. P., *The Scottish Mason and the Mason Word* (Manchester, 1939)

Kratzmann, Gregory, *Anglo-Scottish Literary Relations, 1430–1550* (Cambridge, 1980)

Laing, David, 'An Account of the Scottish Psalter of A.D. 1566', *PSAS*, vii (1866–7), 445–58

Lang, Andrew, 'The Cardinal and the King's Will', *SHR*, iii (1906), 410–22

Lawson, H. A. B., 'The Armorial Register of Sir David Lindsay of the Mount', *The Scottish Genealogist*, iv (1957), 12–19

Lecoq, Anne-Marie, *François Ier imaginaire: symbolique et politique à l'aube de la Renaissance Française* (Paris, 1987)

Lee, M., *James Stewart, Earl of Moray* (New York, 1953)

Lees, J. Cameron, *St. Giles, Edinburgh: Church, College and Cathedral from the Earliest Times to the Present Day* (Edinburgh and London, 1889)

Lees-Milne, James, *The Age of Inigo Jones* (London, 1953)

Lenman, Leah (ed.), *Perspectives in Scottish Social History: Essays in honour of Rosalind Mitchison* (Aberdeen, 1988)

Lewis, Ioan (ed.), *Symbols and Sentiments: Cross-Cultural Studies in Symbolism* (London, 1977)

Loades, David, *The Tudor Court* (Bangor, 1992)

Loades, David, *The Tudor Navy: An Administrative, Political and Military History* (Aldershot, 1992)

Lorimer, Peter, *Patrick Hamilton* (Edinburgh, 1857)

Loveday of Caversham, John, *Diary of a Tour in 1732* (Roxburghe Club, 1890)

Lyall, R. J., 'The Court as a Cultural Centre', *History Today*, xxxiv (Sep. 1984), 28–33

Lyall, R. J., 'The Medieval Scottish Coronation Service: Some Seventeenth-Century Evidence', *IR*, xxviii (1977), 3–21

Lyall, R. J., 'Scottish Students and Masters at the Universities of Cologne and Louvain in the Fifteenth Century', *IR*, xxxvi (1985), 55–73

Lynch, Michael, *Scotland: A New History* (London, 1992)

Lynch, Michael, 'The Origins of Edinburgh's "Toun College": a Revision Article', *IR*, xxxiii (1982), 3–14

Lynch, Michael, 'Court Ceremony and Ritual during the Personal Reign of James VI' in Julian Goodare and Michael Lynch (eds.) *The Reign of James VI* (East Linton, 2000), 71–92

Lynch, Michael, 'Queen Mary's Triumph: the Baptismal Celebrations at Stirling in December 1566', *SHR*, lxix (1990), 1–21

McClure, J. Derrick and Spiller, Michael R. G. (eds.), *Bryght Lanternis: Essays on the Language and Literature of Medieval Scotland* (Aberdeen, 1986)

McClure, J. Derrick (ed.), *Scotland and the Lowland Tongue: Studies in the Language and Literature of Lowland Scotland in honour of David D. Murison* (Aberdeen, 1983)

MacDonald, A. A., 'Catholic Devotion into Protestant Lyric: The Case of *The Contemplacioun of Synnaris*', *IR*, xxxv (1984), 58–83

MacDonald, A. A., 'Mary Stewart's Entry to Edinburgh: an Ambiguous Triumph', *IR*, xlii (1991), 101–10

MacDonald, A. A., 'Anglo-Scottish Literary Relations: Problems and Possibilities', *Studies in Scottish Literature*, xxvi (1991), 172–84

MacDonald, A. A., Lynch, M. and Cowan, I. B. (eds.), *The Renaissance in Scotland: Studies in Literature, Religion, History and Culture Offered to John Durkan* (Leiden, New York, Köln, 1994)

Macdougall, N., *Church, Politics and Society in Scotland, 1428–1929* (Edinburgh, 1983)

Macdougall, N., *James III: a Political Study* (Edinburgh, 1982)

Macdougall, N., *James IV* (Edinburgh, 1988)

Macdougall, N. (ed.), *Scotland and War, AD 79–1918* (Edinburgh, 1991)

Macewen, A. R., *A History of the Church in Scotland* (2 vols, London, 1913)

McFarlane, I. D., *Buchanan* (London, 1981)

McFarlane, I. D., *A Literary History of France: The Renaissance, 1470–1589* (London, 1974)

MacFarlane, L., 'The Book of Hours of James IV and Margaret Tudor', *IR*, xi (1960), 3–21

MacFarlane, L. J., 'Hector Boece and Early Scottish Humanism', *The Deeside Field*, xviii (1984), 65–9

MacFarlane, L. J., *William Elphinstone and the Kingdom of Scotland, 1431–1514* (Aberdeen, 1995)

McGibbon, D. and Ross, T., *The Castellated and Domestic Architecture of Scotland* (5 vols, Edinburgh, 1887–92)

McGibbon, D. and Ross, T., *The Ecclesiastical Architecture of Scotland* (3 vols, Edinburgh, 1896–97)

McGladdery, Christine, *James II* (Edinburgh, 1990)

MacIvor, Iain, *Blackness Castle* (Historic Scotland, 1993)

MacIvor, Iain, *Craignethan Castle* (Historic Scotland, 1993)

MacIvor, Iain, *Edinburgh Castle* (London, 1993)

MacIvor, Iain, *Dumbarton Castle* (Historic Scotland, 1993)

MacIvor, Iain, 'The King's Chapel at Restalrig and St. Triduana's Aisle: A Hexagonal two-storied Chapel of the Fifteenth Century', *PSAS*, xcvi (1962–3), 247–263

McKay, Denis, 'The four heid pilgrimages of Scotland', *IR*, xix (1968), 76–7

McKean, Charles, 'Hamilton of Finnart', *History Today*, xliii (Jan. 1993), 42–47

McKean, Charles, 'Craignethan: the Castle of the Bastard of Arran', *PSAS*, cxxv (1995), 1069–90

McKean, Charles, 'Finnart's Platt', in *Scottish Architects Abroad: Architectural Heritage II: The Journal of the Architectural Heritage Society of Scotland*, ed. D. Howard (1991), 3–17

MacKechnie, Aonghus, 'Stirling's Triumphal Arch', *Welcome: News for Friends of Historic Scotland* (Sept. 1991), unpaginated

Mackenzie, William M., *The Medieval Castle in Scotland* (Edinburgh, 1972)

McKerlie, E. M. H., *Mary of Guise-Lorraine, Queen of Scotland* (London, 1931)

Mackie, A., *Scottish Pageantry* (London, 1967)

Makinson, A., 'Solway Moss and the Death of James V', *History Today*, x (1960), 106–115

Maclean, Ian, *The Renaissance Notion of Woman* (Cambridge, 1980)

MacMillan, Duncan, *Scottish Art, 1460–1990* (Edinburgh, 1990)

MacPhail, J. R. N., 'Hamilton of Kincavil and the General Assembly of 1563', *SHR*, x (1913), 156–61

Macquarrie, Alan, 'Anselm Adornes of Bruges: Traveller in the East and Friend of James III', *IR*, xxxiii (1982), 15–22

MacQueen, John (ed.), *Humanism in Renaissance Scotland* (Edinburgh, 1990)

McRoberts, David (ed.), *Essays on the Scottish Reformation, 1513–1625* (Glasgow, 1962)

McRoberts, David (ed.), *The Medieval Church of St. Andrews* (Glasgow, 1976)

McRoberts, David, *The Heraldic Ceiling of St. Machar's Cathedral, Aberdeen* (Aberdeen, 1976)

McRoberts, David, 'Material Destruction caused by the Scottish Reformation', *IR*, x (1959), 126–72

McRoberts, David, 'Notes on Scoto-Flemish Artistic Contacts', *IR*, x (1959), 91–6

McRoberts, David, 'The Fetternear Banner', *IR*, vii (1956), 69–86

McRoberts, David, 'The Medieval Scottish Liturgy Illustrated by Surviving Documents', *TSES*, vol. xv, pt. 1 (1957), 24–40

McRoberts, David, 'Scottish Sacrament Houses', *TSES*, xv (1965), 33–56

McRoberts, David, 'The Rosary in Scotland', *IR*, xxiii (1972), 81–6

McRoberts, David, 'Some Sixteenth-Century Scottish Breviaries and their place in the History of the Scottish Liturgy', *IR*, iii (1952), 33–48

McRoberts, David, 'The Boy Bishop in Scotland', *IR*, xix (1968), 80–82

McWilliam, C. (ed.), *The Buildings of Scotland: Lothian except Edinburgh* (London, 1978)

Mahoney, M., The Scottish Hierarchy, 1513–1625', *IR*, x (1959), 21–66

Malloch, R. J., 'The Order of the Thistle', *Journal of the Heraldry Society of Scotland*, i (1977–8), 35–46

Mapstone, Sally, 'Was there a Court Literature in Fifteenth-Century Scotland?', *Studies in Scottish Literature*, xxvi (1991), 410–22

Mapstone, Sally, *Scots and their Books in the Middle Ages and the Renaissance*, Bodleian Library exhibition catalogue (Oxford, 1996)

Mapstone, Sally and Wood, Juliette (eds.), *The Rose and the Thistle* (East Linton, 1998)

Margolin, J.-C. (ed.), *Acta Conventus Neo-Latini Turonensis* (Paris, 1980)

Marshall, Rosalind K., *Mary of Guise* (London, 1977)

Marshall, Rosalind K., *Queen of Scots* (Edinburgh, 1988)

Marshall, Rosalind, K., *Virgins and Viragoes. A History of Women in Scotland from 1080 to 1980* (London, 1983)

Marshall, Rosalind K., 'The Jewellery of James V, King of Scots', *Jewellery Studies*, vii (1996), 79–86

Marshall, Rosalind K., 'Jewellery in Scottish Portraits, 1500–1700', *The Connoisseur*, xcvii (1978), 283–91

Marshall, Rosalind K., '"To be the Kingis Grace ane Dowblett": The Costume of James V, King of Scots', *Costume: The Journal of the Costume Society*, xxviii (1994), 14–21

Marshall, Rosalind K., '"Hir Rob Ryall": the Costume of Mary of Guise', *Costume*, xii (1978), 1–12

Marshall, Rosalind. K. and Dalgleish, G. R. (eds.), *The Art of Jewellery in Scotland* (Edinburgh, 1991)

Marwick, Sir James D., *The History of the Collegiate Church and Hospital of the Holy Trinity and the Trinity Hospital, Edinburgh, 1460–1661* (SBRS, 1911)

Mason, Roger A. (ed.), *Scotland and England, 1286–1815* (Edinburgh, 1987)

Mason, Roger A., 'Kingship, Nobility and Anglo-Scottish Union: John Mair's History of Greater Britain (1521)', *IR*, xli (1990), 182–222

Mason, Roger A., *Kingship and the Commonweal: Political Thought in Renaissance and Reformation Scotland* (East Linton, 1998)

Mason, R. A. and Macdougall, N. (eds.), *People and Power in Scotland: Essays in Honour of T. C. Smout* (Edinburgh, 1992)

Mathew, Gevase, *The Court of Richard II* (London, 1968)

Mattingly, Garrett, *Katherine of Aragon* (London, 1950)

Maxwell-Irving, Alastair M. T., 'Cramalt Tower: A Historical Survey and Excavations, 1977–9', *PSAS*, cxi (1981), 421–3

Maxwell-Irving, Alastair M. T., 'Early Firearms and their Influence on the military and domestic architecture of the Borders', *PSAS*, ciii (1970–71), 192–224

Mays, D (ed.), *The Architecture of Scottish Cities: Essays in Honour of David Walker* (East Linton, 1997)

Medcalf, Stephen (ed.), *The Context of English Literature: The Later Middle Ages* (London, 1981)

Meikle, Maureen, 'The World of Women: Review Article', *IR*, xlv (1994), 71–77

Menzies, Walter, 'Robert Galbraith, 148– – 1543', *Aberdeen University Library Bulletin*, vii (June 1929), 205–13

Menzies, Gordon (ed.), *The Scottish Nation* (London, 1972)

Mertes, Kate, *The English Noble Household, 1250–1600: Good Governance and Politic Rule* (Oxford, 1988)

Mill, Anna Jean, *Medieval Plays in Scotland* (Edinburgh and London, 1927)

Millar, A. H., 'Scotland described for Queen Magdalene: A Curious Volume', *SHR*, i (1903–4), 27–38

Millar, Sir Oliver, *The Tudor, Stuart and Early Georgian Pictures in the Collection of Her Majesty the Queen* (2 vols, London, 1963)

Mitchell, W. S., *A History of Scottish Bookbinding, 1432–1650* (Aberdeen, 1955)

Moncrieffe, Sir Iain, *The Royal Palace of Falkland* (NTS, 1989)

Mowat, Sue, *The Port of Leith, its History and People* (Edinburgh, n.d.)

Murray, A. L. 'The Comptroller, 1425–1488', *SHR*, lii (1973), 1–29

Murray, A. L., 'Exchequer and Council in the reign of James V', *Juridical Review*, v (1960), 209–25

Murray, A. L., 'The Lord Clerk Register', *SHR*, liii (1974), 124–56

Murray, A. L., 'The Procedure of the Scottish Exchequer in the early Sixteenth Century', *SHR*, xl (1961), 89–117

Murray, A. L., 'The Revenues of the Bishopric of Moray in 1538', *IR*, xix (1968), 40–56

Murray, Peter and Linda, *The Art of the Renaissance* (London, 1986)

Myers, A. R., *The Household of Edward IV: The Black Book and the Ordinance of 1478* (Manchester, 1959)

Mylne, R. S., *The Master Masons of the Crown of Scotland* (Edinburgh, 1893)

Mylne, R. S., 'Notices of the King's Master Wrights of Scotland with Writs of their Appointments, *PSAS*, xxxiv (1899–1900), 288–96

Oldham, Arthur, 'Scottish Polyphonic Music', *IR*, xiii (1962), 54–61

Oppenheim, M., *A History of the Administration of the Royal Navy* (London, 1896)

Orme, Nicholas, *From Childhood to Chivalry: the Education of the English Kings and Aristocracy, 1066–1530* (London, 1984)

Parsons, John Carmi (ed.), *Medieval Queenship* (Stroud, 1994)

Paterson, J., *James the Fifth: or the "Gudeman of Ballangeich:" his Poetry and Adventures* (Edinburgh, 1861)

Paton, G. C. H. (ed.), *An Introduction to Scottish Legal History* (Stair Society, 1958)

Pimodan, Gabriel de, *La Mère des Guises* (Paris, 1925)

Porteous, J. Moir, *God's Treasure-House in Scotland* (London, 1876)

Porter, Roy and Teich, Mikuláš (eds.), *The Renaissance in National Context* (Cambridge, 1992)

Potter, D., *War and Government in the French Provinces: Picardy, 1470–1560* (Cambridge, 1993)

Prevenier, Walter and Blockmans, Wim, *The Burgundian Netherlands*, trans. Peter King and Yvette Mead (Cambridge, 1986)

Pringle, Denys, *Rothesay Castle and St. Mary's Church* (Edinburgh, 1995)

Purser, John, *Scotland's Music* (Edinburgh, 1992)

Rae, Thomas I., *The Administration of the Scottish Frontier, 1513–1603* (Edinburgh, 1966)

Rait, R. S., *The Parliaments of Scotland* (Glasgow, 1924)

Rait, R. S., *The Scottish Parliament before the Union of the Crowns* (London, 1901)

Reese, Gustave, *Music in the Renaissance* (London, 1954)

Reid, J. J., 'The Scottish Regalia, Anciently Styled the Honours of Scotland', *PSAS*, xxiv (1889–90), 18–48

Reid, Thomas, *History of the Parish of Crawfordjohn, Upper Ward of Lanarkshire, 1153–1928* (Edinburgh, 1928)

Reid, W. Stanford, *Skipper from Leith: The History of Robert Barton of Over Barnton* (Oxford, 1962)

Reid, W. Stanford, 'Clerical Taxation: the Scottish Alternative to the Dissolution of the Monasteries', *Catholic Historical Review*, xxxiv (1948), 129–53

Renaissance Decorative Arts in Scotland, 1480–1650, NMAS and SNPG exhibition catalogue (Edinburgh, 1959)

Renwick, Robert, *A Peebles Aisle and Monastery* (Edinburgh, 1893)

Richardson, J. S., *The Medieval Stone Carver in Scotland* (Edinburgh, 1964)

Richardson, J. S., 'Unrecorded Scottish Wood Carvings', *PSAS*, lx (1925–6), 384–408

Robbins, K. (ed.), *Religion and Humanism, Studies in Church History*, 17 (Oxford, 1981)

Rogers, C., *History of the Chapel Royal of Scotland* (Grampian Club, 1882)

Rogers, C., *Social Life in Scotland from Early to Recent Times* (3 vols, Edinburgh, 1884–6)

Rose, Mary Beth (ed.), *Women in the Middle Ages and the Renaissance* (Syracuse, 1986)

Ross, A., 'Some Scottish Catholic Historians', *IR*, i (1950), 5–21

Ross, D. James, *Musick Fyne: Robert Carver and the Art of Music in Sixteenth Century Scotland* (Edinburgh, 1993)

Ross, T., 'St. Triduana's Well-House', *TSES*, iii (1910–11), 238–46

Russell, J. C., *The Field of Cloth of Gold* (London, 1969)

Russell, J. C., *Peacemaking in the Renaissance* (London, 1986)

Sanderson, M. H. B., *Cardinal of Scotland: David Beaton, c.1494–1546* (Edinburgh, 1986)

Sanderson, J. M., 'Two Stewarts of the Sixteenth Century: Mr William Stewart, Poet, and William Stewart, Elder, Depute Clerk of Edinburgh', *The Stewarts*, xvii (1984), 25–46

Sanger, Keith and Kinnaird, Alison, *Tree of Strings, Crann nan tend: A History of the Harp in Scotland* (Edinburgh, 1992)

Scarisbrick, J. J., *Henry VIII* (London, 1990)

Scattergood, V. J. and Sherborne, J. W. (eds.), *English Court Culture in the Later Middle Ages* (London, 1986)

Scott, Paul H. (ed.) *Scotland: A Concise Cultural History* (Edinburgh, 1993)

Scott, Sir Walter, *Tales of a Grandfather* (Edinburgh, 1872)

Seaby, Peter, and Purvey, P. Frank, *Coins of Scotland, Ireland and the Islands* (London, 1984)

Sedgwick, H. D., *The House of Guise* (London, 1938)

Seton, G., 'Notice of Four Stained Glass Shields of Arms and a Monumental Slab in St. Magdalene's Chapel, Cowgate', *PSAS*, xxi (1886–87), 266–74

Seton, George, *The Law and Practice of Heraldry in Scotland* (Edinburgh, 1863)

Seward, D., *Prince of the Renaissance: The Life of Francis I* (London, 1973)

Shaw, D. W. D., *In Divers Manners: A St. Mary's Miscellany* (St. Andrews, 1990)

Shire, H. M., *Song, Dance and Poetry of the Court of Scotland Under James VI* (Cambridge, 1969)

Simonin, Michel, *Pierre de Ronsard* (Mesnil-sur-l'Estrée, 1990)

Simpson, G. G. (ed.), *Scotland and Scandinavia, 800–1800* (Edinburgh, 1990)

Simpson, W. Douglas, 'A Chronicle History of Dunvegan Castle', *Transactions of the Gaelic Society of Inverness*, xxxvii (1934–6), 370–98

Sinclair, George, A., 'The Scots at Solway Moss', *SHR*, ii (1905), 372–77

Sinclair, John, 'Notes on the Holyrood "Foir-yet" of James IV', *PSAS*, xxxix, (1904–5), 352–362

Sinclair, John, 'Notes on James V's Towers, Holyrood Palace', *PSAS*, xxxiv (1899–1900), 224–41

Slavin, A. S., *Politics and Profit: A Study of Sir Ralph Sadler* (Cambridge, 1966)

Smailes, Helen and Thomson, Duncan, *The Queen's Image* (Edinburgh, 1987)

Smith, Janet M., *The French Background to Middle Scots Literature* (Edinburgh, 1934)

Smith, Pauline M. and MacFarlane, I. D. (eds.), *Literature and the Arts in the Reign of Francis I* (Lexington, 1985)

Smout, T. C. (ed.), *Scotland and Europe, 1200–1850* (Edinburgh, 1986)

Stafford, Pauline, *Queens, Concubines and Dowagers: The King's Wife in the Early Middle Ages* (Athens [USA], 1983)

Stair-Kerr, Eric, *Stirling Castle: Its Place in Scottish History* (Stirling, 1928)

Starkey, David (ed.), *The English Court from the Wars of the Roses to the Civil War* (London, 1987)

Starkey, David (ed.), *Henry VIII: A European Court in England* (London, 1991)

Starkey, David, 'Ightham Mote', *History Today*, xxx (Jan. 1980), 58–60

Starkey, David, 'From Feud to Faction: English Politics c.1450–1550', *History Today*, xxxii (Nov 1982), 16–22

Stevens, John, *Music and Poetry in the Early Tudor Court* (London, 1961)

Stevenson, David, *Scotland's Last Royal Wedding: The Marriage of James VI and Anne of Denmark* (Edinburgh, 1997)

Stevenson, the Revd. Joseph, *Mary Stuart: A Narrative of the First Eighteen Years of her Life Principally from Original Documents* (Edinburgh, 1886)

Stevenson, J. H., *Heraldry in Scotland* (2 vols, Glasgow, 1914)

Stevenson, K. B., 'The Bawbee Issues of James V and Mary', *The British Numismatic Journal*, lix (1989), 120–56

Stevenson, K. B., 'The Groat Coinage of James V, 1526–38', *The British Numismatic Journal*, lxi (1991), 37–56

Stewart, I. H., *The Scottish Coinage* (London, 1955)

Stoddart, Jane T., *The Girlhood of Mary, Queen of Scots* (London, 1908)

Strickland, Agnes, *Lives of the Queens of Scotland and English Princesses* (8 vols, Edinburgh and London, 1850–59)

Stringer, K. J. (ed.), *Essays on the Nobility of Medieval Scotland* (Edinburgh, 1985)

Strong, Roy, *Splendour at Court: Renaissance Spectacle and Illusion* (London, 1973)

Strong, Roy, *Art and Power: Renaissance Festivals, 1450–1650* (Woodbridge, 1984)

Stuart, Marie W., *The Scot who was a Frenchman* (Edinburgh, 1940)

Symms, P., 'Some Aspects of the Sheep-Farming Activities of James V', *Scottish Economic and Social History*, vii (1987), 66–68

Tabraham, C., *Scottish Castles and Fortifications* (Edinburgh, 1990)

Thompson, C. and Campbell, L., *Hugo van der Goes and the Trinity Panels in Edinburgh* (NGS, 1974)

Thomson, D., *Renaissance Paris: Architecture and Growth, 1475–1600* (London, 1984)

Thurley, Simon, *The Royal Palaces of Tudor England: Architecture and Court Life, 1460–1547* (New Haven, 1993)

Thurley, Simon, 'Henry VIII and the Building of Hampton Court Palace: A Reconstruction of a Tudor Palace', *Architect. Hist.*, xxxi (1988), 1–57

Vale, M. G. A., *War and Chivalry* (London, 1981)

Vaughan, R., *Valois Burgundy* (London, 1975)

Verney, Peter, *The Gardens of Scotland* (London, no date)

Walker, Greg, *Plays of Persuasion: Drama and Politics at the Court of Henry VIII* (Cambridge, 1991)

Walker, Greg, 'Henry VIII and the Invention of the Royal Court', *History Today*, xlvii (February 1997), 13–20

Warner, George F., 'The Library of James VI, 1573–1583, From a Manuscript in the hand of Peter Young, his Tutor', *SHS Misc.*, i (SHS, 1893), pp. ix–lxxv

Warrack, John, *Domestic Life in Scotland, 1488–1688* (Edinburgh, 1920)

Waters, D. W. (ed.), *The Rutters of the Sea* (New Haven and London, 1967)

Welsford, Enid, *The Court Masque: A Study in the Relationship between Poetry and the Revels* (Cambridge, 1927)

Wiesner, Merry, E., *Women and Gender in Early Modern Europe* (Cambridge, 1993)

Williams, J. E. H., 'James V, David Lyndsay, and the Bannatyne Manuscript Poem of *The Gyre Carling*', *Studies in Scottish Literature*, xxvi (1991), 164–71

Williams, Janet Hadley (ed.), *Stewart Style, 1513–1542: Essays on the Court of James V* (East Linton, 1996)

Williams, Neville, *Henry VIII and his Court* (London, 1971)

Williams, Peter, *A New History of the Organ from the Greeks to the Present Day* (London, 1980)

Winning, Revd. Thomas, 'Church Councils in Sixteenth-Century Scotland', *IR*, x (1959), 311–37

Withington, Robert, *English Pageantry: An Historical Outline* (2 vols, New York, 1963)

Woodbridge, Kenneth, *Princely Gardens: The Origins and Development of the French Formal Style* (London, 1986)

Woods, Isobel, 'Towards a Biography of Robert Carvor', *The Music Review*, vol. xlix, no. 2 (May 1989), 83–101

Wormald, Jenny, *Court, Kirk and Community: Scotland, 1470–1625* (Edinburgh, 1992)

Wormald, Jenny, *Lords and Men in Scotland: Bonds of Manrent, 1442–1603* (Edinburgh, 1985)

Wormald, Jenny, *Mary Queen of Scots: a Study in Failure* (London, 1991)

Wormald, Jenny (ed.), *Scotland Revisited* (London, 1991)

Wulstan, David, *Tudor Music* (London, 1985)

Yates, Frances A., *Astraea: The Imperial Theme in the Sixteenth Century* (London, 1985)

Yates, Frances A., *The French Academies of the Sixteenth Century* (London, 1947)

Yates, Frances A., *The Valois Tapestries* (London, 1975)

Zeune, Joachim, *The Last Scottish Castles: Investigations with particular reference to domestic architecture from the 15th to 17th centuries*, trans. Silke Böger (Internationale Archäologie, Band 12, Erlbach, 1992)

6. THESES

Cameron, James S., 'Crown-Magnate Relations in the Personal Rule of James V, 1528–1542' (University of St. Andrews Ph.D. thesis, 1994)

Edington, Carol, 'Sir David Lindsay of the Mount: Politics and Religious Culture in Renaissance Scotland' (University of St. Andrews Ph.D. thesis, 1991)

Emond, W. K., 'The Minority of James V, 1513–1528' (University of St. Andrews Ph.D. thesis, 1988)

Finlay, John, 'Professional Men of Law before the Lords of Council, c.1500 – c.1550' (University of Edinburgh Ph.D. thesis, 1998)

Godfrey, Andrew Mark, 'The Lords of Council and Session and the Foundation of the College of Justice: a Study in Jurisdiction' (University of Edinburgh Ph.D. thesis, 1998)

Murray, A. L., 'Exchequer and Crown Revenue of Scotland, 1437–1542' (University of Edinburgh Ph.D. thesis, 1961)

Royan, Nicola, 'The *Scotorum Historia* of Hector Boece: A Study' (University of Oxford D.Phil. thesis, 1996)

Thomas, Andrea, 'Renaissance Culture at the Court of James V, 1528–1542' (University of Edinburgh, Ph.D. thesis, 1997)

Thurley, Simon, 'English Royal Palaces, 1450–1550' (University of London, Ph.D. thesis, 1991–92)

Watry, P. B., 'Sixteenth-Century Printing Types and Ornaments of Scotland with an Introductory Survey of the Scottish Book Trade' (University of Oxford D.Phil. thesis, 1993)

Index

Names and places in the Appendices are not included.